SECURITY+®
PRACTICE TESTS

Mike Chapple

CertMike.com

Get Certified!

Security +

CySA +

CISSP

SSCP

PenTest+

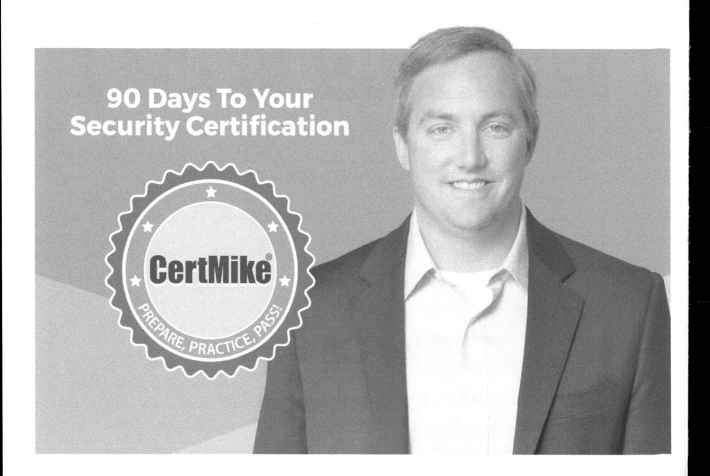

90 Days To Your Security Certification

CertMike®
PREPARE, PRACTICE, PASS!

Mike Chapple offers **FREE ONLINE STUDY GROUPS** that complement this book and will help prepare you for your security certification.

Visit CertMike.com to learn more!

Table of Contents

Introduction

Welcome to the CertMike Security+ SY0-601 Practice Tests! I've prepared these practice tests to help you prepare for the CompTIA Security+ exam and hope that you find them a useful aid as you get ready for test day.

What's in This Book?

In this book, you'll find over 1,000 practice exam questions written using the style and format of the Security+ exam. I've organized the book in a manner designed to help you study effectively. The first five chapters each cover one of the five Security+ domains. Each of those chapters contains practice test questions covering the material from that domain. Chapters 6, 7, 8, and 9 each contain a full-length Security+ practice test that's designed to assess your readiness to take the actual test.

At the end of each chapter, you'll find the answers to all of the questions along with detailed explanations to help reinforce your learning of the material. If you're using the eBook version of this book, you'll find hyperlinks to help you flip back and forth between questions and answers if that's the way you prefer to study.

What is the Security+ Certification?

The Security+ certification is the most popular entry-level certification for cybersecurity professionals. It covers the foundational knowledge in the field and has no work experience requirement, making it accessible to anyone willing to put in the time to prepare for the exam. Sponsored by the Computing Technology Industry Association (CompTIA), the Security+ exam covers five domains of crucial cybersecurity knowledge:

- Threats, Attacks, and Vulnerabilities
- Architecture and Design
- Implementation
- Operations and Incident Response
- Governance, Risk, and Compliance

Today, employers and IT professionals around the world recognize Security+ as a premier certification program that allows candidates to demonstrate a breadth of knowledge in cybersecurity that prepares them for a career in the field.

Security+ Exam Environment

You'll take the computer-based Security+ exam at a *Pearson Vue testing center*, probably not far from your home or office. These centers, typically located in office buildings and strip malls, are nondescript locations that conduct testing for a wide variety of programs. You might find yourself sitting for the exam wedged in between a healthcare professional taking a nursing exam and a student tackling a graduate school admissions test.

When you arrive at the test center, you'll go through a check-in process at the front desk where the exam staff check your identification, take your photograph, and electronically capture your signature. After all, this *is* an information security exam. You didn't expect to get away without multifactor authentication, did you?

Speaking of identification, you'll need to bring two forms of identification along with you to the exam. You will not be admitted to the exam without them. Your primary identification must be a government-issued identification card that contains both a photo and a signature. For example, you might use:

- A Driver's license
- A National or state-issued identification card
- A Learner's permit (if it contains a photo and signature)
- A Passport
- A Military identification card, or
- An Alien registration card

If you have two items on that list, you're good to go. If you can only come up with one of those items, you may use any other form of identification for your second source. Any form of identification that you use must be current -- not expired -- and contain your name and either a photo or a signature. The first and last names on your identification must exactly match the first and last names on your test registration. If you recently changed your name, you must bring proof of a legal name change with you to the testing center.

After completing the identification process, you may have to wait a short time until your testing station is ready for use. Once it's time to sit for the exam, you'll be asked to use a locker to store any personal items that aren't allowed in the exam room and then shown to the system where you will take the exam.

The testing software used for the Security+ exam is the same software used for many exams administered by Pearson. You'll have up to 90 minutes to navigate through the exam and you are allowed to return to previous items and make as many passes through the questions as you would like during that time. Here's a screenshot of the Pearson software to give you a feel for what to expect:

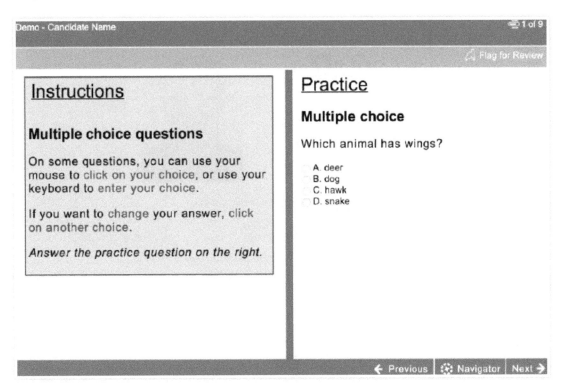

Flag for Review

Instructions

Multiple choice questions

On some questions, you can use your mouse to click on your choice, or use your keyboard to enter your choice.

If you want to change your answer, click on another choice.

Answer the practice question on the right.

Practice

Multiple choice

Which animal has wings?

A. deer
B. dog
C. hawk
D. snake

← Previous | ⚙ Navigator | Next →

Figure 1   Pearson Vue Testing Software

If you have any questions or technical difficulties during the exam, raise your hand and a proctor will assist you. The test center proctors administer many different types of exams and have no specialized knowledge of information security. They can help you with the software but cannot and will not discuss any exam questions with you.

You may take breaks at your own discretion during the exam, but the clock will not stop. You may leave the testing room but may not leave the testing center during your break. You also may not open your locker and access any of your belongings. If you leave the room, the proctor will re-verify your identity before allowing you to return.

When you complete the exam, you'll check out with the front desk and the exam proctor will give you a score report indicating whether you passed the exam. CompTIA will also send you official notification of your results via email.

CompTIA Security+ Certification Exam Score Report SY0-401

CANDIDATE:	MICHAEL J CHAPPLE
CANDIDATE ID:	
REGISTRATION NUMBER:	
EXAM:	CompTIA Security+ Certification Exam
DATE:	8/7/15
SITE NUMBER:	45283
PASSING SCORE:	750
CANDIDATE SCORE:	850
PASS/FAIL:	Pass

The CompTIA Security+ Certification Exam has a scaled score between 100 and 900.

You incorrectly answered one or more questions in the following objective areas.

- 1.2 Given a scenario, use secure network administration principles.
- 2.1 Explain the importance of risk related concepts.
- 2.4 Given a scenario, implement basic forensic procedures.
- 3.6 Analyze a scenario and select the appropriate type of mitigation and deterrent techniques.
- 3.7 Given a scenario, use appropriate tools and techniques to discover security threats and vulnerabilities.
- 6.1 Given a scenario, utilize general cryptography concepts.
- 6.2 Given a scenario, use appropriate cryptographic methods.

For a complete listing of CompTIA Security+ Certification Exam objectives, please visit certification.comptia.org.

Figure 2   CompTIA Score Report

Security+ Question Types

The Security+ exam contains two different types of questions: standard multiple-choice questions and some specialized performance-based questions. Let's look at each of these categories.

The multiple-choice questions are usually pretty straightforward. For most of them, you'll simply be presented with a fact-based question, such as the one shown in Figure 1, and asked to choose the correct answer from four possible choices.

The second type of question you'll face is the performance-based exam question. On some CompTIA exams, such as the A+ exam, you might be asked to perform a task on a simulated computer system. Fortunately, the Security+ exam doesn't currently include these tasks. Instead, you'll find questions where you're asked to drag items into the right order, sort things by category, indicate different components on a network diagram, or perform similar, vendor-agnostic tasks. Figure 3 shows an example of one of these performance-based questions.

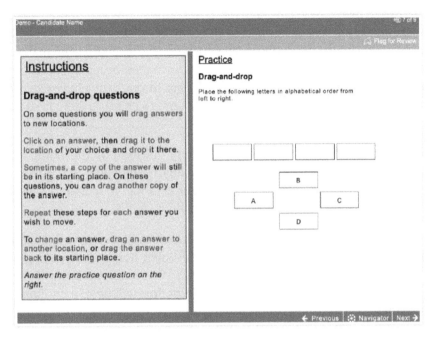

Figure 3 Performance-Based Test Question

When answering exam questions, remember to use solid test taking strategies. Here are a few pointers for you.

First, read the question very carefully. Pay attention to exactly what the question is asking and remember that one or more of the wrong answers may be based upon common misinterpretations of the question. Don't get tricked by the exam because you didn't read the question closely enough!

Second, read all of the answer choices before you commit to the correct one. If you're unsure of the answer, try to eliminate one or more of the answers that you think are obviously incorrect. If you can eliminate two of the answer choices, you just improved your odds from one in four to fifty/fifty!

Third, answer every question, even if you have no idea what the question is asking you! There is no penalty for guessing on the exam, so you might as well answer each one.

Fourth, the exam software offers you the ability to move back and forth between questions and revisit those that you're unsure of. You can mark questions that you'd like to review later. Be sure to use this feature. If you're not confident in your answer, go back later and give it another read.

Finally, make at least three passes through the exam during your 90 minutes. Taking a quick first run through the exam and knocking out the easy questions will build your confidence and help you get a feel for the contents of the entire exam. I've heard from many test-takers that they've encountered exams where all of the performance-based questions appeared in the beginning of the exam. If you don't do a quick pass through the entire exam, you might become very discouraged because these questions tend to be more difficult. It's absolutely fine to just skip them entirely during your first pass.

During your second run-through, try to answer every question on the exam. Finally, your third pass through the exam will help you clean up any errors you made. Answering other questions during the first and second passes might also jog your memory and help you answer questions that were sticking points earlier.

Note: At the time of this writing, CompTIA was also offering a remote testing option that allows Security+ candidates to take the test in their own home. This testing option was introduced in response to the COVID-19 pandemic. We do not yet know if this will be a permanent offering or whether the remote testing option will be discontinued when the pandemic subsides.

Following the CertMike Process

You're welcome to use this book however you'd like. If you're sitting for the exam soon, you might want to skip right to the full-length practice tests found in Chapters 6, 7, 8, and 9 and use them to zero in on areas where you need to study up before the exam.

On the other hand, if you're just getting started with your Security+ certification journey, I encourage you to use a variety of resources as you prepare for the exam. I've created a *video course series on LinkedIn Learning* that walks through all of the knowledge you'll need to pass the exam. I also recommend that you use my *Security+ Study Guide* as a companion reference as you prepare for the exam. Finally, make sure that you have a copy of my *CertMike Security+ Last Minute Review Guide*. It's less than ten bucks and provides all of the crucial knowledge that you should review the night before the exam.

Your Free Bonus: Join My Security+ Study Group

I've helped thousands of students earn their Security+ certifications and I've learned quite a bit about test preparation along the way. I've put together a step-by-step process that guides you through the study process week-by-week, using a combination of this book, my video course series, and my study guide.

As a small token of my thanks for buying this book, I'd like to offer you a free bonus gift. Visit my website at *CertMike.com* and sign up for *my free Security+ Study Group*. I'll email you new assignments each week along with some extra exam tips and practice test questions. You'll get weekly reminders from me that will walk you through the Security+ exam preparation process, step-by-step. You'll also get the opportunity to interact with other technology professionals who are also preparing for the exam.

The assignments I provide use a convenient checklist format that guides you through the week. Here's an example of the checklist from the course:

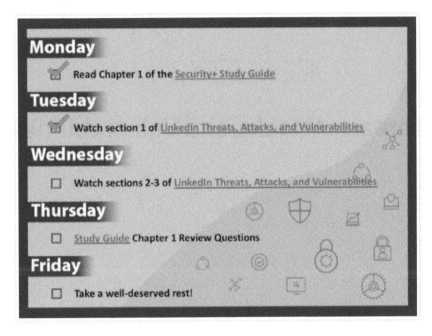

Figure 4 Sample CertMike Study Group Checklist

If you sign up for the free study group, I'll email you a new checklist every Monday and a reminder on Wednesday to help you keep up with the pace of the preparation.

That's it. Good luck with your test preparation!

CHAPTER 1

Threats, Attacks, and Vulnerabilities

Domain 1 Questions

1. After conducting a vulnerability scan of her network, Wendy discovered the issue shown below on several servers. What is the most significant direct impact of this vulnerability?

A. Attackers may eavesdrop on network communications
B. Attackers may use this information to gain administrative privileges
C. Encryption will not protect credentials for this account
D. Automated attacks are more likely to succeed

2. Pete is investigating a domain hijacking attack against his company that successfully redirected web traffic to a third party website. Which one of the following techniques is the most effective way to carry out a domain hijacking attack?

A. ARP poisoning
B. Network eavesdropping
C. DNS poisoning
D. Social engineering

3. Which one of the following characters is most important to restrict when performing input validation to protect against XSS attacks?

A. <
B. !
C. $
D. '

4. Darren is investigating an attack that took place on his network. When he visits the victim's machine and types "www.mybank.com" into the address bar, he is directed to a phishing site designed to look like a legitimate banking site. He then tries entering the IP address of the bank directly into the address bar and the legitimate site loads. What type of attack is likely taking place?

A. IP spoofing
B. DNS poisoning
C. ARP spoofing
D. Typosquatting

5.   During a security exercise, which team is responsible for conducting offensive operations against the target?

   A. Blue Team
   B. Red Team
   C. White Team
   D. Purple Team

6.   What is the purpose of a DNS amplification attack?

   A. Resource exhaustion
   B. Host redirection
   C. Record poisoning
   D. Man-in-the-middle

7.   Which one of the following technologies must be enabled on a wireless network for a Pixie Dust attack to succeed?

   A. SSID broadcasting
   B. WPS
   C. WPA
   D. WEP

8.   During a forensic analysis, Drew discovered that an attacker intercepted traffic headed to networked printers by modifying the printer drivers. His analysis revealed that the attacker modified the code of the driver to transmit copies of printed documents to a secure repository. What type of attack took place?

   A. Refactoring
   B. Shimming
   C. Swapping
   D. Recoding

9.   What type of scan can best help identify cases of system sprawl in an organization?

   A. Database scan
   B. Web application scan
   C. Detailed scan
   D. Discovery scan

10. Scott is reviewing a list of cryptographic cipher suites supported by his organization's website. Which one of the following algorithms is not secure and may expose traffic to eavesdropping attacks?

   A. ECC
   B. 3DES
   C. AES
   D. DES

11. Brenda is selecting the tools that she will use in a penetration test and would like to begin with passive techniques. Which one of the following is not normally considered a passive reconnaissance technique?

    A. Social engineering
    B. Wireless network eavesdropping
    C. Open source intelligence
    D. Domain name searches

12. Scott is a security administrator for a federal government agency. He recently learned of a website that advertises jobs for former government employees. When he accessed the site, the site launched code in his browser that attempted to install malicious software on his system. What type of attack took place?

    A. Denial of service
    B. Watering hole
    C. Spyware
    D. Trojan horse

13. Paul received an email warning him that a new virus is circulating on the Internet and that he needs to apply a patch to correct the problem. The message is branded with a Microsoft header. The virus message is actually a hoax and the patch contains malicious code. What principle of social engineering best describes what the attacker trying to exploit by including the Microsoft header?

    A. Consensus
    B. Scarcity
    C. Trust
    D. Intimidation

14. Kristen conducts a vulnerability scan against her organization's network and discovers a file server with the vulnerability shown below. Which one of the following actions is the best way to remediate this vulnerability?

LOW   FTP Supports Cleartext Authentication   >

Description

The remote FTP server allows the user's name and password to be transmitted in cleartext, which could be intercepted by a network sniffer or a man-in-the-middle attack.

    A. Discontinue the file transfer service
    B. Require strong passwords
    C. Switch to SFTP
    D. Require multifactor authentication

15. Twyla recently completed an assessment of her organization's call center and found that call center representatives discard paper notes from their telephone calls with customers without shredding them. What type of social engineering attack does this practice make her organization vulnerable to?

    A. Shoulder surfing
    B. Dumpster diving
    C. Tailgating
    D. Skimming

16. Frank is the new CISO at a mid-sized business. Upon entering his role, he learns that the organization has not conducted any security training for their sales team. Which one of the following attacks is most likely to be enabled by this control gap?

    A. Buffer overflow
    B. Social engineering
    C. Denial of service
    D. ARP poisoning

17. After conducting security testing, Bruce identifies a memory leak issue on one of his servers that runs an internally developed application. Which one of the following team members is most likely able to correct this issue?

    A. Developer
    B. System administrator
    C. Storage administrator
    D. Security analyst

18. Greg recently detected a system on his network that occasionally begins sending streams of TCP SYN packets to port 80 at a single IP address for several hours and then stops. It later resumes, but directs the packets at a different address. What type of attack is taking place?

    A. Port scanning
    B. DDoS
    C. IP scanning
    D. SQL injection

19. During a security assessment, Ryan learns that the Accounts Receivable department prints out records containing customer credit card numbers and files them in unlocked filing cabinets. Which one of the following approaches is most appropriate for resolving the security issues this situation raises?

    A. Physically secure paper records
    B. Encrypt sensitive information
    C. Modify business process
    D. Monitor areas containing sensitive records

20. Jaime is concerned that users in her organization may fall victim to DNS poisoning attacks. Which one of the following controls would be most helpful in protecting against these attacks?

    A. DNSSEC
    B. Redundant DNS servers
    C. Off-site DNS servers
    D. Firewall rules

21. Irene is reviewing the logs from a security incident and discovers many entries in her database query logs that appear similar to the ones shown below. What type of attack was attempted against her server?

```
SELECT CASE WHEN SUBSTRING(password) = 'a' THEN WAITFOR DELAY
'00:00:10' ELSE NULL END FROM users WHERE id = 1928 ;
SELECT CASE WHEN SUBSTRING(password) = 'b' THEN WAITFOR DELAY
'00:00:10' ELSE NULL END FROM users WHERE id = 1928 ;
SELECT CASE WHEN SUBSTRING(password) = 'c' THEN WAITFOR DELAY
'00:00:10' ELSE NULL END FROM users WHERE id = 1928 ;
SELECT CASE WHEN SUBSTRING(password) = 'd' THEN WAITFOR DELAY
'00:00:10' ELSE NULL END FROM users WHERE id = 1928 ;
```

    A. Error-based SQL injection
    B. Timing-based SQL injection
    C. TOC/TOU
    D. LDAP injection

22. Carl is concerned that his organization's public DNS servers may be used in an amplification attack against a third party. What is the most effective way for Carl to prevent these servers from being used in an amplification attack?

    A. Disable open resolution
    B. Block external DNS requests
    C. Block internal DNS requests
    D. Block port 53 at the firewall

23. Angie is investigating a piece of malware found on a Windows system in her organization. She determines that the malware forced a running program to load code stored in a library. What term best describes this attack?

    A. DLL injection
    B. SQL injection
    C. Pointer dereference
    D. Buffer overflow

24. Which one of the following threat sources is likely to have the highest level of sophistication?

    A. Organized crime
    B. Hacktivist
    C. APT
    D. Script kiddie

25. Alan is assessing the results of a penetration test and discovered that the attackers managed to install a back door on one of his systems. What activity were the attackers most likely engaged in when they installed the back door?

    A. Persistence
    B. Pivoting
    C. Privilege escalation
    D. Lateral movement

26. In which one of the following types of penetration test does the attacker not have any access to any information about the target environment prior to beginning the attack?

    A. Grey box
    B. White box
    C. Red box
    D. Black box

27. Bill is securing a set of terminals used to access a highly sensitive web application. He would like to protect against a man-in-the-browser attack. Which one of the following actions would be most effective in meeting Bill's goal?

    A. Disabling browser extensions
    B. Requiring multifactor authentication
    C. Requiring TLS encryption
    D. Disabling certificate pinning

28. Which one of the following attackers is most likely to understand the design of an organization's business processes?

    A. Script kiddie
    B. APT
    C. Insider
    D. Hacktivist

29. Kevin runs a vulnerability scan on a system on his network and identifies a SQL injection vulnerability. Which one of the following security controls is likely not present on the network?

    A. TLS
    B. DLP
    C. IDS
    D. WAF

30. Maureen is implementing TLS encryption to protect transactions run against her company's web services infrastructure. Which one of the following cipher suites would not be an appropriate choice?

    A. AES256-CCM
    B. ADH-RC4-MD5
    C. ECDHE-RSA-AES256-SHA384
    D. DH-RSA-AES256-GCM-SHA384

31. Val runs a vulnerability scan of her network and finds issues similar to the one shown below on many systems. What action should Val take?

    A. Immediately replace all certificates
    B. Conduct a risk assessment
    C. No action is necessary
    D. Replace certificates as they expire

32. Barry would like to identify the mail server used by an organization. Which one of the following DNS record types identifies a mail server?

    A. MX
    B. A
    C. CNAME
    D. SOA

33. Gina runs a vulnerability scan of a server in her organization and receives the results shown below. What corrective action could Gina take to resolve these issues without disrupting service?

    A. Update RDP encryption
    B. Update HTTPS encryption
    C. Disable the network port
    D. No action is necessary

34. Carl is a help desk technician and received a call from an executive who received a suspicious email message. The content of the email appears below. What type of attack most likely took place?

Claim Your Tax Refund Online

We identified an error in the calculation of your tax from the last payment, amounting to $ 419.95. In order for us to return the excess payment, you need to create a e-Refund account after which the funds will be credited to your specified bank account.

Please click "Get Started" below to claim your refund:

Get Started

We are here to ensure the correct tax is paid at the right time, whether this relates to payment of taxes received by the department or entitlement to benefits paid.

    A. Whaling
    B. Spear phishing
    C. Vishing
    D. Phishing

35. Tina is an independent security researcher who often tests the security of systems belonging to large corporations. She recently entered into a contract with a large automotive supplier to test the security of their systems. What term best describes Tina's work on this engagement?

    A. White hat
    B. Grey hat
    C. Black hat
    D. Blue hat

36. Dan is a cybersecurity analyst. Each day he retrieves log files from a wide variety of security devices and correlates the information they contain, searching for unusual patterns of activity. What security control is likely lacking in Dan's environment?

    A. Firewall management tool
    B. IPS
    C. SIEM
    D. NAC

37. Which one of the following security controls would be MOST effective in combatting buffer overflow attacks?

    A. IDS
    B. VPN
    C. DLP
    D. ASLR

38. Mary believes that her network was the target of a wireless networking attack. Based upon the Wireshark traffic capture shown below, what type of attack likely took place?

```
Frame 981: 26 bytes on wire (208 bits), 26 bytes captures (208 bits)
802.11 radio information
IEEE 802.11 Deauthentication, Flags: ........C
IEEE 802.11 wireless LAN management frame
```

    A. Disassociation
    B. IV accumulation
    C. Replay
    D. Bluesnarfing

39. Gary is concerned about the susceptibility of his organization to phishing attacks. Which one of the following controls will best defend against this type of attack?

    A. Encryption
    B. User training
    C. Firewall
    D. Background checks

40. In which one of the following types of spoofing attack is the attacker often able to establish two-way communication with another device?

    A. E-mail spoofing
    B. MAC spoofing
    C. IP spoofing
    D. RFID spoofing

41. Rob is conducting a penetration test against a wireless network and would like to gather network traffic containing successful authentication attempts but the network is not heavily trafficked and he wants to speed up the information gathering process. What technique can he use?

    A. Replay
    B. Brute force
    C. Rainbow table
    D. Disassociation

42. Joe considers himself a hacker but generally does not develop his own exploits or customize exploits developed by others. Instead, he downloads exploits from hacker sites and attempts to apply them to large numbers of servers around the Internet until he finds one that is vulnerable. What type of hacker is Joe?

    A. 31337 h4x0r
    B. APT
    C. Script kiddie
    D. Penetration tester

43. Julie is beginning a penetration test against a client and would like to begin with passive reconnaissance. Which one of the following tools may be used for passive reconnaissance?

    A. Metasploit
    B. Nmap
    C. Nessus
    D. Aircrack-ng

44. Jake is responsible for the security of his organization's digital certificates and their associated keys. Which one of the following file types is normally shared publicly?

    A. .PEM file
    B. .CRT file
    C. .CSR file
    D. .KEY file

45. Brandon is looking for a security solution that is capable of reacting automatically to security information and performing a variety of tasks across other security solutions. Which one of the following technologies would best meet his needs?

    A. SIEM
    B. CASB
    C. IPS
    D. SOAR

46. Which one of the following malware tools is commonly used by attackers to escalate their access to administrative privileges once they have already compromised a normal user account on a system?

    A. Bot
    B. Rootkit
    C. RAT
    D. Logic bomb

47. Paul detected the vulnerability shown below in one of his systems. He has several other high priority projects waiting for his attention and needs to prioritize this issue. What should he do?

A. Immediately prioritize the remediation of this vulnerability over all other tasks.
B. Take no action.
C. Complete the pressing tasks on his current projects and then correct this vulnerability.
D. Hire a vendor to remediate the vulnerability.

48. Gary recently gained access to a salted and hashed password file from a popular website and he would like to exploit it in an attack. Which one of the following attacks would be most productive if the website has a password policy requiring complex passwords?

A. Offline brute force
B. Online brute force
C. Dictionary
D. Rainbow table

49. Vivian is investigating a website outage that brought down her company's ecommerce platform for several hours. During her investigation, she noticed that the logs are full of millions of connection attempts from systems around the world, but those attempts were never completed. What type of attack likely took place?

A. Cross-site scripting
B. DDoS
C. DoS
D. Cross-site request forgery

50. In which one of the following attacks against Bluetooth technology is the attacker able to steal information from the device?

A. Blueballing
B. Bluejacking
C. Bluesnarfing
D. Bluefeeding

51. What is the most dangerous consequence that commonly occurs as the result of a buffer overflow attack?

    A. Account enumeration
    B. Denial of service
    C. Information disclosure
    D. Arbitrary command execution

52. Which one of the following would not be considered an OSINT tool?

    A. Website perusal
    B. WHOIS lookups
    C. Google searches
    D. Vulnerability scans

53. Which one of the following is not a likely consequence of system sprawl?

    A. Improper input validation
    B. Undocumented assets
    C. Excess costs
    D. Unsupported systems

54. Tonya is developing a web application and is embedding a session ID in the application that is exchanged with each network communication. What type of attack is Tonya most likely trying to prevent?

    A. Man-in-the-middle
    B. Replay
    C. Buffer overflow
    D. SQL injection

55. Which one of the following security testing programs is designed to attract the participation of external testers and incentivize them to uncover security flaws?

    A. Penetration test
    B. Internal vulnerability scan
    C. Bug bounty
    D. External vulnerability scan

56. Carla found the following page on her web server. What type of attacker most likely waged this attack?

A. Hacktivist
B. APT
C. Script kiddie
D. Organized crime

57. Kevin is configuring a vulnerability scan of his network. He would like the scan to be a non-intrusive scan and is using the configuration settings shown below. Which setting should he modify?

A. Enable safe checks
B. Stop scanning hosts that become unresponsive during the scan
C. Scan IP addresses in a random order
D. Slow down the scan when network congestion is detected

58. Frank is responsible for administering his organization's domain names. He recently received a message from their registrar indicating that a transfer request was underway for one of their domains, but Frank was not aware of any request taking place. What type of attack may be occurring?

   A. DNS spoofing
   B. IP spoofing
   C. Domain hijacking
   D. ARP spoofing

59. Morgan is a web developer responsible for implementing an authentication system. She knows that she should store hashed versions of passwords rather than the passwords themselves but chooses to use unsalted passwords. What type of attack does this make the application more susceptible to?

   A. Offline brute force attack
   B. Online brute force attack
   C. Rainbow table
   D. Collision

60. Kelly detected an attack on her network where the attacker used aircrack-ng to create a wireless network bearing her company's SSID. The attacker then boosted the power of that access point so that it was the strongest signal in an executive office area, prompting executive devices to connect to it. What type of attack took place?

   A. Bluesnarfing
   B. Jamming
   C. Evil twin
   D. WPS

61. Which one of the following attributes is NOT a characteristic of APT attackers?

   A. Patience
   B. Large amounts of money
   C. Sophisticated exploits
   D. Brute force

62. Which one of the following security controls is most effective against zero-day attacks?

   A. Vulnerability scans
   B. Signature-based antivirus software
   C. Application control
   D. Intrusion prevention systems

63. Chris is investigating a security incident at his organization where an attacker entered the building wearing a company uniform and demanded that the receptionist provide him access to a network closet. He told the receptionist that he needed to access the closet immediately to prevent a major network disaster. Which one of the following principles of social engineering did the attacker NOT exploit?

    A. Consensus
    B. Authority
    C. Intimidation
    D. Urgency

64. Ann works for an organization that recently opted to discontinue support service on their network devices to control costs. They realized that it would be less expensive to replace devices when they fail than to use the costly replacement plan that was included in their support contract. What should be Ann's primary concern from a security perspective?

    A. Time required to replace a failed device
    B. Cost of replacing devices
    C. Lack of access to vendor patches
    D. Lack of access to vendor support personnel

65. Which one of the following controls would be LEAST effective against a privilege escalation attack?

    A. HIPS
    B. Patching
    C. Data Execution Prevention
    D. Firewall rule

66. Warren is conducting a penetration test and has gained access to a critical file server containing sensitive information. He is now installing a rootkit on that server. What phase of the penetration test is Warren conducting?

    A. Active reconnaissance
    B. Persistence
    C. Escalation of privilege
    D. Pivot

67. Which one of the following security vulnerabilities is NOT a common result of improper input handling?

    A. Distributed denial of service
    B. SQL injection
    C. Cross-site scripting
    D. Buffer overflow

68. What type of access must an attacker have to successfully carry out an ARP poisoning attack against a target?

    A. Access to the target's LAN
    B. Administrative access on the target's system
    C. Normal user access on the target's system
    D. Access to the target's network firewall

69. Which one of the following cryptographic attacks may be used to find collisions in a hash function?

    A. Birthday attack
    B. Meet-in-the-middle attack
    C. Man-in-the-middle attack
    D. Chosen plaintext attack

70. Bob is charged with protecting the service shown below from the attack being waged by Mal. What control would best protect against this threat?

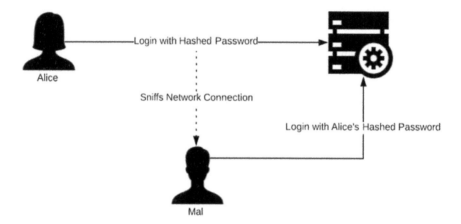

    A. Adding TLS encryption
    B. Changing the hash algorithm
    C. Changing Alice's password
    D. Using a shadow password file

71. After running a vulnerability scan, Charlie identified 10 Windows XP systems running on the network. Those systems support critical business hardware that is over 10 years old and it is not possible to replace the hardware. What is the primary issue that Charlie needs to address?

    A. Obsolete operating system
    B. Incorrectly configured firewall
    C. Outdated hardware
    D. User security awareness

72. Patty is approached by an end user who is trying to visit a banking website and sees the error message below. What type of attack is most likely taking place?

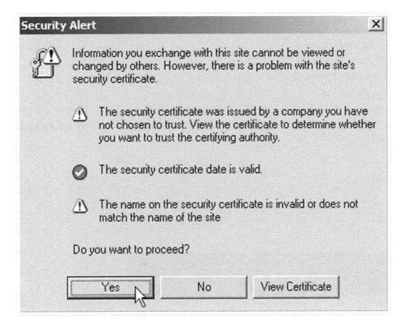

A. Social engineering
B. This is a routine error and no attack is likely
C. Man-in-the-middle
D. Certificate pinning

73. During a security review, Terry identified a system that is using the RC4 cipher with a 40-bit key to protect communications between systems using the Remote Desktop Protocol. Which one of the following findings would it be appropriate for Terry to include in his report on the risk of this service?

A. There is not enough information to reach a conclusion.
B. The key length is too short and should be increased to 1,024 bits.
C. RC4 is an insecure cipher and should not be used.
D. The system is using a secure cipher with an appropriate key length

74. Joan is trying to break a cryptographic algorithm where she has the encryption key but does not have the decryption key. She is generating a series of encrypted messages and using them in her cryptanalysis. Which term best describes Joan's attack?

A. Known plaintext
B. Chosen plaintext
C. Chosen ciphertext
D. Known ciphertext

75. Kristen is investigating wireless signal interference in her building and suspects that jamming might be taking place. Which one of the following actions can help her rule out intentional jamming of her wireless signal?

    A. Moving antenna locations
    B. Changing the WiFi channel
    C. Changing power levels
    D. Testing a variety of devices

76. While investigating a security incident, Ryan discovers that the attacker entered the information shown below in the login box for a web application. What type of attack was likely taking place?

    A. LDAP injection
    B. Blind SQL injection
    C. SQL injection
    D. Cross-site scripting

77. Melanie is designing an authentication scheme for a web application and wishes to protect the site against session hijacking attacks. She would like to ensure that cookies containing session credentials are only sent via encrypted connections. What attribute should she set on cookies used for session identification?

    A. Expire
    B. HttpOnly
    C. SameSite
    D. Secure

78. Ken is conducting a penetration test of one of his organization's clients. He gains access to a web server located in the DMZ using a buffer overflow attack and is now attempting to gain access to systems on the internal network. What stage of the attack has Ken reached?

    A. Reconnaissance
    B. Pivot
    C. Persistence
    D. Escalation of privilege

79. Rob is troubleshooting a production application in his organization. He discovers that after the application has been running for about a week, it begins producing repeated errors. When he reboots the system, it again works fine for another week, until the errors begin recurring. What is the most likely cause of this issue?

    A. Insider attack
    B. Logic bomb
    C. Buffer overflow
    D. Memory leak

80. Vince runs the MD5 hash function against three files on his system. He knows that each of the three files contains log entries from different days. What has occurred?

    ```
    > md5(file1)
    fc3b6237c730b6c527856173ff0a1b28

    > md5(file2)
    dd0e42333f49952523ddf8a33496cf6a

    > md5(file3)
    fc3b6237c730b6c527856173ff0a1b28
    ```

    A. Use of a secure hash function
    B. Decryption
    C. Collision
    D. Syntax error

81. After running an nmap scan of a new web server being commissioned on her network, Karen discovered the results shown below. Which port should Karen prioritize for investigation and remediation?

    ```
    Starting Nmap 7.70 ( https://nmap.org ) at 2018-12-05 18:51 EST
    Nmap scan report for scan1.certmike (192.168.119.84)
    Host is up (0.045s latency).
    Not shown: 996 filtered ports
    PORT     STATE
    22/tcp   open
    23/tcp   open
    80/tcp   open
    443/tcp  open

    Nmap done: 1 IP address (1 host up) scanned in 5.10 seconds
    ```

    A. 443
    B. 22
    C. 80
    D. 23

82. The POODLE attack rendered the SSL protocol insecure and prompted many websites to replace SSL with TLS. What type of attack is POODLE?

   A. Dissassociation
   B. Downgrade
   C. Bluesnarfing
   D. Evil twin

83. Vince is investigating the compromise of a user's account credentials. The user reports that, in addition to her corporate account, the passwords to many of her online banking and bill payment accounts were also compromised. Vince examines her computer and determines that there is an unusual piece of hardware connected between the keyboard and the computer. What type of attack has most likely taken place?

   A. Bot
   B. Spyware
   C. Keylogger
   D. Adware

84. Larry is evaluating a dynamic web application that uses a web server with a database back end, as shown in the image below. The web server is configured to connect to the database server with a database administrative account. Which one of the following statements is correct about this configuration?

   A. The web server should use an OS administrator account to connect to the database.
   B. The web server should use a limited privilege account to connect to the database.
   C. This configuration is reasonable.
   D. The web server should not connect directly to the database server.

85. Which one of the following attacks allows the theft of information from a mobile device over a wireless connection that directly connects the attacker to the device?

   A. Bluejacking
   B. Evil twin
   C. Bluesnarfing
   D. Session hijacking

86. In a recent social engineering attack, the attacker found an employee of the target company at his gym and struck up a friendship there for several months before trying to slowly extract sensitive corporate information from the employee. What principle of social engineering is the attacker trying to exploit?

   A. Consensus
   B. Authority
   C. Urgency
   D. Familiarity

87. During a penetration test, the testers sent the email below to a clerk in an organization's Accounts Payable department. What type of attack took place?

   ---------- Forwarded message ----------
   From: **John Lyons** <jlyons@yourcompany.com>
   Date: Wed, Feb 21, 2018 at 9:29 AM
   Subject: Request
   To: jsmith@yourcompany.com

   Hi Jason,

   I hope you are having a pleasant day.

   I am currently traveling on business in Europe and need to send an urgent wire transfer to one of our business partners here. What information do you need to process the request? Also, what time would you need to have the information in order to send the money prior to the close of business in Europe today?

   I know that this is unusual but appreciate your attending to this right away. It's critical to our relationship with Acme Corp.

   Thanks!
   John Lyons
   President & Chief Executive Office
   YourCompany.com

   A. Spear phishing
   B. Whaling
   C. Vishing
   D. Smishing

88. Which one of the following device types is most susceptible to a pass-the-hash attack?

   A. VPN concentrator
   B. Network firewall
   C. Windows server
   D. Hardware security module

89. Vince is concerned about the execution of SQL injection attacks against the database supporting his organization's e-commerce website. Which one of the following controls would NOT be an effective defense against these attacks?

   A. Parameterized queries
   B. WAF
   C. Indexing
   D. Stored procedures

90. Norm is concerned that his organization may be the target of a theft of trade secrets by a competitor working with an insider to steal sensitive files. What security control would be most helpful in detecting attempts to remove that sensitive information from the organization?

   A. IPS
   B. DLP
   C. Firewall
   D. TLS

91. Elliott is frustrated by the number of false positive reports being returned by his vulnerability scans. Which one of the following actions is MOST likely to reduce the number of false positive reports?

   A. Implement credentialed scanning
   B. Decrease the scan sensitivity
   C. Disable safe checks
   D. Increase the size of the target network

92. During a recent security investigation, Cam discovered the device shown below sewn into a briefcase belonging to a senior executive. What type of transmission was most likely used to communicate with this device?

   A. Cellular
   B. Bluetooth
   C. WiFi
   D. RFID

93. Dave discovers that a piece of malware running on a system has been loading the feeds of strange Twitter accounts that contain tweets similar to the one shown below. What type of malware likely exists on this system?

A. Trojan horse
B. Virus
C. Worm
D. Botnet

94. Rick would like to use vulnerability scanning results as part of a penetration test he is undertaking. The penetration test is scoped as a black box test. Which one of the following scan reports would be most useful and appropriate for Rick to obtain from management before conducting the test?

A. Internal scan report
B. External scan report
C. Credentialed scan report
D. Agent-based scan report

95. After running a vulnerability scan, Carl detects a missing patch on a Windows server. When he investigates the server, he determines that the patch is actually applied. What condition has occurred?

A. True positive
B. False negative
C. False positive
D. True negative

96. After conducting a vulnerability scan, Kaiden discovers the vulnerability shown below on several of his organization's web servers. What is the most likely direct impact of these vulnerabilities?

A. An attacker can disrupt access to the web server
B. An attacker can obtain information about the inner functioning of the web application
C. An attacker can steal information from the database supporting this application
D. An attacker can gain administrative access to the web server

97. Carla noticed unusual spikes in network activity and, upon further investigation, determined that there are an usually high number of outbound DNS query responses. She also noticed that the query responses are significantly larger than the queries themselves. What type of attack should Carla suspect?

A. Cross-site scripting
B. Amplification
C. DNS poisoning
D. Pass-the-hash

98. Shortly after Trish's organization fired a software developer, code on a server activated that determined the developer was no longer employed and deleted the source code from her projects. What type of attack did Trish's organization experience?

A. Logic bomb
B. Trojan horse
C. Worm
D. RAT

99. Dawn is conducting the reconnaissance phase of a penetration test and would like to identify the registered owner of a domain name. Which one of the following tools would be most likely to provide her with this information?

A. Whois
B. Nslookup
C. Dig
D. Ping

100. Which one of the following controls is the most effective way to protect against security-related architectural and design weaknesses?

A. Deploying intrusion prevention systems
B. Carefully maintaining network firewall rules
C. Implementing employee background checks
D. Including security team members in the project management process

101. Barry is the administrator of a message board used by his organization's clients to communicate with each other. One client posted a message on the board that contained script code that caused the browsers of other users to carry out malicious actions when they viewed the message. What type of attack took place?

A. XSRF
B. Reflected XSS
C. DOM XSS
D. Stored XSS

102. Mal is an attacker associated with an advanced persistent threat (APT) organization. Her team recently discovered a new security vulnerability in a major operating system and has not informed anyone of this vulnerability. What type of attack is Mal's organization in a position to wage?

    A. SQL injection
    B. Zero-day
    C. Man-in-the-browser
    D. Spoofing

103. Which one of the following technologies would be most useful in preventing man-in-the-middle attacks?

    A. TLS
    B. SSL
    C. Digital certificates
    D. Input validation

104. Harold is examining the web server logs after detecting unusual activity on the system. He finds the log excerpt shown below. What type of attack did someone attempt against this system based upon the data shown in these logs?

```
10.90.158.182 - - [21/Jan/2018:03:29:56 -0500] "GET /wp-admin HTTP/1.1" 301 241 "-" "Python-url
lib/2.7"
10.90.158.182 - - [21/Jan/2018:03:29:56 -0500] "GET /wp-admin/ HTTP/1.1" 302 - "-" "Python-urll
ib/2.7"
10.90.158.182 - - [21/Jan/2018:03:29:56 -0500] "GET /wp-login.php&uid=20%20UNION%20SELECT%201,2
,3,4,5 HTTP/1.1" 200 7255 "-" "Python-urllib/2.7"
10.90.158.182 - - [21/Jan/2018:03:29:56 -0500] "GET / HTTP/1.1" 200 48816 "-" "Python-urllib/2.
7"
10.90.158.182 - - [21/Jan/2018:03:29:56 -0500] "GET / HTTP/1.1" 301 - "-" "Python-urllib/2.7"
10.196.57.217 - - [21/Jan/2018:03:30:37 -0500] "GET /category/white-papers/feed/ HTTP/1.1" 304
- "https://www.google.com/" "Mozilla/5.0 (Macintosh; U; PPC Mac OS X Mach-O; en-US; rv:1.8.1.7p
re) Gecko/20070815 Firefox/2.0.0.6 Navigator/9.0b3"
```

    A. Cross-site scripting
    B. Domain hijacking
    C. SQL injection
    D. Directory traversal

105. Which one of the following attacks exploits a race condition in a software implementation?

    A. Integer overflow
    B. Buffer overflow
    C. SQL injection
    D. TOC/TOU

106. Which one of the following devices is capable of carrying out a rogue AP attack against a WiFi network with minimal configuration?

    A. Switch
    B. Router
    C. Orange
    D. Pineapple

107. Carla's firm is preparing to deploy a large network of Internet of Things sensors. Which one of the following is the least common security concern with IoT deployments?

   A. Data encryption
   B. Patches to embedded operating systems
   C. Network segmentation
   D. Multifactor authentication

108. Hank ran a vulnerability scan of one of his organization's web servers and found the two vulnerabilities shown below. What is the most expedient way for Hank to correct this issue?

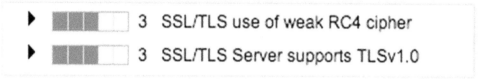

   A. Modify the ciphers used by SSL/TLS
   B. Upgrade to SSL 3.0
   C. Upgrade to TLS 1.2
   D. Replace the digital certificate

109. Mal is engaging in an IP spoofing attack against a target organization over the Internet. Which one of the following limitations does the attack have, if Mal has complete control of her own network?

   A. Mal will not be able to receive responses to requests
   B. Mal will not be able to send packets onto the Internet with spoofed addresses
   C. Mal will not be able to insert a spoofed IP address into her network traffic
   D. Mal will not be able to conduct a denial of service attack

110. Nate is the first person to arrive in the office one morning and he discovers that a piece of malware is spreading from system to system on his network, exploiting the CVE-2019-0708 vulnerability in Microsoft Windows. What term best describes this malware?

   A. Virus
   B. Trojan horse
   C. Worm
   D. Logic bomb

111. Noah is a cybersecurity analyst for a mid-sized business. He is working with the user of a machine that is exhibiting suspicious behavior. The anomalous activity began immediately after the user downloaded and installed software from the Internet and Noah suspects that it contained malware. What term best describes the malware in this situation?

   A. Trojan horse
   B. Virus
   C. Worm
   D. Logic bomb

112. Ryan is reviewing logs for his wireless network controller and discovers that a single system attempted to connect to the wireless network once every minute with incorrect credentials until finally logging in successfully after several hours. In reviewing the logs, Ryan noticed that the system had been used by the same user on the network several days ago. What is the most likely explanation of these log entries?

   A. The user's password was compromised via a brute force attack.
   B. The user fell victim to a social engineering attack.
   C. The user changed his or her password.
   D. The user's device was stolen.

113. Mary's organization uses a specialized statistical software package for their research. Mary discovered that users pass around installation media within their departments rather than deploying the software via a centralized tool. What is the greatest risk facing the organization?

   A. Social engineering
   B. Malware infection
   C. License violation
   D. Faulty software

114. Helen is working with a user who reported that strange messages were appearing on his mobile device. After troubleshooting, Helen determines that the messages were sent over Bluetooth. There is no indication that any information on the device was accessed by the attacker. What type of attack likely took place?

   A. Bluelining
   B. Bluesnarfing
   C. Bluescreening
   D. Bluejacking

115. What type of social engineering attack always occurs via telephone calls?

   A. Spear phishing
   B. Vishing
   C. Smishing
   D. Whaling

116. Hannah is investigating a security incident and discovers that a network client sent false MAC address information to a switch. What type of attack likely took place?

   A. DNS poisoning
   B. ARP poisoning
   C. Man-in-the-middle
   D. Eavesdropping

117. Molly's security team is overwhelmed by the number of sources of security information that they receive. She would like to select a tool that can aggregate and correlate log entries. What tool is most appropriate for her needs?

A. DLP
B. SIEM
C. IPS
D. NAC

118. John would like to identify a subscription service that helps him block known malicious systems from accessing his network by automatically updating his firewall rules. What type of service would best meet this need?

A. Malware signature
B. IP reputation
C. IDS signature
D. Behavioral analysis

119. What is the primary risk associated with storing API keys in a public GitHub code repository?

A. Unauthorized provisioning of resources
B. Theft of sensitive information
C. Unauthorized API use
D. Denial of service attacks

120. Dylan is working to protect his organization against integer overflow attacks. He has a web application that stores the weight of an individual in a database. The weight value is stored as an 8-bit positive integer. What is the maximum weight that may be stored in this field.

A. 255
B. 127
C. 511
D. 1,023

121. Ryan is concerned about integrity attacks against his organization's sales database. Which one of the following SQL commands is least likely to result in an integrity issue?

A. SELECT
B. INSERT
C. UPDATE
D. DELETE

122. Martin is concerned about the misuse of legitimate privileges by employees, otherwise known as the insider threat. Which one of the following activities would best serve as a control against this threat?

A. Privilege auditing
B. Usage auditing
C. Multifactor authentication
D. Credential management

123. Yolanda is concerned about brute force attacks against her Windows system. Which one of the following controls is a good security practice that reduces the likelihood of a successful brute force attack?

   A. Expire the Administrator account password monthly
   B. Rename the Administrator account
   C. Disable the Administrator account
   D. Encrypt the contents of the Administrator account

124. Which one of the following attacks is a critical threat that applies specifically to NTLM authentication?

   A. Rainbow table
   B. Brute force
   C. Pass-the-hash
   D. Man-in-the-middle

125. Which one of the following risk assessment activities does not require advance authorization from the target organization?

   A. Penetration testing
   B. Open source reconnaissance
   C. Social engineering
   D. Vulnerability scanning

126. Darren is an intrusion analyst and feels overwhelmed by the amount of information presented to him by various tools. He would like to find a solution that can correlate information from various other sources. Which one of the following tools would best meet his needs?

   A. DLP
   B. SIEM
   C. IPS
   D. IDS

Domain 1 Answers and Explanations

1. **D.** Most automated attacks assume that a Windows system still contains a default account named Administrator and try to exploit that account. Changing the name makes it less likely that these attacks will stumble upon the account.

2. **D.** In a domain hijacking attack, the attacker changes the registration of a domain with the registrar. DNS and ARP poisoning attacks may redirect web traffic, but they would do so by providing bogus address information, not by hijacking the domain. Network eavesdropping could theoretically be used to steal credentials used to alter information with a registrar, but this is unlikely. The most likely source of a domain hijacking attack is using social engineering with the registrar to gain access to the account used to manage registration information.

3. **A.** Cross-site scripting relies upon embedding HTML tags in stored or reflected input. The < and > characters are used to denote HTML tags and should be carefully managed when seen in user input.

4. **B.** The fact that the legitimate server responds to requests made by IP address indicates that the attacker is not performing IP spoofing or ARP spoofing. There is no indication that the URL is incorrect, so Darren can rule out typosquatting. The most likely attack in this scenario is DNS poisoning. Darren can verify this by manually changing the system to a different DNS server, clearing the system's DNS cache, and attempting to resolve the name again.

5. **B.** During a cybersecurity exercise, the red team is responsible for conducting offensive operations, while the blue team conducts defensive operations. The white team consists of the officials who moderate the exercise and arbitrate rules disputes. Purple teaming occurs after the exercise when the red and blue teams come together to discuss tactics and lessons learned.

6. **A.** DNS amplification is a denial of service technique that sends small queries with spoofed source addresses to DNS servers, generating much larger, amplified, responses back to the spoofed address. The purpose is to consume all of the bandwidth available to the target system, resulting in a resource exhaustion denial of service attack.

7. **B.** Pixie Dust attacks are a specialized attack used to retrieve the WiFi Protected Setup (WPS) PIN code for a network. Pixie Dust attacks will not work if WPS is not enabled on the network.

8. **A.** The two major categories of attack against device drivers are shimming and refactoring. In a shimming attack, the attacker wraps his or her own malicious code around the legitimate driver. Shimming attacks do not require access to the driver's source code. In a refactoring attack, such as this one, the attacker actually modifies the original driver's source code.

9. **D.** Discovery scans are designed to identify systems on the network and can be used to detect undocumented assets that are the result of system sprawl.

10. **D.** The Data Encryption Standard (DES) is an outdated, insecure algorithm that should not be used in modern applications. Triple DES (3DES) is a secure alternative that uses three rounds of DES encryption. The Advanced Encryption Standard (AES) and Elliptic Curve Cryptosystem (ECC) are also modern, secure cipher suites.

11. **A.** Social engineering is an active technique because it involves interaction with the target organization. Attackers may conduct open source intelligence gathering, including domain name searches, using only external resources that will not alert the target organization. Wireless network eavesdropping may also be conducted from a location outside of the organization's facilities without alerting the organization to their presence or interacting with target systems.

12. **B.** This is an example of a watering hole attack. These attacks place malicious code on a website frequented by members of the target audience. There is not sufficient information to determine whether the malicious code was spyware or a Trojan horse, or whether it delivered a denial of service payload.

13. **C.** The social engineer is using the Microsoft header in an attempt to exploit the trust that the recipient has for Microsoft. This attack also exploits the principles of authority, familiarity and urgency. There is no note of scarcity or consensus in the message. The attacker is indeed trying to intimidate the recipient, but the intimidation is contained within the virus hoax message, not the Microsoft header.

14. **C.** The root cause of this issue is that FTP is an insecure protocol and Kristen can resolve the problem by replacing it with a secure alternative, such as SFTP. Requiring strong passwords or multifactor authentication would not resolve the problem, as an attacker could still eavesdrop on those connections and obtain user passwords. Discontinuing the file transfer service would resolve the vulnerability but it is not a good solution because it would unnecessarily disrupt whatever business processes take place on this server.

15. **B.** Discarding notes containing customer information leaves the organization vulnerable to a dumpster diving attack where the attacker retrieves those records from the trash. Twyla should ensure that her organization shreds these records before discarding them.

16. **B.** Social engineering attacks depend upon user error and training can dramatically reduce the success rate of these attacks. Buffer overflow attacks, denial of service attacks, and ARP poisoning attacks are not generally preventable by end users and, therefore, training the sales team would not be an effective defense against them.

17. **A.** A memory leak is a software flaw and, since this is an internally developed application, the developer is the person most likely to be able to correct it. If the issue were in a commercially purchased application, a system administrator may be able to correct the issue by applying a patch but that is not the case in this scenario.

18. **B.** This is a clear example of a distributed denial of service (DDoS) attack. The system is flooding the target with connection requests, hoping to overwhelm it. The port and IP address are not changing, so this is not indicative of a scanning attack. There is no indication that the connection is completed, so it cannot be a SQL injection attack.

19. **C.** All of the controls mentioned in this question would improve the security of this scenario. However, the best way to handle sensitive information is to not retain it in the first place. It is unlikely that there is a valid business reason for storing copies of records containing customer credit card information. Therefore, the most appropriate solution would be to modify the business process to avoid this inappropriate data retention.

20. **A.** DNS poisoning works by injecting false information into a user's local DNS servers. Adding redundant or off-site DNS servers would not reduce the likelihood of a successful attack. Blocking DNS traffic with firewall rules would disrupt the service for legitimate users. The DNSSEC protocol adds a verification layer to ensure that DNS updates come from trusted sources, reducing the likelihood of a successful DNS poisoning attack.

21. **B.** This is an example of a SQL injection attack because the attacker is inserting his or her own commands into a SQL database query. This particular example is slowing down responses when the answer is correct to ferret out the characters of a password, one-by-one. That is an example of a timing-based SQL injection attack.

22. **A.** All of the possible answers have the effect of blocking some DNS requests. The most effective technique to prevent DNS amplification is to disable open resolution so that external users may not make arbitrary recursive requests against the server. Blocking internal requests would have no effect on the attack. Blocking all external requests or blocking port 53 at the firewall would prevent all external requests, preventing the server from fulfilling its purpose as a public DNS server.

23. **A.** This attack is a DLL injection attack. In a DLL injection, the attacker forces an existing process to load a dynamically linked library which contains unauthorized code.

24. **C.** Advanced persistent threats (APTs) are characterized by a high level of sophistication and significant financial and technical resources. Other attackers, including script kiddies, criminals, and hacktivists, are not likely to have anywhere near the same sophistication as an APT attacker (such as a national government).

25. **A.** Back doors are an example of a persistence technique. They are designed to allow the attacker to regain access to the system even after the original flaw they exploited is patched.

26. **D.** In a black box attack, the attacker does not have access to any information about the target environment before beginning the attack. In a grey box attack, the attacker has limited information. In a white box attack, the attacker has full knowledge of the target environment before beginning the attack.

27. **A.** In a man-in-the-browser attack, the attacker manages to gain a foothold inside the user's browser, normally by exploiting a browser extension. This gives him or her access to all information accessed with the browser, regardless of whether the site uses strong authentication or transport encryption (such as TLS). Certificate pinning is a technique used to protect against inauthentic digital certificates and would not protect against a man-in-the-browser attack.

28. **C.** Insider attacks are particularly dangerous because they involve internal employees, contractors, or other individuals with access to systems and knowledge of business processes. Other attackers are less likely to have access to this information.

29. **D.** A web application firewall (WAF), if present, would likely block SQL injection attack attempts, making SQL injection vulnerabilities invisible to a vulnerability scanner. A data loss prevention system (DLP) does not protect against web application vulnerabilities, such as SQL injection. An intrusion detection system (IDS) might identify a SQL injection exploit attempt but it is not able to block the attack. Transport layer security (TLS) encrypts web content but encryption would not prevent an attacker from engaging in SQL injection attacks.

30. **B.** The key to this question is focusing on the encryption algorithms used by each option. Three of the four options use AES 256-bit encryption, which provides strong cryptography. One uses RC4 encryption, which is a weak implementation of cryptography and should be avoided.

31. **B.** The use of self-signed certificates is not, by itself, cause for alarm. It is acceptable to use self-signed certificates for internal use. Val should conduct a risk assessment to identify whether this use is appropriate and replace any certificates used by external users.

32. **A.** The MX record identifies the mail server for a domain. A records are used to identify domain names associated with IP addresses while CNAMES are used to create aliases. Start of Authority (SOA) records contain information about the authoritative servers for a DNS zone.

33. **A.** These vulnerabilities both relate to the encryption of the service running on port 3389, which is used by the Remote Desktop Protocol (RDP). Upgrading this encryption should resolve these vulnerabilities. There is no indication that an HTTPS service is running on this device. Disabling the network port would disrupt the service. Gina should take action because this is an easily corrected vulnerability.

34. **D.** This is most likely a straightforward phishing attack. The message is generic and not targeted at a specific user, as you would find in a spear phishing attack. Although the user is an executive, there is no indication that the message was specifically sent to this user because of his status as an executive, so it is not likely a whaling attack. The attack was sent over email, not the telephone, so it is not an example of vishing.

35. **A.** Tina is working under an authorized contract, so her work is clearly that of a white hat hacker. White hats do not need to be employees of the company being tested; they merely must be authorized to do their work. If Tina was working without permission but intended to report results only to the target company, her work would be considered grey hat. If she had malicious intent, she would be a black hat hacker. Blue hat is not a term commonly used to categorize attackers.

36. **C.** If Dan's organization used a security information and event management (SIEM) solution, Dan would not need to gather information from this wide variety of sources. Instead, the SIEM would collect and correlate this information, providing Dan with a single place to review correlated data.

37. **D.** Address space layout randomization (ASLR) is a security technique that randomizes the location of objects in memory, making a buffer overflow attack less likely to succeed. Virtual private networks (VPN) provide transport encryption and data loss prevention (DLP) systems provide protection against data exfiltration. Neither would be effective against buffer overflow attacks. Intrusion detection systems (IDS) may identify a buffer overflow attack but would not prevent it from succeeding.

38. **A.** The message shown in the capture is a deauthentication message. These messages are often used in disassociation attacks, where the attacker attempts to force the disconnection of a client from a legitimate access point. IV attacks use cryptanalysis on the initialization vectors (IVs) used in establishing a WiFi session. Replay attacks attempt to reuse credentials captured during a legitimate session to establish unauthorized wireless connections. Bluesnarfing attacks leverage Bluetooth technology, which is not in use in this scenario.

39. **B.** Phishing is a form of social engineering and its effectiveness depends upon the susceptibility of users to this type of attack. While some technical controls, such as email content filtering, may be useful against phishing attacks, the most effective defense is user awareness training.

40. **B.** In a MAC spoofing attack, the local switch is normally fooled into believing the spoofed address and will route reply traffic back to the device spoofing an address. IP spoofing and email spoofing work at the application layer and, in most cases, the attacker will not receive any responses to spoofed messages. RFID spoofing is not a common type of attack.

41. **D.** Disassociation attacks intentionally disconnect a wireless user from their access point to force a reauthentication that the attacker may collect with a wireless eavesdropping tool. Brute force attacks, rainbow table attacks and replay attacks do not gather network traffic and, therefore, would not be useful in this scenario.

42. **C.** Joe is a script kiddie because he does not leverage his own knowledge but merely applies tools written by others. Advanced persistent threats or elite hackers (31337 h4x0r) use sophisticated, customized tools. Joe is not a penetration tester because he does not have authorization to perform the scans.

43. **D.** Nmap, Nessus, and Metasploit are all active reconnaissance tools that interact with their target environments. Aircrack-ng may be used to passively gather information about a wireless network and crack a pre-shared key.

44. **B.** Jake may safely share the .CRT file, which contains a copy of the organization's public X.509 certificate. The .KEY and .PEM files contain copies of the organization's private keys, which must be kept secret and secure. The .CSR file is a certificate signing request, which is sent to the CA when requesting a signed digital certificate. There is no need to share this file publicly.

45. **D.** Security orchestration, automation, and response (SOAR) platforms are specifically designed to react to security information and perform workflows across a variety of other systems. Security information and event management (SIEM) platforms are capable of doing this to some degree, but they are not as well suited to the task as SOAR platforms. Cloud access security brokers (CASB) and intrusion prevention systems (IPS) are not designed for this purpose.

46. **B.** Rootkits are specialized attack tools that allow an attacker to escalate privileges. They exploit system vulnerabilities to leverage a normal user account to gain administrative privileges on the system.

47. **B.** This is a very low priority vulnerability. The report shows that it has a severity of one on five-point scale, placing it into the category of informational messages. There are likely hundreds or thousands of similar issues elsewhere on the network. Therefore, there is no need for Paul to take any action.

48. **A.** In this case, Gary should use an offline brute force attack against the password file. An online attack would not leverage the password file that he obtained and would likely be slower and attract attention. A dictionary attack is not effective against a site with a strong password complexity policy. A rainbow table attack suffers the same deficiency as a dictionary attack with the added problem that the site uses salted hashes, rendering the rainbow table ineffective.

49. **B.** This is a clear example of a distributed denial of service (DDoS) attack. The half-open connections indicate the use of a denial of service attack. The fact that the requests came from all over the world

makes it clear that it is more than a standard denial of service attack. There is no indication that there was a web application flaw, such as cross-site request forgery or cross-site scripting.

50. **C.** In a bluesnarfing attack, the attacker establishes a Bluetooth connection to a target device and then retrieves information from that device. Bluejacking attacks only allow the attacker to display a message on the device. Blueballing attacks allow an attacker to break an existing Bluetooth connection between two devices. Bluefeeding attacks do not exist.

51. **D.** While any of these actions may result from a buffer overflow attack, they are all the result of the more general arbitrary command execution capability. After a successful buffer overflow, the attacker can typically execute any commands he or she would like on the system. This effectively gives the attacker full control of the device.

52. **D.** Open source intelligence (OSINT) includes the use of any publicly available information. This would include domain registration records found in WHOIS entries, the contents of public websites, and the use of Google searches. Vulnerability scans are an active reconnaissance technique and would not be considered OSINT.

53. **A.** System sprawl may lead to undocumented systems that are running without the knowledge of the IT organization. These systems may serve no useful purpose, contributing to excess costs. They may also have no assigned IT support personnel, leading to unpatched systems and security vulnerabilities. Input validation is an application security technique and system sprawl would not necessarily lead to increased failures to perform proper input validation.

54. **B.** Session tokens, or session IDs, are used to prevent an eavesdropper from stealing authentication credentials and reusing them in a different session, in what is known as a replay attack. The use of session IDs would not prevent an attacker from carrying out an application layer attack, such as a buffer overflow or injection. It also would not be effective against a man-in-the-middle attack, as the attacker could simply establish a secure session with the server and would, therefore, have access to the session ID.

55. **C.** Bug bounty programs are specifically designed to solicit bug reports from external security testers. Vulnerability scans (whether internal or external) and penetration tests are run by, or on behalf of, an organization's own security team.

56. **A.** This website defacement attack has a clear political message, making the attacker a hacktivist. It is unlikely that an advanced persistent threat or organized crime ring conducted this attack because there is no obvious non-activist motive. There is not enough information to conclude that the attack was waged by a script kiddie because we do not know how the site was compromised.

57. **A.** Enabling safe checks tells the scanner to only use scan plug-ins that are non-intrusive. The other settings would not change the plug-ins used by the scanner. Configuring the scanner to stop scanning hosts that become unresponsive implies that the scan has already disrupted the host. Changing the order or speed of the scan would not change the tests performed.

58. **C.** This is not likely a spoofing attack because there is no evidence that an attacker is falsifying address information in network traffic. However, it is quite possible that an attacker is attempting to steal a domain registration using a domain hijacking attack. Frank should contact the registrar and cancel the request. He should also consider locking the domain to prevent any future unauthorized transfer.

59. **C.** In a rainbow table attack, the attacker computes the hash values of common passwords and then searches the password file for those values. Adding a random salt to the password eliminates the performance benefit of this attack. Brute force attacks (online or offline) would not be more or less effective either way. The use of salting does not decrease the likelihood of a collision.

60. **C.** In this attack, the perpetrator created a false wireless network, otherwise known as an evil twin. Although the attacker boosted the power of the signal to make the evil twin signal stronger than other signals, there is no indication of attempts to jam signals from legitimate access points. There is no indication in the scenario that Bluetooth or WPS technology was involved.

61. **D.** Advanced persistent threat (APT) attackers are sophisticated attackers who generally have the support of a nation-state or other large organization that provides them with significant financial resources and sophisticated tools. They often pursue their targets very patiently until they are able to exploit a vulnerability. APT attackers operate stealthily and would avoid using brute force techniques.

62. **C.** Zero-day attacks are attacks that are not previously known to the security community. Therefore, signature based controls, such as vulnerability scans, antivirus software, and intrusion prevention systems are not effective against these attacks. Application control software may use whitelisting to limit software running on a system to a list of known good applications. This technique may prevent zero-day malware from running on the protected system.

63. **A.** The attacker entered the building wearing a uniform, which is a sign of authority. He threatened the receptionist (intimidation) with an impending network outage (urgency). There is no indication that he tried to build consensus.

64. **C.** While all of these concerns are legitimate, the lack of access to vendor patches should be Ann's primary security concern. Most vendors require a valid support agreement to obtain firmware updates and devices without those updates may have serious security vulnerabilities. Ann should consider pursuing a less costly support agreement that does not include the expensive hardware replacement feature but does provide access to security updates.

65. **D.** Patching operating systems will address security vulnerabilities that may allow privilege escalation attacks. Host intrusion prevention systems (HIPS) may detect and block privilege escalation attempts. Data Execution Prevention (DEP) prevents the system from executing unauthorized code that could result in privilege escalation. Firewalls do not offer an effective defense because an attacker attempting privilege escalation already has a foothold on the system.

66. **C.** Warren is using a rootkit to attempt to gain administrative privileges on the server. This is an example of an escalation of privilege attack.

67. **A.** SQL injection, cross-site scripting, and buffer overflow attacks all occur when applications do not properly screen user-provided input for potentially malicious content. Distributed denial of service attacks use botnets of compromised systems to conduct a brute force resource exhaustion attack against a common target.

68. **A.** ARP poisoning attacks work by broadcasting false MAC address information on the local area network (LAN). ARP traffic does not travel over the Internet or across broadcast domains, so the attacker must have access to the local network segment to carry out an ARP poisoning attack. The attacker does not need access to the target system or any network devices, including firewalls.

69. **A.** A birthday attack is used to find collisions in a hash function. If successful, a birthday attack may be used to find substitute content that matches a digital signature. It takes its name from the mathematical birthday problem, which states that it only takes 70 people in a room to have a 99.9% probability that two will share the same birthday.

70. **A.** The image shows an example of a replay attack, where Mal obtains a copy of Alice's hashed password by sniffing a network connection and then reuses that hash to login to the server. Changing Alice's password or the hash algorithm would prevent Mal from using the hash he already captured, but he could just repeat the attack to obtain the new hash. Using a shadow password file is a good practice but it would not be effective against this attack because Mal is not accessing a password store on the server. Using TLS encryption to protect the session would prevent Mal from sniffing the hashed password.

71. **A.** While any of these issues may exist, the pressing issue that Charlie must resolve is the fact that the computers are running Windows XP, an end-of-life operating system. Microsoft no longer releases security patches for the OS, and this may cause a critical security issue. If Charlie cannot upgrade the operating system, he should implement other compensating controls, such as placing these systems on an isolated network.

72. **C.** This is a serious error, indicating that the name on the certificate does not match the name on the server and that the certificate was not issued by a trusted CA. It is very possible that a man-in-the-middle attack is taking place and the certificate is being presented by an attacker. Patty should warn the user not to visit the site and investigate further.

73. **C.** The RC4 cipher has inherent security vulnerabilities and is not considered secure, regardless of the key length. Therefore, Terry should include a recommendation in his report that the cipher be replaced with a secure alternative.

74. **B.** This is a tricky question, because any of the answers other than chosen ciphertext could be correct. We can rule out that answer because Joan cannot choose her own ciphertext. She can however, choose the plaintext used to create the ciphertext. When she does choose her own plaintext, she must, therefore, have knowledge of the plaintext. Once she encrypts the message, she also has access to the ciphertext. However, the best term to describe this attack is a chosen plaintext attack because it is the most specific of the three names. Every chosen plaintext attack is also a known plaintext and a known ciphertext attack.

75. **B.** While all of these are reliable troubleshooting tools, changing the WiFi channel is the best way to detect intentional interference. If Kristen changes the channel and the interference initially goes away but later reappears, it is possible that an attacker is intentionally jamming her network.

76. **A.** The code shown here is a clear example of an LDAP injection attack. The attacker is attempting to bypass the password security controls of the application by modifying the LDAP query to accept any password provided by the attacker as authentic.

77. **D.** The Secure attribute instructs the browser to only transmit the cookie via an encrypted HTTPS connection. The HttpOnly attribute does not affect encryption but rather restricts scripts from accessing the cookie via DOM objects. The SameSite attribute prevents the cookie from being shared with other domains and the Expire attribute sets an expiration date for the cookie.

78. **B.** Ken is at the pivot stage of the attack. He has gained a foothold on one system and is now attempting to use that access to pivot, or gain access to other systems.

79. **D.** The symptoms described here are the classic symptoms of a memory leak. The system is slowly depleting memory as it runs until it finally runs out of available memory, resulting in errors. When Rob reboots the system, it clears out available memory and begins the cycle anew.

80. **C.** Files 1 and 3 have identical hash values but different content. This is a security issue known as a collision and indicates that the hash function is not secure. There is no syntax error as the hashes were computed properly. Hash functions produce message digests. They do not perform encryption or decryption.

81. **D.** Port 23 is used by telnet, an insecure protocol for administrative connections to a server. This service should be disabled and replaced with SSH, which uses port 22. Ports 80 and 443 are commonly open on a web server.

82. **B.** POODLE is a downgrading attack that forces sites using SSL to revert to insecure cipher suites, rendering their communications susceptible to eavesdropping attacks.

83. **C.** While any type of malware could be responsible for the symptoms described by the user, the compelling piece of evidence in this scenario is that Vince discovered an unusual hardware device attached to the keyboard. This is most likely a keylogger.

84. **B.** This is a common and reasonable architecture for a dynamic web application where the web server initiates a connection to the database server. However, the connection should not take place with an administrative account. Instead, the database administrator should create a limited privilege service account that restricts the activity performed by the web application. This limits the impact of an attack that compromises the web server and takes over the database connection.

85. **C.** Bluesnarfing attacks use Bluetooth connections to steal information stored on the target device. Bluejacking attacks also exploit Bluetooth connections but they only allow sending messages to the device and do not allow the theft of information. Evil twin attacks set up false SSIDs but do not necessarily directly connect the attacker to the target device. Session hijacking attacks do not necessarily take place over a wireless connection and involve a third party website rather than a direct connection.

86. **D.** This is a clear example of familiarity and liking. The attacker built up a relationship over time with the employee until they had a strong bond. He then leveraged that relationship to slowly extract information from the target.

87. **A.** This is an example of a spear phishing attack that was designed specifically for someone in the Accounts Payable department of this firm. It is not a whaling attack because it is targeting a clerk, not a senior executive. It was not conducted by telephone or SMS, so it is not a vishing or smishing attack.

88. **C.** Pass-the-hash attacks exploit a vulnerability in the NTLM authentication protocol, used by Windows systems. The attack is not possible against non-Windows systems.

89. **C.** Web application firewalls are capable of detecting and filtering SQL injection attack attempts and would be an effective control. Stored procedures and parameterized queries both limit the information sent from the web application to the database and also serve as an effective control against SQL

injection attacks. Indexes are used to enhance database performance and would not prevent an injection attack.

90. **B.** Data loss prevention (DLP) systems are designed to detect and block the exfiltration of sensitive information. While an intrusion prevention system (IPS) or firewall may be able to reduce the likelihood of a successful attack, they are not designed for this purpose. The use of TLS encryption would not prevent an attack as it protects data while in transit but not at rest.

91. **A.** Implementing credentialed scanning would improve the quality of the information provided to the scanner and, therefore, would lower the false positive rate. Decreasing the scan sensitivity would lower the threshold for an alert and increase the false positive rate. Disabling safe checks and increasing the size of the target network would both increase the number of scan tests performed and, absent any other change, would have the effect of increasing the number of false positive reports.

92. **D.** This is an example of an radio frequency identification (RFID) transmitter. RFID is a form of near-field communication (NFC) that is used to communicate over short distances. This device could be used to track the physical presence of the executive when within range of a receiver.

93. **D.** These tweets are an example of botnet command and control traffic. The Twitter account is directing the infected system to engage in distributed denial of service attacks.

94. **B.** During a black box test, the attacker should not have access to any non-public information. It is reasonable to assume that any member of the public could conduct an external vulnerability scan, therefore there is no harm in expediting the penetration test by providing Rick with the results of an external scan. However, he should not have access to scans that would require additional access to perform. These include credentialed scans, agent-based scans and internal scans.

95. **C.** A false positive error occurs when a security system reports a condition that does not actually exist. In this case, the vulnerability scanner reported a missing patch, but that report was in error and, therefore, a false positive report.

96. **B.** This issue means that the web server will provide detailed error messages when an error condition occurs. These error messages may disclose information about the structure of the web application and supporting databases to an attacker that the attacker could then use to wage an attack.

97. **B.** The fact that the traffic is exceeding normal baselines and that the responses are much larger than the queries indicates that a DNS amplification attack may be underway. In this type of attack, the attacker sends spoofed DNS queries asking for large amounts of information. The source address on those queries is the IP address of the target system, which then becomes overwhelmed by the response packets.

98. **A.** This is an example of a logic bomb, code that remains dormant until certain logical conditions are met and then releases its payload. In this case, the logic bomb was configured to release if the developer was no longer employed by the organization.

99. **A.** Whois queries provide information about the registered owners of domain names and are a useful open source intelligence tool. The nslookup and dig commands perform standard DNS queries and can determine the IP addresses associated with domain names but do not normally reveal registration information. The ping command is used to test network connectivity.

100. **D.** Including security team members in the project management process allows them to review and comment on proposed system designs and architectures before a project is implemented. This increases the likelihood that the design will be secure. Technical controls, such as firewalls and intrusion prevention systems, may not protect against architectural weaknesses. Design flaws are generally not caused by employee malfeasance, so background checks would not be an effective control.

101. **D.** This type of attack, which causes a user's browser to execute a script, is known as a cross-site scripting (XSS) attack. This particular variant stores the script on the server (in the form of a message board posting) and, therefore, is a stored XSS attack.

102. **B.** Zero-day attacks occur when an attacker exploits a vulnerability for which there is no security patch, leaving users defenseless. As Mal's organization is the only entity aware of the attack, there is no security update from the vendor to resolve the problem. Therefore, she is in a position to conduct a zero-day attack. The question does not provide enough information about the vulnerability to determine whether it would allow SQL injection, man-in-the-browser, or spoofing attacks.

103. **C.** Man-in-the-middle attacks occur when an interloper is able to trick both client and server systems into establishing a connection with the interloper but believing that they are actually communicating with each other. SSL and TLS may be used to protect the contents of communications with encryption but they do not, by themselves, offer protection against man-in-the-middle attacks. If the parties use digital certificates signed by a trusted certificate authority, this provides an added degree of trust and protects against MITM attacks. Input validation is a useful control to protect against application layer attacks but is not helpful against MITM attacks.

104. **C.** The third log entry shows clear signs of a SQL injection attack. Notice that the parameters passed to the web page include an appended SQL command: UNION SELECT 1,2,3,4,5. This is designed to retrieve the first five columns from the database table and will likely succeed if the web application is not performing proper input validation.

105. **D.** Race conditions occur when a security issue exists that allows an attacker to exploit the timing of commands to obtain unauthorized access. A time-of-check/time-of-use (TOC/TOU) attack exploits a time lag between when an application verifies authorization and then allows the use of privileges. Therefore, this timing-based attack exploits a race condition.

106. **D.** A WiFi pineapple is a device specifically designed to carry out rogue AP attacks against wireless networks. The pineapple functions by forcing clients to disassociate from their current access points and connect to a network run by the pineapple.

107. **D.** Generally speaking, IoT deployments do not typically require multifactor authentication. They do, however, call for maintenance of the embedded operating systems, network segmentation, and the encryption of sensitive information.

108. **C.** The core issue underlying these vulnerabilities is that SSL is no longer considered secure and that TLS version 1.0 is also insecure. Therefore, the most expedient way to address the problem is to upgrade to TLS 1.2 and make that the only transport encryption protocol supported by the server.

109. **A.** The main limitation of IP spoofing over the Internet is that the attacker will not be able to receive responses to her requests because they will be routed to a different network location. If Mal controls

her own network, she will be able to bypass any local firewall egress filters that would prevent her from sending the spoofed packets, which she can create with any packet generation tool. IP spoofing is commonly used in denial of service attacks.

110. **C.** Answering this question doesn't require any knowledge of the specific vulnerability described in CVE-2019-0708. Instead, the key is that the worm was spreading overnight while nobody was in the office. The key characteristic of a worm is that it spreads on its own power, without user intervention.

111. **A.** From the description provided, we have sufficient informaton to identify this as a Trojan horse. Trojans are a type of malware that disguise themselves as a benign application, such as a game, but then carry a malicious payload.

112. **C.** While any of these explanations are plausible, this pattern of activity is indicative of a password change. Once the user changed his or her password, authentication began to fail and continued to fail as the device retried the connection automatically. The user eventually noticed and updated the password on the device, allowing it to resume normal connectivity.

113. **C.** The scenario gives us no reason to believe that the installation media is faulty or malicious. However, deploying the software in this way does run the risk of exceeding the organization's licensed allocation, putting them in jeopardy of violating the terms of their license agreement.

114. **D.** In a bluejacking attack, the attacker uses a Bluetooth connection to display messages to the end user. This attack does not grant the attacker access to information stored on the device, as would occur in a bluesnarfing attack. Bluescreening and bluelining are made-up terms in the context of Bluetooth technology.

115. **B.** Vishing, or voice phishing, attacks always take place over telephone calls. Smishing attacks use SMS messages. Spear phishing or whaling attacks normally occur over email but may use any communications mechanism.

116. **B.** Based on the information provided, we can only conclude that an ARP poisoning attack took place. This attack could have been used to conduct eavesdropping or man-in-the-middle attacks but there is not enough information provided to draw that conclusion. There is no evidence that DNS poisoning took place.

117. **B.** Security information and event management (SIEM) solutions aggregate and correlate log entries received from a wide variety of sources. Data loss prevention (DLP) systems seek to prevent the exfiltration of sensitive information from the organization. Intrusion prevention systems (IPS) block potentially malicious network traffic. Network access control (NAC) solutions prevent unauthorized systems from connecting to the network.

118. **B.** IP reputation services are a form of threat intelligence that provide organizations with a frequently updated list of known malicious IP addresses that can be automatically blocked at the firewall. Malware and IDS signature updates are also important security controls but they do not identify known malicious systems but rather identify patterns of suspicious activity. Behavioral analysis systems watch for anomalous patterns of activity rather than relying upon lists of known malicious systems.

119. **C.** This is a tricky question to answer, similar to some of the ones that you'll see on the exam. The reason this is difficult is that all of the answer choices are possible risks associated with storing an API

key in a public code repository. However, the primary risk that occurs in all cases is allowing anyone accessing the key to make unauthorized use of the API using the owner's key. This MIGHT make it possible to steal sensitive information, provision unauthorized resources, or conduct a denial of service attack, but that depends upon the nature of the API, which we do not know in this example.

120. **A.** An 8-bit number can have 256 possible values (calculated as 2 to the 8th power). When used as a positive integer, this means that it can hold values between 0 and 255.

121. **A.** The INSERT, UPDATE, and DELETE commands all have the ability to modify information in a database, potentially resulting in an integrity violation. The SELECT command is used to retrieve, but not modify, information so it is unlikely to result in an integrity issue. The use of the SELECT command is more likely to result in a confidentiality issue.

122. **B.** Martin is concerned about the misuse of legitimately assigned privileges. Credential management and privilege auditing activities would turn up improperly assigned privileges but would not identify the misuse of legitimate privileges. Usage auditing, however, analyzes actual use of privileges and would detect insider misuse.

123. **B.** Yolanda should rename the Administrator account to prevent brute force attempts to guess the password for that account. Expiring the password would limit the effective length of a successful attack but would not prevent an attack from succeeding. Disabling the Administrator account would prevent legitimate administrative access to the system. Encrypting the contents of the account would not prevent someone from accessing the account.

124. **C.** All of these attacks are authentication attacks. Brute force and rainbow table attacks are generic attacks that may be used against any authentication system that stores hashed passwords. Man-in-the-middle attacks are generally used against web applications. Pass-the-hash attacks are specifically effective against NTLM authentication.

125. **B.** Any active testing done against an organization should only be conducted with advance approval. This would include penetration testing, vulnerability scanning, and social engineering. Open source intelligence involves consulting publicly available information sources and is passive in nature. It does not require any prior approval.

126. **B.** A security information and event management (SIEM) system receives information from other security tools and correlates across systems to discover trends and patterns that might indicate an attack. Data loss prevention (DLP) systems, intrusion detection systems (IDS), and intrusion prevention systems (IPS) all generate data that might be fed to a SIEM.

CHAPTER 2

Architecture and Design

Domain 2 Questions

1. Rob is tracking down the unauthorized exfiltration of sensitive information from his organization and found suspicious emails sent by an employee to a Gmail address. The emails seem to only contain photos, but Rob suspects that the photos contain sensitive information. What technique might the employee have used to embed sensitive information within a photograph?

   A. Cartography
   B. Cryptography
   C. Steganography
   D. Psychology

2. Consider the load balanced server situation shown below. The load balancer sent the last user request to Server A. If the server is using round-robin load balancing, which server will receive the next request?

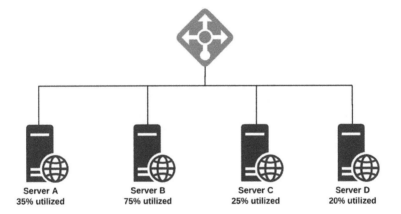

   A. Server A
   B. Server B
   C. Server C
   D. Server D

3. Vince is concerned that attackers might be able to gain access to the password file for a service that he runs and he would like to protect it as much as possible. Which one of the following controls provides the most effective protection against the success of rainbow table attacks?

   A. Salting
   B. Hashing
   C. Shadow passwords
   D. Password expiration

4. Alan is running a system audit and detects a user workstation that deviates from the organization's security standard. What action should he take next?

   A. Identify the cause of the deviation.
   B. Report the issue to his manager.
   C. Reimage the workstation.
   D. Reconfigure the device to meet the baseline.

5. When creating a digital certificate, what person or entity is responsible for creating the digital signature on the certificate?

   A. Registration authority
   B. Certificate authority
   C. Certificate subject
   D. Certificate requestor

6. Ron is selecting an email data loss prevention (DLP) solution for use in his organization. He is specifically concerned about preventing the loss of a set of product plans that are contained in a single repository. Which DLP technology would be most effective at meeting his needs?

   A. Pattern recognition
   B. Watermarking
   C. Host-based
   D. Network-based

7. Alan created a system named PersonnelDatabase that is designed to attract attackers, but there is no real sensitive information on the server. When someone attempts to connect to the system, Alan analyzes their activity. What type of system has Alan created?

   A. Honeypot
   B. Darknet
   C. Sinkhole
   D. Honeynet

8. Tammy is running a set of three load balanced web servers for her domain. The first server is the primary server and handles requests until it reaches capacity, then new requests are assigned to the second server. The third server remains idle unless the other two servers are fully utilized. What IP address should Tammy use for the DNS entry for the domain?

   A. Second server's IP
   B. First server's IP
   C. Virtual IP
   D. Third server's IP

9. Greg is concerned that users might connect USB drives to their workstations in an attempt to steal sensitive information without being detected on the network. What technology can Greg use for blocking USB device use?

   A. Host-based DLP
   B. Network-based DLP
   C. Host-based IPS
   D. Network-based IPS

10. Which one of the following approaches provides the greatest security for a two-factor authentication system based upon the use of mobile devices?

    A. TLS notification
    B. SMS notification
    C. MMS notification
    D. Push notification

11. Juan is running two load balancers in active/passive mode. Which one of the following terms does NOT describe this situation?

    A. High availability
    B. Fully utilized
    C. Fault tolerant
    D. Easily maintained

12. Which one of the following data sanitization techniques uses strong magnetic fields to remove remnant data from a device?

    A. Pulverizing
    B. Degaussing
    C. Wiping
    D. Overwriting

13. Tim is installing a data loss prevention system in his organization and is concerned about the likelihood of false positive reports. Which one of the following techniques is most likely to generate false positive alerts?

    A. Removable media control
    B. Watermarking
    C. Pattern matching
    D. Software updates

14. Samantha would like to add security to her organization's voice over IP (VoIP) telephony system. What protocol is specifically designed to assist with securing VoIP implementations?

    A. SNMP
    B. SRTP
    C. SSH
    D. TLS

15. Which one of the following encryption modes allows a block cipher to function more like a stream cipher?

   A. Authenticated mode
   B. Unauthenticated mode
   C. Counter mode
   D. Blockchain mode

16. Ralph is working with his organization to implement a new cloud storage solution. He would like to protect the data stored in this cloud service against an attack waged by a malicious insider employed by the vendor. What is the best control to provide this defense?

   A. Two-factor authentication
   B. Encryption
   C. Least privilege access controls
   D. Strong passwords

17. Ron is concerned about the potential of attackers exploiting issues in the operating system supporting a virtualization hypervisor to gain access to information stored by guest operating systems. What type of hypervisor can he use to minimize this risk?

   A. Type 1 hypervisor
   B. Type 2 hypervisor
   C. Type 3 hypervisor
   D. Type 4 hypervisor

18. Which one of the following temperature and humidity readings falls outside of the recommended environmental ranges for data centers set by the American Society of Heating, Refrigerating, and Air-Conditioning Engineers (ASHRAE)?

   A. 80 degrees Fahrenheit and 45% relative humidity
   B. 65 degrees Fahrenheit and 55% relative humidity
   C. 60 degrees Fahrenheit and 25% relative humidity
   D. 75 degrees Fahrenheit and 55% relative humidity

19. James would like to implement RAID 5 redundancy for the hard drives he is placing in a server. What is the minimum number of disks necessary to implement this approach?

   A. 1
   B. 2
   C. 3
   D. 5

20. Ed is selecting a load balancing algorithm for use in his organization's web environment. There are substantial differences between the performance characteristics of the servers in the web farm and there are also significant differences in the lengths of user connections. Which load balancing algorithm would produce the best results for Ed?

    A. Weighted Round Robin
    B. Least Connections
    C. Round Robin
    D. Weighted Least Connections

21. Which one of the following biometric security controls requires users to come into the closest physical proximity to the device?

    A. Retinal scanning
    B. Iris scanning
    C. Facial recognition
    D. Voice recognition

22. Which one of the following is a compiled programming language?

    A. JavaScript
    B. C++
    C. R
    D. PHP

23. Which one of the following is an example of a platform-as-a-service (PaaS) computing environment?

    A. Slack
    B. Microsoft Office 365
    C. Amazon EC2
    D. Google App Engine

24. Ingrid is preparing a standby server that her organization will activate to achieve redundancy in the event of a system failure. The server will be placed in the rack in a configured state and may be turned on for immediate functioning when needed. What type of server has Ingrid prepared?

    A. Active spare
    B. Hot spare
    C. Cold spare
    D. Warm spare

25. Bernard is considering using a new cloud service where the vendor offers a managed environment for the execution of customer-supplied code. What term best describes this service?

    A. PaaS
    B. SaaS
    C. IaaS
    D. XaaS

26. Paul's organization has a high availability web server cluster composed of six servers that all handle user requests. In a high availability configuration, how many servers can Paul lose without causing a complete loss of service to end users?

    A. 1
    B. 2
    C. 4
    D. 5

27. In a data center using the hot aisle/cold aisle approach, where should air conditioner vents be positioned to distribute cold air?

    A. Above racks
    B. At the back of racks
    C. At the front and back of racks
    D. At the front of racks

28. What is the main reason to use an ephemeral symmetric session key within a TLS session rather than simply using the asymmetric encryption keys for communication?

    A. Symmetric cryptography is more secure than asymmetric cryptography
    B. Symmetric cryptography is faster than asymmetric cryptography
    C. Asymmetric cryptography may only be used to exchange keys and not to transfer data
    D. Ephemeral keys may be reused

29. Devin manages a shared computing environment for multiple customers and is worried about one of his customers accessing virtual machines owned by other customers. He would like to protect against these virtual machine escape attacks. What is the best control that he can implement?

    A. Hypervisor patching
    B. Network firewall
    C. Input validation
    D. Port security

30. Kassie's company is considering the use of a cloud service to manage their hotel reservations. Employees would use a web interface to access the application located in the vendor data center. The vendor handles all installation tasks, deploys and scales the infrastructure, and maintains the source code. Kassie's company is only responsible for application configuration and authorization control. What type of cloud computing environment is Kassie's organization using?

    A. PaaS
    B. IaaS
    C. SaaS
    D. SecaaS

31. Brandy is using a computer at a hotel business center and she is concerned that the operating system on the device may be compromised. What is the best way for her to use this computer in a secure fashion?

    A. Use live boot media
    B. Run a malware scan
    C. Connect to a VPN
    D. Only access secure websites

32. Katie is conducting testing of a new application and recently completed unit testing. She would now like to run a series of tests designed to confirm that the tested units will work together properly. What type of software testing should Katie run next?

    A. Design testing
    B. Functional testing
    C. Acceptance testing
    D. Integration testing

33. Helen is the developer of a new application that recently completed all testing and now resides in a staging environment. She is ready to release the code into production. Who is the most appropriate person to trigger the code transfer?

    A. Helen's supervisor
    B. Change manager
    C. Another developer on Helen's team
    D. Helen

34. Carl is selecting a computing environment for a machine learning workload. The nature of the workload is that it uses resources intensely for several hours each evening and does not need resources at other times during the day. What computing model would be most cost-effective for this type of workload?

    A. Remote data center
    B. On-premises computing
    C. Cloud computing
    D. Colocation facility

35. When using TLS to secure web communications, what encryption key is used to protect data being sent between the user and the web browser?

    A. Web server's public key
    B. Web server's private key
    C. User's public key
    D. Ephemeral key

36. Tonya is considering the use of a security-as-a-service deployment model for her organization's identity and access management solutions. She is planning to use a well-respected vendor with a mature service. Which one of the following attributes should cause her the greatest concern?

    A. Confidenitiality
    B. Latency
    C. Nonrepudiation
    D. Reliability

37. Devin is a developer who recently received some code from an overseas partner and he is suspicious that it might contain malicious content. He would like to run the code to confirm or deny his suspicion. What environment should he use to perform this testing?

    A. Production
    B. Test
    C. Development
    D. Sandbox

38. In a virtualized environment, what is the easiest way to restore a virtual system to a previous known good state?

    A. Rebuild the system
    B. Restore from full backup and then apply differential backups
    C. Restore from full backup and then apply incremental backups
    D. Revert to a snapshot

39. Katie encounters a fire in her building that appears to have started in a bundle of electrical wires. Which one of the following fire extinguishers would be most appropriate to combat this fire?

    A. Class A
    B. Class B
    C. Class C
    D. Class D

40. Trevor is seeking an open-source version control system for use in his software development environment. Which one of the following tools would not meet his requirements?

    A. Git
    B. Visual SourceSafe
    C. Subversion
    D. CVS

41. Liam is securing a series of endpoints that run Microsoft Windows operating systems. He would like to use an automated mechanism to apply security settings to those systems. What technology can he use to do this?

    A. FQDNs
    B. GPOs
    C. MACs
    D. TLS

42. Which one of the following automation techniques provides a preconfigured baseline version of an operating system that is configured to meet the organization's security standards and is ready for customization to perform workload-specific tasks?

   A. Template
   B. Live boot media
   C. Master image
   D. Standard

43. What type of security control is shown below?

   A. Airgap
   B. Mantrap
   C. Bollard
   D. Hot aisle

44. What do most physical security professionals consider the minimum fence height to slow down a determined intruder?

   A. 12 feet
   B. 4 feet
   C. 6 feet
   D. 8 feet

45. Which one of the following operating environments is least likely to contain a SCADA system?

   A. Energy
   B. Manufacturing
   C. Consulting
   D. Logistics

46. Which one of the following technologies separates applications into their own virtualized environment where each uses the kernel of the underlying operating system?

    A. Type 2 virtualization
    B. Bare metal virtualization
    C. Type 1 virtualization
    D. Application containers

47. What type of hypervisor is shown in the image?

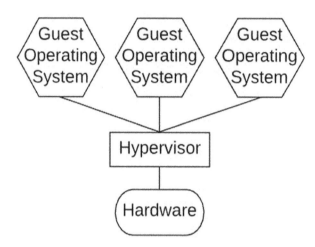

    A. Type 1 Hypervisor
    B. Type 2 Hypervisor
    C. Type 3 Hypervisor
    D. Type 4 Hypervisor

48. Joan is designing the fire suppression system for a new data center in Missouri and would like to choose a system that, if discharged, would be least damaging to the equipment in the data center. What is her best option?

    A. FM-200
    B. Halon
    C. Wet pipe
    D. Dry pipe

49. Florence is installing a concealed CCTV system outside her organization's data center. Which one of the following statements is most likely correct about this system?

    A. The system will be helpful in preventing security violations.
    B. The system will be helpful in deterring security violations.
    C. The system will be helpful in detecting security violations.
    D. The system will be extremely expensive.

50. Rob's organization is considering the deployment of software defined networking (SDN). Which one of the following statements is not correct about SDN?

   A. SDN facilitates network segmentation.
   B. SDN combines the control plane and the data plane.
   C. SDN creates a programmable network environment.
   D. SDN increases network complexity.

51. Ben is designing a network that will support the ICS and SCADA systems at a nuclear power plant. What security technology should he use to segment these networks from other systems?

   A. Physical segmentation
   B. VLANs
   C. VPNs
   D. IPS

52. Jamie is concerned about attackers using a web application to engage in cross-site scripting attacks against her organization. Which one of the following techniques is not a good defense against these attacks?

   A. Server-side input validation
   B. Client-side input validation
   C. Query parameterization
   D. Stored procedures

53. Which one of the following devices would be least likely to run a desktop or server operating system?

   A. Endpoint computing device
   B. Multifunction printer
   C. IoT sensor
   D. Kiosk computer

54. What step in the user lifecycle process should be triggered any time that an employee is terminated?

   A. Management
   B. Provisioning
   C. Deprovisioning
   D. Support

55. Victoria's organization recently adopted git for use by all developers. What term best describes the use of this tool?

   A. Compiler
   B. Load testing
   C. Vulnerability testing
   D. Version control

56. Laura is developing a firewall strategy for her organization using the approach shown below. Which one of the following statements should be Laura's primary concern when selecting firewall products in this scenario?

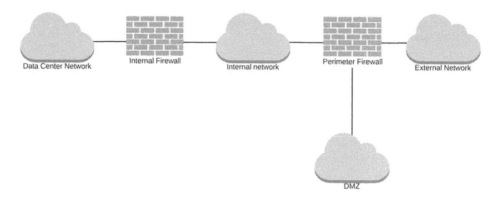

A. Using two different brands of firewall increases expense.
B. Using two different brands of firewalls introduces the opportunity for configuration incompatibility.
C. Using two different brands of firewalls introduces vendor diversity.
D. Using two different brands of firewall increases training requirements.

57. Andy works for an online retailer and has configured his organization's cloud computing environment to automatically purchase additional servers when necessary to meet periods of increased demand. Those servers are automatically deprovisioned when no longer necessary to meet demand. What term best describes what Andy is trying to achieve with this design?

A. Scalability
B. Elasticity
C. Redundancy
D. Flexibility

58. What kind of card reader is shown here?

A. Magnetic stripe card
B. Smart card
C. Proximity card
D. RFID card

59. Paul is helping to develop the security controls for a new high security facility. The requirements specify that some equipment must be housed in a Faraday cage. What is the primary purpose of this control?

A. Block electromagnetic radiation
B. Block physical access to equipment
C. Prevent tailgating attacks
D. Prevent theft of equipment

60. Which one of the following is not a benefit of an infrastructure-as-code approach to computing?

A. Reduced reliance on version control
B. Reduced risk of error
C. Reduction in cost
D. Increase in agility

61. Gavin is part of a consortium of health care providers in his region who are working together to build and host their own cloud computing environment that will be open only to members of the consortium. What type of cloud environment is Gavin helping to build?

A. Community cloud
B. Hybrid cloud
C. Public cloud
D. Private cloud

62. Consider the query shown below:

https://twitter.com/1.1/statuses/user_timeline.json?screen_name=mchapple

What technology is this query using to retrieve information from Twitter?

A. SDK
B. API
C. JSON
D. XML

63. Dennis is evaluating the physical security of a wiring closet inside his office building and would like to implement a preventive control. Which one of the following controls would best meet his needs?

    A. Guard dogs
    B. Warning signs
    C. Intrusion alarms
    D. Door locks

64. John is assisting a senior executive who must store some sensitive files on a USB flash drive for transfer to a remote location. The executive will hand-carry the drive and is the only person who needs to access the contents. Which one of the following encryption technologies would be most appropriate for this application?

    A. TLS
    B. DES
    C. AES
    D. RSA

65. What cryptographic technology enables anonymity in the Tor network?

    A. Quantum cryptography
    B. Perfect forward secrecy
    C. Key stretching
    D. Elliptical curve cryptography

66. Nancy's organization uses the device shown here to store encryption keys in a secure manner. What type of device is this?

    A. HSM
    B. TPM
    C. SSL accelerator
    D. BIOS

67. Air gaps are used by security professionals to perform what information security task?

A. Virtual network implementation
B. Intrusion detection
C. Network separation
D. Nonrepudiation

68. Christina is building a new capability for her organization's data centers that allows the automatic shifting of workloads to Amazon Web Services when the organization's own resources are overwhelmed. What type of environment is Christina building?

A. Public cloud
B. Hybrid cloud
C. Private cloud
D. Community cloud

69. Which one of the following statements is not generally correct about the systems used to control HVAC environments?

A. They often run outdated operating systems
B. They often embed strict host firewalls
C. They often contain security vulnerabilities
D. They often are not actively managed

70. What term is used to describe a network of decoy systems used to attract and study the activity of intruders?

A. Honeypot
B. Honeynet
C. Darknet
D. Darkpot

71. Fred is evaluating the effectiveness of a biometric system. Which one of the following metrics would provide him with the best measure of the system's effectiveness?

A. IRR
B. FAR
C. FRR
D. CER

72. Consider the statistics shown here for a biometric authentication system. What is the system's FRR based upon this data?

	Authorized User	Unauthorized User
Accept	98	16
Reject	2	84

A. 1%
B. 2%
C. 8%
D. 16%

73. Victoria is implementing an authentication system where the user is asked to speak a predefined passcode into a microphone. The system then verifies that the speaker's voice matches their enrollment sample and that the passcode is correct. How many authentication factors are at play in this scenario?

A. Zero
B. One
C. Two
D. Three

74. Which one of the following assertions can NOT be made by validating the card authentication certificate on a US government PIV card?

A. The holder of the credential is the same individual the card was issued to.
B. The card is not expired.
C. The card has not been revoked.
D. The card was issued by an authorized entity.

75. Which one of the following networking technologies would be most appropriate for a home automation system?

A. 5G
B. 4G
C. Satellite
D. Zigbee

76. Review the Google Authenticator screenshot shown below. What protocol is being used to generate passcodes by this software token?

A. LOTP
B. HOTP
C. KOTP
D. TOTP

77. Which one of the following biometric technologies is most likely to be affected by a person's race?

    A. Facial recognition
    B. Fingerprint recognition
    C. Iris recognition
    D. Hand geometry

78. Tina is designing a recovery mechanism for her organization's authentication system and provides each user with a card containing several one-time use passwords for use in the event their smartphone app malfunctions. What type of authentication factor are these one-time passwords?

    A. Something you have
    B. Something you know
    C. Somewhere you are
    D. Something you are

79. Corey would like to implement a multifactor authentication system for physical access to his data center. He is currently using a fingerprint scan. Which one of the following would be the best second authentication technique to use in combination with the fingerprint scan?

    A. Voiceprint analysis
    B. Security question
    C. ID card
    D. Retinal scan

80. Which one of the following techniques is the least secure approach to a "something you have" authentication factor?

    A. SMS message
    B. Physical token
    C. Smartphone app
    D. Smartcard

81. Erin would like to assess the impact of several overlapping Windows GPOs and determine the effective result of those policies. Which tool is best suited for this task?

    A. dcpromo
    B. gpedit
    C. gpresult
    D. gpupdate

82. Roger uses his fingerprint to unlock his laptop. What authentication factor was used in this example?

    A. Biometric authentication
    B. Token-based authentication
    C. Location-based authentication
    D. Knowledge-based authentication

83. Which one of the following biometric access control mechanisms generally takes the longest time to recognize a user?

   A. Fingerprint scan
   B. Iris scan
   C. Facial recognition
   D. Retinal scan

84. Before accessing a wire transfer website, Harry's bank requires that he provide a password, a security PIN, and answer several security questions. How many distinct authentication factors is this system using?

   A. 0
   B. 1
   C. 2
   D. 3

85. Which one of the following is not a constraint commonly found in specialized IoT devices?

   A. Lack of connectivity
   B. Inability to patch
   C. Limited power
   D. Limited compute

86. Lisa is evaluating a set of Group Policy Objects applied to a Windows account. Which one of the following policies will be processed first?

   A. Organizational Unit policy
   B. Site policy
   C. Domain policy
   D. Local policy

87. Greg is designing authentication controls for a system that is accessed by employees in branch offices. There is no need for mobile or remote users to access the system. What authentication factor could Greg implement to prevent users from accessing the system remotely?

   A. Something you have
   B. Something you are
   C. Somewhere you are
   D. Something you know

88. Tom is deciding whether to implement a standard account naming practice for his organization. Which one of the following statements best reflects the accepted best practices on this topic?

   A. Organizations should adopt standard naming conventions to make account identification easier.
   B. Organizations should not adopt standard naming conventions because it makes account names easy to guess.
   C. Organizations should not adopt standard naming conventions because it facilitates social engineering.
   D. Organizations should not adopt standard naming conventions because because it violates the principle of security through obscurity.

89. Group Policy Objects (GPOs) are a component of what access control system?

   A. Active Directory
   B. Kerberos
   C. RADIUS
   D. TACACS+

90. Tonya is considering the use of a voice recognition system for authentication purposes. She is concerned about the use of recordings to fool the system. What technology can she include in her design to best reduce the risk of this type of attack?

   A. Passcode
   B. Hashing
   C. Encryption
   D. Challenge/response

91. This diagram shows the results of testing the accuracy of a biometric authentication system. In this diagram, what characteristic is designated by the arrow?

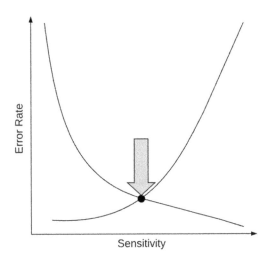

A. FAR
B. CER
C. FRR
D. IRR

92. When you enter a password into a system, what activity are you engaged in?

    A. Authentication
    B. Identification
    C. Authorization
    D. Accounting

93. Which one of the following statements about iris recognition technology is incorrect?

    A. Iris recognition technology has a very low false acceptance rate.
    B. Iris patterns may be recognized from a distance.
    C. Iris patterns change gradually during a person's lifetime.
    D. Iris recognition scanners can be fooled by an image of a face.

94. Carrie approaches the door to a physical facility and places her finger on a scanner. When she does so, the scanner displays the message "OK" and the door unlocks. Which one of the following steps has not occurred?

    A. Authentication
    B. Authorization
    C. Identification
    D. Two factor authentication

95. Which one of the following technologies is not commonly used in embedded systems?

    A. Raspberry Pi
    B. Arduino
    C. SELinux
    D. FPGA

96. Which one of the following is an example of a biometric authentication control?

    A. Password
    B. Fingerprint scan
    C. Smart card
    D. Keyfob token

97. After a user enters an incorrect password, many authentication systems record this activity in an authentication log. What phase of the identity and access management process is taking place?

    A. Identification
    B. Authentication
    C. Accounting
    D. Authorization

98. Randy is building a multifactor authentication system that requires users to enter a passcode and then verifies that their face matches a photo stored in the system. What two factors is this system using?

A. Something you know and something you have
B. Something you have and something you know
C. Something you have and something you are
D. Something you know and something you are

99. Which one of the following authentication factors is the most difficult to practically implement?

A. Something you are
B. Something you do
C. Something you have
D. Something you know

100. What type of security card is shown here?

A. Proximity card
B. Smart card
C. Magnetic stripe card
D. Common access card (CAC)

101. Consider the statistics shown here for a biometric authentication system. What is the system's FAR based upon this data?

	Authorized User	Unauthorized User
Accept	45	2
Reject	5	48

A. 2%
B. 4%
C. 5%
D. 10%

102. Consider the OpenLDAP password hashes shown here. Which user has the most secure password storage mechanism?

User 1
userPassword: {MD5}af14621b429c5a5cb94e2f46ddd52885

User 2
userPassword: {SSHA}hnN1pfl+13Pg8H/wr6Z7YqyC4PJLYtFx

User 3
userPassword: {SHA}6EDC6DEAB58E4C149032FE96981F20B708678769

User 4
userPassword: {CRYPT}bIxoer4WdlS3Y

A. User 1
B. User 2
C. User 3
D. User 4

103. Andy is developing requirements for a disaster recovery site and needs the ability to recover operations as quickly as possible. Which one of the following recovery site options provides the quickest activation time?

A. Warm site
B. Mobile site
C. Hot site
D. Cold site

104. Jake is helping his organization move out of an office complex they are leaving and has a large quantity of sensitive paper records to dispose. Which one of the following destruction methods would not be appropriate to sufficiently destroy the information?

A. Degaussing
B. Burning
C. Pulping
D. Shredding

105. Brynn is concerned about the risks associated with web application attacks and wishes to perform input validation. What is the best place to perform this task?

A. In the user's browser via HTML
B. In the user's browser via JavaScript
C. On the web server
D. On the database server

106. Gordon is considering a variety of techniques to remove information stored on hard drives that are being discarded by his company and donated to a charity for reuse. Which one of the following techniques would not be an effective way to meet this goal?

    A. Wiping
    B. Encryption
    C. Degaussing
    D. Purging

107. Which one of the following elements would not be found at a warm disaster recovery site?

    A. Computing hardware
    B. Electrical infrastructure
    C. Current data
    D. Software

108. Vincent is tasked with establishing a disaster recovery site but is charged with providing bare-bones functionality at minimal cost. Which option should he consider?

    A. Hot site
    B. Cold site
    C. Warm site
    D. Mobile site

109. Harold is designing an access control system that will require the concurrence of two system administrators to gain emergency access to a root password. What security principle is he most directly enforcing?

    A. Two-person control
    B. Least privilege
    C. Separation of duties
    D. Security through obscurity

110. Which one of the following data destruction technique requires the use of chemicals?

    A. Pulverizing
    B. Pulping
    C. Degaussing
    D. Wiping

111. Ron has a hard disk that contains sensitive information. He tried connecting the drive to a computer but a component failure will not allow him to access the drive. Which one of the following destruction techniques would be most effective?

    A. Wiping
    B. Purging
    C. Degaussing
    D. Pulping

112. When choosing an appropriate off-site storage location for backup media, which one of the following factors is most important when choosing the distance between the storage location and the primary facility?

   A. Facility usage fees
   B. Nature of the risk
   C. Convenience
   D. Transportation fees

113. Randy is working within a virtualized server environment and would like to back up complete images of his virtual servers so that he may easily restore them in the event of failure. What type of backup is most appropriate for his needs?

   A. Full backup
   B. Snapshot backup
   C. Differential backup
   D. Incremental backup

114. What is the primary risk associated with using motion detectors to automatically unlock a data center door when a person is attempting to exit?

   A. An employee may exit the facility with unauthorized materials.
   B. An intruder may attempt to trigger the motion detector from the outside to gain entry.
   C. The motion detector may not work during a power failure.
   D. The motion detector may not sense some employees based upon their physical characteristics.

115. Brian recently completed the change approval process for code that he developed and is waiting for the change control team to release the code for users. What environment is the code most likely in at this point?

   A. Production
   B. Staging
   C. Test
   D. Development

116. Which one of the following techniques for destroying physical records is considered the least secure?

   A. Pulping
   B. Incineration
   C. Straight-cut shredding
   D. Cross-cut shredding

117. Bob is performing regular backups of a system and is asked by his boss to create an emergency backup. Which one of the following backup types will consume the most disk space?

   A. Full backup
   B. Differential backup
   C. Incremental backup
   D. Transaction log backup

118. Helen is examining the contract for a new SaaS provider and is scrutinizing a clause about data sovereignty. What is her primary concern?

    A. Vendor viability
    B. Resiliency
    C. Fault tolerance
    D. Retaining ownership of data

> **Questions 119–121 refer to the following scenario.**
>
> John's organization performs full backups at midnight on the first day of every month and incremental backups every night at midnight (other than the first night of the month). The organization also performs differential backups every two hours beginning at 2AM and ending at 10PM each day.
>
> John is working to restore a system that failed at 9:30AM on Wednesday, November 14th.

119. How many different backups must John apply to restore the system to the most current possible status?

    A. 1
    B. 3
    C. 6
    D. 15

120. How long is the time period where data may have been permanently lost?

    A. 30 minutes
    B. 90 minutes
    C. 2 hours
    D. 9.5 hours

121. If the system failure occurred at 12:30AM instead of 9:30AM, how many backups would John have needed to restore?

    A. 1
    B. 2
    C. 3
    D. 14

122. Carla is concerned about the exfiltration of sensitive information from her corporate network by employees. Which one of the following controls would be least effective at meeting this requirement?

    A. Encrypting data in transit
    B. Blocking the use of personal email accounts
    C. Implementing data loss prevention systems
    D. Building least privilege access controls

123. Which one of the following backup types typically takes the shortest amount of time to perform when done several times per day?

    A. Complete backup
    B. Full backup
    C. Incremental backup
    D. Differential backup

124. Adam created a message and then computed a message digest based upon that message. He then altered a single character at the end of the message and then recomputed the message digest. Which one of the following statements about the second message digest is correct?

    A. The second message digest should be one character different than the first digest.
    B. The second message digest will be completely different from the first digest.
    C. There may be minor differences in the second message digest but they will be toward the end of the digest.
    D. The two digests will be substantially the same, with minor differences.

125. Greg recently designed a new IT architecture that is able to respond to both increases and decreases in demand by adding and removing resources. What term best describes this environment?

    A. Scalable
    B. Redundant
    C. Resilient
    D. Elastic

126. Which one of the following encryption algorithms relies upon the difficulty of factoring large prime numbers to achieve its secrecy?

    A. RSA
    B. Quantum
    C. ECC
    D. Diffie Hellman

127. Helen is concerned about an attack that may retrieve credit card numbers from memory in a point-of-sale terminal. What term best describes this scenario?

    A. Data-in-transit
    B. Data-at-rest
    C. Data-in-use
    D. Data-on-disk

128. Renee would like confidentiality protection on the message that she sends Mike and would like to achieve this by encrypting the message. What key should she use to encrypt the message?

    A. Mike's public key
    B. Mike's private key
    C. Renee's public key
    D. Renee's private key

129. When Mike receives the message, what key must he use to decrypt it?

    A. Mike's public key
    B. Mike's private key
    C. Renee's public key
    D. Renee's private key

130. Renee would also like to achieve non-repudiation by applying a digital signature to the message. What key does she use to encrypt the message digest?

    A. Mike's public key
    B. Mike's private key
    C. Renee's public key
    D. Renee's private key

131. When Mike receives the message, he would like to verify the digital signature. What key should he use to decrypt the signature?

    A. Mike's public key
    B. Mike's private key
    C. Renee's public key
    D. Renee's private key

132. Which one of the following statements about the Blowfish algorithm is incorrect?

    A. The algorithm is covered by a patent.
    B. The algorithm uses a 64-bit block size.
    C. The algorithm allows the use of any length key between 32 and 448 bits.
    D. The developer of the algorithm does not recommend it for use today.

133. Norm would like to allow users to memorize passwords that may be used to protect strong encryption keys. What technique may he use to generate strong keys from those relatively short passwords?

A. Key stretching
B. Key escrow
C. Key exchange
D. Key revocation

134. Which one of the following properties should NOT be found in a cryptographic hash function?

A. Defined range
B. One-way
C. Collision
D. Reproducible

135. As you increase the length of a key by a single bit, how much more resilient does that key become against a brute force attack?

A. Twice as strong
B. One percent stronger
C. Ten times stronger
D. Four times stronger

136. David encountered a cryptographic implementation using the RC4 stream cipher with a weak key and he would like to secure this implementation. What action should he take?

A. Apply the algorithm three times
B. Increase the key length
C. Replace the cipher algorithm
D. Apply the algorithm twice

137. Which one of the following block cipher modes of operation may NOT be used to turn a block cipher into a stream cipher?

A. OFB
B. GCM
C. CTM
D. ECB

138. Which one of the following statements about block and stream ciphers is correct?

A. Most modern ciphers are block ciphers.
B. Stream ciphers commonly use Feistel networks.
C. Block ciphers are faster than equivalent stream ciphers.
D. Block ciphers encrypt one byte at a time.

139. When configuring cipher suites for a web server, which one of the following key exchange approaches would produce the strongest security?

   A. DHE Group 1
   B. DHE Group 2
   C. Export cipher suite
   D. ECDHE

140. Which one of the following message digest sizes is supported by the SHA-3 hash algorithm?

   A. 256 bits
   B. 224 bits
   C. SHA-3 supports any size digest
   D. 384 bits

141. Alan is developing a new application that will rely upon cryptography. Which one of the following techniques is the best way for him to ensure that the cryptography is properly implemented?

   A. Write the cryptographic code directly in his application
   B. Hire a vendor to develop a custom cryptographic module
   C. Use a popular open-source cryptographic module
   D. Test the software prior to use

142. Greg is using a pseudorandom number generator (PNRG) to create cryptographic keying material. Which element of the algorithm must be varied each use to prevent against reproduction attacks?

   A. Hash
   B. Algorithm
   C. Key
   D. Seed

143. What block size is used by the Advanced Encryption Standard when encrypting and decrypting data?

   A. 64 bits
   B. 128 bits
   C. 192 bits
   D. 256 bits

144. When designing an encryption algorithm, which elements of the algorithm should be preserved as secrets?

   A. Both keys and encryption techniques should be kept secret
   B. Encryption techniques
   C. Decryption techniques
   D. Cryptographic keys

145. Andy is implementing a new VPN server and would like to use the Diffie-Hellman algorithm. Which one of the following DH groups is most secure?

A. Group 2
B. Group 14
C. Group 19
D. Group 5

146. Rob is sending a message to Gary and, as part of that communication, he computes the hash value of the message using the SHA-1 algorithm. Which of the following options best describes the set of people who are able to compute that hash value if they have the original message?

A. Only Rob can compute the hash
B. Anyone can compute the hash
C. Only Rob or Gary can compute the hash
D. Only someone with the encryption key can compute the hash

147. Seth is encrypting a document to provide confidentiality using a symmetric encryption algorithm. He is sending the document to Helena. Which key should he use to perform this encryption?

A. Shared secret key
B. Seth's public key
C. Seth's private key
D. Helena's public key

148. Which one of the following cryptographic algorithms was chosen as the winner of the contest to implement the Advanced Encryption Standard (AES)?

A. Twofish
B. Rijndael
C. Blowfish
D. Serpent

149. When storing passwords in a password file, what term is used to describe a random value combined with the password to reduce the risk of rainbow table attacks?

A. Cream
B. IV
C. Nonce
D. Salt

150. Don would like to ensure that traveling users are provided with encryption services for all of their network connections while on the road. Which one of the following cryptographic technologies would best meet this need?

A. SSH
B. Encrypted web proxy
C. Web browser supporting HTTPS
D. VPN

151. Bill is designing a security solution that must be able to encrypt network traffic without introducing a delay into the transmission of that traffic. What term best describes Bill's requirement?

    A. Low resiliency
    B. High latency
    C. Low latency
    D. High resiliency

152. Nick is using AES encryption to protect files stored on his network. What is the simplest step he can take to improve the strength of that encryption?

    A. Apply a second encryption algorithm on top of AES
    B. Change algorithms
    C. Increase the key length
    D. Use two rounds of AES encryption

153. Vincent and Fred would like to communicate with each other using the 3DES encryption algorithm. What key must Vincent have in order to successfully communicate with Fred?

    A. Vincent's private key
    B. Shared secret key
    C. Fred's public key
    D. Fred's private key

154. Ben is conducting a forensic analysis and discovers an image stored on a computer titled "Drug Formula." When he opens the file, he sees the image shown here. If someone did embed a formula in the file, what technique did they likely use?

    A. Stream cipher
    B. Hashing
    C. Obfuscation
    D. Steganography

155. The Tor network allows both participants in a communication to remain anonymous by filtering traffic through a number of relay nodes. What term describes the technology used by Tor to ensure anonymity?

A. Perfect forward secrecy
B. Security through obscurity
C. Obfuscation
D. Non-repduation

156. How many times must the DES encryption algorithm be applied to data in order to achieve a reasonable level of security?

A. 1
B. 2
C. 3
D. It is not possible to implement DES in a secure manner

157. Brian is designing a communications system for the exchange of stock transactions. He wants to implement a system where a customer can not later claim that someone else placed an order on their behalf. What goal of cryptography is he attempting to achieve?

A. Integrity
B. Authentication
C. Confidentiality
D. Nonrepudiation

158. Victor is evaluating the encryption algorithm options available for use in his organization. Of the options presented below, which would provide Victor with the strongest level of encryption?

A. AES
B. 2DES
C. DES
D. RC4

159. Which mode of cipher operation is shown here?

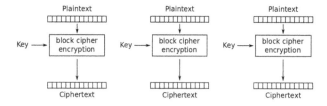

A. OFB
B. CFB
C. ECB
D. CBC

160. Which one of the following keying options creates the most secure implementation of the 3DES encryption algorithm?

    A. K1=K2=K3
    B. K1, K2, and K3 are independent
    C. K1=K2, K2 is not equal to K3
    D. K2=K3, K1 is not equal to K3

161. Which one of the following is not a secure technique for exchanging encryption keys?

    A. Emailed key
    B. Diffie-Hellman algorithm
    C. Digital certificates
    D. In-person exchange

162. What encryption key length is used by the original Data Encryption Standard (DES)?

    A. 16 bits
    B. 56 bits
    C. 112 bits
    D. 128 bits

163. Bill is configuring a web server to use TLS cryptography. When the server is up and running, how many users will share each ephemeral session key?

    A. 1
    B. 2
    C. 4
    D. All users use the same session key

Questions 164 and 165 refer to the following scenario.

Ryan is evaluating potential encryption algorithms for use in his organization and would like to choose an approach that provides strong security.
---

164. Ryan would like to ensure that the relationship between the encryption key and the ciphertext is quite complex to avoid reverse engineering. What property is he seeking to enforce?

    A. Diffusion
    B. Collusion
    C. Obfuscation
    D. Confusion

165. Ryan would also like to prevent statistical analysis attacks by choosing an algorithm that prevents patterns in the plaintext from also appearing in the ciphertext. What property is he seeking to enforce?

    A. Diffusion
    B. Collusion
    C. Obfuscation
    D. Confusion

1. **C.** Steganography is a set of techniques used to hide information within other files, in plain sight. The most common application of steganography is hiding information within images.

2. **B.** In round-robin load balancing, the load balancer assigns requests to servers sequentially. The load balancer does not use capacity information to determine scheduling. It simply assigns each incoming request to the next server in line.

3. **A.** Rainbow table attacks use precomputed hash values to identify commonly used passwords in password files. They are quite effective against password files or shadow password files that contain passwords that have been hashed but have not been salted. Password expiration limits the length of time that a compromised password may be used but does not prevent rainbow table attacks from being successful.

4. **A.** There are sometimes legitimate reasons for a system to deviate from a security baseline. Alan should investigate this issue and determine the reason for the deviation before taking more drastic action.

5. **B.** The digital signature on a certificate is created by the certificate authority using that certificate authority's private key. Anyone using the certificate can verify the signature with the certificate authority's public key.

6. **B.** There is not enough information in the scenario to determine whether host-based or network-based DLP would be more appropriate. The main choice facing Ron is whether to use pattern matching or watermarking. Pattern matching looks for data that matches the format of known sensitive data elements, such as Social Security numbers or credit card numbers. Watermarking tags sensitive documents and then watches for those tags in network traffic. In this case, Ron has a specific set of documents that he would like to protect so watermarking would be the best solution.

7. **A.** Honeypots are systems that are deliberately designed to attract attackers and monitor their activity. Honeynets are entire networks of decoy systems. Darknets are unused portions of IP space used to identify scanning attempts. Sinkholes are false DNS entries created to prevent users from accidentally contacting malicious systems.

8. **C.** When registering DNS entries for a load balanced service, administrators should assign the entry to a virtual IP address that maps to the public interface of the load balancer.

9. **A.** Data loss prevention systems are designed to prevent the exfiltration of sensitive information, while intrusion prevention systems are designed to block attack traffic. Since Greg is attempting to block the exfiltration of sensitive information, he should choose a DLP solution. The threat that Greg wants to defend against does not use the network, so he should choose a host-based DLP that offers USB blocking capabilities.

10. **D.** Push notification uses a secure mechanism to notify users of mobile devices. The Apple Push Notification Service (APNS) is an example of a secure push notification mechanism. SMS (text messaging) notification has insecurities, particularly when used with VoIP numbers. MMS is used for

multimedia messages and is not appropriate for an authentication solution. TLS is a generic transport-layer security protocol and cannot be used to directly deliver notifications to mobile devices.

11. **B.** In an active/passive configuration, one load balancer remains unused while the other load balancer handles all traffic. If the active load balancer fails, the passive load balancer takes over. This is a high availability, fault tolerant configuration and it is easily maintained. It does not, however, use the full capacity of both devices.

12. **B.** Degaussing applies strong magnetic fields to a storage device in order to remove the data that is stored magnetically on that device.

13. **C.** Data loss prevention systems that use pattern matching are most likely to generate false positive reports because data in a file might match a pattern by happenstance. Watermarking and removable media control techniques do not typically generate false positive reports. Software updates would not be detected by a DLP system.

14. **B.** The Secure Real Time Protocol (SRTP) is a secure, encrypted protocol designed specifically to support VoIP communications. The Simple Network Management Protocol is designed to facilitate management of network devices. Secure Shell (SSH) is a tool for encrypted administrative connections to systems. Transport Layer Security (TLS) may be used to encrypt VoIP communications but it is a general purpose encryption protocol and is not specifically designed to secure VoIP communications.

15. **C.** Counter mode ciphers incorporate a changing counter value into the encryption process, allowing a block cipher to function in the same manner as a stream cipher.

16. **B.** Ralph should use encryption to protect the data and then store the encryption keys in a location other than the cloud service. With this control in place, a rogue employee of the cloud service may be able to access the organization's data, but will not be able to decrypt it. The other controls listed are all good security practices, but an insider may be able to bypass them.

17. **A.** In a type 1 hypervisor, the hypervisor runs directly on the system hardware, eliminating the need for an underlying operating system and reducing the environment's attack surface. Type 2 hypervisors require the use of a host operating system. Type 3 and 4 hypervisors do not exist.

18. **C.** ASHRE recommends that data centers maintain temperatures within the range of 64.4 and 80.6 degrees Fahrenheit and keep relative humidity between 8% and 80%.

19. **C.** RAID level 5 is also known as disk striping with parity. This approach requires a minimum of two disks for data storage and an additional disk for parity, requiring a total of three disks, minimum. It is important to note that RAID 5 actually distributes parity information across all of the disks to prevent a single disk from becoming a bottleneck, but it does require the use of three disks.

20. **D.** The fact that the servers have different performance characteristics indicate that Ed should choose a weighted algorithm that allows him to specify that some servers should handle more load than others. The fact that users have sessions of differing length indicates that he should use a least connections approach that tracks the number of active sessions instead of a round robin approach that simply balances the number of assignments made. Therefore, Ed should choose the Weighted Least Connections algorithm.

21. **A.** Facial and voice recognition can normally be done from a distance without requiring close user interaction. Retina and iris recognition both require the user to expose his or her eye to the reader, however iris scanning can often be done from a distance while retinal scanning requires intrusive interaction with the scanner.

22. **B.** Compiled languages are converted from source code into machine language before execution using a program called a compiler. C++ is an example of a compiled language. Interpreted languages run the source code directly using an interpreter. JavaScript, R, and PHP are all examples of interpreted languages.

23. **D.** In a platform-as-a-service (PaaS) computing environment, the vendor maintains an environment where customers can develop, run, and manage their own applications. The vendor manages all of the infrastructure and the code execution environment. Google App Engine is an example of a PaaS service. Microsoft Office 365 and Slack are software-as-a-service (SaaS) services. Amazon's Elastic Compute Cloud (EC2) is an infrastructure-as-a-service (IaaS) environment.

24. **D.** A warm spare server is configured and ready to operate but is not turned on until it is needed. Hot spare (or active spare) servers are identically configured but are powered on and ready to take over operations, perhaps on an automated basis. Cold spare servers are on hand but not yet configured.

25. **A.** This environment, where customers supply code and vendors supply managed infrastructure, is known as platform as a service (PaaS) computing.

26. **D.** Because these servers are configured in a high availability manner, the web cluster will continue to operate as long as at least one server is functioning properly and answering user requests. The server may not be able to handle the full load, but there will not be a complete loss of service unless all six servers are lost.

27. **D.** In a hot aisle/cold aisle layout, cold air should be distributed at floor level in the front of racks (cold aisle) so that it is pulled into the front of equipment and vented out the back into the hot aisle.

28. **B.** The main reason that TLS uses asymmetric cryptography to establish a session and then switches over to symmetric cryptography using an ephemeral key is that symmetric cryptography is much faster than asymmetric cryptography. One approach is not necessarily more secure than the other and both may be used to exchange data. Ephemeral keys are intended for use during a single session and should not be reused.

29. **A.** Virtual machine (VM) escape attacks target vulnerabilities in the hypervisor supporting a virtualized environment. The strongest control to protect hypervisors against these attacks is to keep them patched. Network firewalls and port security are network security controls that occur outside of the virtualized environment and would not be effective in this case. Input validation is an application security control.

30. **C.** In a software-as-a-service (SaaS) environment, the customer is only responsible for configuring the application and managing authorization controls. The vendor develops and maintains the application and infrastructure environment.

31. **A.** If Brandy's major concern is a compromised operating system, she can bypass the operating system on the device by booting it from live boot media and running her own operating system on the hardware. Running a malware scan may provide her with some information but may not detect all

compromises and Brandy likely does not have the necessary permissions to correct any issues. Using a VPN or accessing secure sites would not protect her against a compromised operating system, as the operating system would be able to view the contents of her communication prior to encryption.

32. **D.** Integration testing occurs after unit testing and is designed to confirm that units of code will work together properly. Functional testing takes place upon the conclusion of requirements development, while design testing occurs after the design is complete. Both functional and design testing should be completed before, not after, unit testing. Acceptance testing occurs as the next step after successful integration testing.

33. **B.** Development environments are designed for active use by developers who are creating new code. These environments are the only location where code should be modified. Once code is ready for testing, it is released from the development environment into a test environment for software testing. After the completion of user acceptance testing, the code is moved from the test environment into a staging environment where it is prepared for final deployment into the production environment. Developers should never have permission to move code themselves but should only be able to move code between environments through the use of a managed change control system.

34. **C.** Cloud computing environments provide on-demand computing and allow users to pay for resources on an as-needed basis. In that model, Carl can power down servers that are not needed and reduce his costs. Other computing models have high fixed costs that would not be as cost-effective for this type of bursty workload.

35. **D.** When using TLS encryption, data sent during a session is encrypted using an ephemeral key created specifically for use during that session. That key is generated and encrypted using asymmetric encryption, but the normal communication switches over to using faster, symmetric encryption with the ephemeral key.

36. **B.** If the service is not designed and/or implemented well, any of these issues could become a concern. However, a mature service from a well-respected vendor should not have design flaws that cause confidentiality, non-repudiation, or reliability concerns. Latency is a potential issue with any cloud service and should be carefully evaluated in an identity and access management deployment.

37. **D.** Testing of suspicious software should only take place within an isolated sandbox environment that is specifically designed for testing suspicious code in a manner where it cannot impact other systems. Test, development, and production environments should never be used for testing potentially malicious software.

38. **D.** All of the options presented here are possible ways to restore a system to a previously known good state, but the simplest way to do so is to restore the system from a snapshot, as this is a file that captures the complete state of the system. Applying backups or rebuilding the system may achieve the same goal but would be more time-consuming.

39. **C.** Class C fire extinguishers are designed for use against electrical fires. Class A extinguishers are for ordinary combustible materials, such as wood. Class B are for flammable liquids, such as grease, while Class D are specialized extinguishers for flammable metals.

40. **B.** Git, Subversion (SVN), and Concurrent Versions System (CVS) are all open-source version control systems. Visual SourceSafe is a version control system from Microsoft but it is not open-source.

41. **B.** Group Policy Objects (GPOs) may be used to automatically assign security settings to systems through Active Directory. Fully qualified domain names (FQDNs) are not used to apply security settings. Neither are media access control (MAC) addresses or Transport Layer Security (TLS).

42. **C.** A master image is a preconfigured version of an operating system that meets the organization's standard configuration requirements and may be customized for workload-specific use. A template or standard may contain information about the organization's security requirements but does not provide a working copy of the operating system. Live boot media is a media device that contains an operating system and may be used to boot a device. It does not necessarily meet the organization's security configuration requirements.

43. **C.** The image shows an example of a bollard: a physical barrier placed near a street to block vehicle access without inhibiting pedestrian access.

44. **D.** Most security professionals consider eight feet to be the minimum height for a fence protecting critical assets. It is trivial for an intruder to climb a fence of six feet or less. A fence that stands twelve feet high is likely unnecessary and aesthetically unpleasant. For added security, organizations may add barbed wire to the top of the fence.

45. **C.** SCADA systems are used to control industrial and logistics processes. These systems are commonly found in facilities environments, industrial settings, manufacturing plants, energy infrastructure, and logistics operations. Those are the SCADA environments referenced by CompTIA in the exam objectives and you should be familiar with them. SCADA systems are not likely to be found in a consulting practice.

46. **D.** Application containers virtualize the user space for an application but each container uses the kernel of the underlying operating system. In type 1 or type 2 virtualization, the hypervisor supports different guest operating systems but does not perform application isolation. Bare metal virtualization is another term for type 1 virtualization.

47. **A.** In a Type 1 hypervisor, the hypervisor runs directly on the physical hardware. In a Type 2 hypervisor, the hypervisor runs on a host operating system which, in turn, runs on the physical hardware. In both cases, guest operating systems run on top of the hypervisor.

48. **A.** Wet pipe and dry pipe systems both use water and may damage or destroy equipment in the data center if discharged. FM-200 and Halon systems both use gas that is not likely to damage equipment, but it is illegal to construct new Halon systems in the United States. Therefore, Joan should choose an FM-200 system.

49. **C.** Closed-circuit television (CCTV) systems are useful controls for monitoring a facility and detecting potential intrusions. Therefore, Florence's system is best described as a detective control. CCTV may be a deterrent control as well, but this system is concealed, so it has no deterrent purpose. A video surveillance system can not actually stop an intrusion, so it is not a preventive control. CCTV systems are usually fairly cost effective and not overwhelmingly expensive.

50. **B.** Software defined networking does facilitate network segmentation. It allows the rapid realignment of network functionality by creating a programmable network, but this flexibility also adds complexity to the network. SDN separates, rather than combines, the data and control planes of the network.

51. **A.** Virtual LANs (VLANs), Virtual Private Networks (VPNs), and physical segmentation are all technologies that can isolate networks. However, the extremely sensitive nature of industrial control systems (ICS) and supervisory control and data acquisition (SCADA) systems in a nuclear power plant call for the greatest degree of segmentation possible -- physical segmentation. This approach is usually too costly for most applications, but it is appropriate in this case. An intrusion prevention system (IPS) does not provide the required functionality.

52. **B.** Query parameterization and stored procedures store the SQL code on the database server, preventing a user from supplying additional code through a web application. Input validation is used to filter out potentially malicious input, but it must be performed on the server to prevent attackers from tampering with the validation code.

53. **C.** Kiosk computers and endpoint computing devices all commonly run desktop and server operating systems. Multifunction printers often have embedded computer systems running standard operating systems. Internet of Things (IoT) sensors usually do not have the memory or processing power to run a standard operating system and normally run specialized operating systems designed for IoT applications.

54. **C.** Provisioning is the process of adding a new user to the organization and should be triggered for new hires. Deprovisioning is the process of removing a user from the organization and should be triggered on termination. Management and support are ongoing activities.

55. **D.** Git is a version control tool, used to manage the development and release of source code. It does not perform any testing itself and does not have the ability to compile code, although it may be used in conjunction with other tools that accomplish those tasks.

56. **C.** All of the statements listed in this scenario may be true to one extent or another. However, Laura's overriding concern here should be introducing vendor diversity into the environment to provide additional security. Using two different products increases the likelihood that her data center network will be robustly defended following a defense-in-depth strategy. Watch out for questions like this on the exam, as CompTIA stresses the need for vendor diversity in the exam objectives.

57. **B.** Andy may very well be attempting to achieve all of these goals. However, the term elasticity best describes this environment because it both provisions new servers when necessary and deprovisions them when they are no longer needed. Scalability is a very similar term but it describes the provisioning of servers to meet demand but does not include the deprovisioning of unnecessary servers.

58. **B.** The card reader shown requires the user to insert the card into the reader and leave it there. This indicates that the card is a smart card containing a chip that interacts with the reader. Magnetic stripe cards are swiped through a reader and do not remain in the reader. Proximity and RFID cards are waved in front of the reader.

59. **A.** Faraday cages are enclosures designed to prevent electromagnetic radiation from entering or leaving an area. They are used to shield very sensitive equipment and to prevent electromagnetic signals that might be intercepted from leaving a facility.

60. **A.** Infrastructure-as-code approaches reduce risk by decreasing manual work, lower costs by automating activity, and increase agility by providing rapid flexibility. However, they increase, rather

than decrease, the importance of using version control systems to manage the code that defines infrastructure.

61. **A.** In a public cloud environment, providers offer services on the same shared computing platform to all customers. Customers do not necessarily have any relationship to, or knowledge of, each other. In a private cloud environment, an organization builds its own computing environment. In a hybrid cloud environment, an organization combines elements of public and private cloud computing. In a community cloud environment, a group of related organizations builds a shared cloud environment that is not open for general public use.

62. **B.** This query is using the Twitter application programming interface (API) to retrieve data for the user with the Twitter handle mchapple. We can tell that this is an API call because the query is in a HTTP request. A software development kit (SDK) would use function calls in the language of the SDK. The query is retrieving results in JSON format, rather than XML format, but this is the standard used to format the results, not the technology used to retrieve them.

63. **D.** All of the controls listed here are physical security controls. However, warning signs are a deterrent control and an intrusion alarm is a detective control. Neither are preventive controls. Guard dogs and door locks may both be considered preventive controls but it is not normally practical to have guard dogs in an office building. Therefore, the best choice for Dennis is to use hardware door locks.

64. **C.** Because the executive is the only person who needs access to the information, the simplest solution would be to use a symmetric encryption algorithm, such as the Advanced Encryption Standard (AES). The Data Encryption Standard (DES) is also a symmetric algorithm, but it is insecure and not suitable for use. The Rivest, Shamir, Adelman (RSA) algorithm would work for this application, but it is asymmetric and has unnecessary complexity. Transport Layer Security (TLS) is designed for use on data in transit over a network and not data stored on a device.

65. **B.** The Tor network depends upon perfect forward secrecy to enable true anonymity. In this approach, each link in the Tor chain only knows the identity of the immediately adjacent links in the chain.

66. **A.** Hardware security modules (HSMs), such as the one shown here, are used to protect encryption keys and perform cryptographic processing. Trusted Platform Modules (TPMs) do store encryption keys for use in disk encryption but they are chips contained within another device, rather than a standalone device. SSL accelerators and BIOS chips do not serve as key repositories.

67. **C.** Air gaps are a security control that uses physical separation between networks to prevent the flow of information or network traffic between the networks. Air gapping is used in high security environments to protect critically sensitive systems from the potential of external access and other threats.

68. **B.** In a public cloud environment, providers offer services on the same shared computing platform to all customers. Customers do not necessarily have any relationship to, or knowledge of, each other. In a private cloud environment, an organization builds its own computing environment. In a hybrid cloud environment, an organization combines elements of public and private cloud computing. In a community cloud environment, a group of related organizations builds a shared cloud environment that is not open for general public use.

69. **B.** The controllers for heating, ventilation, and air conditioning (HVAC) systems often run on outdated hardware and software and contain security vulnerabilities because they are commonly not actively managed. These systems do not usually have host firewalls and should be segmented on a specialized network.

70. **B.** Honeynets are networks of decoy systems designed to attract intruders so that security analysts may study their activity. Honeypots are single systems designed for the same purpose. Darknets are unused portions of IP address space designed to detect scanning activity when a scanner attempts to access those unused addresses. Darkpots are what occur when I attempt to cook and leave a pot unattended on the stove for too long.

71. **D.** The false rejection rate (FRR) identifies the number of times that an individual who should be allowed access to a facility is rejected. The false acceptance rate (FAR) identifies the number of times that an individual who should not be allowed access to a facility is admitted. Both the FAR and FRR may be manipulated by changing system settings. The crossover error rate (CER) is the rate at which the FRR and FAR are equal and is less prone to manipulation. Therefore, the CER is the best measure for Fred to use. IRR is not a measure of biometric system effectiveness.

72. **A.** The false rejection rate (FRR) of a system is calculated by dividing the number of false rejections by the total number of authentication attempts. In this dataset, there are 200 total authentication attempts, of which 2 were false rejections of an authorized user. Therefore, the false acceptance rate is 1%.

73. **C.** This does qualify as multifactor authentication, because it is based upon a passcode known only to the user (something you know) and the user's voice (something you are). However, it is not an ideal solution because an attacker could record the user speaking the passcode and replay it to gain access to the system.

74. **A.** PIVs contain four digital certificates. The card authentication certificate is used to verify that the PIV credential was issued by an authorized entity, has not expired, and has not been revoked. The PIV authentication certificate is used to verify that the PIV credential was issued by an authorized entity, has not expired, has not been revoked, and holder of the credential (YOU) is the same individual it was issued to. The digital signature certificate allows the user to digitally sign a document or email, providing both integrity and non-repudiation. The encryption certificate allows the user to digitally encrypt documents or email.

75. **D.** Zigbee is a short-range wireless networking technology designed specifically for use in home automation applications. 4G and 5G communications are cellular technologies designed for longer range communications. Satellite communications are most appropriate for communication to distant areas.

76. **D.** The two main technologies used to generate one-time passwords are the HMAC-based One Time Password (HOTP) algorithm and the Time-based One Time Password (TOTP) algorithm. HOTP passcodes are generated sequentially and do not expire until use. TOTP passcodes are based upon the time of authentication and expire frequently. Google Authenticator uses TOTP expiring passcodes, as shown by the pie chart icons to the right of each code.

77. **A.** Academic studies have demonstrated that the accuracy of facial recognition technology may be significantly affected by a person's race. Ethnicity is less likely to impact other biometric techniques, such as fingerprint recognition, iris recognition, and hand geometry analysis.

78. **A.** This is a difficult question, as it is likely many people will automatically assume that this is a knowledge-based factor because it involves passwords. However, since those passwords are provided on a card, this approach is considered a possession-based approach (something you have). For a reference on this, see page 15 of NIST SP800-63b.

79. **C.** Retinal scans and voiceprint analysis are both examples of biometric controls and, when used in combination with a fingerprint scan, would not constitute multifactor authentication. Security questions are a knowledge-based factor but would be difficult to implement for physical access and are generally not a very secure authentication technique due to the ease of a third party discovering correct answers in many cases. ID cards are a "something you have" factor and would be an ideal pairing for the fingerprint scan.

80. **A.** SMS-based approaches to authentication are vulnerable to attacks where the attacker hijacks the telephone number associated with an individual and then uses that hijacked number to receive an authentication message. The other techniques listed here are all considered secure.

81. **C.** The gpresult command computes and displays Resultant Set of Policy (RSoP) information for a remote user and computer. This allows administrators to determine the end result of a set of policies applied to a user account.

82. **A.** This use of a fingerprint scan is an example of a measurement of Roger's physical body, or "something you are" authentication. Therefore, it is an example of a biometric authentication technique.

83. **D.** Retinal scans are generally perceived as the slowest and most intrusive biometric techinque because they require that the individual make physical contact with an eye scanner. Iris scanning and facial recognition can typically be accomplished from a distance. Fingerprint scanning does require physical contact with the scanner but is generally faster than retinal scanning.

84. **B.** All of the authentication techniques described in this scenario are knowledge-based authentication techniques. Therefore, the only factor being used in this scenario is "something you know."

85. **A.** IoT devices are often limited in size and power capacity, limiting their on-board functionality, including their compute capacity. They also often are difficult to patch and maintain to current security standards. They do, by design, normally have sufficient network capacity so that they can connect back to more powerful systems and cloud networks.

86. **D.** Group Policy Objects are processed in the following order: local policies are processed first, followed by site GPOs, domain GPOs, and Organizational Unit (OU) GPOs.

87. **C.** While these are all valid authentication factors, the only one that would implement Greg's location-based requirement is "somewhere you are" authentication that takes the user's physical location into account. These factors may be used to implement context-based authentication that either blocks user access or requires additional authentication measures based upon location.

88. **A.** Security professionals generally agree that the transparency benefits of standard naming conventions outweighs any risks associated with the practice by making it easier to identify users. It is true that naming conventions might make it easier to guess usernames or conduct social engineering, but these risks are generally minimal compared to the benefits of easy user identification.

89. **A.** Active Directory uses Group Policy Objects to assign permissions and policy controls to groups of user accounts and systems.

90. **D.** Hashing and encryption are not practical for an interactive system, because the human speaking cannot perform these operations. The use of a passcode does not protect against this attack if someone is able to record the person saying the passcode Challenge/response systems prompt the user to answer a simple, randomly generated question, similar to a CAPTCHA. They increase the difficulty of a replay attack.

91. **B.** The accuracy of a biometric authentication system is described using three metrics. The false acceptance rate (FAR) is the frequency at which the system admits a person who should not be admitted. The false rejection rate (FRR) is the frequency at which the system denies access to an authorized user incorrectly. The FAR can be improved by increasing the sensitivity of the system, while the FRR can be improved by decreasing the sensitivity of the system. Because of this, the best measure of accuracy is the crossover error rate (CER), which is the sensitivity point at which the FAR and FRR are equal.

92. **A.** Identification occurs when a user makes a claim of identity. This claim is then proven during the authentication phase, through the use of one or more authentication factors, such as a password, smart card, or biometric reading. The system then determines the specific activities that the authenticated user is authorized to engage in by consulting access control lists (ACLs) and other mechanisms and then tracks user access in an accounting system.

93. **C.** Iris recognition technology is a widely used biometric authentication technique because it is nonintrusive and has a low false positive rate. Iris patterns remain stable throughout a person's life and may be scanned from a distance. One disadvantage to this technology is that scanners may be fooled by an image of a person's face.

94. **D.** When Carrie places her finger on the scanner, she is using this as both a identification and authentication technique. The fact that the door opens means that authentication was successful and Carrie was authorized to access the facility. Carrie did not provide a PIN, ID card, or other authentication technique, so this is only single-factor authentication.

95. **C.** Security Enhanced Linux (SELinux) is a security-focused version of the Linux operating system. It is not commonly used in embedded systems because it has significant overhead and complexity. Raspberry Pis, Arduinos, and field-programmable gate arrays (FPGA) are all hardware platforms that are easily reconfigurable for use in embedded systems.

96. **B.** A fingerprint scan is a measurement of an individual's physical characteristics and, therefore, is a biometric security control. Passwords are an example of something you know. Smart cards and keyfobs are examples of something you have.

97. **C.** Logging is an example of an accounting mechanism, creating an unalterable record of authentication activity. The user already completed the identification and authentication phases and authentication was unsuccessful, so no authorization takes place.

98. **D.** Facial recognition technology is an example of a biometric authentication technique, or "something you are." A passcode is an example of a knowledge-based authentication technique, or "something you know."

99. **B.** The most commonly used authentication factors are something you know (such as a password), something you have (such as an authentication token or smartcard), and something you are (such as a fingerprint). Behavioral factors, known as something you do, are more difficult to measure and implement effectively.

100. **A.** This is an example of a proximity card. It lacks the magnetic strip that would be found on a magnetic swipe card or the integrated circuit that would be found on a smart card or CAC.

101. **A.** The false acceptance rate (FAR) of a system is calculated by dividing the number of false acceptances by the total number of authentication attempts. In this dataset, there are 100 total authentication attempts, of which 2 were false acceptances of an unauthorized user. Therefore, the false acceptance rate is 2%.

102. **B.** User 2's password is stored using the salted SHA algorithm, which is resistant to both brute force and dictionary attacks. The unsalted MD5 and SHA algorithms are vulnerable to dictionary attacks. The MD5 and CRYPT algorithms are vulnerable to brute force attacks.

103. **C.** Cold sites have only basic infrastructure available and require the longest period of time to activate operations. They are also the cheapest option. Warm sites add hardware, and possible software, to the mix but do not have a current copy of the data running. They require hours to activate. Hot sites are up and running at all times and can assume operations at a moment's notice. They are the most expensive option. Mobile sites are transportable on trailers and are a good choice for a last-minute recovery plan.

104. **A.** Burning, shredding, and pulping are all acceptable ways to destroy paper records. Degaussing is a magnetic destruction technique that is only appropriate for digital records.

105. **C.** Input validation should always be performed on the web server. Database servers do not see the full input provided by the user and are not well-situated to perform input validation. Input validation should never be performed at the web browser because a malicious user can disable that validation code.

106. **C.** Purging/wiping uses overwriting to remove data from a disk and is an acceptable technique. Encryption renders data inaccessible and is acceptable, provided that strong encryption is used. Degaussing can destroy data on the drive but it also will likely destroy the drive, preventing reuse by the charity.

107. **C.** Cold sites have only basic infrastructure available and require the longest period of time to activate operations. They are also the cheapest option. Warm sites add hardware, and possible software, to the mix but do not have a current copy of the data running. They require hours to activate. Hot sites are up and running at all times and can assume operations at a moment's notice. They are the most

expensive option. Mobile sites are transportable on trailers and are a good choice for a last-minute recovery plan.

108. **B.** Cold sites have only basic infrastructure available and require the longest period of time to activate operations. They are also the cheapest option. Warm sites add hardware, and possible software, to the mix but do not have a current copy of the data running. They require hours to activate. Hot sites are up and running at all times and can assume operations at a moment's notice. They are the most expensive option. Mobile sites are transportable on trailers and are a good choice for a last-minute recovery plan.

109. **A.** Systems that require two individuals to concur before performing a single action follow the principle of two-person control. There is no indication in the question that the control also enforces separation of duties or least privilege. There is also no indication that the mechanism relies upon the dangerous practice of security through obscurity.

110. **B.** Pulping reduces paper to a slurry of fibers and requires the use of chemicals and water. Degaussing and wiping are digital destruction techniques and require no chemicals. Pulverizing reduces an object to dust and does not require the use of chemicals.

111. **C.** Degaussing uses strong magnetic fields to destroy data on a device and will work even if the drive is not functioning properly. Purging or wiping will not work if the drive is not accessible. Pulping is effective only on paper records.

112. **B.** All of these factors are important when performing off-site storage facility location selection. However, the primary consideration should be the nature of the risk. The off-site facility must be located far away enough from the primary facility that it would not be impacted by the same disaster.

113. **B.** A snapshot backup is a specialized type of backup that takes a complete image of the system, rather than just storing files from the file system. This approach is commonly used in virtualized environments because the virtualization platform can launch a new system directly from that image.

114. **B.** The primary risk associated with automated exit motion detectors is that an intruder outside the facility may be able to gain access by triggering the motion detector. For example, if it is possible to slide a piece of paper under the door, it may be possible to forcefully push the paper through so it flies up in the air and triggers the detector.

115. **B.** The fact that Brian has completed the change approval process means that the code is most likely in a staging environment. This staging environment is where code resides until change managers release it into the production environment. Code is moved to staging after being created in a development environment and evaluated in a test environment. Once code is in production, it is available to users.

116. **C.** Straight-cut shredding produces long strips of paper that may be reassembled and, therefore, is not considered a secure document destruction technique. Cross-cut shredding, pulping, and incineration are all considered secure.

117. **A.** Full backups always include all data stored on the backed up media and, therefore, are always at least as large as any other backup type. This system is being regularly backed up, so other backup types will be smaller than a full backup.

118. **D.** While Helen is right to be concerned about all of these issues while examining a vendor contract, her primary concern here is data sovereignty. This means that she wishes to ensure that her company retains ownership of data that is stored in the vendor's systems and has the ability to retrieve that data when necessary.

119. **D.** John must first restore the full backup from November 1st and then apply the incremental backups from each of the 13 days up until the morning of November 14th. He then must apply the differential backup from 8AM. This is a total of 15 backups that he must restore.

120. **B.** The most recent backup occurred at 8AM. There is no way for John to recover any information that was created or modified between 8:00 and the failure time at 9:30, an interval of 90 minutes.

121. **D.** The only difference in this scenario is that there are no differential backups to apply. Therefore, John only needs to restore the full backup and the 13 incremental backups.

122. **A.** Carla should implement least privilege access controls to limit the amount of information available to any individual user. She can also use a data loss prevention (DLP) system to detect the exfiltration of sensitive information. Blocking the use of personal email accounts limits a common method for exfiltrating sensitive information. Adding encryption in transit is not likely to reduce the risk of internal theft, as employees may still access stored sensitive information.

123. **C.** Incremental backups only back up files that were changed since the most recent full or incremental backup. Therefore, they are faster than full/complete backups, which would back up all files. Differential backups contain all files modified since the last full or incremental backup and would therefore take longer, as each differential backup in a series grows larger by including all files from previous incremental backups. Each differential backup in a series contains all of the files included in prior differential backups, while each file is only contained in one incremental backup from a series.

124. **B.** Message digests are one-way functions where it is not possible to reproduce the input by observing the output. To facilitate this, the digests produced by messages with even slight differences are completely different from each other. There is no way to assess the similarity of two messages by comparing their message digests.

125. **D.** Elasticity is the ability to both add and release resources as demand changes. Scalability is only the ability to add resources. While this system is both scalable and elastic, the term elasticity best describes it because it covers both activities. There is no indication in the scenario that the system is redundant or resilient.

126. **A.** The Rivest Shamir Adelman (RSA) algorithm depends upon the difficulty of the prime factorization problem to achieve secrecy. The Elliptic Curve Cryptography (ECC) algorithm does not use prime numbers and instead depends upon the mathematical properties of an elliptic curve. The Diffie Hellman algorithm depends the difficulty of the discrete logarithm problem. Quantum encryption is not yet a practical approach to encryption but, regardless, it also does not use the prime factorization problem.

127. **C.** Data stored in memory is considered data-in-use and is the most difficult scenario to protect against. Data at rest is data stored on a disk or other storage device, while data in transit is data being sent over a network.

128. **A.** In an asymmetric encryption algorithm, the sender of a message achieves confidentiality by encrypting the message with the recipient's public key.

129. **B.** In an asymmetric encryption algorithm, the recipient of a message decrypts the message by using the recipient's private key.

130. **D.** In an asymmetric encryption algorithm, the sender of a message may achieve non-repudiation by digitally signing the message. To do this, the sender creates a message digest using a secure hash function and then signs that message digest with his or her own private key.

131. **C.** In an asymmetric encryption algorithm, the recipient of a digitally signed message decrypts the digital signature using the sender's public key. The recipient then computes the hash of the message using the same hash function used by the sender and compares the hash with the decrypted signature. If the hash and decrypted signature are identical, the message is authentic.

132. **A.** Bruce Schneier designed the Blowfish algorithm as an open-source alternative to other patented encryption algorithms. The algorithm does support a 64-bit block size and variable length keys between 32-448 bits. Schneier does not recommend that people use Blowfish today, instead recommending the Twofish algorithm.

133. **A.** Key stretching is a cryptographic technique used to turn a relatively weak key, such as a short password, into a stronger cryptographic key used to protect the confidentiality of information.

134. **C.** Collisions occur when a hash function produces the same output for two different input values. This is a serious failure of the algorithm. Hash functions should have a defined range, as they often produce fixed-length output values. They should be one-way functions, meaning that it is not possible to obtain the plaintext from the hash. They should also be reproducible, meaning that anyone using the same hash function on the same input should receive the same hash value as output.

135. **A.** Adding a single bit to a cryptographic key doubles the number of possible keys, making the new key length twice as strong as the previous key length.

136. **C.** The RC4 algorithm has inherent insecurities and should not be used under any circumstances. David should replace RC4 with another algorithm that meets modern security standards.

137. **D.** The counter mode (CTM), Galois/counter mode (GCM), and output feedback (OFB) modes of operation may all be used to turn a block cipher into a stream cipher. The electronic codebook (ECB) mode retains the characteristics of a block cipher.

138. **A.** It is true that block ciphers make up the vast majority of modern encryption algorithms. Stream ciphers are faster, not slower, than block ciphers. Block ciphers may make use of Feistel networks, while stream ciphers cannot. Block ciphers work on chunks of data, rather than a single byte at a time.

139. **D.** The Elliptic Curve Diffie Hellman algorithm (ECDHE) is a strong, modern approach to key exchange. Export cipher suites are intentionally weak and should always be avoided. DHE groups 1 and 2 are also outdated and inappropriate for use in modern applications.

140. **C.** The SHA-3 algorithm differs from earlier versions of SHA in that it supports an arbitrary message digest length.

141. **C.** Alan should rely upon a widely-used and scrutinized cryptographic module because that code has likely been tested by thousands of users and many flaws already resolved. If Alan attempts to write or purchase custom code, it is highly likely that he will make a mistake and nobody will continue the development of the code win an ongoing basis. While Alan should test his software prior to use, this testing is unlikely to uncover subtle flaws in the cryptographic implementation.

142. **D.** It is quite difficult to generate a truly random number, so modern computing applications use pseudorandom numbers. PNRGs depend upon a starting point, known as a seed value, to generate their sequence of random values. This seed value must be carefully selected and never reused to prevent against an attacker attempting to generate the same pseudorandom sequence.

143. **B.** The Advanced Encryption Standard uses a 128-bit fixed block size. This should not be confused with the AES key length options of 128 bits, 256 bits, or 512 bits.

144. **D.** Good security practice dictates that encryption and decryption algorithms should be open to public scrutiny to ensure their security. All of the secrecy in a cryptographic function should come from preserving the secrecy of the cryptographic keys.

145. **C.** Diffie-Hellman group 19 uses a strong 256-bit elliptic curve key and is the best option of those presented here. Groups 2 and 5 use 1024-bit and 1536-bit modulus keys, respectively, and are not considered secure. Group 14 uses a 2048-bit key and is minimally secure but is weaker than group 19.

146. **B.** Hash functions do not provide secrecy and the results of a hash operation may be repeated by anyone with access to the hashed content. There are no encryption keys involved in computing a hash function. You may encrypt a hash value with a private key to create a digital signature, but there is no encryption or secrecy involved in creating the hash itself.

147. **A.** In a symmetric encryption algorithm, all encryption and decryption is performed using a shared secret key. Public and private keys only exist in asymmetric encryption algorithms.

148. **B.** The Rijndael algorithm won the AES competition and is the basis for the current AES. Twofish and Serpent were also competitors in the AES selection process. Twofish was a follow-on algorithm to Blowfish, which was not in the competition.

149. **D.** A cryptographic salt is a value combined with a plaintext value prior to encryption or hashing to prevent the use of a rainbow table attack that precomputes encrypted or hashed values.

150. **D.** All of these techniques will provide some degree of cryptographic security. However, the best approach is to use a VPN that will tunnel all communications to the main office over a secure encrypted tunnel. A proxy using HTTPS will only support the specific applications that are proxied. The HTTPS web browser will only encrypt web communications. SSH will only provide encrypted terminal sessions between systems.

151. **C.** Delays introduced into communications due to the overhead from encryption or other processing are known as latency. In a case where latency is unacceptable, architects should seek out low latency technologies.

152. **C.** The simplest way to improve the security of an already strong encryption algorithm is to increase the length of the key used by the algorithm. This is easier than switching algorithms, which would require new software.

153. **B.** Triple DES (3DES) is a symmetric encryption algorithm and, therefore, uses a shared secret key for communication. Public and private keys are only used by asymmetric encryption algorithms and are not relevant here.

154. **D.** Individuals seeking to hide the existence of their communications may use a technique called steganography to hide data within another file. This is often done with image files by subtly altering the pixels of an image to encode the data in a manner that is imperceptible to the human eye.

155. **A.** The Tor network uses perfect forward secrecy (PFS) to allow the relay nodes to forward communications to their end destination without knowing the identity of the sender or the receiver of the message.

156. **C.** The DES algorithm may be made secure by applying it at least three times using at least two independent keys. This mode of operation is known as triple DES or 3DES.

157. **D.** Nonrepudiation is the goal of ensuring that someone can not later disclaim an action that they engaged in. It provides the ability for any third party to conclusively demonstrate the original source.

158. **A.** The Advanced Encryption Standard (AES) is a modern, secure algorithm. The Data Encryption Standard (DES) and Rivest Cipher 4 (RC4) are outdated and insecure. You may improve the security of DES by applying it to data three times (3DES) but for technical reasons, applying it twice (2DES) does not improve security.

159. **C.** This image illustrates the Electronic Code Book (ECB) mode of cipher operation. You can determine this by noting that there is no link at all between the encryption operations.

160. **B.** The most secure implementation of 3DES uses three independent keys. This approach creates a key with 168 (56x3) independent bits. When all three keys are the same, the key length is only 56 bits. When only two keys are independent, the key length is 112 bits.

161. **A.** Email is an insecure data transfer mechanism and should not be used to transfer cryptographic keying material. Two parties wishing to communicate may use digital certificates to exchange public keys, establish a shared secret key using the Diffie Hellman algorithm, or even exchange keys in person.

162. **B.** The Data Encryption Standard uses a 56-bit key. This short key length, along with some insecurities in the algorithm's design, makes it vulnerable to brute force key attacks.

163. **A.** Web servers using TLS generate a new session key for each user that accesses the web server. Session keys are not reused to preserve confidentiality between user sessions.

164. **D.** The two main properties of any cryptographic cipher are confusion and diffusion. Confusion ensures that the relationship between the cryptographic key is extremely complex, while diffusion takes any statistical patterns found in the plaintext and prevents them from appearing in the ciphertext. Obfuscation and collusion are not properties of ciphers.

165. **A.** The two main properties of any cryptographic cipher are diffusion and confusion. Diffusion takes any statistical patterns found in the plaintext and prevents them from appearing in the ciphertext, while confusion ensures that the relationship between the cryptographic key is extremely complex. Obfuscation and collusion are not properties of ciphers.

CHAPTER 3

Implementation

1. In which one of the following mobile device deployment models does the organization allow employees to use corporate owned devices for personal use?

   A. BYOD
   B. CYOD
   C. COPE
   D. Corporate owned

2. Bruce would like to implement an authentication mechanism that requires that users connecting via mobile devices use a second authentication factor when they are connecting from an unfamiliar IP address. What term best describes this technique?

   A. Context-based authentication
   B. Role-baed authentication
   C. Rule-based authentication
   D. Device-based authentication

3. Brad received a call from the Help Desk that users are suddenly calling to report that they are receiving an Access Denied message when trying to access several popular websites, although they are able to access other sites. It seems that everyone in the organization is experiencing the same symptoms on different devices and operating systems and the sites blocked are consistent from user to user. Of the components listed below, which is the most likely culprit?

   A. Content filter
   B. Network firewall
   C. GPO
   D. IPS

4. Sandra is deploying cellular devices to her firm's salesforce. She is concerned that the employees will install apps on the devices that jeopardize security. Which one of the following technologies will allow her to control the configuration of the device and prevent the installation of unwanted apps?

   A. ERP
   B. BYOD
   C. MDM
   D. CRM

5. Katie would like to use a single digital certificate to secure the following websites:

   mywebsite.com
   www.mywebsite.com
   myotherwebsite.com

   Which one of the following certificate attributes can she use to meet this need?

A. CN
B. EV
C. SAN
D. Wildcard

6. Which one of the following tools would be most helpful in detecting missing operating system patches?

A. Documentation review
B. Network vulnerability scanner
C. Port scanner
D. Configuration management tool

7. Tina is deploying a NAC solution for a university network and she wishes to perform host health checking. The network has many unmanaged student machines and students do not want to have software installed on their systems that remains behind after they leave the network. Which one of the following approaches would be best for Tina to use?

A. Dissolvable NAC
B. Permanent NAC
C. Captive portal
D. Active Directory NAC

8. Which one of the following elements of an LDAP entry can be reconstructed to determine the domain name of a system?

A. CN
B. OU
C. DC
D. ST

9. Charlie received an alert from file integrity monitoring software running on a server in his organization. Which one of the following is NOT a likely reason for this alert?

A. Operating system update
B. CPU failure
C. Application update
D. Security incident

10. Which one of the following features is not typically supported by mobile device management solutions?

A. Remote wiping
B. Carrier unlocking
C. Application management
D. Configuration management

11. Tim is planning the deployment of a new VPN that is illustrated in the high-level diagram shown here. What type of VPN is Tim deploying?

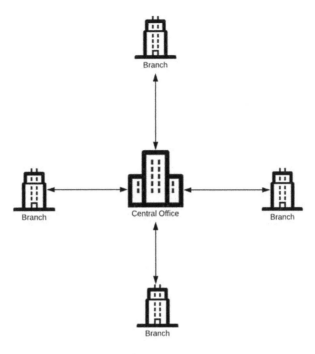

A. TLS VPN
B. Remote access VPN
C. Site-to-site VPN
D. IPsec VPN

12. Which one of the following techniques often reveals both the type and version of a service running on a particular port?

A. Traceroute
B. Port scanning
C. Steganography
D. Banner grabbing

13. Jena would like to configure her organization's switches so that they do not allow systems connected to a switch to spoof MAC addresses. Which one of the following features would be helpful in this configuration?

A. Loop protection
B. Port security
C. Flood guard
D. Traffic encryption

14. What type of proxy server is shown in the illustration below?

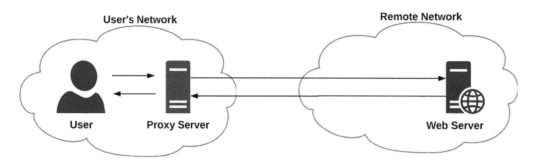

A. Caching proxy
B. Reverse proxy
C. Content filtering proxy
D. Forward proxy

15. Carla is configuring a security policy for a cloud storage bucket. There are currently no bucket or access point policies applied to the bucket that allow public access, but there are some that allow cross-account access. She wants to preserve cross-account access and also prevent any future policies or ACLs from accidentally allowing public access. What boxes should she check?

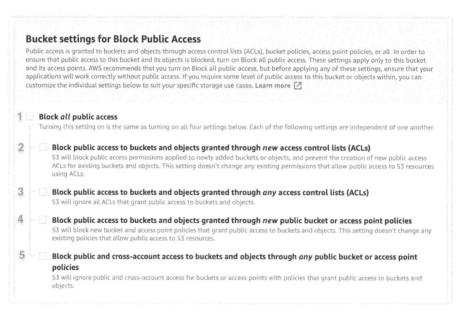

A. 1
B. 2 and 3
C. 2, 3, and 4
D. 2, 3, 4, and 5

16. Bill is inspecting a new tablet computer brought to him by an employee wishing to connect it to the network. The device has the logo shown below on its back panel. What does this logo indicate?

   A. The device has the ability to upload data to cloud services.
   B. The device is portable.
   C. The device allows for recharging through the USB port.
   D. The device may be used as a server to access other USB devices.

17. Drew is concerned that users in his organization may send customers sensitive email messages that travel over the Internet in unencrypted form. What technology can he use to intercept these messages and provide encrypted delivery to the recipient?

   A. Firewall
   B. Email gateway
   C. IPS
   D. TLS

18. Brian recently established a transport mode IPsec connection between his system and a remote VPN concentrator. Which one of the following statements is correct about this connection?

   A. The payload of the packet is not encrypted.
   B. The IP header of the packet is not encrypted.
   C. The connection supports NAT traversal.
   D. No encryption is in use.

19. What type of WiFi antenna is shown in the picture below?

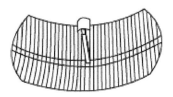

   A. Omnidirectional
   B. Parabolic
   C. Pulse width
   D. Yagi

20. Helen would like to sideload an app onto an Android device. What format must the application be in for her to successfully sideload it?

   A. EXE
   B. IPA
   C. ZIP
   D. APK

21. Raj is troubleshooting authentication problems with his organization's VPN. All users are receiving password authentication failures. What is the most likely cause of this problem?

   A. Password expiration
   B. Incorrect passwords
   C. RADIUS server failure
   D. VPN server failure

22. Carla learns that a user in her organization is about to be terminated at 3:00 and she wants to properly time the disablement of that user's account. What would be the best time to terminate access?

   A. During the termination conversation
   B. Immediately
   C. At the end of the day
   D. Tomorrow morning

23. Ricky is configuring a directory server that must be accessible to users passing through a firewall. He would like to allow only encrypted LDAPS sessions through the firewall. What port should Ricky enable?

   A. TCP port 3389
   B. TCP port 389
   C. TCP port 636
   D. TCP port 443

24. Which one of the following security controls can best protect against the risk of unauthorized software installation?

   A. Content filters
   B. Application blacklisting
   C. Host firewalls
   D. Application whitelisting

25. Rob's organization uses a variety of different cloud vendors. He is looking for a security solution that would allow him to enforce security policies consistently across those different vendors. Which one of the following technologies would best meet his needs?

   A. CASB
   B. SIEM
   C. SOAR
   D. VDI

26. During a security audit of his organization's web environment, Robert discovers that his web server supports SSL v2.0. What action should he recommend based upon this information?

    A. The organizations should replace SSL with TLS.
    B. The organization should disable SSL v2.0 and support only SSL v3.0 or higher.
    C. The organization should replace SSL with SSH.
    D. No action is necessary.

27. Ryan is experiencing interference on his WiFi network. Which one of the following options is not an effective solution to the problem?

    A. Change wireless channels
    B. Relocate access points
    C. Increase bandwidth
    D. Relocate wireless clients

28. When creating a role-based access control system, what mechanism can best be used to assign permissions to individuals in the same job role?

    A. Policy templates
    B. Group policy
    C. Standard procedures
    D. Administrator training

29. Ricky works for a defense contractor that would like to disable the use of cameras on all mobile devices owned by the organization. They are doing this to prevent the theft of confidential information through device cameras. What technology can Ricky use to best enforce this requirement?

    A. IPS
    B. DLP
    C. MDM
    D. WAF

30. Libby is reviewing the logs generated by her organization's application whitelisting system. Which one of the following circumstances is most likely to generate a false positive alert?

    A. Software update to authorized application
    B. Downloading software from the web
    C. Execution of malware on a system
    D. Installation of a rootkit

31. Which one of the following statements about IPsec protocols is correct?

    A. AH supports authentication, integrity and confidentiality. ESP supports confidentiality and authentication.
    B. AH supports authentication, integrity and confidentiality. ESP supports confidentiality and integrity.
    C. AH supports authentication and integrity. ESP supports confidentiality, authentication, and integrity.
    D. AH supports authentication and confidentiality. ESP supports integrity and authentication.

32. Colleen's company is considering deploying a BYOD mobile device strategy. She is concerned about the intermingling of corporate and personal data on mobile devices. What security control can help resolve this situation?

    A. Application control
    B. Full device encryption
    C. Storage segmentation
    D. Multifactor authentication

33. Renee ran a wireless network scan in her office and found the results shown in the image below. Which one of the following networks has the strongest signal?

Network Name	^ BSSID	Security	Protocol	RSSI	Noise	Channel
CAFwifi	1c:b9:c	WPA2 Personal	802.11b/g/n	-67	0	9
CAFwifi-Guest	1c:b9:c	WPA2 Personal	802.11b/g/n	-74	0	4
CAFwifi-Guest	1c:b9:c	WPA2 Personal	802.11ac	-89	0	36
CAFwifi-Guest	1c:b9:c	WPA2 Personal	802.11b/g/n	-73	0	4
CAFwifi-Guest	1c:b9:c	WPA2 Personal	802.11ac	-81	0	157
CAFwifi-Guest	1c:b9:c	WPA2 Personal	802.11b/g/n	-68	0	9
cathy	f8:a0:9	WPA/WPA2 Personal	802.11ac	-89	-99	48
CBCI-3CD8-2.4	20:25:	WPA/WPA2 Personal	802.11b/g/n	-69	0	6
CBD	1c:b9:c	WPA2 Personal	802.11b/g/n	-78	0	4
CBD	1c:b9:c	WPA2 Personal	802.11ac	-88	0	36
CNA_Corporate	68:bd:	WPA2 Enterprise	802.11a/n	-83	0	60
CornerBakeryCafeWiFi	00:11:7	Open	802.11ac	-72	0	1
CornerBakeryCafeWiFi	00:11:7	Open	802.11ac	-83	-99	48

    A. CAFwifi-Guest
    B. cathy
    C. CornerBakeryCafeWiFi
    D. CAFwifi

34. Dylan is helping his organization select a secure videoconferencing solution that will be used to meet both internally and with customers. He would like to choose a technology that uses a protocol that supports secure videoconferencing and will most likely be allowed through the network firewalls of customer organizations. Which one of the following protocols is his best option?

    A. RTPS
    B. HTTPS
    C. H.323
    D. SIP

35. Tom's company produces software for use by consumers. Users installing the software on Macs receive the warning message shown below. What technology, if used, would remove this warning?

A. Certificate stapling
B. Code review
C. Code signing
D. Forensic imaging

36. Sally is planning to deploy an advanced malware protection system. What feature of these systems would allow Sally to leverage information obtained from malware monitoring conducted by other customers of the same vendor?

A. Sandboxing
B. Threat intelligence
C. Quarantining
D. Behavioral detection

37. Visitors to Patricia's organization's website are seeing the error message below. What is the simplest way that Patricia can resolve this issue?

A. Require the use of TLS
B. Renew the certificate
C. Replace the certificate
D. Block insecure ciphers

38. Tom would like to deploy NAC technology that is capable of constantly monitoring the configuration of endpoint machines and quarantining machines that fail to meet a security baseline. Which technology would be most appropriate for Tom to deploy?

    A. Dissolvable NAC
    B. Agentless NAC
    C. Captive portal
    D. Agent-based NAC

39. Flo is investigating an alert generated by her organization's NIDS. The system alerted to a distributed denial of service attack and Flo's investigation revealed that this type of attack did take place. What type of report has the system generated?

    A. False positive
    B. True negative
    C. True positive
    D. False negative

40. Which one of the following IP addresses should never be seen as the destination address of a packet leaving an organization's network over the Internet?

    A. 192.168.10.6
    B. 12.8.1.42
    C. 129.53.100.15
    D. 154.42.190.5

41. Trevor is planning the deployment of a WiFi network. Which one of the following encryption technologies provides the highest level of security?

    A. WPA2
    B. WEP
    C. TKIP
    D. WPA

42. Wendy is deploying mobile devices to field workers who must travel in rural areas and require constant data service availability. Which one of the following technologies can provide that access?

    A. Cellular
    B. SATCOM
    C. WiFi
    D. Bluetooth

43. Tim is concerned about the integrity of log records written by a database that stores sensitive information. What technology can he use to best prevent unauthorized changes to log entries?

    A. TLS
    B. Crypographic hashing
    C. File integrity monitoring
    D. WORM

44. Brian would like to restrict access to his WiFi network to three specific devices that he controls. This network is small and Brian would like to control costs and preserve simplicity. What is the best way to restrict access?

A. PSK
B. MAC filtering
C. NAC
D. Kerberos

45. Jen is evaluating the security group shown below, which is applied to a cloud-based web server that she administers. Which one of the following rules is most problematic?

Inbound rules   Edit inbound rules

	Type	Protocol	Port range	Source	Description - optional
1	HTTP	TCP	80	0.0.0.0/0	-
2	SSH	TCP	22	0.0.0.0/0	-
3	RDP	TCP	3389	67.162.132.232/32	-
4	HTTPS	TCP	443	0.0.0.0/0	-

A. 1
B. 2
C. 3
D. 4

46. Carrie is setting up a site-to-site VPN between two of her organization's offices and wishes to establish the connection using IPsec-based VPN concentrators. Which IPsec mode should Carrie use?

A. Tunnel mode
B. Transport mode
C. Split tunnel
D. TLS

47. Maddox is configuring an internal firewall that will restrict access to a network subnet populated with database servers. Which one of the following ports is not commonly associated with database traffic?

A. 1433
B. 1521
C. 1701
D. 3306

48. Alan is checking the NTFS permissions for a file and finds that the permissions for a problematic user are as shown below. What is the end result of these permissions?

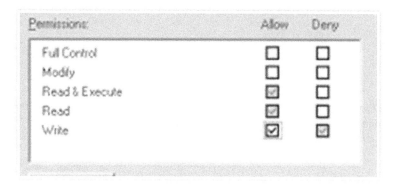

A. The user cannot read or write the file.
B. The user can read the file but not write to it.
C. The user can write to the file but cannot read it.
D. The user can read and write the file.

49. Laurie is considering using the S/MIME standard to provide secure email capability for her organization. Which one of the following statements best describes the security capabilities of S/MIME?

A. S/MIME provides confidentiality, integrity, and non-repudiation.
B. S/MIME provides confidentiality and integrity, but not non-repudation.
C. S/MIME provides integrity and non-repudiation, but not confidentiality.
D. S/MIME provides confidentiality and non-repudiation, but not integrity.

50. Tom is conducting a security audit of network devices in a hospital and discovers that the devices are using SNMPv3 for management. What conclusion can he reach from this information alone?

A. SNMPv3 is insecure because it contains injection vulnerabilities.
B. SNMPv3 is insecure because it uses plaintext community strings.
C. SNMPv3 is insecure because it transfers commands in unencrypted form.
D. The hospital is using a secure network management protocol.

51. Dave's organization uses Android devices from a manufacturer who is very slow to provide operating system updates. Users in his organization are very tech-savvy and want the most recent version of Android. What technique might they wind up adopting to obtain those updates that might also jeopardize Dave's ability to manage them through his MDM platform?

A. Custom firmware
B. Application sideloading
C. Bluejacking
D. Bluesnarfing

52. Scott is creating a VPN policy for end users. He would like to provide maximum protection for mobile devices running Windows by automatically establishing VPN connections when users of those devices open applications that are known to process sensitive data. What technology can best assist Scott with this task?

    A. Split tunnel VPN
    B. TLS VPN
    C. IPsec VPN
    D. Always on VPN

53. Alan's organization is deploying a BYOD policy for mobile devices and he would like to protect corporate data stored on those devices in the event of a compromise. Which one of the following features would be least appropriate for meeting this goal?

    A. Remote wiping
    B. Containerization
    C. Geofencing
    D. Encryption

54. Which feature of Microsoft operating systems prevents the execution of code stored in regions of memory not specifically designated for executable code?

    A. PCI
    B. ASLR
    C. DEP
    D. PGP

55. Gina would like to restrict the access that different technologists in her organization have to provision cloud resources from the company's IaaS provider. What is the best way for her to achieve this goal?

    A. ACL
    B. CASB policy
    C. Resource policy
    D. Security group

56. Carl is configuring security permissions for his network and comes across the ruleset shown below. What type of device is most likely executing this policy?

```
access-list 100 deny ip 10.0.0.0 0.255.255.255 any
access-list 100 deny ip 172.16.0.0 0.15.255.255 any
access-list 100 deny ip 192.168.0.0 0.0.255.255 any
access-list 100 deny ip 127.0.0.0 0.255.255.255 any
access-list 100 permit ip any any
```

    A. IDP
    B. Firewall
    C. DLP
    D. Router

57. In the image below, what term is used to describe the WiFi network names being displayed to the user?

A. Broadcast name
B. MAC
C. IP address
D. SSID

58. Greg is reviewing smartphone security controls for users who take photos at sensitive locations. He is concerned about the type of information that might be included in the EXIF metadata associated with each image. Which one of the following data elements is not commonly included in EXIF metadata?

A. Ambient temperature
B. GPS coordinates
C. Camera model
D. Shutter speed

59. Which one of the following firewall types is capable of monitoring connection status by tracking the stages of the TCP handshake and then using that information when deciding whether to allow future packets that are part of an active connection?

    A. Stateless firewall
    B. Packet filter
    C. Stateful inspection
    D. Router ACL

60. Barbara is the cybersecurity manager for a retail chain that is considering deploying contactless payment systems that support Apple Pay, Google Wallet, and similar solutions. What type of communication technology do these solutions use to communicate between a user's smartphone and the payment terminal?

    A. NFC
    B. Bluetooth
    C. Infrared
    D. WiFi

61. After reviewing the results of a system scan, Mike determines that a server in his organization supports connections using the FTP service. What is the primary risk associated with this service?

    A. Buffer overflow
    B. Unencrypted credentials
    C. Cross-site scripting
    D. Privilege escalation

62. Tina is selecting a firewall for her organization and would like to choose a technology that is capable of serving as her organization's front line connection to the Internet and blocking a variety of attacks, including SYN floods, TCP probes, and SQL injection. Which one of the following devices would best meet her needs?

    A. Packet filter
    B. Next generation firewall
    C. Router ACL
    D. Web application firewall

63. Sam is reviewing the logs from his organization's unified threat management system. Which one of the following functions is not typically performed by a UTM device?

    A. Sandboxing
    B. Content filter
    C. Firewall
    D. Intrusion prevention

64. Jaime is creating a firewall ruleset that is designed to allow access from external networks to a web server that responds to both encrypted and unencrypted requests. What ports should Jaime fill for the boxes currently labeled X and Y on the diagram?

Rule	Source IP	Source Port	Dest IP	Dest Port	Action
1	any	any	10.0.0.1	X	allow
2	any	any	10.0.0.1	Y	allow
3	any	any	any	any	block

A. 80 and 443
B. 80 and 8080
C. 53 and 443
D. 53 and 80

65. Yolanda would like to find a secure mechanism for managing keys in her cloud environment. She wants to protect key material from access by her own staff and the cloud vendor. What approach would best meet her needs?

A. Storing keys on a separate key server
B. Storing keys on the same servers where they are used
C. Storing keys in a password vault
D. Using an HSM

66. Tom purchased a mobile device from a carrier under a contract that expired last year. He attempted to transfer the device to a new carrier but was told that the device is locked. Who must unlock the device in order for Tom to complete the transfer?

A. The new carrier
B. The original carrier
C. Tom's employer
D. Tom

67. Norma is comparing the security characteristics of different WiFi networks. Which one of the following types of WiFi network allows the use of enterprise authentication protocols?

A. PSK
B. WPA
C. Ad Hoc
D. Direct

68. Which one of the following network device features is NOT used to prevent routing loops from occurring in a network or to correct them when they do occur?

   A. Split horizon
   B. Loop prevention
   C. Flood guard
   D. Hold-down timers

69. Which one of the following services is not normally performed by email security gateways?

   A. Network firewall
   B. Data loss prevention
   C. Encryption
   D. Spam filtering

70. In the firewall ruleset shown here, what name is typically used to refer to rule number 4?

Rule	Source IP	Source Port	Dest IP	Dest Port	Action
1	any	any	10.0.0.1	25	allow
2	any	any	10.0.0.1	465	allow
3	10.0.0.0/24	any	any	any	allow
4	any	any	any	any	block

   A. SMTP
   B. Stealth
   C. Promiscuous
   D. Implicit deny

71. Ralph runs a large-scale WiFi network and is having difficulty with interference between access points. What is the most effective and efficient way for Ralph to address these issues?

   A. Use a WiFi controller
   B. Modify access point power levels
   C. Reposition access points
   D. Modify access point antenna configuration

72. Gavin is choosing a model that will allow employees to access corporate systems remotely. He would like to allow employees to use their own devices but would like to provision access in a way that allows them to use the data through a corporate-controlled computing environment without transferring data to their own devices. Which one of the following models would best meet Gavin's needs?

   A. COPE
   B. CYOD
   C. BYOD
   D. VDI

73. Nina is assisting a user who reports that he cannot connect to the wireless network in his building. The network continually pops up a message requesting a network password. What is the most likely issue with this connection?

    A. Expired user account
    B. Incorrect PSK
    C. Incorrect user password
    D. Incorrect SSID

74. An attacker already compromised a system on an organization's local network and has set up an encrypted tunnel to that system. He is now attempting to pivot by exploiting a zero-day vulnerability on a system located on the same LAN as the already-compromised system. What type of intrusion detection system would be the most likely to detect the pivot attack?

    A. Signature HIDS
    B. Heuristic HIDS
    C. Heuristic NIDS
    D. Signature NIDS

75. Which one of the following techniques speeds up the certificate verification process by including an OCSP response with the initial presentation of a certificate?

    A. Certificate chaining
    B. Certificate linking
    C. Certificate pinning
    D. Certificate stapling

76. Greg is working with remote users to troubleshoot issues that they are experiencing with VPN connections when traveling to customer sites. He believes that customer firewalls are interfering with the VPN connection and is considering altering the VPN configuration to prevent this issue. What type of VPN connection is least susceptible to this problem?

    A. TLS
    B. IPsec
    C. Split tunnel
    D. Full tunnel

77. Mark is analyzing host antivirus logs in the aftermath of a system compromise. He discovers that the antivirus software did not detect malicious software that infected the system. Which one of the following is the least likely cause of this failure?

    A. Antivirus software failure
    B. Outdated antivirus signatures
    C. Zero-day attack
    D. APT attack

78. Which one of the following approaches to hard drive encryption uses a drive that performs the encryption itself?

    A. Chipset FDE
    B. Enclosed FDE
    C. SED
    D. Bridge FDE

79. Betty is responsible for managing the digital certificates on her organization's servers. The certificate on the main public web server is about to expire. What must Betty do?

    A. Obtain a new certificate from the CA
    B. Generate a new certificate using the server's private key
    C. Renew the certificate using the server's private key
    D. Place the certificate on the CRL

80. Gina is preparing an application server that will be used by employees within her organization to manage payroll. Review the basic network diagram shown below. Gina will place the server on a protected subnet of one of these network zones. Which zone is most appropriate?

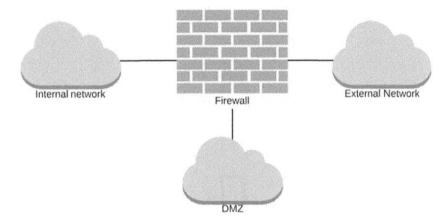

    A. Internal network
    B. External network
    C. DMZ
    D. None of the above

81. Denise is reviewing the security of her network's management plane against the vendor's security baseline. Which one of the following protocols should she not expect to see allowed on the management plane?

    A. RADIUS
    B. NTP
    C. SSH
    D. RTP

82. Refer to the network shown here. What technology must be supported by the firewall in order for this network to function properly?

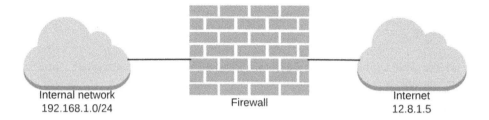

Internal network
192.168.1.0/24

Firewall

Internet
12.8.1.5

A. IPS
B. NAC
C. NAT
D. WAF

83. Barry is designing a site-to-site VPN to support remote office access to corporate resources, as shown below. Which one of the following devices would be the best place to terminate the VPN connection at the central office?

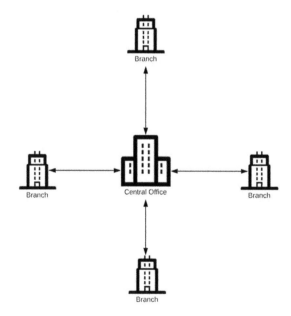

A. VPN server
B. Router
C. Firewall
D. VPN concentrator

84. Gina receives a piece of digitally signed code from one of her suppliers and would like to verify the digital signature on the code. What key should she use to verify the signature?

    A. Her own public key
    B. The supplier's private key
    C. The supplier's public key
    D. Her own private key

85. Tom is considering an intrusion prevention solution for his IaaS environment and is concerned about vendor diversity and resiliency. Which one of the following approaches would best allow him to continue outsourcing IPS work while meeting his goals?

    A. IPS solution provided by his IaaS vendor
    B. Open source IPS built in an IaaS environment
    C. Third-party cloud IPS
    D. Third-party on-premises IPS

86. Paul's company offers an unencrypted wireless network for use by visitors to their chain of retail stores. Employees sometimes use this network for convenience because the secured wireless network is known to have authentication issues. When an employee connects to the unencrypted network, what network zone should they be placed onto?

    A. Guest network
    B. Intranet
    C. Extranet
    D. DMZ

87. Tony would like to use input validation to prevent SQL injection attacks against his organization's web applications. Where should Tony place input validation code to ensure maximum effectiveness?

    A. Within JavaScript code
    B. Database server
    C. Endpoint systems
    D. Web server

88. Elaine is installing an intrusion detection system and would like to ensure that her device sees all network traffic crossing a link. She is also concerned about the system causing a network outage if it fails. Which installation approach would be most appropriate in this situation?

    A. TAP
    B. SPAN
    C. Port mirroring
    D. Inline installation

89. Which one of the following security tools is best able to perform file integrity monitoring?

    A. Wireshark
    B. Snort
    C. Tripwire
    D. QRadar

90. Upon booting a laptop, Yvonne sees the password prompt shown below. What is presenting this prompt?

    A. Active Directory
    B. BIOS
    C. TPM
    D. HSM

91. Which one of the following characteristics does not describe a hardware root of trust?

    A. It should be secure by design.
    B. It should be implemented in hardware.
    C. It should contain as much of the operating system as possible.
    D. It should be trusted by components at higher layers of abstraction.

92. Fran is working with her organization's IT operations team troubleshooting an issue on their web servers. They are discovering that the CPU load on all of their web servers is quite high and they would like to reduce that load without purchasing additional web servers. Which one of the following technologies would best address this situation?

    A. Weighted least connections load balancing
    B. Round-robin load balancing
    C. SSL acceleration
    D. Web application firewall

93. Martha is placing an IPS sensor on her network and would like to place it in a location where it will receive the least traffic but is likely to intercept any SQL injection attack that might reach the web server located in the DMZ. Which network location is the best place to position the sensor, given the network diagram shown here?

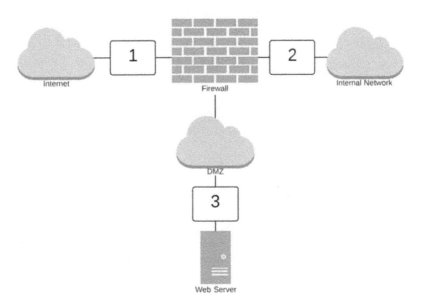

A. Location 1
B. Location 2
C. Location 3
D. Both Locations 1 and 2

94. Which one of the following security devices is least likely to perform content filtering services to protect end users against malware infections?

   A. IPS
   B. Firewall
   C. Proxy
   D. Router

95. Jessica is creating a virtual private cloud (VPC) with a private subnet in her IaaS environment. Which one of the following IP address ranges would not be appropriate for this subnet?

   A. 10.16.0.0/16
   B. 172.16.0.0/16
   C. 181.10.0.0/16
   D. 192.168.0.0/16

96. When configuring access control lists (ACLs) on a Cisco router, what limitation of standard ACLs does not exist for extended ACLs?

   A. Standard ACLs cannot perform outbound filtering.
   B. Standard ACLs cannot filter based upon source IP address.
   C. Standard ACLs cannot perform inbound filtering.
   D. Standard ACLs cannot filter based upon destination IP address.

97. What IPSec mode is most commonly used to create site-to-site VPNs between locations?

    A. Tunnel mode
    B. Transport mode
    C. Internet key exchange mode
    D. Security association mode

98. Zack is concerned about the potential for DDoS attacks against his organization that may consume all of their available network bandwidth. What entity is in the best position to implement controls to limit the impact of these attacks?

    A. Zack's ISP
    B. Zack's organization
    C. Nobody is able to mitigate the impact of a distributed attack
    D. Attacker's ISP

99. Carla is the firewall administrator for a large university. She has recently seen a flurry of activity from student networks sending spam print jobs to printers located in administrative offices. She would like to block printer traffic between network segments using the standard HP JetDirect port. What port should she block?

    A. UDP port 9100
    B. TCP port 9100
    C. TCP port 8080
    D. UDP port 8080

100. Tim is performing input validation for a free-text field in a web application. He would like to protect against SQL injection attacks. Which one of the following characters is most crucial to sanitize?

    A. >
    B. "
    C. <
    D. '

101. Travis is placing a new web server on his organization's network. The server will provide information to the general public. Which network zone is the most appropriate placement for this server?

    A. Extranet
    B. Intranet
    C. DMZ
    D. Guest network

102. When deploying a wireless network, which network zone offers the most appropriate placement for wireless users?

    A. Wireless users should be placed onto the extranet.
    B. Wireless users should be placed onto the guest network.
    C. Wireless users should be placed onto the intranet.
    D. Wireless users should be placed on the same network zone they would be placed on if they connected to a wired network.

103. When using Windows BitLocker in transparent operation mode, what is used to decrypt the key protecting data stored on the disk?

    A. USB Key
    B. Active Directory
    C. User Password
    D. Trusted Platform Module

104. Which one of the following features is not normally included in a proxy server?

    A. Caching
    B. Content filtering
    C. Route optmization
    D. Anonymization

105. Dylan is creating a cloud architecture that requires connections between systems in two different private VPCs. What would be the best way for Dylan to enable this access?

    A. Internet gateway
    B. Public IP address
    C. VPC endpoint
    D. VPN connection

106. Wanda would like to disable unnecessary services on a Windows 10 system in her organization. What tool should she use to do this?

    A. Event Viewer
    B. Programs and Features
    C. Computer Management
    D. Disk Management

107. Tim is designing a remote access VPN for use by employees traveling to customer sites on sales calls. His primary objective is to ensure that employees will be able to access the VPN from customer networks without requiring that the customer reconfigure their networks to allow this access. What type of VPN would best meet Tim's needs?

    A. TLS
    B. IPSec
    C. PPTP
    D. L2TP

108. Consider the application input shown below:

    \uFE64script\uFE65

    What technique should a developer use prior to submitting this string for input validation?

    A. Normalization
    B. Concatenation
    C. Tokenization
    D. Substitution

109. Why should administrators only allow employees to download digitally signed applications to mobile devices?

    A. Digitally signed applications are certified to function properly
    B. Digitally signed applications are free of malware
    C. Digitally signed applications come from known sources
    D. Digitally signed applications are guaranteed by Apple

110. Fran recently completed development of a new code module and the module successfully completed user acceptance testing. Now that testing is complete, she would like to request that the module be moved to the next step in the process. What environment is most appropriate for the code at this stage of the process?

    A. Staging environment
    B. Development environment
    C. Production environment
    D. Test environment

111. Joe is responsible for providing end user computing to a large organization that allows a BYOD approach for most users. He needs to provide users with a way to access a very expensive desktop software package that has limited licenses and may not be installed on personally-owned devices due to license restrictions. He wants to provide users with a desktop environment where they can log in and interact with the software while being isolated from each other. What type of environment is most appropriate for this purpose?

    A. DLP
    B. Web-based client
    C. VPN-based client
    D. VDI

112. Joyce is planning to implement a cloud access security broker and would like to deploy the technology using a model that will function with the largest possible variety of cloud applications. Which one of the following approaches should Joyce select?

    A. Forward proxy
    B. Reverse proxy
    C. API
    D. Firewall

113. Katie is reviewing the security of a web server used by her organization. She discovers each of the items listed below. Which one of these items poses the greatest security risk and should be prioritized for remediation?

    A. The server runs Apache and MySQL.
    B. The server supports access on port 80.
    C. The server supports access on port 443.
    D. The server uses TLS 1.2.

114. Randy wishes to segment his organization's network to enforce isolation between different classes of users. Users are scattered around the building and Randy must support each of these network segments anywhere within the facility. Which one of the following technologies will best meet Randy's needs?

  A. WAF
  B. Physical segmentation
  C. VPN
  D. VLANs

115. Jake would like to find a security solution that protects users from malicious content hosted on websites that they visit and allows him to perform content filtering according to his company's policy. Which one of the following solutions would best meet his needs?

  A. CASB
  B. IPS
  C. NGFW
  D. SWG

116. Consider the firewall rulebase shown here. Assuming the firewall is positioned to intercept the request, if a user on a system located at 192.168.100.1 attempts to make an HTTPS connection to the web server located at 192.168.15.5, how will the firewall react?

Rule	Source IP	Source Port	Dest IP	Dest Port	Action
1	any	any	192.168.15.5	80	allow
2	any	any	192.168.15.5	443	allow
3	192.168.100.1	any	192.168.15.5	any	deny
4	any	any	any	any	deny

  A. The firewall will allow the traffic according to rule 1
  B. The firewall will allow the traffic according to rule 2
  C. The firewall will deny the traffic according to rule 3
  D. The firewall will deny the traffic according to rule 4

117. What static code analysis technique seeks to identify the variables in a program that may contain user input?

  A. Signature detection
  B. Lexical analysis
  C. Control flow analysis
  D. Taint analysis

118. Sarah's boss asked her to identify a security technology that can block users from installing three specific pieces of undesirable software on their laptops without affecting other uses of the devices. Which one of the following security technologies would best meet this requirement?

    A. Application blacklisting
    B. Application whitelisting
    C. Host firewall
    D. Host IPS

119. Kevin is an application developer and would like to digitally sign code so that users know that it originated from his organization. What key should Kevin use to sign the code?

    A. The web server's private key
    B. The company's public key
    C. The company's private key
    D. The web server's public key

120. What software security technique can be added to a Secure DevOps approach to automate the evaluation of how software will respond to mutated input?

    A. Decompilation
    B. Penetration testing
    C. Vulnerability scanning
    D. Fuzz testing

121. Which one of the following tools can be used to easily determine the patch level of Windows systems across an enterprise?

    A. APT
    B. Windows Update
    C. Yum
    D. SCCM

122. What technology do Mac OS X systems use to prevent applications downloaded from the App Store from directly accessing critical system resources?

    A. Sandboxing
    B. TCP wrappers
    C. Virtualization
    D. Taint analysis

123. Which one of the following technologies is not commonly used as part of a single sign-on (SSO) implementation?

    A. OAuth
    B. IPSec
    C. OpenID
    D. SAML

124. In an authentication system using the mandatory access control (MAC) model, who determines what users may access an object?

    A. The user
    B. The object owner
    C. The system administrator
    D. The system

125. Ryan is building out a cloud web architecture and wishes to provide the maximum possible degree of fault tolerance while still working with a single IaaS vendor. Which one of the following solutions would best meet his needs?

    A. Creating redundant web servers in different regions
    B. Creating redundant web servers in different availability zones
    C. Creating redundant web servers in the same availability zone
    D. Creating redundant web servers across multiple vendors

126. TJ is designing the authentication system for an online gambling website that is restricted for use by residents of a single U.S. state. What type of access control should TJ implement to ensure that his organization does not run afoul of the law?

    A. Role-based access control
    B. Multifactor authentication
    C. Token-based authentication
    D. Location-based access control

127. Thelma is configuring a new web server running Apache. Apache requires an account to read the files contained in the /var/www directory. What type of account should Thelma use for this access?

    A. Root account
    B. Guest account
    C. Service account
    D. Administrator account

128. Helen's organization has a password policy that does not enforce complexity requirements. What is the major disadvantage to this approach?

    A. Attackers can use social engineering to extract simple passwords from users.
    B. Attackers can easily brute force passwords that are short.
    C. Attackers can easily brute force passwords that draw from a limited character set.
    D. Attackers may use reverse hashing to decrypt simple passwords.

129. Lila is concerned about the security of a database table that contains Social Security Numbers. The organization needs to maintain this information for tax reporting purposes, but Lila wants to make sure that database administrators are not able to access this very sensitive field. Which one of the following security controls would best meet Lila's need?

    A. Database activity monitoring
    B. Field-level hashing
    C. Database access controls
    D. Field-level encryption

130. Which one of the following account types should be assigned the highest priority for account activity logging?

    A. Temporary user accounts
    B. Guest accounts
    C. Service accounts
    D. Standard user accounts

131. Colleen's company would like to manage administrator credentials by creating them in a manner such that nobody has knowledge of the root password for a system and the password is stored in an electronic vault. What mechanism should Colleen implement to ensure that administrators are not locked out of the system in the event of an access control failure?

    A. Emergency access procedure
    B. Redundant passwords
    C. Provide a manager with the passwords
    D. Multifactor authentication

132. Carla is examining a point-of-sale terminal and sees the pre-populated login screen shown here. What type of account is most likely being used in this scenario?

    A. Privileged account
    B. Shared account
    C. Guest account
    D. Superuser account

133. Tim is a member of several NTFS groups and is attempting to access a file stored on an NTFS volume. The set of permissions that apply from each of his group memberships are shown here. What is the end result of these permissions when Tim attempts to access the file?

Accounting Group
Inherited deny read and write permission

Tim's Account
Explicit allow read and write permission

Managers Group
Explicit deny write permission

    A. Tim can't read or write the file.
    B. Tim can read the file but not write to it.
    C. Tim can write to the file but not read it.
    D. Tim can both read and write the file.

134. What network port is used for communications related to the Kerberos authentication process?

    A. UDP port 636
    B. TCP port 88
    C. UDP port 88
    D. TCP port 636

135. Paula is reviewing her organization's account management lifecycle. She is paying particular attention to the timeliness of account management activities and would like to prioritize areas that have the greatest risk. Which one of the following activities should be her highest priority?

    A. Access modifications
    B. Onboarding
    C. Access reviews
    D. Offboarding

136. Nancy is configuring a user account and is setting permissions as shown here. What type of permissions is Nancy setting?

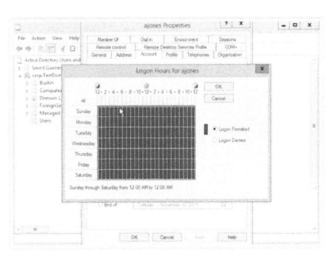

    A. Location-based restrictions
    B. Content-based restrictions
    C. Role-based restrictions
    D. Time-based restrictions

137. When using CHAP authentication, what does the server send to the client in the second step of the handshake?

    A. Password
    B. Hash
    C. Challenge
    D. Certificate

138. Brian is implementing geofencing as a component of his access control system. What type of control is he implementing?

    A. Role-based access control
    B. Group-based access control
    C. Location-based access control
    D. Time-based access control

139. Molly's organization has a shared account that they use to provide access to vendors. What is the primary security objective that is sacrificed using this model, assuming that the password is not shared with unauthorized individuals?

    A. Integrity
    B. Least privilege
    C. Confidentiality
    D. Accountability

140. When digital certificates are used for the authentication of a user to a server, what is the primary purpose of the digital certificate?

    A. To convey a signed copy of the server's public key
    B. To convey a signed copy of the user's private key
    C. To convey a signed copy of the user's public key
    D. To convey a signed copy of the server's private key

141. Taylor is accessing a website that would like to access information stored in her Google account. The site makes a request to access that information using the oAuth protocol. In this scenario, who is the oAuth resource owner?

    A. Taylor
    B. Google
    C. Website
    D. Both Google and the website

142. What is the primary feature that distinguishes a smart card from other types of access card?

    A. Presence of a magnetic stripe
    B. Presence of an integrated circuit
    C. Requirement to enter a PIN or password
    D. Compatibility with biometric authentication

143. Consider the U.S. government personal identity verification (PIV) card shown here. When the individual presents a card to an appropriate system for verification, what element allows the validator to verify the identity of the PIV user?

A. Encryption certificate
B. Card authentication certificate
C. Digital signature certificate
D. PIV authentication certificate

144. Barry is troubleshooting authentication problems for his organization's VPN. The VPN uses a RADIUS backend for authentication and Barry would like to monitor this traffic. What ports are associated with RADIUS?

A. UDP ports 1812 and 1813
B. TCP ports 1812 and 1813
C. UDP ports 1433 and 1521
D. TCP ports 1433 and 1521

145. Which of the following services are supported by the TACACS+ protocol?

A. Authentication, authorization, and accounting
B. Authentication only
C. Authentication and authorization
D. Authentication and accounting

146. Tim recently set the attribute shown here on a group of Windows user accounts. His organization has the following security requirements:

1. Passwords must be at least 10 characters.

2. Passwords must contain characters from three different character classes.

3. Passwords may not contain the user's account name.

Which of these requirements are met by the setting shown here?

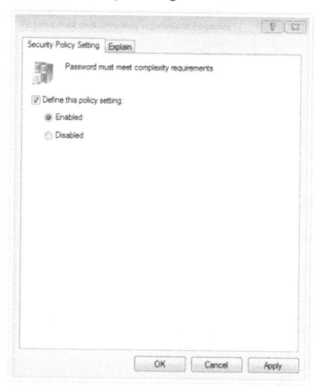

A. Requirements 1 and 2
B. Requirements 2 and 3
C. Requirements 1, 2, and 3
D. Requirements 1 and 3

147. Carl would like to implement a recertification process for vendors with accounts allowing access to systems in his organization. What access management control can best facilitate this?

A. Password complexity
B. Account expiration
C. Least privilege
D. Job rotation

148. Which one of the following protocols is considered secure for use in an authentication system without the use of any compensating controls?

   A. PAP
   B. MS-CHAP
   C. MS-CHAP v2
   D. Kerberos

149. Tom is designing a password reset mechanism for his organization and would like to require a personal visit to a help desk. Which one of the following statements is not correct?

   A. Users should be permitted to reset passwords in person.
   B. Users reporting to the help desk should be asked for proof of identification
   C. Use of a help desk reset approach is burdensome on both users and staff.
   D. Users reporting to the help desk should provide an old, expired password if possible.

150. Which one of the following is a best practice for the management of privileged accounts on a server?

   A. Privileged accounts should be shared between administrators.
   B. Administrative users should have both privileged and unprivileged accounts.
   C. Privileged accounts should not be protected by passwords.
   D. Privileged accounts should be exempted from standard password management practices.

151. Frank would like to set his organization's password length requirements to align with industry best practices. What should he set as the maximum password length?

   A. 8 characters
   B. 16 characters
   C. 255 characters
   D. No maximum

152. Which one of the following is an implementation of a mandatory access control system?

   A. SELinux
   B. NTFS
   C. Google Drive
   D. Mac OS X

153. Taylor works for an organization that experiences high turnover in employees, particularly at their call center and retail stores. She would like to implement an access control system that minimizes work. Which one of the following actions will best reduce the workload on the access management team while maintaining security?

   A. Implement group-based access control
   B. Implement a permissive access control model
   C. Implement mandatory access control
   D. Implement personalized access control for each employee

154. In a normal RADIUS authentication session, what is the first message sent by the client to the server?

   A. Access-Reject
   B. Access-Request
   C. Access-Challenge
   D. Access-Accept

155. In a discretionary access control (DAC) system, who is primarily responsible for assigning permissions to access objects for a user?

   A. User
   B. Object owners
   C. System administrator
   D. The system itself

156. What type of access control is performed by a standard network firewall?

   A. Role-based access control
   B. Rule-based access control
   C. Mandatory access control
   D. Attribute-based access control

157. Brenda is assisting a user who is traveling on business and is unable to access a critical system. Brenda is able to access the system herself and the user was able to access it last week from the office. The user connected to the VPN and is still having the same issue. What type of access restriction is most likely in place?

   A. Role-based restriction
   B. Time-based restriction
   C. Location-based restriction
   D. Content-based restriction

158. When using an attribute-based access control (ABAC) model, what attributes are available to the authorization system for analysis?

   A. User and system attributes only
   B. User attributes, system attributes, and environmental attributes
   C. User attributes only
   D. System attributes only

159. Which one of the following principles describes the basic concept of access control that should be enforced by every network firewall?

   A. Explicit deny
   B. Implicit deny
   C. Implicit allow
   D. Explicit allow

160. In a Kerberos authentication scheme, the client sends an authenticator to the ticket-granting server (TGS) when requesting a service ticket. How does the client encrypt this authenticator?

    A. The client encrypts the authenticator with the client's private key.
    B. The client encrypts the authenticator with the TGS public key.
    C. The client encrypts the authenticator with the TGS session key.
    D. The client does not encrypt the authenticator

161. In a network using 802.1x authentication, which device normally contains the 802.1x supplicant?

    A. Authenticator
    B. End user system
    C. Authentication server
    D. Service server

162. Which one of the following authentication protocols is an appropriate protocol for performing administrator authentication on network devices?

    A. STACACS
    B. XTACACS
    C. TACACS
    D. TACACS+

163. Ryan attempts to log into AcmeSocial, a social networking website. The website allows him to login with his HMail account through the use of SAML authentication. In this scenario, who is the SAML principal?

    A. Both HMail and Acme Social
    B. AcmeSocial
    C. HMail
    D. Ryan

164. What protocol is normally used for communication between an authenticator and authentication server on a network using 802.1x authentication?

    A. XTACACS
    B. TACACS
    C. RADIUS
    D. TACACS+

165. Thomas is configuring the security for a specialized computing system that will be used in a high security environment. This system will assign tags to each file based upon their classification and users will only be able to access information that matches their security clearance. What type of security model is Thomas implementing?

    A. ABAC
    B. DAC
    C. MAC
    D. RBAC

166. Which one of the following is a reasonable approach to handling failed authentication attempts against a password-based authentication system?

    A. Disablement of a user account after three incorrect attempts
    B. Require an exponentially increasing timeout period between login attempts
    C. Lockout of a user account after five incorrect login attempts
    D. Require 5 seconds between login attempts

167. Riley is securing an application that uses PAP authentication. Which one of the following statements is correct about PAP?

    A. PAP can't perform reliable, repeatable authentication.
    B. PAP does not encrypt credentials and is insecure.
    C. PAP implementations are only possible on Token Ring networks.
    D. PAP is widely used for VPN authentication.

168. Gavin is managing the access control system for his organization. Users often change jobs and he would like to select an approach that will make it easy to reassign permissions when users move around the organization. Which access control model is best suited for his needs?

    A. MAC
    B. ABAC
    C. DAC
    D. RBAC

169. Kip is preparing to conduct a privilege usage audit of his organization's database servers. Which one of the following data sources would be least helpful to him in this exercise?

    A. Organization chart
    B. Database access logs
    C. Network firewall logs
    D. Asset classification information

170. Ron is designing a user awareness program intended to improve password security practices. Of the practices listed below, which poses the greatest risk to organizations?

    A. Use of passwords that are more than a year old
    B. Use of passwords less than 12 characters
    C. Use of passwords that do not contain special characters
    D. Reuse of passwords on multiple sites

171. When creating a web application based upon the oAuth 2.0 standard, what authentication protocol is often the simplest choice?

    A. Digital certificates
    B. RADIUS
    C. Kerberos
    D. OpenID Connect

172. Val would like to configure her organization's password security policy to comply with industry best practices. How many passwords should she keep in a password history to prevent password reuse?

    A. 0
    B. 1
    C. 5
    D. 8

173. Which one of the following devices is most likely to serve as an authenticator in an 802.1x network authentication scenario?

    A. Laptop with a wireless connection
    B. Desktop with a wired connection
    C. Wireless access point
    D. RADIUS server

174. Beth used the sign-in with Facebook feature to access a website hosted by The Washington Post. This feature uses SAML-based authentication. In this scenario, what is the role played by The Washington Post?

    A. Identity provider
    B. User agent
    C. Service provider
    D. Certificate authority

175. In Kerberos authentication, which one of the following components is responsible for verifying that a user's password (or other credentials) is valid and correct?

    A. Client
    B. AS
    C. Service
    D. TGS

176. Gina is configuring an access control system for a college that will examine a user's identity profile when determining whether to grant access to resources. Students will be granted access to limited files, while faculty and staff will have broader access. Faculty and staff access may be further segmented based upon their department, title, and other identity attributes. What type of access control system is Gina designing?

    A. ABAC
    B. DAC
    C. MAC
    D. SLAC

177. Jane is seeking to enforce role-based access restrictions in her organization. Which one of the following technologies would allow her to enforce these restrictions across a variety of systems?

    A. Oracle database permissions
    B. NTFS access control lists
    C. Cisco access controls lists
    D. Active Directory group policy

178. John approaches a security guard and hands her the smart card shown here. The guard conducts a physical inspection of the card and pulls up an image of it on her system to verify that it is authentic. How many authentication factors has John successfully completed at this point?

A. Zero
B. One
C. Two
D. Three

179. Which one of the following is not an example of a privileged account on a server?

A. Shared account
B. Root account
C. Service account
D. Administrator account

180. Paul is designing a system that will allow users from Acme Corporation, one of his organization's vendors, to access Paul's accounts payable system using the accounts provided by Acme Corporation. What type of authentication system is Paul attempting to design?

A. Single sign-on
B. Transitive trust
C. Federated authentication
D. Multifactor authentication

181. During an incident response effort, Tony discovers that many systems on his network have different times set on their internal clocks. He wants to avoid the hassle of recording time offsets during future investigations by synchronizing clocks. What protocol would meet this need?

   A. NTP
   B. TLS
   C. SMTP
   D. BGP

182. Carol is designing a wireless network for use in a coffee shop. Her primary concern is ensuring that users have easy access to the network. Which one of the following wireless network types is most appropriate for her needs?

   A. WPA-PSK
   B. Open
   C. WPA-Enterprise
   D. WPA2-Enterprise

183. Darryl is concerned about the level of security provided by the encryption of Microsoft Office documents. What component of Windows can he upgrade to allow the use of stronger encryption with these documents?

   A. CRL
   B. CSP
   C. PKI
   D. SP

184. When creating a digital certificate, what key does the certificate authority use to prevent public disclosure of the certificate's public key?

   A. Certificate owner's private key
   B. CA's private key
   C. CA's public key
   D. No key

185. Will is creating a digital certificate for his web server. He will request the certificate from his internal corporate CA, which is an intermediate CA validated by the Geotrust root CA. Who would create the CSR in this case?

   A. Geotrust creates the CSR after receiving a request from Will
   B. Will creates the CSR on the Geotrust website
   C. Will creates the CSR on the web server
   D. The internal CA creates the CSR after receiving a request from Will.

186. Which one of the following approaches to cryptography is least useful for data in transit over a network?

   A. FDE
   B. File encryption
   C. TLS
   D. AES

187. Kaitlyn is selecting a wireless encryption algorithm for use in her organization. If she is able to choose from the following options, which would be the best choice?

A. WPA
B. WPA2
C. WEP
D. WPS

188. Ron is troubleshooting an application that is having trouble communicating with a RADIUS authentication server to validate user credentials. He believes that the issue may be a firewall problem. What port should he verify is accessible through the firewall from the application to the RADIUS server?

A. 1812
B. 1521
C. 1433
D. 3389

189. Paul is sending a message to Kathy using asymmetric cryptography. In the final stage of the process, he uses Kathy's public key to encrypt the message. What goal(s) of cryptography are met by this encryption?

A. Confidentiality, integrity, and nonrepudiation
B. Confidentiality only
C. Nonrepudiation only
D. Confidentiality and integrity only

190. Harold is connecting to a wireless network that uses the 802.1x protocol. What term best describes the operating system component on his computer that interacts with the 802.1x service?

A. Authentication server
B. Client
C. Supplicant
D. Access server

191. What encryption protocol does the WPA2 algorithm use to provide confidentiality for wireless communications?

A. 3DES
B. TKIP
C. DES
D. CCMP

192. What is the most commonly used secure message digest length with the RIPEMD algorithm?

A. 128 bits
B. 160 bits
C. 256 bits
D. 320 bits

193. What protocol was designed as an efficient and secure replacement for the use of CRLs to determine whether a digital certificate has been revoked by the certificate authority?

A. CSR
B. OCSP
C. CSP
D. TACACS

194. Carl connects to a wireless network that is using strong encryption and encounters the message shown here. Which type of network might be be connecting to?

A. WPA2-PSK
B. WPA-Enterprise
C. WEP2-PSK
D. WEP-Enterprise

195. Zack is purchasing a digital certificate for his organization's web server from a trusted certificate authority. He would like to choose the certificate that provides the highest degree of trust to site visitors. Which certificate type should he choose?

A. EV
B. OV
C. DV
D. NV

196. Which one of the following is not a disadvantage of using a CRL to revoke digital certificates?

A. Fails open if the client can't retrieve the CRL
B. Slow updating
C. Does not work for EV certificates
D. Requires that the client search the CRL

197. Which one of the following risks would be addressed by applying full disk encryption to a computer?

    A. Malware infection on the device
    B. Theft of the device
    C. Eavesdropping on the network segment used by the device
    D. Insider attack

198. Sam is designing a new certificate authority (CA). He creates an initial CA and uses that CA to authorize several subordinate CAs that issue certificates to end users. He then disconnects the initial CA from the network to protect it against attack. Which one of the following terms best describes the initial CA?

    A. Online CA
    B. Intermediate CA
    C. Offline CA
    D. Unauthorized CA

199. Brianne is accessing a website over a TLS connection. When her browser retrieves the digital certificate from the website, what key should she use to verify that the certificate may be trusted?

    A. CA's public key
    B. CA's private key
    C. Website's public key
    D. Website's private key

200. Carla is examining her wireless access point and notices that it bears the logo shown here. What technology does this access point support?

    A. WPS
    B. WPA2
    C. WPA
    D. WEP

201. What does the PGP algorithm use to facilitate the trusted exchange of public keys between users?

    A. Certificate authorities
    B. Web of trust
    C. Central key management server
    D. Bittorrent

202. What standard is used to define the format of a digital certificate?

    A. X.509
    B. 802.1x
    C. RFC 1918
    D. RFC 793

203. What mathematical principle does the RSA algorithm rely upon for security?

    A. Cosine law
    B. Prime factorization
    C. Elliptic curve
    D. Ohm's law

204. Barry is configuring 802.1x authentication for his wireless network. In a typical wireless authentication scenario, what device would act as the 802.1x client?

    A. Back-end authentication server
    B. Mobile devices connecting to the network
    C. Router
    D. Wireless access point

205. Frank accesses a website over HTTPS using a standard web browser. After his browser retrieves the site's digital certificate and validates the signature, what piece of critical information does it extract from the certificate to continue the communications session?

    A. Web server's private key
    B. Web server's public key
    C. CA's public key
    D. CA's private key

206. What technology does the PEAP protocol combine with EAP to provide secure communication of authentication credentials?

    A. IDEA
    B. SSL
    C. LEAP
    D. TLS

207. Shannon is assisting a business unit with the implementation of an approach that may be used to verify the integrity and authenticity of a message. Which one of the following algorithms would best meet this need?

    A. SHA-3
    B. AES
    C. SHA-2
    D. HMAC

208. Jerry is examining the cipher suites available for use on his organization's web server and finds the following supported options. Which one of these is it most important for him to remove?

    A. TLS_DHE_RSA_WITH_AES_128_GCM-SHA256
    B. TLS_RSA_WITH_RC4_128_SHA
    C. TLS_ECDHE_ECDSA_WITH_AES_128_CBC_SHA
    D. TLS_RSA_WITH_3DES_EDE_CBC_SHA

209. Riley would like to perform port-based authentication on her network and is seeking an authentication protocol specifically designed for this purpose. Which protocol would best meet her needs?

    A. RADIUS
    B. 802.1x
    C. Kerberos
    D. TACACS

210. Mike accesses the wireless network in a local coffee shop and sees the login screen shown here. What type of authentication is in use on this network?

    A. WPA-PSK
    B. WPA-Enterprise
    C. Captive portal
    D. WPA2-Enterprise

211. Examine the digital certificate shown here. What organization is asserting that the public key presented in this certificate actually belongs to Bank of America?

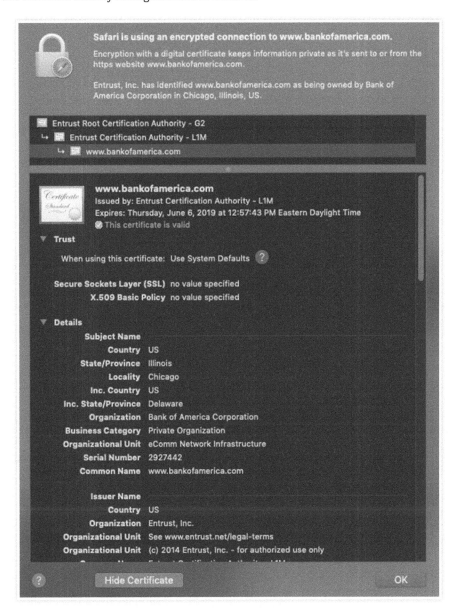

A. No such assertion is being made
B. Bank of America Corporation
C. eComm Network Infrastructure
D. Entrust Certification Authority

212. What cipher does EAP use to protect the confidentiality of authentication credentials passed using the protocol?

  A. 3DES
  B. AES
  C. No cipher
  D. RC4

213. Which one of the following digital certificate types offers the lowest degree of assurance?

  A. EV
  B. OV
  C. DV
  D. XV

214. Examine the digital certificate shown here. Which one of the following URLs would not be covered by this certificate?

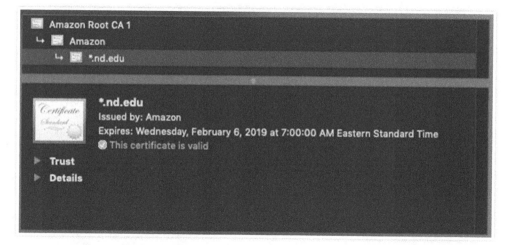

  A. https://www.mike.nd.edu/
  B. https://www.nd.edu/
  C. https://www.nd.edu/mike
  D. https://mike.nd.edu/

215. Ray is configuring a highly secure web application that is being used by a limited number of users. He would like to apply a client-side control that informs the client browser exactly what certificate to expect from the server. Which one of the following controls meets his requirement?

  A. Certificate stapling
  B. Certificate pinning
  C. Certificate folding
  D. Certificate chaining

216. Consider the digital certificate shown here. What format is the file used for this digital certificate?

```
-----BEGIN RSA PRIVATE KEY-----
MIIEowIBAAKCAQEAmxYcf8/qYv9kvXKatOpanz+f/Bq6yZbfCdAz+XnlA7iokSb8ZmZ/N7/pBmYo
HIkrPTnUpAKuHllyiiot4GpkLttQNRrND8gYQOmn1MHZJIvr52DLuBUjzbFu1+rKQLUmyVt9oHOp
3aBdpWcz3d4MjgmzQPgJAC0tSD0LKMzP3JbHkoK70gEqc4cBEfCL4MlZsAYkqhWnQ/QgYnrII278
l7CanwFFlinFNp0EPeN3uvoslM1W81k7ie1/T2VLVLlFtB1PZY+df5o7vLweF4fFfbaUilvBLCSn
xHk/FSiWF3d9XQePUhjInKbG9UeJZCczSbWXH9cV2dAgPqo7VIWpZwIDAQABAoIBACicFKBfSEfe
CnoVLW+cQlia54CzWx/4crT2IPX9tjtqOguwAr2przxg81rqmyxFut3Qa976mK93aqdlPhgao9sl
MI6HUxUD214AESOEEyEfxokS7qVoW7S79oNxhr6E8QAfBfli8CMJn9jr+kXRXEZBQgAMMwcpzUay
PV7UqsVfCb+Xy3i2y//YXZkYbOWLAFjuLh28nXvx/NcGTJ2SmIU3Cj3suqIQ0L4u7OX784Cw9p3x
BEa4FFB84aWbImrFciRmoGOFU7nvrYTgDbTxAR6HqQkD1NIZZPhia3D7XEvqzbL9lXzLaXLVXPuW
HoZMENAiDTWF5dUKz1EpAPlGMtkCgYEAzjP5yrnXJjaDgR7zJGMrRWZAWllReRW+DXkIZaHVHZch
LTcWf6qEKPbHmW8ayD8xzSwQs38hg9ItqgrKiV5GgWmqflfPxR07Fckzm7dLsmn0iTFlsKTJhT5W
ibvRp83AyuR5pw+KUWzef2rw4b1tfA569JZPS+pCW/VQ+4ZATI0CgaEAwIn3etXdakC81CqxDm7r
f4vdSORhI7cHJX+9L82taWUkEuqnppjCIrOCXrnTt5qgD5Y2BPGvDrkt0Li55c+bNXCcbL71jHNY
4EiRuPXogh+ELD7bg4d1C6xwIg/jdwDLkpC7P9r20I8jWpNvyhcRh6vX9xTQX05YXxnrxHLLQsMC
gYA/S5sQjI0rUK57MxnlgIIqD2IPmb01kuP81LssH0oAxERN0cwZMilRPbc1NPKepy9NUIpr3slV
4m1cLogxtHuNbWcFU04Wt4tMe61YzCHzSSzj9ALH/z1QprsAGmQrwaO7w/hHrLBzoByINjZswkzX
eMZrT7xVjDoaakAKhUI1fQKBgQCxTxzi0Qum4E1E0d/l283x0prBItg2LLpfFSjjWfTlh2fWJ9Sm
fiziCg/4LgdEIRhf4kPy/6Ln2y7O9R70/OABMahMGPtGEX96ZDoWbBcLjpiIqoY6tUbbrjxBkgI2
uDvAyJo3mTlA0r6LDhW3tNDG8UDcYIWYDy0gv104t0JqQwKBgHXfmoLKG8iGCjn8AB6KryK7BTiK
ULHuklkIcHHFh8mdQJd9VzoAlilqvny7b9aTwq0RB9c8PvBAbexD6v5ti+0KiPCJfiZiNIS2K07q
9ICEyB2dPA1kYLKfAfRVr0P6oIKN1l7PMCY/6PykRc1/xVZ+klWecBR5CtRSfxsqMcv9
-----END RSA PRIVATE KEY-----
```

A. .DER
B. .PEM
C. .P12
D. .PFX

Domain 3 Answers and Explanations

1. **C.** The corporate-owned, personally enabled (COPE) model allows employees to make personal use of corporate-owned devices. While choose-your-own-device (CYOD) and corporate-owned models do not preclude personal use, they do not necessarily allow it. Bring-your-own-device (BYOD) models use personally-owned equipment, rather than corporate-owned equipment.

2. **A.** The use of different authentication requirements depending upon the circumstances of the user's request is known as context-based authentication. In this scenario, authentication requirements are changing based upon the user's IP address, making it an example of context-based authentication.

3. **A.** Any of these devices could conceivably be the culprit, but the most likely case is that a content filter is suddenly blocking sites that should be allowed. This often happens when the filter policy is incorrectly configured. A network firewall is less likely to block traffic based upon the identity of the website. An intrusion prevention system (IPS) may be conducting this type of filtering, but it is a less likely candidate than the content filter. A GPO could also be restricting access to websites but this is not likely to happen across different operating systems, as GPOs are a Windows technology.

4. **C.** Mobile device management (MDM) solutions allow administrators to set policies that manage the configuration of mobile devices as well as control the apps installed on those devices.

5. **C.** Katie can achieve this goal by listing the alternate domains on the certificate using the Subject Alternate Name (SAN) attribute. A wildcard certificate would not work in this case because the websites use two different domains (mywebsite.com and myotherwebsite.com). She could use a wildcard certificate if all sites had the same domain name (e.g. *.mywebsite.com).

6. **D.** All of these tools may be useful in detecting missing patches. However, the most useful tool is a configuration management system. These tools have the ability to directly query the operating system to obtain real-time information on their patch level.

7. **A.** Dissolvable NAC uses a temporary agent that is removed immediately after the health check completes. This would be the best solution for Tina to deploy. A captive portal solution does not necessarily have the ability to perform health checking unless it is combined with a dissolvable agent. Permanent NAC would install software that remains on the student computers. Active Directory NAC would not be appropriate because the systems are unmanaged and, therefore, not accessible through AD.

8. **C.** The domain component (DC) of an LDAP entry contains portions of the domain name of a system. The OU component contains information about the organizational unit while the CN component contains the common name. The ST component contains information about the state or territory.

9. **B.** Operating system updates and application updates frequently trigger file integrity alerts, as do system compromises. A CPU failure would result in a system crash, rather than a file integrity alert.

10. **B.** Mobile device management products do typically support remote wiping, application management, and configuration management, among other features. They do not provide carrier unlocking functionality, as this may only be performed by the wireless carrier that activated the device.

11. **C.** The illustration shows a VPN that connects multiple branches of the organization to a central office. This is a site-to-site VPN. Remote access VPNs are used to connect individual devices. It is not possible to tell from the diagram whether the VPN is using TLS or IPsec transport.

12. **D.** Banner grabbing queries a service for header information provided to clients. This information often includes the specific service running on a port as well as version information. Port scanning will reveal the existence of a service on a port but port scanning alone cannot identify version information unless it is supplemented with banner grabbing information. Steganography is a technique for hiding data within images or other binary files. Traceroute is a command used to find the path between two systems on a network.

13. **B.** Port security restricts the number of unique MAC addresses that may originate from a single switch port. It is commonly used to prevent someone from unplugging an authorized device from the network and connecting an unauthorized device but may also be used to prevent existing devices from spoofing MAC addresses of other devices.

14. **D.** This is a forward proxy because the proxy server is located on the same network as the user. It connects to remote web servers on behalf of the end user. It is not possible to determine whether this proxy server is performing caching and/or content filtering based upon this illustration.

15. **C.** Carla should check boxes 2, 3, and 4 to block all public access to objects stored in this bucket. Checking box 5 would disable the existing cross-account access that she wishes to preserve, as would checking box 1. Checking only boxes 2 and 3 would allow new public access to be granted through a bucket or access point policy.

16. **D.** While all of the attributes listed in the scenario may be true of the device, the USB on-the-go logo indicates that the device supports the USB OTG standard for acting as a host server for other devices, such as cameras, flash drives, or peripherals.

17. **B.** One of the functions provided by email gateways is the interception of sensitive messages destined for external locations. The gateway then informs the recipient that they have a secure message and the recipient logs into a website to receive the message over an HTTPS protected connection. Firewalls and intrusion prevention systems do not provide this technology. While TLS is used in this solution, TLS alone is not capable of intercepting messages.

18. **B.** VPN connections established in transport mode encrypt the payload of data packets, but do not provide encryption for packet headers. Transport mode connections do not support NAT traversal.

19. **B.** The antenna shown is an example of a parabolic antenna.

20. **D.** Android applications must be in Android Application Package (APK) format to sideload onto a device. IPA files are used for iOS applications, not Android applications. EXE files are applications designed for use on Windows systems. The ZIP format is a generic file compression format that is used in APK files, but Android applications are not stored in pure ZIP format.

21. **C.** The most likely problem is that the RADIUS server is not properly authenticating accounts. It is not likely a VPN server problem because users are able to contact the server but are failing at the authentication step. It is unlikely that users are entering their passwords incorrectly or using expired passwords because the issue is occurring for all users.

22. **A.** The primary risk that Carla must avoid is that the user may have access to systems after being terminated. In addition, Carla should avoid tipping off the user to the pending termination. Therefore, she should wait until she can verify that the termination meeting has started and then cut off the user's access during the meeting.

23. **C.** Encrypted LDAPS sessions use TCP port 636. Unencrypted LDAP sessions use TCP port 389. Port 3389 is used for GUI connections to devices using the Remote Desktop Protocol (RDP). Port 443 is used for encrypted web connections using HTTPS.

24. **D.** Application whitelisting prevents the installation of any software that is not on a list of preapproved applications and would prevent users from installing software that is not on the authorized list. Blacklisting takes the opposite approach, where administrators list the software that may not be installed. Host firewalls and content filters do not generally block the installation of software.

25. **A.** Cloud access security brokers (CASB) are designed to enforce security policies across cloud services. Security information and event management (SIEM) and security orchestration, automation, and response (SOAR) platforms are designed to aggregate, analyze, and react to security events. Virtual desktop infrastructure (VDI) offers desktop computing to end users in a virtualized manner.

26. **A.** The Secure Sockets Layer (SSL) is now considered an insecure protocol and should no longer be used. The secure replacement for SSL is Transport Layer Security (TLS). The Secure Shell (SSH) protocol is a secure means for establishing connections between two systems, but it does not provide the same transport-layer functionality as SSL and TLS.

27. **C.** Moving the access point or the client may resolve the interference, as might changing the wireless channel/band in use. Increasing bandwidth will only provide more capacity. Additional capacity will not resolve interference.

28. **B.** While all of these techniques may be used to assign user permissions, the best way to achieve this goal is to use group policy to assign permissions to role-based groups and then add users to the appropriate group(s) for their role.

29. **C.** Mobile device management (MDM) technology allows administrators to control the configuration of mobile devices, such as disabling device cameras. Data loss prevention (DLP) systems may be useful in preventing the theft of confidential information but cannot disable device cameras. Intrusion prevention systems (IPS) and web application firewalls (WAF) are also good security controls but do not manage mobile device configurations.

30. **A.** The most common false positive report for application whitelisting results from an unexpected update from the software vendor that changes the signature of the application. A user downloading software from the web should generate an alert, so this would not be a false positive. The same thing is true for malicious activity, such as the execution of malware or the installation of a rootkit.

31. **C.** The Authentication Headers (AH) protocol supports only authentication and integrity for IPsec connections. The Encapsulating Security Payload (ESP) protocol supports confidentiality, integrity, and authentication.

32. **C.** Storage segmentation provides separate storage areas on the mobile device for personal and corporate information, preventing the two from becoming intermingled. Application control would limit the applications that users may install on devices but would not control where those applications

store data. Full device encryption would add security to all data stored on the device but would not differentiate between personal and corporate data. Multifactor authentication does add a layer of security to the device but does not distinguish between categories of information.

33. **D.** When measuring RSSI, the network with the strongest signal is the one with the highest value. Since RSSI is measured in negative numbers, this will be the number closest to zero which, in this case, is -67, corresponding to the CAFwifi network.

34. **B.** All of the protocols listed have the capability of supporting secure videoconferencing. Of the options, HTTPS is the most likely to be fully supported by customer firewalls because it is the same port used for secure web connections. Therefore, this would be the best option for Dylan to choose.

35. **C.** This message indicates that the code lacks a trusted digital signature. The Mac is configured to only allow software downloaded from the App Store or authorized developers. If the developer registers a certificate with Apple and signs the code, this message will go away.

36. **B.** All of the capabilities listed here are features of advanced malware prevention systems. However, only threat intelligence directly leverages information obtained from systems deployed at other customer sites.

37. **C.** This error message indicates that the website is using a certificate from an untrusted certificate authority. Patricia should replace the certificate with one from a trusted CA.

38. **D.** Tom should deploy an agent-based NAC solution or, more specifically, a permanent agent. This technology leaves software running on the endpoint that may remain in constant contact with the NAC solution. Agentless NAC, captive portal solutions, and dissolvable agents do not maintain a constant presence on the system and would not meet Tom's requirements.

39. **C.** In a true positive report, the system reports an attack when an attack actually exists. A false positive report occurs when the system reports an attack that did not take place. A true negative report occurs when the system reports no attack and no attack took place. A false negative report occurs when the system does not report an attack that did take place.

40. **A.** The IP address 192.168.10.6 falls within the private IP address range of 192.168.0.0/16. This address range is only for use on a local area network and should never be seen on a public network, such as the Internet. The other addresses provided in this question are all valid public IP addresses.

41. **A.** WiFi Protected Access version 2 (WPA2) uses the AES encryption standard and provides the highest level of security for a WiFi network. WPA version 1 uses the Temporal Key Integrity Protocol (TKIP), which is secure but not as strong as WPA2. Wired Equivalent Privacy (WEP) is an insecure encryption technique.

42. **B.** Satellite communications (SATCOM) have the widest availability, as they may be used from any region of the world with satellite coverage. For large satellite networks, this covers the entire planet. Cellular signals do travel long distances but may not have constant availability in rural areas. WiFi and Bluetooth are only useful over short distances and would not be appropriate for this scenario.

43. **D.** Write once, read many (WORM) storage devices allow the writing of data in a permanent fashion where modification is impossible. Cryptographic hashing and file integrity monitoring solutions may

detect unauthorized changes but they are unable to prevent unauthorized changes. Transport layer security (TLS) is an encryption protocol that would not prevent changes to stored data.

44. **A.** Brian can use a preshared key (PSK) known only by him to restrict network access. Kerberos or NAC authentication would require configuration and costly infrastructure. MAC address filtering is easily defeated and should not be relied upon for secure network access controls.

45. **B.** The second rule allows SSH access from anywhere in the world. This rule should be tightened to restrict access to specific networks, as the RDP rule is configured. The HTTP and HTTPS rules allow public access to the web server, which is a typical configuration.

46. **A.** IPsec has two modes of operation: tunnel mode and transport mode. Tunnel mode is primarily used for site-to-site connections, such as the one that Carrie is establishing here. Transport mode is normally used for connections involving endpoint devices.

47. **C.** Port 1433 is commonly associated with Microsoft SQL Server databases, while port 1521 is used by Oracle databases. Port 3306 is the default port for MySQL databases. Port 1701 is used by the L2TP protocol, which is associated with VPN access, not databases.

48. **D.** In this case, the explicit permission granted to the user to write the file overrides the deny permission which is inherited (denoted by the grey shading). Therefore, the user can both read and write the file.

49. **A.** The S/MIME secure email standard allows organizations to achieve confidentiality, integrity, and non-repudiation for email communications.

50. **D.** SNMPv3 is the current standard for network management and is a secure protocol. Older versions of SNMP did not provide secure authentication due to their use of plaintext community strings.

51. **A.** Users may bypass the manufacturer's installed operating system by installing their own custom firmware on the device. This may remove any MDM configuration that Dave places on the device before providing it to the user. Application sideloading can install illicit applications on a device but does not replace the operating system. Bluejacking and Bluesnarfing are attacks against Bluetooth connections but do not alter the operating system on a device.

52. **D.** In this scenario, Scott would like to choose a technology that automatically triggers VPN connections based upon security policies. Microsoft Always On VPN technology provides this feature. TLS and IPsec VPNs are different VPN protocols but they do not inherently have the ability to trigger a VPN connection. Split tunneling policies control what information is routed through the VPN connection but they do not have the ability to require or initiate a VPN connection.

53. **C.** Mobile device management products do support all four of these features. Containerization may be used to isolate corporate content from personal content. Remote wiping may be used to remove data from a lost or stolen device. Encryption may be used to protect data from theft. Geofencing does not prevent the theft of data.

54. **C.** Data execution prevention (DEP) requires the explicit marking of memory regions as executable, preventing malicious attacks that seek to execute code out of other regions of memory.

55. **C.** Resource policies are cloud-native controls designed to restrict the use of IaaS services by particular users. That would be the best way for Gina to achieve her goal. It might be possible to achieve this goal using a CASB, but that would add an unnecessary layer of complexity. Security groups and ACLs are used to restrict network access, not resource use.

56. **D.** This is an example of an access control list from a router. Of the devices listed, only routers and firewalls perform network filtering of the type that would be defined by these types of rules. However, if these rules had come from a firewall, they would contain more detail, including source and destination ports.

57. **D.** WiFi networks use the service set identifier (SSID) to broadcast a network name to all devices in the area. SSID broadcasting advertises the presence of the WiFi network.

58. **A.** EXIF metadata includes a wide variety of technical and environmental information about photos shot with digital cameras and smartphones. This information does commonly include geolocation information obtained from the device's GPS as well as the camera make and model, shutter speed, and other technical characteristics. It does not normally include temperature information, as these devices typically do not include thermometers that measure ambient temperature.

59. **C.** Stateful inspection firewalls monitor connection status by tracking the TCP handshake. They maintain a table of active connections and automatically allow traffic that is part of an established connection without requiring the reevaluation of the ruleset for each packet. The other firewall types listed are more primitive and do not track connection status. They simply reevaluate every packet that they receive.

60. **A.** Apple Pay, Google Wallet and similar contactless payment technologies rely upon near field communication (NFC) to facilitate communications between a user's smartphone and the payment terminal.

61. **B.** The primary issue with FTP is that it does not support the use of encryption. Credentials and other information sent via FTP are transmitted in cleartext and are open to eavesdropping attacks.

62. **B.** Next generation firewalls (NGFW) are traditional firewalls with advanced capabilities, including defense against application-layer attacks, such as SQL injection. Of the choices listed, a NGFW is the best solution to meet all of these requirements. Packet filters and router ACLs would not be effective against all of the attacks listed. A web application firewall does not normally contain the routing technology necessary to be the organization's main connection to the Internet.

63. **A.** UTM solutions typically perform a wide variety of security functions, including content filtering, intrusion prevention, and firewalling. They do not typically perform sandboxing, as this is typically a capability of more advanced malware prevention systems.

64. **A.** Web servers use port 80 for unencrypted communications using the HTTP protocol and port 443 for encrypted communications using the HTTPS protocol. Those are the two ports that Jaime should allow through the firewall. Port 53 is used for DNS, while port 8080 is a nonstandard port sometimes used for proxies or as an alternate location for web services. Neither of those situations is mentioned in the scenario.

65. **D.** Using a cloud-based hardware security module (HSM) provides the key management that Yolanda desires, protecting keys from viewing by anyone. The other approaches all expose keys to vendor staff

and/or Yolanda's own team and would not provide the same high level of secrets management as an HSM.

66. **B.** Mobile devices purchased under contract are locked by the carrier to prevent transfers to other carriers while the contract is in place. After the expiration of the contract, the original carrier must unlock the device before the user may transfer it to another carrier.

67. **B.** Ad hoc and direct WiFi networks allow the establishment of WiFi connectivity between devices without the use of enterprise infrastructure. Therefore, these WiFi operating modes do not support the use of enterprise authentication. WiFi networks using preshared keys (PSK) use these preshared keys in lieu of enterprise authentication. WPA and WPA2 both support the use of enterprise authentication in place of a preshared key.

68. **C.** Flood guard technology is used to block denial of service attacks on a network. Loop prevention, hold-down timers, and split horizon are all used to prevent and correct routing loops.

69. **A.** Email security gateways commonly perform spam filtering, malware filtering, data loss prevention and encryption. They do not typically serve as a network firewall.

70. **D.** The implicit deny rule is the last rule found in a firewall rulebase and is part of the firewall's default configuration. It specifies that any traffic that was not explicitly allowed by an earlier rule should be blocked.

71. **A.** Any of the solutions presented may resolve the issue that Ralph is experiencing, but deploying a WiFi controller is the most efficient approach. Wireless controllers allow the automated modification of access point settings to adapt to the changing radio frequency environment.

72. **D.** Virutal Desktop Infrastructure (VDI) environments allow employees to access a remote desktop computing environment and work within that environment without transferring data to the device used to access the VDI desktop. The choose-your-own-device (CYOD) and corporate-owned, personally enabled (COPE) models do not involve employee-owned devices. The bring-your-own-device (BYOD) model does allow the use of personal devices but does not necessarily prevent the transfer of corporate information to the device.

73. **B.** The use of a network password indicates that this network is using a preshared key (PSK) rather than user authentication. Therefore, the most likely issue is that the user is entering the PSK incorrectly.

74. **B.** This attack is taking place between two systems located on the same LAN, so it is unlikely that a network-based IDS (NIDS) would detect the traffic. A host-based IDS (HIDS) would be much more likely to do so. Signature-based systems are not capable of detecting zero-day attacks, so a heuristic system would be the most likely to detect the attack.

75. **D.** In certificate stapling, the subject of a digital certificate includes a copy of a current OCSP response with the certificate when providing that certificate to a user, allowing the user to complete verification without issuing its own OCSP request. This process speeds the validation of digital certificates.

76. **A.** TLS VPNs typically use port 443, the same port used for HTTPS web traffic. This port is commonly allowed full outbound access through firewalls. IPsec VPNs use UDP port 500 as well as IP protocols 50 and 51. It is much more likely that this traffic will be blocked at a firewall. It is irrelevant whether

Greg uses a split tunnel or full tunnel policy in this case, as the policy will not help establish the connection through the firewall, it will only control what traffic is routed through the VPN connection once it is established.

77. **A.** There is no indication in the scenario that Mark discovered log entries indicating any type of software failure. The failure most likely resulted from the use of malware for which the scanner did not have current signatures. This could be because the scanner had not been updated or it may be because the attacker used a zero-day/APT attack.

78. **C.** Self-encrypting drives (SEDs) contain encryption technology built into the drive and, therefore, provide a high degree of security. Enclosed full disk encryption (FDE) technology uses a standard drive that is bundled with an encryption module. Chipset and bridge FDE place a bridge that performs encryption between the computer and the drive.

79. **A.** Betty must obtain a new certificate from a certificate authority (CA). While this may be called "renewing" the certificate, it requires obtaining a new certificate that replaces the expiring certificate. She should not place the certificate on the certificate revocation list (CRL) unless it has been compromised.

80. **A.** An application server designed only for use by internal users should be placed on the internal network. The DMZ is only appropriate for servers which require external access, while the external network zone is not an appropriate place to host any servers, as it is not protected by the firewall from external access.

81. **D.** The Real Time Protocol (RTP) is an application protocol used for videoconferencing and should not be found on a management plane. The Network Time Protocol (NTP), Secure Shell (SSH), and Remote Access Dial In User Service (RADIUS) are all administrative protocols that would be expected traffic on a management plane.

82. **C.** This network uses a private IP range (192.168.1.0/24) on the internal network and a public IP address (12.8.1.5) on the external network. The firewall must support Network Address Translation (NAT) to convert between public and private addresses or this network will not function properly. The firewall may also support Intrusion Prevention System (IPS) and Web Application Firewall (WAF) technology, but those are not required for proper network functioning. Network Admission Control (NAC) is normally performed by switches, rather than firewalls.

83. **D.** Any of the devices listed is capable of serving as an endpoint for a VPN connection. However, a VPN concentrator is specifically well-suited for this task because it contains dedicated hardware optimized for performing the cryptographic calculations required by a VPN. This would place an unnecessary burden on a firewall or router. A VPN server is also dedicated to this purpose, but does not contain the specialized, optimized hardware of a VPN concentrator.

84. **C.** Digital signatures are always verified using the public key of the individual or organization who created the signature. In this case, Gina should use the supplier's public key to verify the signature.

85. **C.** Any one of these solutions is capable of providing IPS service for Tom's environment. However, many of them fail to meet other goals. Building an open-source IPS or using an on-premises solution would not meet his goal of outsourcing the IPS. Using the IaaS vendor's IPS capability would not meet his goal of vendor diversity. Therefore, the best solution for Tom is a third-party cloud IPS solution.

86. **A.** In almost all cases, users should be placed into network zones based upon their role in the organization. However, this scenario presents the exception to that rule. Because employees are connecting to an unsecured wireless network, they should be placed into a guest zone where they will not have access to sensitive information. If employees need to access sensitive information, they should either connect to a secured wireless network or use a VPN to make an external connection to the secured network.

87. **D.** Input validation should always be performed on the web server. If it is placed on the endpoint or within Javascript code, the attacker may modify or remove the input validation code. Input validation cannot be performed on the database server because the database server will not be able to tell the difference between SQL code provided by the web server and code provided by the user as part of the attack.

88. **A.** Elaine should use a network terminal access point (TAP) to create a monitor port that allows the intrusion detection system to see all network traffic. Port mirroring (also known as SPAN) would allow the IDS to see network traffic but it runs the risk of dropped packets. Inline installation would not have this disadvantage but does pose a higher risk of network interruption if the IDS fails to pass traffic properly.

89. **C.** Tripwire is a file integrity monitoring solution that is also able to perform system configuration monitoring. It is the most appropriate tool for this task. Snort is an intrusion detection and prevention system. Wireshark is a network packet sniffing tool. QRadar is a security information and event management (SIEM) system.

90. **B.** The password shown here is a BIOS password presented through the UEFI interface. This is not an especially secure way of securing access to a system, as there are many techniques to bypass BIOS passwords.

91. **C.** The hardware root of trust is a core building block of the security of a system and must be designed securely so that system components that build upon it (operating at higher levels of abstraction) may trust it. The root of trust should be implemented in hardware and it should be as small as possible. The root of trust should not be large and, therefore, should not contain the operating system.

92. **C.** SSL acceleration uses hardware to reduce the computational burden on web servers and other devices using Transport Layer Security (TLS). Note that this technology is still called SSL acceleration even through SSL has been replaced by TLS. Load balancing strategies would not be effective in this case because all of the servers are experiencing the problem equally. There is no indication in the scenario that a web application firewall (WAF) would reduce the load.

93. **C.** Placing the sensor on the DMZ allows it to see traffic before it reaches the web server but minimizes the amount of traffic that it sees because the sensor will not observe traffic that is blocked first by the network firewall. Placing the sensor on the external network would still allow it to see external attacks but would expose it to traffic destined to be blocked by the firewall. Placing it on the internal network would not allow it to see external traffic headed to the web server.

94. **D.** Firewalls, proxy servers, and intrusion prevention systems all offer content filtering functionality. Routers generally do not perform content filtering, as they do not operate at the application layer.

95. **C.** The following address ranges are available for use on private networks and subnets: 10.0.0.0-10.255.255.255, 172.16.0.0-172.31.255.255, and 192.168.0.0-192.168.255.255. Three of the subnets presented in this question fall into these ranges while the fourth, 181.10.0.0/16 does not. That subnet is a public address range assigned to a particular user and should not be used on a private subnet.

96. **D.** Standard ACLs are able to filter traffic based only upon source address. They cannot filter based upon the destination address. Extended ACLs do not have this limitation. Both standard and extended ACLs may apply to either inbound or outbound traffic.

97. **A.** Organizations deploying IPsec for site-to-site VPNs typically use tunnel mode to connect two VPN concentrators to each other and then route traffic through that tunnel in a manner that is transparent to the communicating devices. Transport mode is more commonly used for remote access VPNs. Internet key exchange (IKE) and security associations (SAs) are not modes of IPSec VPN operation.

98. **A.** Internet service providers are best positioned to mitigate the effects of an attack against their customers by blocking the traffic before it reaches the customer network.

99. **B.** HP JetDirect printer traffic uses TCP port 9100 to transfer data from clients to printers.

100. **D.** The single quotation mark (') is commonly used to escape a SQL query and should be carefully handled during input validation. The greater-than and less-than (< >) characters should also be handled carefully, but they are used in cross-site scripting (XSS) rather than SQL injection attacks.

101. **C.** Servers that provide services to the general public should be placed in the DMZ. Intranet servers should have access restricted to internal users. Extranet servers may be accessed by vendors and other business partners. Guest networks are designed for visitors to a facility to gain Internet access.

102. **D.** When assigning users to network zones, the method of accessing the network (wired or wireless) should not be a primary concern. Rather, users should be placed into network zones based upon their role in the organization and security policies. These zone assignments should be consistent across wired and wireless networks.

103. **D.** In transparent operation mode, BitLocker uses the Trusted Platform Module (TPM) to decrypt the encryption key. Active Directory does not store disk encryption keys. User passwords are used to protect the key in user authentication mode, while USB keys are used in USB Key Mode.

104. **C.** Proxy servers do not perform route optimization, as this is the function of network routing devices. They do accept requests from users for websites, anonymize those requests, and pass them to the remote site. This allows the proxy server to perform anonymization to protect the identity of the end user and content filtering to block access to undesirable content.

105. **C.** The easiest and most secure way for Dylan to enable this access is through the use of a VPC endpoint that allows direct connections between the VPCs without leaving the cloud provider's secure network. The other solutions proposed here would allow the access but would require crossing public networks, reducing security and adding inefficiency.

106. **B.** Wanda can disable services using the Windows Programs and Features tool.

107. **A.** TLS VPNs are unique because they rely upon the same Transport Layer Security protocol used by HTTPS connections. Because of this, most customer networks will allow the access by default. Other VPN types would likely require configuration of customer firewalls to allow access.

108. **A.** String normalization processes input in different Unicode character sets and converts it to a standard format prior to performing input validation. Normalizing the string shown here results in the input <script>, which may be part of a cross-site scripting attack.

109. **C.** Digital signatures validate that the application came from the entity that signed the application. Security professionals should not draw any other conclusions from the fact that an application is digitally signed.

110. **A.** Development environments are designed for active use by developers who are creating new code. These environments are the only location where code should be modified. Once code is ready for testing, it is released from the development environment into a test environment for software testing. After the completion of user acceptance testing, the code is moved from the test environment into a staging environment where it is prepared for final deployment into the production environment. Developers should never have permission to move code themselves but should only be able to move code between environments through the use of a managed change control system.

111. **D.** In a virtual desktop infrastructure (VDI) approach, each user logs in to the system and has access to his or her own interactive desktop. This approach best meets Joe's requirements. The software being used is desktop software, so there is no reason to believe that a web-based client is available. Using a VPN-based approach would require installing the software on the devices connecting to the VPN, which is prohibited by the license agreement. Data loss prevention (DLP) systems are not relevant in this scenario.

112. **A.** A forward proxy approach can work with any type of cloud application and would best meet Joyce's requirements. Reverse proxies and API-based approaches work with a limited subset of applications. Firewall is not a CASB deployment model.

113. **A.** One of the basic server security principles is that each server should support only one primary function. Best practice dictates separating the web server (Apache) from the database server (MySQL). It is normal and standard for a web server to support both unencrypted access on port 80 and encrypted access on port 443. TLS 1.2 is a modern version of the protocol and is secure and acceptable for use.

114. **D.** Virtual LANs (VLANs) provide the segmentation Randy desires at the logical level, allowing them to appear anywhere in the building. Physical segmentation is likely too costly and inflexible for these requirements. Virtual private networks (VPNs) are unwieldy and unnecessary in a fixed office environment. Web application firewalls (WAFs) do not provide the required segmentation functionality.

115. **D.** It is possible that an intrusion prevention system (IPS) or next generation firewall (NGFW) could provide this functionality. However, a secure web gateway (SWG) is purpose-built for filtering user web traffic and, therefore, would be the best solution in this scenario. Cloud access security brokers (CASB) do not perform web content filtering.

116. **B.** Firewall rules are always processed in a top-down fashion, with the first rule matching the network traffic taking precedence. In this case, rule 1 does not apply because the request is for HTTPS traffic,

which takes place on port 443, while rule 1 is for port 80. Rule 2 does apply because the destination IP address and port match. Therefore the traffic is allowed. Rules 3 and 4 would also match this traffic, but they are not effective in this case because rule 2 supersedes them.

117. **D.** Taint analysis traces variables that may contain user input and ensures that they are sanitized before being used by a potentially vulnerable function. Lexical analysis converts source code into a tokenized form. Control flow analysis traces the execution path of code. Signature detection looks for known patterns of malicious activity.

118. **A.** Application blacklisting is used to block specific applications from devices. Sarah has a list of three specific applications she must block and blacklisting would be the least disruptive way to achieve her goal. Application whitelisting would block all applications not on an approved list and would likely cause unintended disruptions. Host firewalls and intrusion prevention systems generally do not block the installation and use of software.

119. **C.** When digitally signing code, the developer uses the private key belonging to the organization that is vouching for the code. In this case, Kevin should sign the code using the organization's private key.

120. **D.** Fuzz testing specifically evaluates the performance of applications in response to mutated input combinations. Penetration testing is a manual, not automated, process. Vulnerability scanning may be automated but does not necessarily include the use of mutated input. Decompilation attempts to reverse engineer code.

121. **D.** Windows System Center Configuration Manager allows administrators to easily determine the patch level of multiple systems. Windows Update is an updating mechanism for individual systems that does not provide automated monitoring. Yum and APT are package managers allowing updates for Linux systems.

122. **A.** Sandboxing isolates an application preventing it from accessing protected system resources. Mac OS X uses sandboxing for all applications installed through the App Store. TCP wrappers is a firewall technology. Virtualization is a general term used to refer to running multiple operating systems on a single hardware platform. Taint analysis is a technique used to trace user input through code execution.

123. **B.** OAuth is commonly used to provide API-based SSO for web applications. OpenID is used for consumer-grade SSO implementations, while SAML is used for enterprise-grade SSO implementations. IPSec is a network security protocol used for VPN connections, among other purposes, but is not associated with SSO implementations.

124. **D.** In a mandatory access control (MAC) model, the system determines access authorization based upon the security labels applied to objects.

125. **A.** The most fault-tolerant solution would involve multiple vendors, but Ryan specified that he wanted to work with a single vendor, so this is not an acceptable solution. Therefore, Ryan should strive for the solution that has the greatest geographic and logical redundancy within his vendor's environment. The best solution would be to use redundant servers in multiple regions. Availability zones are subsets of regions and provide less redundancy. Operating servers in the same availability zone would create multiple single points of failure.

126. **D.** All of the options presented here are good security practices and TJ should consider each of them. However, only location-based access control will help prevent TJ's organization from running afoul of the law restricting access to residents of a single state.

127. **C.** Service accounts are used to provide applications with access to resources necessary for the provision of their services. This example clearly calls for a service account. Guest accounts should never be used on a server barring extenuating circumstances. The web server service should not run with unrestricted root/administrator access.

128. **C.** The major issue with simple passwords is that they are far easier to break in a brute force attack than complex passwords that draw from multiple character classes. Complexity requirements do not affect the minimum length of a password or make passwords less susceptible to social engineering. Reverse hashing is not possible for any password, as secure hash functions are not reversible.

129. **D.** Lila should encrypt the Social Security Number field using an encryption key that is not known to the database administrators. Hashing is not a good solution because it would not be possible to reverse the hash and retrieve the SSN for tax reporting purposes. Database access controls would not be effective against a database administrator, who likely has the privileges necessary to bypass those controls. Database activity monitoring might detect unauthorized access but cannot prevent it.

130. **C.** Service accounts are an example of privileged accounts and should be subject to strict logging requirements. Activity from other account types may certainly be logged, but this is not as high a priority as it is for privileged accounts.

131. **A.** Colleen should implement an emergency access procedure to allow access to the passwords. A common way to do this is to require the concurrence of two authorized individuals to retrieve the password from the vault. Providing a manager with the passwords would defeat the design requirement of nobody having knowledge of the password. Multifactor authentication would still require knowledge of the password. Redundant passwords are not a security mechanism.

132. **B.** An account with a generic role-based name, such as cashier, is most likely shared among many users. There is no reason to believe that this is an privileged administrator or superuser account. There is also no reason to believe that non-employee guests have access to this account.

133. **B.** In NTFS permissions, explicit permissions always take precedence over inherited permissions and deny permissions take precedence over allow permissions. Therefore, in this case, the explicit deny from the manager's group blocks Tim from writing to the file, regardless of any other permissions. Then, the explicit permission assigned to Tim's account to read the file takes precedence over the inherited deny read permission on the accounting group.

134. **C.** Kerberos uses UDP port 88 for authentication-related communications. Port 636 is associated with the secure LDAP (LDAPS) protocol.

135. **D.** The offboarding process is the area of greatest risk to the organization because failure to execute deprovisioning activities in a prompt manner may mean that employees who have left the organization retain access to sensitive information or systems.

136. **D.** In this image, Nancy is setting logon hours restrictions for the ajones account. This is an example of a restriction based upon the time of day.

137. **C.** In the Challenge Handshake Authentication Protocol (CHAP), the client makes an authentication request and the server responds with a challenge message. The client must then combine its password with the challenge message and hash it, providing this hashed response to the server.

138. **C.** Geofencing places specific geographic constraints around access to a system or resource. This is, therefore, an example of a location-based access control.

139. **D.** If the password remains known only to authorized individuals, this does not violate the principles of confidentiality or integrity. There is no indication from the scenario that the account has excess privileges, so least privilege is not violated. However, the use of a shared account prevents security staff from determining which individual performed an action, violating the principle of accountability.

140. **C.** When a user presents a digital certificate for authentication purposes, the primary purpose of that certificate is to provide a signed copy of the user's public key.

141. **A.** In this scenario, the website would like to access information in Taylor's Google account. This makes Taylor, as the account owner, the resource owner. Google, the service that maintains the account, is the resource provider, and the third-party website is the application.

142. **B.** Smart cards contain an integrated circuit that interactively authenticates with the reader. They do not necessarily contain a magnetic stripe. There is no requirement that a smart card be combined with a PIN/passcode or biometric authentication, although this is often done to achieve multifactor authentication.

143. **D.** PIVs contain four digital certificates. The card authentication certificate is used to verify that the PIV credential was issued by an authorized entity, has not expired, and has not been revoked. The PIV authentication certificate is used to verify that the PIV credential was issued by an authorized entity, has not expired, has not been revoked, and holder of the credential (YOU) is the same individual it was issued to. The digital signature certificate allows the user to digitally sign a document or email, providing both integrity and non-repudiation. The encryption certificate allows the user to digitally encrypt documents or email.

144. **A.** RADIUS uses UDP port 1812 for authentication and UDP port 1813 for accounting services. TCP ports 1433 and 1521 are associated with Microsoft SQL Server and Oracle databases, respectively.

145. **A.** TACACS+ is a AAA protocol. Therefore, it supports authentication, authorization, and accounting services.

146. **B.** The passwords must meet complexity requirements setting establishes a policy that user passwords must contain characters from three different character classes and that the password may not contain the user's account name or display name. It does not enforce a minimum password length.

147. **B.** Recertification requires that a user's access be renewed periodically to ensure that a business need still exists. The best way that Carl can enforce this is to implement account expiration controls on the vendor accounts and require that the account sponsor recertify the need on a periodic basis to extend the expiration date. Accounts that are not recertified will then be automatically disabled.

148. **D.** Kerberos is a widely used authentication system that is considered secure by modern standards. The Password Authentication Protocol (PAP) is an insecure protocol that does not encrypt passwords as they are transmitted over the network. The Microsoft Challenge Handshake Authentication Protocol

(MS-CHAP) and MS-CHAP v2 both have known security vulnerabilities that make them unacceptable for standalone use today.

149. **D.** The use of a help desk password reset process is burdensome on staff and users but does provide security if users are asked to prove their identity with documentation. Users should never be asked to provide a current or expired password, as this promotes poor password security practices.

150. **B.** It is a standard practice for administrative users to have both privileged and non-privileged accounts. They may then use the non-privileged account for routine activities and only use the privileged access when necessary. There is no reason that privileged accounts should not be protected by passwords. They should not be shared by multiple users or exempted from password management policies.

151. **D.** The best source for guidance on passwords and other authentication techniques is NIST Special Publication 800-63B: Digital Identity Guidelines. In the most recent revision of this document, NIST states that users should not be subjected to a maximum password length requirement and should be allowed to choose passwords as lengthy as they would like.

152. **A.** Most modern file systems, including the Windows NTFS, Mac OS X, and cloud services such as Google Drive, allow the owner of objects to set the access permissions for those objects. These are examples of discretionary access control (DAC). Security-enhanced Linux (SELinux) allows the system owner to set authorization based upon security labels. This is an example of mandatory access control.

153. **A.** The most effective way to implement access controls in this situation is to use group-based access control. This way, every new user is simply added to the appropriate group and then receives the necessary permissions. Permissive access control would violate the security principle of least privilege. Mandatory and personalized access control approaches would increase the burden on staff, rather than reduce it.

154. **B.** The RADIUS Access-Request message is sent by a client to the server requesting RADIUS authentication. The server then normally responds with an Access-Accept or Access-Reject message, depending upon whether the authentication was successful or unsuccessful. When a system is using two-factor authentication, the RADIUS server may respond to the client's request with an Access-Challenge message asking for additional authentication.

155. **B.** In a discretionary access control (DAC) system, the owners of individual objects are delegated the authority to grant other users access to those objects. This is the primary means of managing authorization on most modern systems.

156. **B.** Rule-based access control uses a standard set of rules to determine what access is authorized. This is the access control mechanism enforced by a firewall, which consults a rule base each time a network connection request is received.

157. **C.** The only factor that changed is the user's location, making a location-based restriction the most likely culprit. This type of restriction can apply even when a user connects to a VPN. We know that it is not a content-based restriction or role-based restriction because the user was able to access the same system when in the office. We also can surmise that it is not likely a time-based restriction because Brenda is able to access the system at the same time.

158. **B.** When making attribute-based authorization decisions, the ABAC system may analyze user attributes (such as job position or group membership), system attributes (such as the sensitivity level of information processed), and environmental attributes (such as the date or time).

159. **B.** The implicit deny principle is the cornerstone of firewall access control. This principle states that any activity that is not explicitly authorized should be blocked. Explicit allow does describe the way that access is granted, but this is only effective if the firewall uses the implicit deny principle as its foundation.

160. **C.** When a Kerberos client requests a session key, the client creates an authenticator consisting of the client's ID and a timestamp. The client then encrypts this authenticator with the TGS session key, which the client obtained earlier from the authentication server.

161. **B.** In 802.1x authentication, the end user's system contains a component called the supplicant that initiates the authentication process. The supplicant connects to the authenticator, normally a network switch or wireless access point, that then reaches out to an authentication server to confirm the user's identity. The communication between the authenticator and authentication server normally takes place using the RADIUS and EAP protocols.

162. **D.** The TACACS+ protocol is an authentication protocol developed by Cisco for use with network devices. It replaced the older TACACS and XTACACS protocols, which should no longer be used. STACACS is not a protocol.

163. **D.** In SAML authentication the user requesting authentication (Ryan) is the principal. The organization providing the request service (AcmeSocial) is the service provider and the organization providing the login account (HMail) is the identity provider.

164. **C.** In 802.1x authentication, the end user's system contains a component called the supplicant that initiates the authentication process. The supplicant connects to the authenticator, normally a network switch or wireless access point, that then reaches out to an authentication server to confirm the user's identity. The communication between the authenticator and authentication server normally takes place using the RADIUS and EAP protocols.

165. **C.** In a mandatory access control (MAC) system, such as the one that Thomas is implementing, the system itself sets authorizations based upon object labels. In a discretionary access control (DAC) system, file owners set authorizations for other users. In an attribute-based access control (ABAC) system, authorization is set based upon user attributes. In a role-based access control system (RBAC), authorization is based upon the role of a user in the organization.

166. **B.** Best practices in authentication security dictate that user accounts should be subject to an exponentially increasing login delay after failed login attempts. This greatly reduces the effectiveness of brute force password guessing attacks. Locking out or disabling user accounts after a small number of incorrect logins is likely to cause false positive alerts when users accidentally lock themselves out. That approach also facilitates denial of service attacks where an attacker can easily trigger the lockout mechanism, denying users access to their accounts.

167. **B.** The Password Authentication Protocol (PAP) is a legacy protocol that was commonly used for authentication many years ago but is no longer used today because it does not use encryption to

protect passwords in transit. There are no issues with PAP's reliability or use on Ethernet networks, but is it not widely used for any purpose today.

168. **D.** This situation calls for role-based access control, where authorizations are assigned based upon a user's role in the organization. This approach would allow Gavin to simply change a user's role when they switch jobs and then the permissions would automatically update based upon the user's new role.

169. **C.** During a privilege usage review, Kip will determine whether any employees misused legitimately assigned privileges. To do this, he would need access logs that detail privilege usage. It would also be helpful for him to have access to an organizational chart to determine employee job roles and asset classification information to identify sensitive assets. Firewall logs would not likely be helpful in this situation because he is looking for insider misuse, which would appear to be legitimate activity from a network perspective.

170. **D.** One of the greatest risks to password security occurs when users reuse passwords across multiple sites. If an attacker compromises a third-party site, he or she may attempt to reuse those passwords on other sites. NIST password security guidelines recommend a minimum password length of 8 characters, so a 12-character password does not pose excessive risk. Those guidelines also call for using non-expiring passwords and not requiring enhanced complexity requirements, such as the use of special characters. These practices reduce the likelihood that users will remember their passwords.

171. **D.** OpenID connect is an authentication protocol built directly on top of the oAuth 2.0 framework, making it the simplest choice for user authentication.

172. **A.** Current guidance from the National Institute for Standards and Technology suggests that user passwords should not expire as a matter of best practice. Therefore, users should also not be prohibited from reusing prior passwords, unless those passwords are known to be compromised.

173. **C.** In 802.1x authentication, the end user's system contains a component called the supplicant that initiates the authentication process. The supplicant connects to the authenticator, normally a network switch or wireless access point, that then reaches out to an authentication server to confirm the user's identity. The communication between the authenticator and authentication server normally takes place using the RADIUS and EAP protocols.

174. **C.** In SAML authentication, the user agent is the web browser, application, or other technology used by the end user. The service provider is the service that the user would like to access. The identity provider is the organization providing the authentication mechanism. The certificate authority issues digital certificates required to secure the connections.

175. **B.** In Kerberos authentication, the authentication server (AS) is responsible for validating user credentials. The ticket granting server (TGS) issues authentication tickets to clients after the authentication server completes this validation. The client then provides authentication tickets to the service as proof of identity, rather than providing the service with authentication credentials directly.

176. **A.** There is not enough information provided to determine whether this system uses mandatory access control (MAC) where permissions are set only by the system or discretionary access control (DAC), where permissions are set by resource owners. We can determine based upon the analysis of the user's identity that this system is using attribute-based access control (ABAC). SLAC is not an access control model.

177. **D.** All of these technologies enable the enforcement of access controls, but most are limited to a specific domain, such as Windows file systems, Oracle databases, or network access. Active Directory group policies, on the other hand, may apply across a wide variety of Windows-based systems and applications.

178. **C.** While John and the guard are not using the smart capabilities of this card, they have still achieved multifactor authentication. John has presented a physical token (the card) and has also passed a biometric screening when the guard performed facial recognition by comparing him to the photo in her database.

179. **A.** Administrative (or root) accounts are clear examples of privileged accounts due to their superuser privileges. Service accounts also have elevated privilege levels. Shared accounts do not normally have privileged access and should not be used on secured servers.

180. **C.** This type of authentication, where one domain trusts users from another domain, is called federation. Federation may involve transitive trusts, where the trusts may be followed through a series of domains, but this scenario only describes the use of two domains. The scenario only describes use of credentials for a single system and does not describe a multiple-system scenario where single sign-on would be relevant. There is no requirement described for the use of multifactor authentication, which would require the use of two or more diverse authentication techniques.

181. **A.** The Network Time Protocol (NTP) is used to synchronize system clocks. Transport Layer Security (TLS) is used to encrypt network communications. The Simple Mail Transfer Protocol (SMTP) is used to exchange email messages. The Border Gateway Protocol (BGP) is used to coordinate network routing.

182. **B.** In an open environment such as a coffee shop, the most effective approach is likely to use an unauthenticated, unencrypted network that users can connect to easily and simply. While this leaves communications unsecured, it minimizes support and increases the likelihood that users will successfully connect. In this setup, users are responsible for providing their own encryption, if desired. This is an excellent example of conducting a risk/benefit analysis -- the most secure option is not always the best choice!

183. **B.** Cryptographic Service Providers (CSPs) are components of Microsoft Windows that add support for specific encryption algorithms. Darryl can ensure that his systems are configured to use strong CSPs.

184. **D.** The purpose of a digital certificate is to share a public key freely with the world. Therefore, the public key is not encrypted at all - it is freely given to anyone who receives the certificate.

185. **C.** In the process of creating a digital certificate, the requester creates a certificate signing request (CSR) on the device that will receive the certificate and then sends this CSR to the CA for use in creating the certificate.

186. **A.** Full disk encryption is designed to protect data stored on a disk and would not affect data transmitted over a network. Transport Layer Security (TLS) is designed specifically to protect data being sent over network connections. File encryption may also be used to protect the contents of files being sent over a network. TLS and file encryption may both make use of the Advanced Encryption Standard (AES) to provide encryption and decryption functionality.

187. **B.** The WPA2 algorithm is the current best practice standard for wireless encryption. The WPA algorithm is also considered secure, but is not the current best practice. The WiFi Protected Setup (WPS) protocol is used to establish a wireless connection and is not an encryption standard. The Wired Equivalent Privacy (WEP) protocol is an outdated wireless encryption standard.

188. **A.** RADIUS authentication may take place over TCP or UDP and uses port 1812 in either case. TCP port 1521 is reserved for Oracle database communication, while TCP port 1433 is reserved for Microsoft SQL Server. TCP port 3389 is used by the Remote Desktop Protocol (RDP).

189. **D.** When Paul encrypts the message with Kathy's public key, he provides confidentiality for the message because Kathy is the only one with the corresponding decryption key. When Kathy decrypts the message successfully, she also receives a guarantee of integrity because the message would not decrypt properly if it were altered. There is no guarantee of nonrepudiation because Paul did not digitally sign the message.

190. **C.** In an 802.1x connection, the device that is actually attempting to connect to the network runs a software component known as the supplicant. This communicates with the network device performing the authentication, which is the client. That network device then communicates with the back-end authentication server.

191. **D.** WPA uses the Temporal Key Integrity Protocol (TKIP) to rapidly cycle encryption keys and overcome the weaknesses of WEP. WPA2 uses the Counter Mode Cipher Block Chaining Message Authentication Code Protocol (CCMP) to provide enhanced security using AES.

192. **B.** The RIPEMD algorithm supports all four of these message digest lengths. The 160-bit digest is the most commonly used approach because it provides equivalent security to the 256 and 320 bit versions and stronger security than the insecure 128 bit version.

193. **B.** The Online Certificate Status Protocol (OCSP) is a dynamic protocol designed to allow real-time verification of digital certificates by end user devices. OCSP allows the immediate revocation of digital certificates without the lag time associated with the use of certificate revocation lists (CRLs).

194. **A.** This message is prompting the user to enter a pre-shared key (PSK) and, therefore, the network is in PSK mode. The question indicates that the network is secure, ruling out the use of WEP.

195. **A.** Extended validation (EV) certificates are the most difficult to obtain but provide the highest degree of trust to end users. Organization validated (OV) certificates do verify the business name but offer a lesser degree of trust than EV certificates. Domain validated (DV) certificates only verify the domain name and provide the lowest degree of trust. NV certificates do not exist.

196. **C.** Certificate revocation lists (CRLs) have several disadvantages. They do require that the client search the CRL for the serial number of a certificate to determine if it was revoked. CRL implementations do fail open so that a user will trust a certificate if the CRL is unavailable. They also are slow to update. CRLs do support EV certificates. They do not support OV or DV certificates.

197. **B.** Full disk encryption is effective against data-at-rest situations where the data is not being actively accessed. For example, full disk encryption protects the contents of a lost or stolen device. Full disk encryption is not effective when a user has accessed the device legitimately, so it would not be effective against an insider attack or against malware running within a user account. It also does not protect data in transit so it would not be effective against an eavesdropping attack.

198. **C.** This certificate authority is a root CA, as it was the initial element in the chain of trust. The root CA was then used to create several intermediate CAs, but the root CA itself is not an intermediate CA. The root CA is disconnected from the network, so it is an offline CA, not an online CA. There is no indication that Sam was not authorized to create this CA, so it is not unauthorized.

199. **A.** Digital certificates are signed by a certificate authority (CA). When a user or browser wishes to verify a digital certificate, it does so by validating the digital signature using the CA's public key.

200. **A.** This logo indicates that the router supports WiFi Protected Setup (WPS) for the establishment of a wireless connection.

201. **B.** The PGP package uses a concept known as the web of trust to provide assurances that keys are accurate. This decentralized model requires having keys vouched for by trusted individuals within the network and eschews a centralized approach.

202. **A.** The digital certificate format is set out in the X.509 standard. RFC 1918 contains the standard for private IP addressing, while RFC 793 defines the TCP standard. IEEE 802.1x is a standard for wireless authentication.

203. **B.** The RSA algorithm depends upon the difficulty of factoring the products of large prime numbers in order to achieve cryptographic security.

204. **D.** In an 802.1x wireless network, the wireless access point or wireless controller typically serves as the 802.1x client, sending authentication requests to a back-end authentication server.

205. **B.** The purpose of a digital certificate is to share a web server's public key. Frank's browser would extract this key from the certificate and use it to send the server an ephemeral session key to use for the remainder of the session.

206. **D.** The Protected Extensible Authentication Protocol (PEAP) runs the standard EAP protocol within a TLS session to provide secure communications.

207. **D.** The hash-based message authentication code (HMAC) algorithm supports both message integrity and authenticity. Hash algorithms without message authentication, such as MD5, SHA-2, and SHA-3, also support integrity but not authenticity.

208. **B.** Of these cipher suites, the only one using an insecure algorithm is TLS_RSA_WITH_RC4_128_SHA, which makes use of the outdated RC4 algorithm.

209. **B.** The 802.1x protocol is an authentication protocol that is specifically designed to provide port-based authentication for wired networks as well as authentication for wireless networks.

210. **C.** The screen displayed here is a captive portal that is intercepting communications and requiring that the user complete the authentication process before gaining access to the network.

211. **D.** This digital certificate is a valid digital certificate for www.bankofamerica.com and does include the organization name Bank of America. Therefore, the certification authority, in this case Entrust, is making an assertion that the public key does indeed belong to Bank of America.

212. **C.** The EAP protocol does not provide encryption capability and, therefore, must be run within a communications channel protected by other means.

213. **C.** Domain validated (DV) certificates only assure the recipient that the certificate authority has validated that the certificate holder has possession of the domain name validated in the certificate. Extended validation (EV) and organizational validation (OV) certificates go beyond this, requiring additional proof of identity. XV certificates do not exist.

214. **A.** This certificate is a wildcard certificate with the wildcard character (*) put in place as a subdomain of nd.edu. Therefore, the certificate will work for any URL following the format https://*.nd.edu followed by any other directories or document names. This would apply to both mike.nd.edu and www.nd.edu and any folders or documents contained under those domains. It would not apply to www.mike.nd.edu because that is a second-level subdomain. A wildcard certificate covering that domain would need to be of the format https://*.mike.nd.edu.

215. **B.** Certificate pinning is a control that provides the client browser with instructions about the certificate(s) that it may accept from a specific web server. Certificates not matching the pinned certificate are rejected.

216. **B.** The certificate shown here is in ASCII format. The PEM file format is the only answer choice that is an ASCII format. The .DER, .P12, and .PFX certificate files are all binary formats and are not presentable as standard text.

CHAPTER 4

Operations and Incident Response

Domain 4 Questions

1. Ben would like to identify all of the active network connections and services listening for connections on a Linux system that he is analyzing. What command-line utility can he use to meet this need?

   A. pstools
   B. tcpdump
   C. netstat
   D. netcat

2. Nick runs a vulnerability scan on his server and the scanner reports the issue shown below. What action should he take?

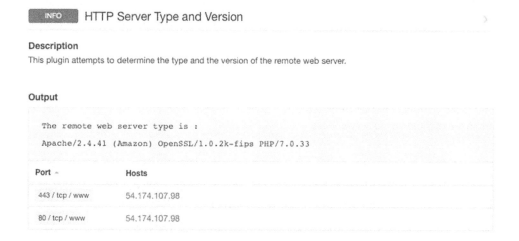

   A. The web server should be updated
   B. The operating system should be updated
   C. The firewall rule should be adjusted
   D. No action is necessary

3. Consider the file listing shown below. Who has permission to read and write to the encode.py file?

```
-rw------- 1 mchapple staff      75 Jul  2 2018 ages.py
-rw------- 1 mchapple staff      73 Jul  2 2018 ages.rb
-rw------- 1 mchapple staff      88 Jul  2 2018 ages.sh
-rw------- 1 mchapple staff 1536219 Aug  8 2018 c11-LW-MC.pdf
-rw------- 1 mchapple staff   43638 Jun 21 2018 c11f001.png
-rw------- 1 mchapple staff   42687 Jun 21 2018 c11f002.png
-rw------- 1 mchapple staff   41886 Jun 21 2018 c11f003.png
-rw------- 1 mchapple staff     108 Jul  2 2018 cupcake.py
-rw------- 1 mchapple staff     106 Jul  2 2018 cupcake.rb
-rw------- 1 mchapple staff     113 Jul  2 2018 cupcake.sh
-rw------- 1 mchapple staff      76 Jun 11 2018 else.sh
-rw------- 1 mchapple staff     182 Jul  2 2018 encode.py
```

A. Only the user mchapple
B. Only members of the staff group
C. Both mchapple and members of the staff group
D. Anyone with an account on the system

4. Carl is troubleshooting a Windows device that is having issues connecting to the network. He runs the ipconfig commands and finds the information shown below for the problematic interface. How did the system receive this IP address?

```
Ethernet adapter Ethernet 3:

    Connection-specific DNS Suffix  . :
    Link-local IPv6 Address . . . . . : fe80::d50a:1b66:8185:4ae3
    IPv4 Address. . . . . . . . . . . : 169.254.188.19(Preferred)
    Subnet Mask . . . . . . . . . . . : 255.255.0.0
    Default Gateway . . . . . . . . . :
```

A. Active Directory preferred address
B. DHCP
C. Static assignment
D. APIPA

5. Refer to the Wireshark packet capture below. Based on this packet capture, what services can we be certain are running on the server located at 3.84.33.224?

213	14.074782	192.168.1.5	3.84.33.224	TCP	78	58036 → 443 [SYN] Seq=0 Win=65535 Len=0 MSS…
216	15.075928	192.168.1.5	3.84.33.224	TCP	78	[TCP Retransmission] 58036 → 443 [SYN] Seq=…
221	16.076700	192.168.1.5	3.84.33.224	TCP	78	[TCP Retransmission] 58036 → 443 [SYN] Seq=…
224	17.077934	192.168.1.5	3.84.33.224	TCP	78	[TCP Retransmission] 58036 → 443 [SYN] Seq=…
225	18.078985	192.168.1.5	3.84.33.224	TCP	78	[TCP Retransmission] 58036 → 443 [SYN] Seq=…
226	19.081075	192.168.1.5	3.84.33.224	TCP	78	[TCP Retransmission] 58036 → 443 [SYN] Seq=…
254	21.087864	192.168.1.5	3.84.33.224	TCP	78	[TCP Retransmission] 58036 → 443 [SYN] Seq=…
336	25.105961	192.168.1.5	3.84.33.224	TCP	78	[TCP Retransmission] 58036 → 443 [SYN] Seq=…
550	33.159849	192.168.1.5	3.84.33.224	TCP	78	[TCP Retransmission] 58036 → 443 [SYN] Seq=…
11…	48.972814	192.168.1.5	3.84.33.224	TCP	78	58042 → 80 [SYN] Seq=0 Win=65535 Len=0 MSS=…
11…	49.979912	192.168.1.5	3.84.33.224	TCP	78	[TCP Retransmission] 58042 → 80 [SYN] Seq=0…
11…	50.980022	192.168.1.5	3.84.33.224	TCP	78	[TCP Retransmission] 58042 → 80 [SYN] Seq=0…
11…	51.983622	192.168.1.5	3.84.33.224	TCP	78	[TCP Retransmission] 58042 → 80 [SYN] Seq=0…
12…	52.988216	192.168.1.5	3.84.33.224	TCP	78	[TCP Retransmission] 58042 → 80 [SYN] Seq=0…
12…	53.990455	192.168.1.5	3.84.33.224	TCP	78	[TCP Retransmission] 58042 → 80 [SYN] Seq=0…
12…	55.994452	192.168.1.5	3.84.33.224	TCP	78	[TCP Retransmission] 58042 → 80 [SYN] Seq=0…
13…	64.300303	192.168.1.5	3.84.33.224	TCP	78	58045 → 22 [SYN] Seq=0 Win=65535 Len=0 MSS=…
13…	64.340714	3.84.33.224	192.168.1.5	TCP	74	22 → 58045 [SYN, ACK] Seq=0 Ack=1 Win=26847…
13…	64.340830	192.168.1.5	3.84.33.224	TCP	66	58045 → 22 [ACK] Seq=1 Ack=1 Win=131712 Len…
13…	64.343019	192.168.1.5	3.84.33.224	SSH…	87	Client: Protocol (SSH-2.0-OpenSSH_7.9)
13…	64.388090	3.84.33.224	192.168.1.5	SSH…	87	Server: Protocol (SSH-2.0-OpenSSH_7.4)
13…	64.388151	192.168.1.5	3.84.33.224	TCP	66	58045 → 22 [ACK] Seq=22 Ack=22 Win=131712 L…
13…	64.390670	3.84.33.224	192.168.1.5	TCP	66	22 → 58045 [ACK] Seq=22 Ack=22 Win=26880 Le…
13…	64.390718	192.168.1.5	3.84.33.224	SSH…	14…	Client: Key Exchange Init
13…	64.426301	3.84.33.224	192.168.1.5	SSH…	13…	Server: Key Exchange Init
13…	64.426407	192.168.1.5	3.84.33.224	TCP	66	58045 → 22 [ACK] Seq=1414 Ack=1302 Win=1304…
13…	64.470816	3.84.33.224	192.168.1.5	TCP	66	22 → 58045 [ACK] Seq=1302 Ack=1414 Win=2969…
13…	64.470880	192.168.1.5	3.84.33.224	SSH…	114	Client: Diffie-Hellman Key Exchange Init
13…	64.527501	3.84.33.224	192.168.1.5	SSH…	430	Server: Diffie-Hellman Key Exchange Reply, …
13…	64.527610	192.168.1.5	3.84.33.224	TCP	66	58045 → 22 [ACK] Seq=1462 Ack=1666 Win=1306…
13…	64.534257	192.168.1.5	3.84.33.224	SSH…	82	Client: New Keys

A. SSH

B. SSH and HTTPS

C. HTTP and HTTPS

D. SSH, HTTP, and HTTPS

6. Kevin would like to obtain a listing of the MAC addresses of systems on his local network, similar to the one shown below. What command can he use to generate this listing?

```
? (192.168.1.1) at a0:40:a0:55:2f:c0 on en0 ifscope [ethernet]
? (192.168.1.4) at b0:39:56:6f:d0:3d on en0 ifscope [ethernet]
? (192.168.1.23) at e8:b2:ac:40:a9:c4 on en0 ifscope [ethernet]
? (192.168.1.37) at 54:e4:3a:a5:7b:44 on en0 ifscope [ethernet]
```

A. arp

B. ifconfig

C. netstat

D. ping

7. What transport protocol is used by the traceroute command by default?

A. No transport protocol is used

B. ICMP

C. TCP

D. UDP

8. Which one of the following is not a normal task of a SIEM?

A. Aggregate log entries

B. Block unwanted traffic

C. Correlate records

D. Identify trends

9. Brenda recently participated in an incident response training program where members of the team met in a conference room to discuss their roles in an incident using the context of a simulated emergency situation. What term best describes this event?

A. Full activation

B. Partial activation

C. Tabletop

D. Walkthrough

10. Nancy issues the command shown below to determine whether a system is live on the network. What type of packet is sent out by her system?

```
$ ping 10.36.16.1
PING 10.36.16.1 (10.36.16.1): 56 data bytes
64 bytes from 10.36.16.1: icmp_seq=0 ttl=255 time=46.363 ms
64 bytes from 10.36.16.1: icmp_seq=1 ttl=255 time=2.172 ms
64 bytes from 10.36.16.1: icmp_seq=2 ttl=255 time=1.613 ms
64 bytes from 10.36.16.1: icmp_seq=3 ttl=255 time=6.930 ms
64 bytes from 10.36.16.1: icmp_seq=4 ttl=255 time=2.834 ms
64 bytes from 10.36.16.1: icmp_seq=5 ttl=255 time=1.612 ms
^C
--- 10.36.16.1 ping statistics ---
6 packets transmitted, 6 packets received, 0.0% packet loss
round-trip min/avg/max/stddev = 1.612/10.254/46.363/16.251 ms
$
```

A. ICMP Echo Reply
B. ICMP Echo Request
C. ICMP Information Request
D. ICMP Information Reply

11. Alex is reviewing alerts generated by his organization's SIEM and determines that the SIEM is generating too many false positive alerts. What parameter can he alter to reduce the number of false positives?

A. Increase the SIEM sensitivity
B. Reduce the SIEM sensitivity
C. Increase the SIEM capacity
D. Reduce the SIEM capacity

12. Which one of the following mechanisms offer the most immediate way to invalidate a compromised digital certificate?

A. CRL
B. OCSP
C. Changing the private key
D. Changing the public key

13. Laura is performing a DNS query using the nslookup command and she would like to identify the SMTP server(s) associated with a domain. What type of records should she retrieve?

A. MX
B. A
C. CNAME
D. NS

14. Paul is looking for a free solution that will aggregate the security logs from devices across his organization. Which one of the following tools would best meet his needs?

    A. Journalctl
    B. NXlog
    C. Syslog
    D. Wireshark

15. Which of the following types of information may be collected by a mobile device management (MDM) solution?

    A. Call history only
    B. Applications installed and call history
    C. User identity, applications installed, and call history
    D. User identity, geographic location, applications installed, and call history

16. Barry is reviewing log records in the wake of a security incident. He suspects that the attackers attempted a SQL injection attack that was blocked. Which one of the following log sources is likely to contain the best information about the attempted attack?

    A. Host firewall logs
    B. Web server logs
    C. Database logs
    D. Web application firewall logs

17. What metric would a SOC use to measure the amount of time that elapses between a security incident occurring and the SOC identifying the incident?

    A. MITRE
    B. MTBF
    C. MTTD
    D. MTTR

18. Carolyn is working with her team to develop her organization's disaster recovery plan. What stage of the planning process provides the information necessary to prioritize recovery efforts by service?

    A. Business impact assessment
    B. Design
    C. Implementation
    D. Preparation

19. After implementing a SIEM solution, Amanda discovers that the timestamps on log entries are not synchronized. What protocol can Amanda deploy in her organization to ensure clock synchronization?

    A. DHCP
    B. DNS
    C. NTP
    D. BGP

20. Chris would like to send a custom-crafted TCP packet to a remote system. What utility can he use to meet this requirement?

A. ping
B. hping
C. pathping
D. tcpdump

21. What is the purpose of the Python script shown below?

```
import socket

net = '192.168.1.'

for hst in range(0,256):
        ip= net + str(hst)
        print(ip, ': ', socket.gethostbyaddr(ip), '\n')
```

A. Display the IP addresses of all hosts in the 192.168.1.9/16 network
B. Display the IP addresses of all hosts in the 192.168.1.9/24 network
C. Display the hostnames of all hosts in the 192.168.1.9/16 network
D. Display the hostnames of all hosts in the 192.168.1.9/24 network

22. Dennis is reviewing the logs from a content filter and notices that a user has been visiting pornographic websites during business hours. What action should Dennis take next?

A. Take no action.
B. Discuss the issue with the user.
C. Block access to the websites.
D. Report the issue to management.

23. In order to improve the security of his network, Tony is placing systems onto small subnets that are designed for systems that share a common purpose. What term best describes this technique?

A. Isolation
B. Segmentation
C. Shimming
D. Refactoring

24. Which one of the following fields would NOT be found in a NetFlow record?

A. Destination address
B. Payload
C. Source address
D. Timestamp

25. Review the ifconfig results shown below. What is the primary IP address for this machine?

```
lo0: flags=8049<UP,LOOPBACK,RUNNING,MULTICAST> mtu 16384
        options=1203<RXCSUM,TXCSUM,TXSTATUS,SW_TIMESTAMP>
        inet 127.0.0.1 netmask 0xff000000
        inet6 ::1 prefixlen 128
        inet6 fe80::1%lo0 prefixlen 64 scopeid 0x1
        nd6 options=201<PERFORMNUD,DAD>
gif0: flags=8010<POINTOPOINT,MULTICAST> mtu 1280
stf0: flags=0<> mtu 1280
XHC20: flags=0<> mtu 0
en0: flags=8863<UP,BROADCAST,SMART,RUNNING,SIMPLEX,MULTICAST> mtu 1500
        ether 98:e0:d9:87:8a:73
        inet 10.36.23.22 netmask 0xfffff800 broadcast 10.36.23.255
        media: autoselect
        status: active
p2p0: flags=8843<UP,BROADCAST,RUNNING,SIMPLEX,MULTICAST> mtu 2304
        ether 0a:e0:d9:87:8a:73
        media: autoselect
        status: inactive
awdl0: flags=8943<UP,BROADCAST,RUNNING,PROMISC,SIMPLEX,MULTICAST> mtu 1484
        ether 62:9f:a8:6b:94:08
        inet6 fe80::609f:a8ff:fe6b:9408%awdl0 prefixlen 64 scopeid 0x9
        nd6 options=201<PERFORMNUD,DAD>
        media: autoselect
        status: active
en1: flags=8963<UP,BROADCAST,SMART,RUNNING,PROMISC,SIMPLEX,MULTICAST> mtu 1500
        options=60<TSO4,TSO6>
        ether 9a:00:01:99:02:70
        media: autoselect <full-duplex>
        status: inactive
bridge0: flags=8863<UP,BROADCAST,SMART,RUNNING,SIMPLEX,MULTICAST> mtu 1500
        options=63<RXCSUM,TXCSUM,TSO4,TSO6>
        ether 9a:00:01:99:02:70
        Configuration:
                id 0:0:0:0:0:0 priority 0 hellotime 0 fwddelay 0
                maxage 0 holdcnt 0 proto stp maxaddr 100 timeout 1200
                root id 0:0:0:0:0:0 priority 0 ifcost 0 port 0
                ipfilter disabled flags 0x2
        member: en1 flags=3<LEARNING,DISCOVER>
                ifmaxaddr 0 port 10 priority 0 path cost 0
        nd6 options=201<PERFORMNUD,DAD>
        media: <unknown type>
        status: inactive
utun0: flags=8051<UP,POINTOPOINT,RUNNING,MULTICAST> mtu 2000
        inet6 fe80::1f19:7c86:94a1:3708%utun0 prefixlen 64 scopeid 0xd
        nd6 options=201<PERFORMNUD,DAD>
utun1: flags=8051<UP,POINTOPOINT,RUNNING,MULTICAST> mtu 1380
        inet6 fe80::c277:463f:341a:4c99%utun1 prefixlen 64 scopeid 0xe
        nd6 options=201<PERFORMNUD,DAD>
```

A. 127.0.0.1
B. 10.36.23.255
C. 10.36.23.22
D. 98:e0:d9:87:8a:73

26. Brian is reviewing a Wireshark packet capture and finds the packets shown below. What type of activity most likely caused this traffic?

```
Source          Destination     Protocol    Info
10.21.12.73     10.21.12.20       SIP        Request: REGISTER sip:10.21.12.20:5060
10.21.12.73     10.21.12.20       SIP        Request: REGISTER sip:10.21.12.20:5060
10.21.12.102    10.21.12.73       SIP        Status: 401 Unauthorized      (0 bindings)
10.21.12.102    10.21.12.73       SIP        Status: 401 Unauthorized      (0 bindings)
10.21.12.73     10.21.12.20       SIP        Request: REGISTER sip:10.21.12.20:5060
10.21.12.73     10.21.12.20       SIP        Request: REGISTER sip:10.21.12.20:5060
10.21.12.102    10.21.12.73       SIP        Status: 200 OK      (1 bindings)
10.21.12.102    10.21.12.73       SIP        Status: 200 OK      (1 bindings)
10.21.12.73     10.21.12.20     SIP/SDP      Request: INVITE sip:580@10.21.12.20, with session description
10.21.12.102    10.21.12.73       SIP        Status: 401 Unauthorized
10.21.12.73     10.21.12.20       SIP        Request: ACK sip:580@10.21.12.20
10.21.12.73     10.21.12.20     SIP/SDP      Request: INVITE sip:580@10.21.12.20, with session description
10.21.12.102    10.21.12.73       SIP        Status: 100 Trying
10.21.12.102    10.21.12.73       SIP        Status: 180 Ringing
10.21.12.102    10.21.12.73     SIP/SDP      Status: 200 OK, with session description
10.21.12.73     10.21.12.20       SIP        Request: ACK sip:580@10.21.12.20
10.21.12.102    10.21.12.73       SIP        Request: BYE sip:530@10.21.12.73:54911;transport=udp
10.21.12.73     10.21.12.102      SIP        Status: 200 OK
```

A. ARP queries
B. Network maintenance
C. Routing changes
D. VoIP calls

27. Tom is a forensic analyst conducting a security investigation at his company after the firm experienced a data breach. He is planning to speak with some employees to gather evidence and suspects they may have been complicit in the breach. Which one of the following statements is incorrect about these conversations?

A. Tom should ask employees difficult questions during the interview
B. Tom should be friendly and non-aggressive
C. Tom should consult Human Resources before speaking with employees who may have been involved in the incident
D. Tom may not speak with employees without first advising them of their rights because he suspects they were involved in a security incident

28. Kyle would like to capture network traffic to assist with troubleshooting a firewall issue. What command line utility can he use to capture traffic?

A. netcat
B. Wireshark
C. nmap
D. tcpdump

29. Review the firewall ruleset shown below. If a system at 10.18.100.3 attempts an SSH connection to the server at 192.168.10.5, what would be the result?

Rule	Source IP	Source Port	Dest IP	Dest Port	Action
1	any	any	192.168.10.5	1443	allow
2	any	any	192.168.10.6	1521	allow
3	10.18.100.3	any	192.168.10.6	22	deny
4	any	any	any	any	deny

A. The traffic will be allowed by rule 1
B. The traffic will be allowed by rule 2
C. The traffic will be blocked by rule 3
D. The traffic will be blocked by rule 4

30. Review the firewall ruleset below. If a system with the IP address 10.18.100.4 attempts to access the server at 10.18.1.4 over a standard HTTP connection, what would be the result?

Rule	Source IP	Source Port	Dest IP	Dest Port	Action
1	any	any	10.18.1.4	80	allow
2	any	any	10.18.1.4	443	allow
3	10.18.100.3	any	10.18.1.4	any	deny
4	any	any	any	any	deny

A. The traffic will be allowed by rule 1
B. The traffic will be allowed by rule 2
C. The traffic will be blocked by rule 3
D. The traffic will be blocked by rule 4

31. Which one of the following tools is an exploitation framework commonly used in penetration testing?

A. Metasploit
B. Cain & Abel
C. Nessus
D. Sysinternals

32. What intrusion analysis approach is illustrated in the diagram below?

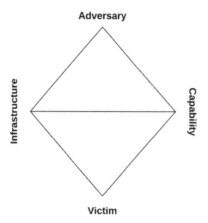

A. ATT&CK framework
B. Cyber Kill Chain
C. Diamond model
D. TTP sequencing

33. Refer to the packet capture shown below. Which packet indicates the end of a TCP connection?

No.	Time	Source	Destination	Protocol	Length	Info
206	14.724769	74.125.132.189	192.168.1.5	TCP	66	443 → 58898 [ACK] Seq=309 Ack=1487 Win=410 …
207	14.813510	18.214.96.169	192.168.1.5	TLS…	420	Application Data
208	14.813514	18.214.96.169	192.168.1.5	TLS…	97	Encrypted Alert
209	14.813580	192.168.1.5	18.214.96.169	TCP	66	58903 → 443 [ACK] Seq=1 Ack=355 Win=2042 Le…
210	14.813580	192.168.1.5	18.214.96.169	TCP	66	58903 → 443 [ACK] Seq=1 Ack=387 Win=2041 Le…
211	14.813688	192.168.1.5	18.214.96.169	TLS…	97	Encrypted Alert
212	14.814330	192.168.1.5	18.214.96.169	TCP	66	58903 → 443 [FIN, ACK] Seq=32 Ack=387 Win=2…
213	14.816023	192.168.1.5	192.168.1.1	DNS	95	Standard query 0x3df4 A ss-prod-ue1-notif-5…
214	14.816491	192.168.1.5	34.196.150.241	TCP	78	58911 → 443 [SYN] Seq=0 Win=65535 Len=0 MSS…
215	14.842543	192.168.1.1	192.168.1.5	DNS	143	Standard query response 0x3df4 A ss-prod-ue…
216	14.855940	34.196.150.241	192.168.1.5	TCP	74	443 → 58911 [SYN, ACK] Seq=0 Ack=1 Win=2684…
217	14.855942	18.214.96.169	192.168.1.5	TCP	54	443 → 58903 [RST] Seq=387 Win=0 Len=0
218	14.855943	18.214.96.169	192.168.1.5	TCP	54	443 → 58903 [RST] Seq=387 Win=0 Len=0
219	14.856022	192.168.1.5	34.196.150.241	TCP	66	58911 → 443 [ACK] Seq=1 Ack=1 Win=131712 Le…
220	14.856375	192.168.1.5	34.196.150.241	TLS…	293	Client Hello
221	14.900330	34.196.150.241	192.168.1.5	TLS…	15…	Server Hello
222	14.900334	34.196.150.241	192.168.1.5	TCP	15…	443 → 58911 [ACK] Seq=1449 Ack=228 Win=2816…
223	14.900335	34.196.150.241	192.168.1.5	TLS…	14…	Certificate, Server Key Exchange, Server He…
224	14.900432	192.168.1.5	34.196.150.241	TCP	66	58911 → 443 [ACK] Seq=228 Ack=2897 Win=1288…
225	14.900432	192.168.1.5	34.196.150.241	TCP	66	58911 → 443 [ACK] Seq=228 Ack=4330 Win=1274…
226	14.900479	192.168.1.5	34.196.150.241	TCP	66	[TCP Window Update] 58911 → 443 [ACK] Seq=2…
227	14.909832	192.168.1.5	34.196.150.241	TLS…	141	Client Key Exchange
228	14.909883	192.168.1.5	34.196.150.241	TLS…	72	Change Cipher Spec
229	14.909883	192.168.1.5	34.196.150.241	TLS…	111	Encrypted Handshake Message
230	14.919491	Netgear_6f:d0…	IEEE-1905.1-C…	iee…	34	Topology notification
231	14.929985	Netgear_6f:d0…	IEEE-1905.1-C…	iee…	34	Topology notification
232	14.955136	34.196.150.241	192.168.1.5	TCP	66	443 → 58911 [ACK] Seq=4330 Ack=354 Win=2816…
233	14.955139	34.196.150.241	192.168.1.5	TLS…	117	Change Cipher Spec, Encrypted Handshake Mes…
234	14.955204	192.168.1.5	34.196.150.241	TCP	66	58911 → 443 [ACK] Seq=354 Ack=4381 Win=1310…

A. 211
B. 217
C. 233
D. 234

34. Barry is using nmap to scan systems and is experiencing difficulty because some systems are not responding to ping requests. He knows the hosts are active. What flag can he use to skip the discovery step entirely?

    A. -Pn
    B. -PS
    C. -PA
    D. -PU

35. Referring to the NIST Incident Response diagram shown below, during what step in the process would the team normally conduct a lessons learned session?

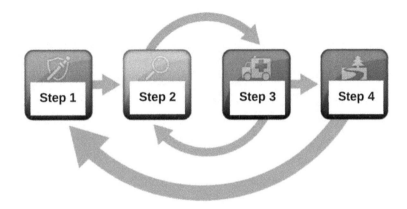

    A. Step 1
    B. Step 2
    C. Step 3
    D. Step 4

36. Frances would like to conduct purple teaming as part of her organization's next cybersecurity exercise. Which exercise participants should participate in the purple teaming effort?

    A. Red team members
    B. Blue team members
    C. Red and blue team members
    D. All participants

37. Eric would like to determine whether users on his network are transmitting sensitive information without the use of encryption. What technology, of the following choices, can best assist Eric in completing this task?

    A. Exploitation framework
    B. Port scanner
    C. Protocol analyzer
    D. Honeypot

38. At what point in a legal dispute should an organization involved in the dispute issue a litigation hold for evidence related to the dispute?

    A. As soon as they believe a lawsuit might occur
    B. As soon as a lawsuit is filed
    C. As soon as they receive a subpoena or other court order
    D. As soon as they believe evidence is at risk of destruction

39. Roger's organization recently activated their disaster recovery plan in response to a facility emergency. At what point would the organization typically deactivate the plan?

    A. When the organization completes the initial response effort
    B. When the organization has a stable operating environment set up in an alternate facility
    C. When the organization is returned to its normal operating environment
    D. When senior leaders arrive on scene to take command

40. Bev is analyzing host IPS logs from endpoints in her network and notices that many are receiving port scans from external hosts. Which one of the following circumstances is likely present?

    A. Compromised internal system
    B. Misconfigured host firewall
    C. Misconfigured IPS
    D. Misconfigured network firewall

41. Kevin would like to restrict users from accessing a list of prohibited websites while connected to his network. Which one of the following controls would best achieve his objective?

    A. DLP solution
    B. IP address block
    C. IPS solution
    D. URL filter

42. Harry believes that an employee of his organization launched a privilege escalation attack to gain root access on one of the organization's database servers. The employee does have an authorized user account on the server. What log file would be most likely to contain relevant information?

    A. Database application log
    B. Firewall log
    C. IDS log
    D. Operating system log

43. Justin is searching for rogue systems on his network and would like to detect devices that are responding to network requests but are not on his approved list. What tool can he use to identify the systems on a network that are responding to requests?

    A. sqlmap
    B. openssl
    C. netcat
    D. nmap

44. Referring to the NIST Incident Response process diagram shown below, what is the proper order for the steps of the incident response process?

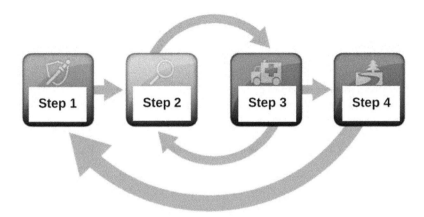

A. Detection & Analysis; Preparation; Containment, Eradication & Recovery; Post-Incident Activities
B. Preparation; Containment, Eradication & Recovery; Detection & Analysis; Post-Incident Activities
C. Preparation; Detection & Analysis; Containment, Eradication & Recovery; Post-Incident Activities
D. Detection & Analysis; Containment, Eradication & Recovery; Post-Incident Activities; Preparation

45. Which file stores the contents of virtual memory on a Windows system?

A. config.sys
B. hiberfil.sys
C. pagefile.sys
D. swapfile.sys

46. Which one of the following tools can be used to perform DNS queries on a Windows system without requiring the installation of non-standard software?

A. dig
B. nslookup
C. nbtstat
D. arp

47. Peter is analyzing network flow logs and finds that a server in his organization is sending a large amount of traffic to a single destination. Upon further investigation, he sees that the server is receiving very small repeated requests from the same source on UDP port 53 and sends very large responses. What type of attack should Peter suspect?

A. ARP spoofing
B. ARP amplification
C. DNS spoofing
D. DNS amplification

48. Carmen recently collected evidence from a variety of sources and is concerned that the clocks on the systems generating the evidence may not be synchronized. What would be her best course of action?

   A. Record the time offsets for each device
   B. Modify the system clocks
   C. Configure the systems to use an NTP server
   D. Modify the timestamps in the evidence to match real time

49. Greg believes that a recently departed employee is likely to sue the company for employment law violations because the employee threatened to do so during an exit interview. When should the company issue a legal hold to preserve evidence?

   A. When the employee issues a formal notice of intent to sue
   B. When a lawsuit is filed
   C. When they receive a subpoena
   D. Immediately

50. Which one of the following next generation SIEM capabilities is focused on automating portions of the incident response workflow?

   A. Dashboards
   B. SOAR
   C. Threat hunting
   D. UEBA

51. Frank is loading evidence from several hard drives into a forensic analysis system. As he reviews the evidence, he wants to organize it in several different ways: by device, by investigative theory, and by user. What method would best allow him to organize the data in this way?

   A. File names
   B. Folders
   C. Printouts
   D. Tags

52. When capturing a system image for forensic purposes, what tool should the analyst use to avoid unintentionally altering the original evidence?

   A. Write blocker
   B. Imaging software
   C. Clean media
   D. Labels

53. Which one of the following data loss prevention (DLP) rule actions is least likely to disrupt normal business processes?

   A. Alert
   B. Block
   C. Encrypt
   D. Quarantine

54. Jodie is helping her organization move services into a new cloud-based service. This includes transferring PII about her company's customers. She is concerned about the regulatory impact of that move. What country/countries may have jurisdiction over customer PII used in the new cloud service?

A. The country where Jodie's company is headquartered
B. The country where the customer resides
C. The country where Jodie's company is headquartered, and the customer resides
D. The country where the data is stored, Jodie's company is headquartered, and the customer resides

55. Consider the NIST incident response process shown here. Which step in the process is indicated by the question mark?

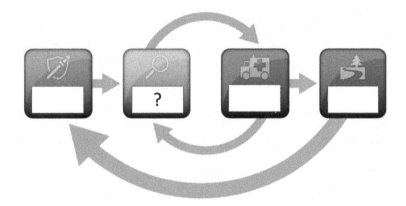

A. Post-incident Activity
B. Preparation
C. Containment, Eradication, & Recovery
D. Detection & Analysis

56. Wyatt would like to retrieve a web page and store it in a file using a command that works at the Linux command line. What command can he use to meet this need?

A. curl
B. ftp
C. tcpdump
D. wireshark

57. Alison is preparing to testify in court about the results of a forensic investigation conducted after a security breach. As an expert witness, she will be sharing her interpretation of the evidence collected by others. What type of evidence will Alison be giving?

A. Documentary
B. Hearsay
C. Tangible
D. Testimonial

58. Bill is concerned about his organization's practices regarding the timing of disposing records that are no longer necessary for business purposes. Which one of the following policies would be most relevant to this issue?

A. Data retention policy
B. Data encryption standards
C. Data access policy
D. Acceptable use policy

59. In which stage of the incident response process should incident responders work to isolate affected systems from the rest of the network?

A. Preparation
B. Detection & Analysis
C. Containment, Eradication, and Recovery
D. Post-Incident Activity

60. Which one of the following protocols is an open, industry standard protocol for the exchange of network flow records?

A. IPFIX
B. IPFlow
C. NetFlow v5
D. NetFlow v9

61. Kate is conducting an investigation of activity on her network. She is looking for an information source that might provide the identity of the systems that a user connected to and the times of those connections. Which one of the following data sources is LEAST likely to have this information?

A. Wireless access point logs
B. NetFlow logs
C. Firewall logs
D. Content filter logs

62. Review the Wireshark packet capture shown below. What is the most significant security issue present in these results?

No.	Time	Source	Destination	Protocol	Length	Info
81	2.700683	192.168.1.5	10.0.0.1	TCP	78	58864 → 80 [SYN] Seq=0 Win=65535 Len=0 MSS=…
82	2.707517	10.0.0.1	192.168.1.5	TCP	74	80 → 58864 [SYN, ACK] Seq=0 Ack=1 Win=28960…
83	2.707588	192.168.1.5	10.0.0.1	TCP	66	58864 → 80 [ACK] Seq=1 Ack=1 Win=131712 Len…
84	2.707958	192.168.1.5	10.0.0.1	HTTP	416	GET / HTTP/1.1
91	2.712598	10.0.0.1	192.168.1.5	TCP	66	80 → 58864 [ACK] Seq=1 Ack=351 Win=30080 Le…
123	3.093328	10.0.0.1	192.168.1.5	TCP	15…	80 → 58864 [ACK] Seq=1 Ack=351 Win=30080 Le…
124	3.093333	10.0.0.1	192.168.1.5	TCP	15…	80 → 58864 [ACK] Seq=1449 Ack=351 Win=30080…
125	3.093334	10.0.0.1	192.168.1.5	TCP	15…	80 → 58864 [ACK] Seq=2897 Ack=351 Win=30080…
126	3.093335	10.0.0.1	192.168.1.5	TCP	15…	80 → 58864 [ACK] Seq=4345 Ack=351 Win=30080…
127	3.093336	10.0.0.1	192.168.1.5	TCP	15…	80 → 58864 [ACK] Seq=5793 Ack=351 Win=30080…
128	3.093337	10.0.0.1	192.168.1.5	TCP	15…	80 → 58864 [ACK] Seq=7241 Ack=351 Win=30080…
129	3.093338	10.0.0.1	192.168.1.5	TCP	15…	80 → 58864 [ACK] Seq=8689 Ack=351 Win=30080…
130	3.093440	192.168.1.5	10.0.0.1	TCP	66	58864 → 80 [ACK] Seq=351 Ack=2897 Win=12883…
131	3.093440	192.168.1.5	10.0.0.1	TCP	66	58864 → 80 [ACK] Seq=351 Ack=5793 Win=12595…
132	3.093441	192.168.1.5	10.0.0.1	TCP	66	58864 → 80 [ACK] Seq=351 Ack=8689 Win=12307…
133	3.093481	192.168.1.5	10.0.0.1	TCP	66	58864 → 80 [ACK] Seq=351 Ack=10137 Win=1310…
134	3.094509	10.0.0.1	192.168.1.5	TCP	15…	80 → 58864 [ACK] Seq=10137 Ack=351 Win=3008…
135	3.094513	10.0.0.1	192.168.1.5	TCP	15…	80 → 58864 [ACK] Seq=11585 Ack=351 Win=3008…
136	3.094514	10.0.0.1	192.168.1.5	TCP	15…	80 → 58864 [ACK] Seq=13033 Ack=351 Win=3008…
137	3.094583	192.168.1.5	10.0.0.1	TCP	66	58864 → 80 [ACK] Seq=351 Ack=13033 Win=1281…
138	3.094624	192.168.1.5	10.0.0.1	TCP	66	58864 → 80 [ACK] Seq=351 Ack=14481 Win=1310…
139	3.095924	10.0.0.1	192.168.1.5	TCP	15…	80 → 58864 [ACK] Seq=14481 Ack=351 Win=3008…
140	3.100733	10.0.0.1	192.168.1.5	TCP	15…	80 → 58864 [ACK] Seq=15929 Ack=351 Win=3008…
141	3.100737	10.0.0.1	192.168.1.5	TCP	15…	80 → 58864 [ACK] Seq=17377 Ack=351 Win=3008…
142	3.100738	10.0.0.1	192.168.1.5	TCP	15…	80 → 58864 [ACK] Seq=18825 Ack=351 Win=3008…
143	3.100739	10.0.0.1	192.168.1.5	HTTP	12…	HTTP/1.1 200 OK (text/html)
144	3.100815	192.168.1.5	10.0.0.1	TCP	66	58864 → 80 [ACK] Seq=351 Ack=17377 Win=1296…
145	3.100816	192.168.1.5	10.0.0.1	TCP	66	58864 → 80 [ACK] Seq=351 Ack=20273 Win=1267…
146	3.100856	192.168.1.5	10.0.0.1	TCP	66	58864 → 80 [ACK] Seq=351 Ack=21434 Win=1255…

A. 10.0.0.1 supports an outdated encryption protocol
B. 10.0.0.1 allows unencrypted connections
C. 192.168.1.5 supports an outdated encryption protocol
D. 192.168.1.5 allows unencrypted connections

63. Beth is using the Cyber Kill Chain approach to analyze the actions of an intruder on her network. She finds evidence that the most recent activity of the attacker was to successfully use a buffer overflow attack to gain control of a system. What stage is the attacker in?

A. Command and Control
B. Exploitation
C. Installation
D. Weaponization

64. Wanda is developing an incident response team for her organization. Which one of the following individuals would be the best person to have direct oversight of the team's activities?

A. CEO
B. CIO
C. CISO
D. CFO

65. What Linux command allows you to view the contents of the system journal that are currently stored in memory?

    A. journalctl
    B. journalview
    C. syslogd
    D. sysview

66. After running a vulnerability scan of one of her organization's web servers, Morgan discovers the issue shown below. What is the most significant risk directly posed by this issue?

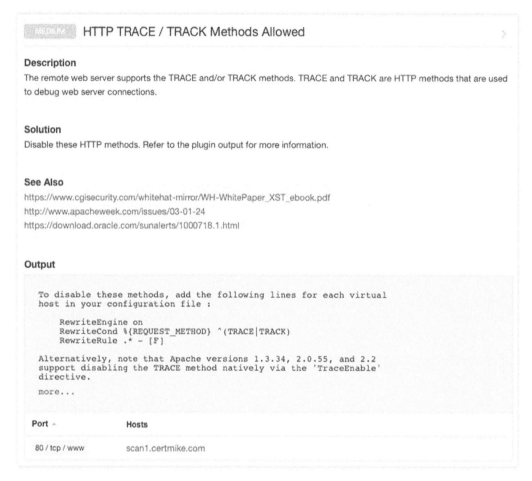

    A. Denial of service
    B. Information disclosure
    C. Server compromise
    D. Website defacement

67. Which one of the following disaster recovery exercise types will have the greatest impact on an organization's operations?

A. Parallel test
B. Full interruption test
C. Checklist review
D. Structured walkthrough

68. When operating in a cloud environment, what cloud deployment model provides security teams with the greatest access to forensic information?

A. FaaS
B. IaaS
C. PaaS
D. SaaS

69. Review the firewall rules shown below. If the system at 10.18.100.3 attempts a standard HTTPS connection to 10.18.1.4, what will be the result?

Rule	Source IP	Source Port	Dest IP	Dest Port	Action
1	any	any	10.18.1.4	80	allow
2	any	any	10.18.1.4	443	allow
3	10.18.100.3	any	10.18.1.4	any	deny
4	any	any	any	any	deny

A. Allowed by rule 1
B. Allowed by rule 2
C. Blocked by rule 3
D. Blocked by rule 4

70. Which one of the following statements is correct about evidence gathering and litigation holds?

A. Attorneys should review documents for privilege during the collection phase.
B. Most litigation holds never move forward to the production phase.
C. System administrators do not need to disable log file deletion during a litigation hold if the deletion process is part of a standard business practice.
D. Corporate attorneys bear primary responsibility for preserving evidence during a litigation hold

71. During what stage of the eDiscovery process does the organization share evidence with opposing parties?

A. Analysis
B. Collection
C. Preservation
D. Production

72. In a NetFlow implementation, what term is used to describe the network devices, such as routers and firewalls, that generate NetFlow records?

    A. Flow aggregator
    B. Flow analyzer
    C. Flow collector
    D. Flow exporter

73. Consider the evidence log shown here. What is the primary purpose of this tool during a forensic investigation?

EVIDENCE LOG
(For Non-Photographic Evidence)

Incident Identification: _____

Evidence Custodian: _____

Description of Item	Evidence ID #	Name of Person Logging Item Out	Name & Signature of Person Receiving Item	Date Item Received	Name & Signature of Person Receiving Item Back In	Date Item Received

    A. Ensure evidence is timely
    B. Prevent the alteration of evidence
    C. Document the chain of custody
    D. Ensure evidence is relevant

74. Vickie recently gathered digital evidence and would like to be able to provide future users of that evidence with the ability to verify nonrepudiation. How can she provide this?

    A. Digitally sign the evidence
    B. Encrypt the evidence
    C. Generate a checksum from the evidence
    D. Generate a hash value from the evidence

75. Helen is concerned about eavesdropping on a network that she manages. If a user on the network accesses only HTTPS sites, what information would an eavesdropper be able to determine about the sites that the user visits?

    A. IP addresses only
    B. IP addresses and site domains
    C. IP addresses, site domains, and site content
    D. An eavesdropper would not be able to gather any of this information

76. Wayne was called to visit the workstation of a user who believes that an attacker is remotely controlling his computer. Which one of the following evidence gathering techniques would best document what is appearing on the user's screen?

   A. Witness interview
   B. Operating system logs
   C. Screen capture
   D. CCTV

77. Randi is conducting a penetration test on behalf of one of his organization's clients and is using the Internet to gather email addresses of employees at the client organization. What phase of the Cyber Kill Chain includes Randi's activity?

   A. Actions on Objectives
   B. Delivery
   C. Reconnaissance
   D. Weaponization

78. Which one of the following groups is not normally part of an organization's cybersecurity incident response team?

   A. Cybersecurity experts
   B. Law enforcement
   C. Management
   D. Technical subject matter experts

79. Steven is conducting a forensic investigation and believes that a hard drive may contain critical evidence. Which one of the following statements correctly describes how Steven should analyze this evidence?

   A. Steven should not attempt to make a forensic image because it may tamper with the evidence.
   B. Steven should make a forensic image of the drive, lock away the image, and conduct analysis on the original.
   C. Steven should make a forensic image of the drive, lock away the original, and conduct analysis on the image.
   D. Steven should create two forensic images, one for storage and one for analysis, and return the original drive to the user immediately.

80. Which one of the following statements about modern implementations of syslog is incorrect?

   A. The syslog-ng daemon is newer than the rsyslog daemon
   B. The rsyslog daemon does not support encryption
   C. The syslog-ng daemon only supports UDP, not TCP
   D. The rsyslog daemon limits message sizes to 1,024 characters

81. What command was used to generate the output below?

```
1  192.168.1.1 (192.168.1.1)  5.962 ms  4.730 ms  4.017 ms
2  10.0.0.1 (10.0.0.1)  4.638 ms  5.687 ms  8.768 ms
3  96.120.26.197 (96.120.26.197)  16.062 ms  22.077 ms  16.983 ms
4  96.110.154.45 (96.110.154.45)  14.532 ms  18.488 ms  15.994 ms
5  96.108.35.202 (96.108.35.202)  13.439 ms  24.754 ms  13.422 ms
6  50-235-119-214-static.hfc.comcastbusiness.net (50.235.119.214)  14.686 ms  1
3.039 ms  12.288 ms
7  129.74.248.68 (129.74.248.68)  13.286 ms  22.657 ms  22.851 ms
8  172.21.255.130 (172.21.255.130)  13.593 ms  15.546 ms  15.192 ms
9  172.21.0.138 (172.21.0.138)  14.899 ms  15.377 ms  17.018 ms
```

A. ifconfig
B. ping
C. netstat
D. traceroute

82. Which one of the following is the biggest disadvantage to relying upon witness interviews during a forensic investigation?

A. Witness testimony is not admissible in civil court.
B. Witnesses usually want to deceive the interviewer.
C. Witnesses interviews are costly.
D. Witnesses have unreliable memories.

83. Gavin has been tasked with collecting several types of forensic information from a system involved in a security incident. Which one of the choices below lists the preferred order in which he should collect this evidence, from first to last?

A. Virtual memory, RAM, SSD, backups
B. RAM, virtual memory, SSD, backups
C. RAM, virtual memory, backups, SSD
D. Virtual memory, RAM, backups, SSD

84. What type of information is shown on the graph below?

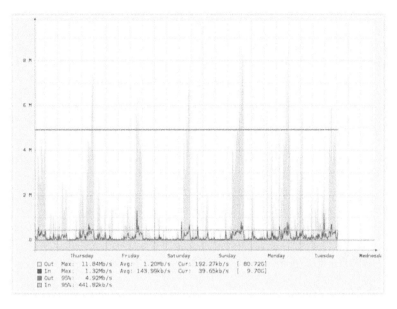

A. Bandwidth consumption
B. CPU consumption
C. Memory consumption
D. Storage consumption

85. Which one of the following sources of evidence contains the least volatile information?

A. Archival media
B. Memory contents
C. Files stored on disk
D. ARP tables

86. Matthew is reviewing the web server logs shown below. What type of attack should he suspect after reviewing them?

```
3.227.24.236 - - [27/Apr/2020:10:05:16 -0400] "GET / HTTP/1.1" 200 45770 "-" "Python-urllib/2.7"
45.143.220.144 - - [27/Apr/2020:10:05:20 -0400] "GET / HTTP/1.1" 301 - "-" "-"
69.162.124.231 - - [27/Apr/2020:10:05:38 -0400] "GET / HTTP/1.1" 200 11222 "http://mike.chapple.org" "M
ozilla/5.0+(compatible; UptimeRobot/2.0; http://www.uptimerobot.com/)"
36.250.185.216 - - [27/Apr/2020:10:07:31 -0400] "GET /endpoint-threat-detection-for-dummies/ HTTP/1.1"
200 7959 "-" "Mozilla/5.0 (Windows NT 6.1; Trident/7.0; rv:11.0) like Gecko"
36.250.185.216 - - [27/Apr/2020:10:07:36 -0400] "GET /endpoint-threat-detection-for-dummies/ HTTP/1.1"
200 7959 "-" "Mozilla/5.0 (Windows NT 6.1; Trident/7.0; rv:11.0) like Gecko"
69.162.124.231 - - [27/Apr/2020:10:08:30 -0400] "GET /wp-admin HTTP/1.1" 301 241 "http://mike.chapple.o
rg/wp-admin" "Mozilla/5.0+(compatible; UptimeRobot/2.0; http://www.uptimerobot.com/)"
69.162.124.231 - - [27/Apr/2020:10:08:30 -0400] "GET /wp-admin/ HTTP/1.1" 302 - "http://mike.chapple.or
g/wp-admin" "Mozilla/5.0+(compatible; UptimeRobot/2.0; http://www.uptimerobot.com/)"
```

A. Brute force attack
B. Directory traversal attack
C. File inclusion attack
D. There is no indication of attack in this log file

87. After running a vulnerability scan, Dave discovers the vulnerability shown below on one of his organization's web servers. Who would be in the best position to correct this vulnerability?

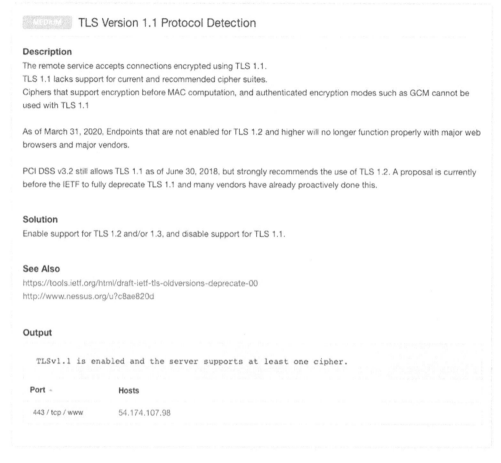

A. Database server administrator
B. Network engineer
C. Web application developer
D. Web server administrator

88. Frank is collecting digital evidence and would like to use a technical control that would allow him to conclusively demonstrate that the evidence he later presents in court is identical to the evidence he collected. Which one of the following controls would best meet this requirement?

A. Digital certificates
B. Hashing
C. Write blocking
D. Evidence logs

89. Brynn is conducting a forensic analysis of a network switch and would like to obtain a copy of the switch's operating system. Where would she most likely find this data?

    A. Backups
    B. Firmware
    C. Hard disk
    D. RAM

90. Which one of the following commands, when used in its default configuration, will display the last ten lines of a specified log file?

    A. cat
    B. grep
    C. head
    D. tail

91. Roger is wrapping up an incident response effort. The business is now functioning normally again and affected systems and data are restored. What activity should come next in the process?

    A. Containment
    B. Recovery
    C. Eradication
    D. Lessons learned

92. Kim is reviewing the logs on a Linux server that she administers and finds the records shown below. What conclusion should she draw from these logs?

```
Apr 27 09:15:17 ip-172-30-0-80 sshd[3420]: Received disconnect from 107.161.172.118 port 47126:11: Bye Bye [preauth]
Apr 27 09:15:17 ip-172-30-0-80 sshd[3420]: Disconnected from 107.161.172.118 port 47126 [preauth]
Apr 27 09:15:18 ip-172-30-0-80 sshd[3416]: Invalid user bsnl from 122.51.255.33 port 11880
Apr 27 09:15:18 ip-172-30-0-80 sshd[3416]: input_userauth_request: invalid user bsnl [preauth]
Apr 27 09:15:18 ip-172-30-0-80 sshd[3416]: Received disconnect from 122.51.255.33 port 11880:11: Bye Bye [preauth]
Apr 27 09:15:18 ip-172-30-0-80 sshd[3416]: Disconnected from 122.51.255.33 port 11880 [preauth]
Apr 27 09:16:18 ip-172-30-0-80 sshd[3422]: Received disconnect from 222.186.175.23 port 22679:11:  [preauth]
Apr 27 09:16:18 ip-172-30-0-80 sshd[3422]: Disconnected from 222.186.175.23 port 22679 [preauth]
Apr 27 09:18:13 ip-172-30-0-80 sshd[3433]: Received disconnect from 188.131.211.207 port 49658:11: Bye Bye [preauth]
Apr 27 09:18:13 ip-172-30-0-80 sshd[3433]: Disconnected from 188.131.211.207 port 49658 [preauth]
Apr 27 09:19:33 ip-172-30-0-80 sshd[3442]: Invalid user ubuntu from 47.17.177.110 port 56998
Apr 27 09:19:33 ip-172-30-0-80 sshd[3442]: input_userauth_request: invalid user ubuntu [preauth]
Apr 27 09:19:33 ip-172-30-0-80 sshd[3442]: Received disconnect from 47.17.177.110 port 56998:11: Bye Bye [preauth]
Apr 27 09:19:33 ip-172-30-0-80 sshd[3442]: Disconnected from 47.17.177.110 port 56998 [preauth]
Apr 27 09:20:37 ip-172-30-0-80 sshd[3448]: Invalid user lei from 152.136.159.231 port 39444
Apr 27 09:20:37 ip-172-30-0-80 sshd[3448]: input_userauth_request: invalid user lei [preauth]
Apr 27 09:20:37 ip-172-30-0-80 sshd[3448]: Received disconnect from 152.136.159.231 port 39444:11: Bye Bye [preauth]
Apr 27 09:20:37 ip-172-30-0-80 sshd[3448]: Disconnected from 152.136.159.231 port 39444 [preauth]
Apr 27 09:20:45 ip-172-30-0-80 sshd[3450]: Received disconnect from 89.154.4.249 port 46680:11: Bye Bye [preauth]
Apr 27 09:20:45 ip-172-30-0-80 sshd[3450]: Disconnected from 89.154.4.249 port 46680 [preauth]
Apr 27 09:21:59 ip-172-30-0-80 sshd[3466]: Received disconnect from 222.186.175.23 port 53192:11:  [preauth]
Apr 27 09:21:59 ip-172-30-0-80 sshd[3466]: Disconnected from 222.186.175.23 port 53192 [preauth]
Apr 27 09:22:13 ip-172-30-0-80 sshd[3468]: Received disconnect from 222.186.52.131 port 39536:11:  [preauth]
Apr 27 09:22:13 ip-172-30-0-80 sshd[3468]: Disconnected from 222.186.52.131 port 39536 [preauth]
Apr 27 09:23:05 ip-172-30-0-80 sshd[3470]: Invalid user cortex from 139.59.60.220 port 47998
Apr 27 09:23:05 ip-172-30-0-80 sshd[3470]: input_userauth_request: invalid user cortex [preauth]
Apr 27 09:23:05 ip-172-30-0-80 sshd[3470]: Received disconnect from 139.59.60.220 port 47998:11: Bye Bye [preauth]
Apr 27 09:23:05 ip-172-30-0-80 sshd[3470]: Disconnected from 139.59.60.220 port 47998 [preauth]
Apr 27 09:23:55 ip-172-30-0-80 sshd[3480]: Invalid user zy from 111.229.226.212 port 32884
Apr 27 09:23:55 ip-172-30-0-80 sshd[3480]: input_userauth_request: invalid user zy [preauth]
Apr 27 09:23:55 ip-172-30-0-80 sshd[3480]: Received disconnect from 111.229.226.212 port 32884:11: Bye Bye [preauth]
```

A. The server was the victim of a successful SSH attack
B. The server was targeted with an unsuccessful SSH decryption attack
C. The server was targeted with an unsuccessful SSH brute force attack
D. These logs represent normal activity that was likely authorized

93. Refer to the Wireshark packet capture shown below. Which one of the following statements is correct about this traffic?

No.	Time	Source	Destination	Protocol	Length	Info
45	2.098014	192.168.1.5	3.84.33.224	TCP	78	57927 → 22 [SYN] Seq=0 Win=65535 Len=0 MSS=…
46	2.141097	3.84.33.224	192.168.1.5	TCP	74	22 → 57927 [SYN, ACK] Seq=0 Ack=1 Win=26847…
47	2.141224	192.168.1.5	3.84.33.224	TCP	66	57927 → 22 [ACK] Seq=1 Ack=1 Win=131712 Len…
48	2.142828	192.168.1.5	3.84.33.224	SSH…	87	Client: Protocol (SSH-2.0-OpenSSH_7.9)
49	2.183533	3.84.33.224	192.168.1.5	TCP	66	22 → 57927 [ACK] Seq=1 Ack=22 Win=26880 Len…
50	2.189644	3.84.33.224	192.168.1.5	SSH…	87	Server: Protocol (SSH-2.0-OpenSSH_7.4)
51	2.189762	192.168.1.5	3.84.33.224	TCP	66	57927 → 22 [ACK] Seq=22 Ack=22 Win=131712 L…
52	2.191623	192.168.1.5	3.84.33.224	SSH…	14…	Client: Key Exchange Init
59	2.236633	3.84.33.224	192.168.1.5	SSH…	13…	Server: Key Exchange Init
60	2.236714	192.168.1.5	3.84.33.224	TCP	66	57927 → 22 [ACK] Seq=1414 Ack=1302 Win=1304…
65	2.276896	3.84.33.224	192.168.1.5	TCP	66	22 → 57927 [ACK] Seq=1302 Ack=1414 Win=2969…
66	2.277003	192.168.1.5	3.84.33.224	SSH…	114	Client: Diffie-Hellman Key Exchange Init
67	2.321874	3.84.33.224	192.168.1.5	TCP	66	22 → 57927 [ACK] Seq=1302 Ack=1462 Win=2969…
68	2.326641	3.84.33.224	192.168.1.5	SSH…	430	Server: Diffie-Hellman Key Exchange Reply, …
69	2.326746	192.168.1.5	3.84.33.224	TCP	66	57927 → 22 [ACK] Seq=1462 Ack=1666 Win=1306…
70	2.333398	192.168.1.5	3.84.33.224	SSH…	82	Client: New Keys
71	2.421936	3.84.33.224	192.168.1.5	TCP	66	22 → 57927 [ACK] Seq=1666 Ack=1478 Win=2969…
72	2.422035	192.168.1.5	3.84.33.224	SSH…	110	Client: Encrypted packet (len=44)
73	2.468728	3.84.33.224	192.168.1.5	TCP	66	22 → 57927 [ACK] Seq=1666 Ack=1522 Win=2969…
74	2.468732	3.84.33.224	192.168.1.5	SSH…	110	Server: Encrypted packet (len=44)
75	2.468813	192.168.1.5	3.84.33.224	TCP	66	57927 → 22 [ACK] Seq=1522 Ack=1710 Win=1310…
76	2.468908	192.168.1.5	3.84.33.224	SSH…	134	Client: Encrypted packet (len=68)
77	2.522539	3.84.33.224	192.168.1.5	SSH…	142	Server: Encrypted packet (len=76)
78	2.522601	192.168.1.5	3.84.33.224	TCP	66	57927 → 22 [ACK] Seq=1590 Ack=1786 Win=1309…
79	2.532169	192.168.1.5	3.84.33.224	SSH…	718	Client: Encrypted packet (len=652)
80	2.614163	3.84.33.224	192.168.1.5	SSH…	94	Server: Encrypted packet (len=28)
81	2.614275	192.168.1.5	3.84.33.224	TCP	66	57927 → 22 [ACK] Seq=2242 Ack=1814 Win=1310…
82	2.614750	192.168.1.5	3.84.33.224	SSH…	178	Client: Encrypted packet (len=112)
83	2.652857	3.84.33.224	192.168.1.5	SSH…	566	Server: Encrypted packet (len=500)

A. It is a successful SSH connection attempt to the server at 3.84.33.224
B. It is an unsuccessful SSH connection attempt to the server at 3.84.33.224
C. It is a successful SSH connection attempt to the server at 192.168.1.5
D. It is an unsuccessful SSH connection attempt to the server at 192.168.1.5

94. Which one of the following actions would not normally occur during the recovery phase of an incident response effort?

A. Remediate vulnerabilities
B. Restore from backups
C. Shutting down systems
D. Modify firewall rules

95. Gina is reviewing the header information attached to an email message that was used in a phishing scam. She retrieved this header information from her own organization's email server. Which one of the following pieces of information in the header is the most reliable?

A. Sender's name
B. Sender's email address
C. IP address of the system originating the message
D. IP address of the system that forwarded the message to her organization's email server

96. Review the firewall ruleset shown below. If a system at 10.18.100.3 attempts to access the Microsoft SQL Server database on the server at 192.168.10.5, what would be the end result?

Rule	Source IP	Source Port	Dest IP	Dest Port	Action
1	any	any	192.168.10.5	1443	allow
2	any	any	192.168.10.6	1521	allow
3	10.18.100.3	any	192.168.10.6	22	deny
4	any	any	any	any	deny

A. The traffic will be allowed by rule 1
B. The traffic will be allowed by rule 2
C. The traffic will be blocked by rule 3
D. The traffic will be blocked by rule 4

97. After an incident responder identifies that a security incident is in progress, what is the next step in the incident response process?

A. Eradication
B. Containment
C. Recovery
D. Preparation

98. Alyssa recently completed an incident investigation and is conducting the cleanup effort before closing out the incident. She has a large quantity of evidence collected during the incident and wishes to use secure disposal techniques to destroy it. When should she do so?

A. Alyssa should securely destroy the files now, as the incident is closed
B. Alyssa should await instructions from law enforcement
C. Alyssa should follow the instructions in her organization's retention policy
D. Alyssa should preserve the files indefinitely

99. What type of information is classified in the MITRE ATT&CK framework?

A. Adversary tactics
B. Indicators of compromise
C. Threat actors
D. Threat vectors

100. Henry would like to capture network packets from the command line. What command would best meet his needs?

A. dd
B. FTK
C. tcpdump
D. Wireshark

Domain 4 Answers and Explanations

1. **C.** The netstat command lists all of the active network connections on a system as well as the status of ports that are listening for requests. The tcpdump command captures network traffic and would see active network connections but does not identify ports that are listening without an active connection. The pstools comand is used to find infomration about processes running on a system but does not provide network port or version information. The netcat command is used to send information via a network pipe.

2. **D.** This is an informational report, merely telling the user that the scanned system is running a web server. It does not indicate any vulnerability requiring remediation.

3. **A.** This file is open only to read and write access by the file owner, mchapple. The chmod command can be used to alter these permissions to allow access by members of the staff group or other system users.

4. **D.** Addresses in the range 169.254.0.0/16 are assigned by the Automatic Private IP Assignment (APIPA) protocol when a system is unable to receive an address via other means. An address received via DHCP or static assignment would override this address. Active Directory preferred address is not a valid IP address assignment mechanism.

5. **A.** This network traffic shows two unsuccessful connection attempts on ports 80 (HTTP) and 443 (HTTPS) and a successful connection attempt on port 22 (SSH). Therefore, we can conclude that the server is running the SSH service. However, we do not have enough information to draw any conclusions about HTTP or HTTPS, as the traffic may be blocked by a firewall rule.

6. **A.** The arp command is capable of accessing Address Resolution Protocol (ARP) information to display the Ethernet (MAC) addresses of systems visible on the local network.

7. **D.** By default, the traceroute command uses UDP connections. This is different from the ping command, which uses ICMP by default.

8. **B.** SIEM platforms are responsible for collecting, aggregating, and correlating log records and using them to identify potential security events and trends. They do not block traffic, as they are a reporting and analysis tool.

9. **C.** Tabletop exercises are informal sessions that gather team members to discuss how they would respond in a given scenario. Walkthroughs are instructional sessions designed to familiarize team members with their roles and are not structured around a scenario. Activations (full or partial) only occur in response to an actual incident.

10. **B.** The ping command transmits an ICMP Echo Request message to the target system, which may then respond with an ICMP Echo Reply message.

11. **B.** To alter the false positive rate, Alex should adjust the SIEM sensitivity. Increasing the sensitivity of the SIEM reduces the threshold for an alert and would increase the number of false positives. Decreasing the sensitivity of the SIEM would increase the threshold for an alert and decrease the

number of false positives. Adjusting the SIEM capacity would adjust the amount of information that it can process and store, rather than changing the false positive rate.

12. **B.** The two possible methods for invalidating a digital certificate are adding it to a certificate revocation list (CRL) or using the online certificate status protocol (OCSP). Of these two methods, the OCSP is immediate, while using a CRL has a time delay. Changing the keys associated with a certificate would not invalidate the certificate, as an imposter would still be able to use the certificate with the old keys.

13. **A.** Mail eXchanger (MX) records contain information about the SMTP servers associated with a domain. A records are standard address mapping records. Canonical name (CNAME) records are used to create aliases for DNS names. Name Server (NS) records are used to identify DNS servers for a domain.

14. **B.** NXlog is a log management tool available in a free, open-source edition that would meet Paul's needs. Syslog is a format used to exchange log messages and not a log aggregation solution. Journalctl is a command-line utility used to view system logs. Wireshark is a protocol analyzer used to sniff network traffic.

15. **D.** Mobile device management (MDM) solutions have deep access to mobile devices and are capable of collecting any information available on the device. This may include call history, user identity, geographic location, and application data. The specific capabilities will depend upon the MDM solution used.

16. **D.** The web application firewall is the device that most likely blocked the attack and would contain detailed information about the attack. If the WAF blocked the attack, records would not appear in the logs of the web server or the database server or the host firewalls on any devices.

17. **C.** The mean time to detection (MTTD) is the typical time taken to detect a security incident. The mean time to repair (MTTR) and mean time between failures (MTBF) are business continuity metrics. MITRE is a security consulting firm and government think tank.

18. **A.** The business impact assessment (BIA) stage of the disaster recovery planning process assesses services used by the organization and prioritizes their recovery based upon their potential impact on the business.

19. **C.** The Network Time Protocol (NTP) performs clock synchronization across devices. The Domain Name Service performs translations between domain names and IP addresses. The Dynamic Host Configuration Protocol (DHCP) provides IP addresses to systems. The Border Gateway Protocol (BGP) is used to configure network routing.

20. **B.** The hping command may be used to send custom-crafted packets to a remote destination. The ping and pathing commands can generate packets but do not allow full customization. They only allow some configuration. The tcpdump command is used to capture network traffic.

21. **D.** This script uses the gethostbyaddr() command to look up the host names for each IP address in the range 192.168.1.0 through 192.168.1.255. That is equivalent to the 192.168.1.0/24 subnet.

22. **D.** Dennis should consult with his manager to determine appropriate next steps. He should not confront the user directly. While his manager may direct him to block the websites, this is a management decision that Dennis should not take himself.

23. **B.** Segmentation is a term used to describe placing systems onto specialized subnets, rather than having them all on a larger network. Isolation disconnects a system from all other networked devices. Refactoring and shimming are terms related to device drivers and not network structure.

24. **B.** NetFlow records only contain summary information about network connections. They do not contain the actual content, or payload, from the connection. Think of NetFlow as similar to a telephone bill. You get a record of communications, but not the actual communications themselves.

25. **C.** The IP address for this machine is shown in the record for the Ethernet interface en0. It is 10.36.23.22. The address 10.36.23.255 is the broadcast address associated with that adapter and not the IP address of the machine. 127.0.0.1 is the local loopback address for any system. 98:e0:d9:87:8a:73 is the MAC address for the en0 interface and not an IP address.

26. **D.** The key fact to note here is the use of the Session Initiation Protocol (SIP). SIP is used in Voice over Internet Protocol (VoIP) digital telephony. Therefore, this traffic is most likely related to VoIP calls.

27. **D.** One of the keys to answering this question is understanding the difference between interviews and interrogations. In an interview, Tom may ask difficult questions, but should do so in a non-confrontational manner. If Tom gets more aggressive, he crosses the line from interview to interrogation. Tom should always consult with Human Resources before involving employees in an investigation, but he does not need to advise employees of their rights because he is not a law enforcement officer.

28. **D.** Both the tcpdump and Wireshark utilities can be used to capture network traffic. Of those two, only tcpdump is a command-line utility. Wireshark uses a graphical interface. Nmap is a network port scanner and netcat is used to redirect data to a network connection. Neither nmap nor netcat can capture traffic.

29. **D.** While rule 3 might seem to apply to this traffic at first glance, careful inspection of the rule reveals that it is for the server at 192.168.10.6, not 192.168.10.5. Therefore, there is no rule governing the port 22 SSH connection in this scenario, so the implicit deny rule (rule 4) applies.

30. **A.** Rule 1 allows any system to access the server at 10.18.1.4 over a standard HTTP connection on port 80.

31. **A.** Metasploit is an exploitation framework commonly used in penetration testing. Cain & Abel is a password cracking utility. Nessus is a vulnerability scanner. Sysinternals is a set of Windows system administration tools.

32. **C.** The Diamond Model is an approach to intrusion analysis that seeks out connections between adversaries, infrastructure, capabilities, and victims. It uses diagrams similar to the one shown in this question to help analysts identify missing components of an attack investigation.

33. **B.** The end of a TCP connection may occur in two different ways. The first is a three-way handshake using three sequential packets with the FIN, FIN/ACK, and ACK flags set, respectively. This sequence

does not occur in the packet capture. The second way is an abrupt termination by one system, indicated by a single packet with the RST flag set. This occurs in lines 217 and 218.

34. **A.** The -Pn flag disables the host discovery step and scans every specified system. The -PS flag conducts a TCP SYN ping, while the -PA flag conducts a TCP ACK ping. The -PU flag conducts a UDP ping.

35. **D.** Lessons learned sessions are conducted during the final stage of the incident response process, post-incident activities.

36. **D.** Purple teaming efforts seek to learn from the experiences of the exercise. All exercise participants, including red, white, and blue team members, should participate in the purple teaming session.

37. **C.** Eric can use a protocol analyzer to sniff network traffic and search the contents for unencrypted sensitive information. A data loss prevention (DLP) solution could automate this work, but that is not one of the options available to Eric.

38. **A.** The standard defined by the courts for litigation holds is that an organization must issue one as soon as they "reasonably anticipate" litigation.

39. **C.** Disaster recovery plans guide work during all stages of a disaster, from the initial response through the restoration of normal activity. The plan remains active until the organization is restored to its normal operating environment.

40. **D.** Hosts on an internal network should never see port scans coming from external networks. The fact that these packets are reaching the host indicates that the network perimeter firewall is improperly configured.

41. **D.** The best way to restrict website traffic is through the use of URL and content filtering. IP-based restrictions are unreliable because sites may change IP addresses or use multiple IP addresses, making it difficult to maintain a current block list. Data loss prevention (DLP) systems do not filter web traffic. It is possible to use an intrusion prevention system (IPS) to filter web traffic, but this is not as simple and reliable as a dedicated URL/content filtering solution.

42. **D.** A privilege escalation attack takes place against the operating system and information relevant to this attack is most likely found in the operating system logs. It is unlikely that the database application itself would be involved, so that application's logs would not likely contain relevant information. The user has authorized access to the system, so the firewall and IDS logs would simply show that authorized access taking place.

43. **D.** The nmap tool performs network mapping and is the ideal way for Justin to develop a list of systems providing network services. Openssl is an encryption tool that would not help Justin meet his goal. Netcat lists the open connections and listening services on a single system but does not do this across a network. The sqlmap tool is used to scan database applications for vulnerabilities.

44. **C.** The four steps of the NIST Incident Response process, in order, are: Preparation, Detection & Analysis, Containment, Eradication & Recovery, and Post-Incident Activities.

45. **C.** The page file (pagefile.sys) is used to store the contents of virtual memory and is useful when conducting forensic analysis. The hibernation file (hiberfil.sys) is used to store the contents of memory when the system hibernates. The swap file (swapfile.sys) is used for process swapping data.

46. **B.** The nslookup and dig utilities both perform domain name resolution, b ut dig is not included on Windows systems by default and must be manually installed. Nbtstat is used for NetBIOS name lookups while ARP is used for MAC address lookups.

47. **D.** UDP port 53 is used by the Domain Name Service (DNS). The attack described in this scenario is indicative of an amplification attack, where the DNS requests are spoofed with a false source address belonging to the attack victim. This causes the DNS server to flood the victim with traffic. While this attack does use IP spoofing to insert a false source address, it is not a DNS spoofing attack because no DNS information is tampered with during the attack.

48. **A.** At this point, Carmen has already collected the evidence, so changing the system clocks (manually or through NTP) would have no effect. Carmen should never modify evidence that has already been collected, so her best course of action is to record the time offsets and make the adjustments in her analysis.

49. **D.** An organization is required to issue a legal hold as soon as they have reason to believe that they may have evidence that will be used in a legal proceeding.

50. **B.** All of these capabilities are options in advanced security information and event management (SIEM) solutions. However, only security orchestration, automation, and response (SOAR) is focused on automating the incident response workflow.

51. **D.** Tags are the best approach here because Frank may apply multiple tags to the same evidence. Using file or folder names would require placing multiple copies of the evidence in different files or folders and would be difficult to manage. Using printouts of the evidence is an unnecessary burden.

52. **A.** An analyst capturing a forensic image should use all of the tools listed here. However, the write blocker is the only tool specifically designed to preserve the original evidence by preventing the system creating the image from accidentally altering the original drive.

53. **A.** A DLP rule with an action of "alert" merely notifies system administrators of rule violations. Blocking, quarantining, and encrypting rules alter that traffic and, therefore, have greater potential to disrupt normal business activity.

54. **D.** The use of cloud services is complicated from a regulatory perspective. It is possible that each of the countries involved has some jurisdiction over the data. These include the country where the cloud provider has its data centers, the country where the customer resides, and the home country of Jodie's company.

55. **D.** The first phase in the NIST incident response process is preparation, this is followed by the detection and analysis phase, The final two phases are containment, eradication, & recovery and post-incident activity.

56. **A.** The curl command is used to retrieve files from remote URLs and may be used to store those files on the local system. The FTP command is used to retrieve files from an FTP server, not a remote web URL. The tcpdump and Wireshark utilities are used to capture network traffic.

57. **D.** Expert witness evidence is best described as testimonial evidence, where a witness is making statements about their own observations and experience. The scenario does not specify that Alison will be introducing any documents or tangible objects herself. Hearsay would only apply if Alison makes statements about what other people said to her, which is also not described in the scenario.

58. **A.** Data retention policies govern the maintenance and disposal of records and normally reference retention schedules that specify the minimum and maximum retention periods for different categories of information.

59. **C.** Isolating affected systems is one of the first steps toward containing an incident. It occurs after the incident is detected during the containment, eradication, and recovery phase of incident response.

60. **A.** The commonly used NetFlow standard is a proprietary Cisco standard. The Internet Protocol Flow Information Export (IPFIX) standard is an open alternative made available by the Internet Engineering Task Force (IETF).

61. **A.** Wireless access points are generally not configured to log network traffic. They typically record only diagnostic information. The other data sources are far more likely to contain network traffic records.

62. **B.** In this packet capture, we see an unencrypted HTTP connection from 192.168.1.5 to 10.0.0.1. Therefore, we can conclude that the server at 10.0.0.1 supports unencrypted connections and should most likely be upgraded to only support HTTPS connections. We cannot draw any conclusions about the connections allowed to 192.168.1.5. We also can't draw any conclusions about what encryption protocol(s) 10.0.0.1 might support.

63. **B.** The stages of the Cyber Kill Chain are reconnaissance, weaponization, delivery, exploitation, installation, command-and-control, and actions on objectives. The exploitation stage is where the attacker exploits a vulnerability to execute code on the victim's system. That is the stage where a buffer overflow attack gains control of a system.

64. **C.** The incident response team should be overseen by an executive with authority and responsibility for cybersecurity activities. Of the choices presented, the Chief Information Security Officer (CISO) is the individual who most directly meets these requirements.

65. **A.** The journalctl command is used to view the contents of the system journal, which is stored in memory. Syslogd is the daemon used to write syslog entries to disk. Sysview and journalview are not Linux commands.

66. **B.** This vulnerability indicates that the attacker may be able to obtain debugging information from the server. The primary risk involved is that an attacker may be able to retrieve information about the web server. The attacker could use this information in another attack, but the direct risk posed here is one of information disclosure.

67. **B.** The full interruption test has the potential to disrupt all of the business activities of an organization by moving processing to the alternate facility. A parallel test also activates the alternate facility but does not switch over operations to that facility. A structured walkthrough gathers everyone together to discuss an exercise in a tabletop format. A checklist review is the least disruptive test because people simply review their disaster recovery checklists on their own time.

68. **B.** Infrastructure as a service (IaaS) environments provide analysts with access to the operating system, allowing deeper forensic analysis than other cloud platforms that operate higher in the stack.

69. **B.** This network traffic would be allowed by rule 2, which authorized any system to connect to 10.18.1.4 using port 443 (HTTPS). Rule 3, which attempts to block access for requests from 10.18.100.3 is a shadowed rule that would never trigger because it is positioned beneath a more general rule that allows access.

70. **B.** Litigation holds occur quite often, but very few of them actually move to the production phase. Attorneys should review documents for privilege prior to production, but it would be unnecessarily costly and time-consuming to do this during the collection phase. System administrators must disable automatic deletion of logs or other materials subject to a litigation hold. It is the responsibility of all employees, not just attorneys, to preserve evidence when a litigation hold is in place.

71. **D.** The preservation, collection, and analysis phases of eDiscovery all take place internally and do not involve sharing evidence with opposing parties. Evidence is not shared until the production phase.

72. **D.** The routers, firewalls, and other network devices that generate network flow records are known as flow exporters. Flow exporters send records to flow collectors, which may then be reviewed by cybersecurity analysts using a flow analyzer.

73. **C.** While all of these goals are important for those handling forensic evidence, the primary purpose of an evidence log is to document the chain of custody from the time of collection to the time of use.

74. **A.** Vickie can provide nonrepudiation by digitally signing the evidence with her private key. Using a hash value or checksum can verify that the evidence was not altered but does not provide nonrepudiation. Encrypting the evidence protects it from unauthorized disclosure and also verifies integrity, but it does not provide nonrepudiation.

75. **A.** HTTPS traffic is protected by Transport Layer Security (TLS). An eavesdropper would be able to determine the IP addresses of sites visited by the user but would not be able to see any information from inside the connection, such as the site domain or content.

76. **C.** Screen capture technology allows the analyst to capture what is appearing on a user's screen directly and is a good evidence source. Operating system logs may provide information about the activity but they will not directly document what the user saw. Witness interviews may be useful, but the user's memory is not as reliable as a screen capture. It is unlikely that a CCTV camera would be positioned in such a manner as to capture activity on a user's screen.

77. **C.** Harvesting email addresses from the Internet is passive reconnaissance that takes place during the early stages of a penetration test.

78. **B.** The incident response team normally includes a wide range of internal experts, including those from cybersecurity and other technical disciplines. It also includes management representation. The team would not normally include outside organizations, such as representatives of law enforcement, although it may interact with those groups through a liaison function.

79. **C.** In order to ensure preservation of evidence, Steven should make a forensic image of the original drive and lock the original away for safekeeping. He should then perform his analysis on the image.

If the end user needs the drive back immediately, Steven should provide the user with another drive made from the image and should retain the original drive as evidence.

80. **A.** Modern implementations of syslog avoid many of the limitations of the original protocol. Both rsyslog and syslog-ng support TCP communications and encryption. They are also not subject to the 1,024-character limit of the original protocol. The rsyslog daemon (2004) is, however, newer than syslog-ng (1998).

81. **D.** This output shows the network path between two hosts. The traceroute (or tracert on Windows) command performs this task.

82. **D.** Generally speaking, witnesses are not trying to deceive the interviewer unless they are accused of wrongdoing. They do generally want to assist, but suffer from unreliable memories. Interviews are generally not expensive to conduct and are definitely admissible in court.

83. **B.** The order of volatility says that you should first collect the evidence most likely to be destroyed first. The proper ordering of these evidence sources in order of volatility is RAM first, as the contents of RAM are deleted when the system is turned off. The next step is to collect the virtual memory paging file, as this file is frequently modified. Next, Gavin should collect other files stored on the SSD disk. Backups are the least volatile item and they can be collected last.

84. **A.** The key fact here is that the unit of measure is in megabytes per section (Mb/s). This is a unit of measuring network traffic and this chart, therefore, shows network bandwidth consumption.

85. **A.** Volatile information is information that is likely to be altered or lost as time passes. Archival media is designed for long-term storage and is the least volatile data source listed here. ARP tables in a router and the contents of system memory may change frequently and are the most volatile. Files stored on disk fall in between these two extremes.

86. **D.** These log entries represent normal access to a web server. There is no indication in these records of any malicious activity.

87. **D.** This vulnerability indicates that the web server is supporting an outdated version of TLS. This is a server configuration issue and would best be corrected by the server administrator. Web application developers generally would not have access to this type of server configuration even if their applications are deployed on the server. There is no reason to believe that a network engineer or database administrator would have any access to the server.

88. **B.** If Frank takes a hash of the evidence as he collects it, he may then take a hash at a later date. If the two hashes match, he can demonstrate that the evidence was not altered. A write blocker may prevent tampering but it does not provide a means for Frank to demonstrate the integrity of the evidence.

89. **B.** Most network devices keep their operating system in firmware, where it can be stored in a rapidly accessible, yet non-volatile form. Network switches do not normally have hard disks and would not keep the operating system in volatile RAM storage.

90. **D.** The tail command is used to display the last lines of a file. By default, it displays ten lines, although this value is configurable. It is quite useful when attempting to view the most recent records in a log file. The head command is used to display the first lines of a file. The grep command is used to search a file and the cat command is used to display an entire file, by default.

91. **D.** At the conclusion of an incident response, the organization should conduct a thorough lessons learned designed to evaluate the response and identify opportunities for improvement.

92. **C.** These log files show repeated, unsuccessful attempts to log onto the server via SSH using different usernames. There are no successful attempts. This is most likely due to an unsuccessful SSH brute force attack.

93. **A.** We can key in on two packets here to determine the nature of this traffic. The first packet, labeled as number 45 in the capture, is the opening packet of the communication. We can tell this because only the SYN flag is set on the packet. Therefore, the source of this packet (192.168.1.5) is the client and the destination of the packet (3.84.33.224) is the server. We can also tell from the fact that the connection is being made to port 22 on the server that this is an SSH connection. We can then look at packet 47, where we see the completion of the three-way handshake, as identified by the ACK flag. This tells us that the connection was successful. We can also surmise that the user successfully authenticated due to the number of encrypted packets exchanged, but we cannot tell this for certain from the data provided.

94. **C.** According to the NIST incident response guide, shutting down systems would normally occur during the containment phase. In the recovery phase, administrators restore systems to normal operation, confirm that the systems are functioning normally, and (if applicable) remediate vulnerabilities to prevent similar incidents. Recovery may involve such actions as restoring systems from clean backups, rebuilding systems from scratch, replacing compromised files with clean versions, installing patches, changing passwords, and tightening network perimeter security (e.g., firewall rulesets, boundary router access control lists).

95. **D.** When interpreting email headers, analysts must be careful to take most information they contain with a grain of salt. Any information added by servers earlier in the chain usually can't be trusted, as it is open to manipulation. This includes information about the sender (such as their name and email address) as well as any IP addresses of systems earlier in the chain. Analysts can generally trust information added by their own servers, such as the IP address of the system that forwarded the message to the server.

96. **A.** Microsoft SQL Server uses TCP port 1443. Therefore, the connection request described in this scenario matches rule 1 in the rule base and will be allowed.

97. **B.** After identifying an incident, the team should next move into the containment phase where they seek to limit the damage caused by the incident. Containment occurs prior to the eradication and recovery phases. The preparation phase occurs before incident identification.

98. **C.** This is a tricky question, as many of the answers sound reasonable. However, the best answer to this question is that Alyssa should follow the mandates of her organization's retention policy. That policy should, in turn, take factors such as law enforcement interest into account.

99. **A.** The MITRE ATT&CK framework documents common tactics, techniques, and procedures used by advanced persistent threats (APTs). The term is an acronym for Adversarial Tactics, Techniques, and Common Knowledge.

100. **C.** Tcpdump is a command-line packet capture utility. Wireshark is also a packet capture utility, but it is designed for interactive use through a GUI. FTK and dd are forensic utilities used to capture disk images, not network packets.

CHAPTER 5

Governance, Risk, and Compliance

Domain 5 Questions

1. Gwen is crafting a social media policy for her organization and is considering including the following provisions. Which one of these provisions is most likely to be problematic from a legal perspective?

   A. Restricting use of personal social media accounts outside of working hours
   B. Requiring disclosure of company affiliation on social media
   C. Requiring approval of posts sent out via corporate social media accounts
   D. Blocking social media sites at the perimeter firewall

2. Victor's organization is experiencing a rash of misplaced devices. What IT management discipline can help them maintain an accurate inventory?

   A. Configuration management
   B. Asset management
   C. Change management
   D. Firewall management

3. Barry was reviewing his organization's perimeter firewall ruleset and determined that it contains rules that allow unnecessary access. What type of control flaw has Barry discovered?

   A. Corrective
   B. Detective
   C. Deterrent
   D. Preventative

4. Which one of the following combinations of controls introduces control diversity across the major control categories?

   A. Background checks and security training
   B. DLP and IPS
   C. IPS and backups
   D. DLP and background checks

5. Barry's organization follows the Center for Internet Security's benchmarks for Windows Server security. He is working with a developer who insists that a security setting must be changed to allow an application to function properly. What should Barry do next?

   A. Allow the change
   B. Implement a compensating control
   C. Deny the change
   D. Evaluate the change and determine whether it is appropriate

6. Rob recently learned this his organization is not performing backups of critical systems on a routine basis. What type of control gap has Rob identified?

    A. Corrective
    B. Deterrent
    C. Physical
    D. Preventative

7. Which element of the NIST Cybersecurity Framework, shown below, involves the development and implementation of appropriate safeguards to ensure the delivery of critical services?

    A. Identify
    B. Protect
    C. Respond
    D. Recover

8. Which one of the following is not an example of a physical security control?

    A. Exterior lighting
    B. System ACL
    C. Secure equipment enclosures
    D. Faraday cages

9. Jorge is putting a process in place to ensure that the organization reviews intrusion prevention system logs on a regular basis. What category of control is this?

    A. Compensating
    B. Managerial
    C. Operational
    D. Technical

10. Norma is employed by an online retailer that processes credit card payments thousands of times each day. Which one of the following regulations definitely applies to her organization?

    A. PCI DSS
    B. HIPAA
    C. FERPA
    D. Sarbanes-Oxley

11. Brian is designing a security awareness training program for his organization. Which one of the following statements is not true about awareness training best practices?

    A. Users should receive initial training shortly after joining the organization.
    B. Employees in some job categories do not need to receive awareness training.
    C. Awareness training efforts should be customized based upon an individual's role in the organization.
    D. Privileged users should be singled out for focused training efforts.

12. Which set of organizational policies and procedures would best describe the process for moving modified source code into production?

    A. Acceptable use
    B. Asset management
    C. Change management
    D. Data governance

13. Wanda is concerned about the likelihood of privilege creep in her organization. Which one of the following activities is likely to uncover the most comprehensive listing of privilege creep situations which may then be remediated?

    A. Permission auditing
    B. Usage auditing
    C. Policy review
    D. User termination audit

14. Helen recently moved from the marketing department to the sales department and retained the permissions assigned to her previous job, despite the fact that they are no longer necessary. What security principle does this violate?

    A. Security through obscurity
    B. Separation of duties
    C. Two-person control
    D. Least privilege

15. Ty is planning a cybersecurity exercise where the goal of the attacking team will be to gain access to a secret code stored in a text file on a secured server. What type of exercise is he running?

    A. Blue team
    B. Capture the flag
    C. Purple team
    D. Walkthrough

16. During what stage of the account management lifecycle should a user receive his or her first exposure to security awareness training?

    A. Onboarding
    B. Deprovisioning
    C. Renewal
    D. Privilege assignment

17. Ryan is developing a security awareness training program and would like to include information about the person employees should approach if they need to clarify who may access different types of information. What role in an organization has this responsibility?

    A. Privileged user
    B. System owner
    C. Data owner
    D. Executive user

18. Yolanda recently sent a request to a company asking them to delete all personal information collected about her, exercising her "right to be forgotten." What law includes this provision?

    A. FERPA
    B. GDPR
    C. GLBA
    D. HIPAA

19. Which one of the following statements is not true about security awareness programs?

    A. Some categories of employee do not require any security training
    B. System administrators should receive specialized technical training
    C. Awareness training should be customized to a user's role in the organization
    D. Training updates should occur when there are significant new threats

20. Belinda is negotiating with an Internet Service Provider (ISP) on the terms of service they will provide to her organization. Belinda would like the agreement to spell out the specific requirements for the service and include financial penalties if the service does not meet those requirements. What tool would best meet Belinda's needs?

    A. SLA
    B. BPA
    C. ISA
    D. MOU

21. Carla discovered a set of incident response records from six years ago. What should she do with those records?

    A. Leave the records where they are
    B. Maintain the records indefinitely in a secure location
    C. Destroy the records in a secure manner
    D. Consult the organization's data retention policy

22. Which one of the following statements about risk management is true?

    A. Risk acceptance should only be done after careful analysis of other options.
    B. Insurance policies are an example of risk avoidance.
    C. Firewalls and intrusion prevention systems are examples of risk avoidance.
    D. Risk avoidance is always preferable to risk acceptance.

23. Sonia is concerned that users in her organization are connecting to corporate systems over insecure networks and begins a security awareness campaign designed to encourage them to use the VPN. What category of control has Sonia implemented?

    A. Technical
    B. Operational
    C. Physical
    D. Managerial

24. Which ISO standard contains specific guidance on the privacy of personally identifiable information?

    A. ISO 27001
    B. ISO 27002
    C. ISO 27701
    D. ISO 31000

Questions 25 through 28 refer to the following scenario:

Gary is conducting a business impact assessment for his organization. During this assessment, he identifies the risk of a power supply failure in a critical database server. He determines that the power supply is likely to fail once every three years and that it will take 2 days to obtain and install a replacement part.

After consulting with functional experts, Gary determines that the database server is crucial to business functions and would cause considerable disruption if it were down for more than a day. No new transactions would occur during a failure. In the event of a failure, clerks could retrieve the last four hours of transactions from an application log file and use those to recover lost data. Therefore, it would be acceptable to lose four hours of information prior to the failure.

---

25. What is the MTTR in this scenario?

    A. 4 hours
    B. 1 day
    C. 2 days
    D. 3 years

26. What is the MTBF in this scenario?

    A. 4 hours
    B. 1 day
    C. 2 days
    D. 3 years

27. What is the RTO in this scenario?

    A. 4 hours
    B. 1 day
    C. 2 days
    D. 3 years

28. What is the RPO in this scenario?

    A. 4 hours
    B. 1 day
    C. 2 days
    D. 3 years

29. Mary is developing a new risk assessment process for her organization. What category of control does this represent?

    A. Compensating
    B. Managerial
    C. Operational
    D. Technical

30. Under the NIST Cloud Computing Reference Architecture, who is the principal stakeholder for a cloud computing service?

    A. Cloud broker
    B. Cloud carrier
    C. Cloud consumer
    D. Cloud provider

31. Rhonda is preparing a role-based awareness training program and recently developed a module designed to raise awareness among users of wire transfer fraud schemes where the attacker poses as a business leader seeking to transfer money to a foreign account. Of the following audiences, which would be the most likely to need this training?

    A. System administrator
    B. Executive user
    C. Accounts payable clerk
    D. Sales director

32. Tom is conducting an incident response effort and believes that a crime may have been committed against his organization involving the theft of intellectual property. Which one of the following statements best describes Tom's obligation based upon the information available at this point?

    A. Tom must contact federal law enforcement.
    B. Tom must contact local law enforcement.
    C. Tom does not have a specific legal obligation to report the incident to anyone outside the organization.
    D. Tom must notify customers of the breach.

33. During a security assessment, Karen discovers that server cabinets containing sensitive equipment were left unlocked in the data center. What type of control gap has Karen discovered?

    A. Compensating
    B. Corrective
    C. Detective
    D. Physical

34. Scott's company is entering into a joint venture with another organization and he would like to create a document that spells out the relationship between the two firms. Scott would like the agreement to be enforceable in court. What type of document would be best suited for this task?

    A. SLA
    B. BPA
    C. ISA
    D. MOU

35. Brenda is a security analyst and is reviewing the alerts generated by a content filtering system on her corporate network. She notices that one employee has accessed a large number of sports gambling websites. What action should Brenda take next?

    A. Disable the employee's account pending an investigation
    B. Inform the employee that this activity is not acceptable
    C. Consult with her manager
    D. Take no action, as this would be an invasion of the employee's privacy

36. Darlene is concerned about the level of security at a cloud service provider that her organization is considering using and would like to review the results of an independent audit that verifies that the cloud provider has appropriate controls in place and that they are operating efficiently and effectively. What type of audit report would provide this assurance?

    A. SOC 1 Type 1
    B. SOC 1 Type 2
    C. SOC 2 Type 1
    D. SOC 2 Type 2

37. Howard is conducting an asset valuation exercise as part of his organization's risk assessment process. He would like to ensure that the valuations included in insurance policies are sufficient to cover the restoration of operations after asset destruction. Which one of the following asset valuation techniques is most appropriate for Howard's use?

    A. Replacement cost
    B. Original purchase price
    C. Depreciated value
    D. Subject matter expert estimated value

38. Jane is designing an inventory control system and wants to reduce the risk of employee theft. She designs the access controls such that a person who has the ability to order supplies from vendors does not also have the ability to log received shipments into the system. This attempts to prevent someone from ordering supplies, diverting them for their own use, and logging them into the inventory system as received. What principle is Jane most directly enforcing?

A. Least privilege
B. Two person control
C. Job rotation
D. Separation of duties

39. Morgan's business handles sensitive personal information belonging to residents of the European Union. What data privacy law most likely applies to this information?

A. CCPA
B. GDPR
C. GLBA
D. HIPAA

40. Which one of the following data governance roles would normally be assigned to someone of the most senior rank in the organization?

A. Data custodian
B. Data steward
C. Data owner
D. Data user

41. When labeling sensitive information using the U.S. military classification scheme, which one of the following is the lowest level of classification?

A. Confidential
B. Secret
C. Top Secret
D. Top Secret SCI

42. Cesar is modifying the rules on his organization's firewall to accommodate a new mail server that they recently installed. What category of control does this represent?

A. Compensating
B. Managerial
C. Operational
D. Technical

43. Which one of the following categories of information is explicitly governed by HIPAA's security and privacy rules?

A. PDI
B. PCI
C. PII
D. PHI

44. Which one of the following activities would not typically be a component of an employee onboarding process?

    A. Deprovisioning accounts
    B. Security training
    C. Computer issuance
    D. Credential generation

45. Gina is reviewing the configuration of an Apache Ubuntu web server environment and would like to review appropriate security configuration guides. Which one of the following guides would be least relevant to her situation?

    A. Apache web server configuration guide
    B. Firewall configuration guide
    C. Web application firewall configuration guide
    D. Windows operating system configuration guide

46. Who has primary responsibility for ensuring that the security requirements for a system are designed in a manner that is consistent with the organization's security policy?

    A. System owner
    B. Business owner
    C. System administrator
    D. Data owner

47. Don maintains a database of information about the spending habits of individual consumers. Which term would best describe this information?

    A. PHI
    B. PII
    C. PCI
    D. PDI

48. Which one of the following is NOT a function under the NIST Cybersecurity Framework?

    A. Detect
    B. Deter
    C. Identify
    D. Respond

49. Tom is attempting to comply with a requirement of the Payment Card Industry Data Security Standard (PCI DSS) that requires that credit card information not be stored in a system. He is unable to remove the data due to a variety of technical issues and works with regulators to implement encryption as an interim measure while he is working to fully comply with the requirement. What term best describes this control?

    A. Detective control
    B. Corrective control
    C. Preventive control
    D. Compensating control

50. Sandy is working with her leadership team on documenting the relationship between her firm and a new partner who will be co-marketing products. They would like to document the relationship between the firms but do so in a less formal way than a contract. Which tool would be most appropriate for this task?

    A. ISA
    B. BPA
    C. MOU
    D. SLA

51. Dennis recently received a SOC 2 Type 1 report from a cloud service provider. What assurance should he be able to gain from this report?

    A. The cloud provider has appropriate controls in place to protect privacy and security of data.
    B. The cloud provider has appropriate controls in place to protect privacy and security of data and those controls are operating effectively.
    C. The cloud provider has appropriate controls in place to protect the accuracy of Dennis' firm's financial reports.
    D. The cloud provider has appropriate controls in place to protect the accuracy of its own financial reports.

52. Thomas is considering using guard dogs to patrol the fenced perimeter of his organization's data processing facility. What category best describes this control?

    A. Corrective
    B. Deterrent
    C. Compensating
    D. Preventive

53. Which one of the following regulations contains specific provisions requiring that the organization maintain the availability of protected information to facilitate medical treatment?

    A. GDPR
    B. PCI DSS
    C. HIPAA
    D. GLBA

54. You are seeking to secure a Windows Server and would like to find a security standard that is independent of both government agencies and the vendors involved in providing your operating system and software. Which one of the following sources would best meet your needs?

    A. CIS
    B. Microsoft
    C. NIST
    D. NSA

55. Gavin is planning to upgrade the operating system on a production server and would like to obtain approval from the change advisory board. What type of document should he submit to obtain this approval?

    A. CRC
    B. RFP
    C. RFC
    D. CMA

56. Matt is ranking systems in his organization in order of priority for disaster recovery. Which one of the following systems should have the highest impact rating?

    A. Enterprise resource planning
    B. Routing and switching
    C. Fire suppression
    D. Customer relationship management

57. Which one of the following frameworks provides a mapping of cloud-specific security controls to security standards, best practices, and regulations?

    A. ISO 27001
    B. ISO 31000
    C. CCM
    D. CSF

58. Which one of the following elements is least likely to be found in a security awareness training program designed for end users?

    A. Confidentiality requirements
    B. Password management requirements
    C. Social engineering education
    D. Patching requirements

59. What type of risk assessment focuses on evaluating the security controls put in place by vendors and contractors?

    A. Penetration test
    B. Quantitative assessment
    C. Supply chain assessment
    D. Qualitative assessment

60. Gavin recently posted signs around his organization's facility warning visitors that the area is under 24-hour video surveillance. What term best describes this control?

    A. Corrective
    B. Detective
    C. Deterrent
    D. Preventative

61. What is the asset value (AV) in this scenario?

    A. $20,000
    B. $100,000
    C. $2 million
    D. $12 million

62. What is the annualized rate of occurrence (ARO) in this scenario?

    A. 0.01
    B. .1
    C. 1
    D. 100

63. What is the single loss expectancy in this scenario?

    A. $20,000
    B. $100,000
    C. $2 million
    D. $12 million

64. What is the annualized loss expectancy in this scenario?

    A. $20,000
    B. $100,000
    C. $2 million
    D. $12 million

65. Which one of the following statements best describes the risk situation Tonya is in?

    A. Tonya should recommend that the business always purchase insurance for any risk with an ALE greater than 0.005.
    B. The purchase of insurance in this scenario is not cost effective from a purely financial viewpoint.
    C. The purchase of insurance in this scenario makes good financial sense.
    D. Tonya should recommend against the purchase of insurance because the SLE is less than the AV.

66. At what point does good security practice dictate that an organization should no longer use a software application?

    A. Vendor end of launch
    B. Vendor end of promotion
    C. Vendor end of sales
    D. Vendor end of support

67. Gordon is considering the implementation of exit interviews for staff who voluntarily resign from his organization. Who would be best suited to perform this exit interview?

    A. Immediate supervisor
    B. Second-level supervisor
    C. Human Resources representative
    D. Co-worker

68. Where is the most appropriate place for an organization to keep track of risks across a wide variety of risk management disciplines?

    A. Audit reports
    B. Risk assessment reports
    C. Incident tracking system
    D. Risk register

69. Randi runs a credit card processing network for her organization. During an assessment, she notices that the organization uses a protocol that transmits passwords in unencrypted form over a local network. Correcting the situation will take several months of reengineering. While the situation exists, she implemented a requirement for multifactor authentication on internal network connections. What term best describes this control?

    A. Compensating
    B. Corrective
    C. Detective
    D. Deterrent

70. Which one of the following security policies is specifically designed to prevent the unintentional unauthorized observation of sensitive information?

    A. Mandatory vacations
    B. Separation of duties
    C. Least privilege
    D. Clean desk policy

71. Renee is reviewing the diagram shown here for a critical web application used by her company. She is performing a SPOF analysis on this environment. In the context of this analysis, what should raise the most concern?

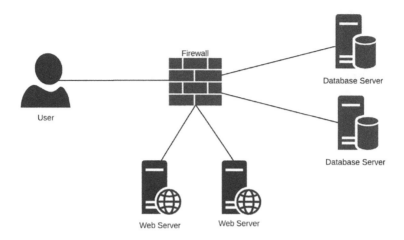

A. User
B. Firewall
C. Web server
D. Database server

72. When designing a security awareness program for employees, which one of the following groups would generally receive the most technical security training?

A. Users
B. System administrators
C. Data owners
D. Executives

73. Wendy is seeking to design a compensating control for a PCI DSS requirement that she cannot meet. Which one of the following statements is incorrect about compensating controls in this situation?

A. The compensating control must meet the intent of the original control.
B. The compensating control may be used to meet another PCI DSS requirement simultaneously.
C. The compensating control must be commensurate with the additional risk introduced by failing to meet the original requirement.
D. The compensating control must meet the rigor of the original control.

74. Which one of the following is the best example of a technical security control?

A. Firewall rules
B. Employee credit checks
C. Asset inventory
D. Fire detection system

75. Which one of the following activities is the best example of a corrective security control?

    A. Vulnerability remediation
    B. Perimeter protection
    C. Background checks
    D. Intrusion prevention system

76. Gwen is reviewing her organization's security policies and would like to update them to restrict the web browsing of employees. Specifically, she would like to prohibit the use of pornographic websites. Where would be the most common place to detail this type of restriction?

    A. AUP
    B. NDA
    C. BYOD
    D. This type of policy is an invasion of privacy and should not be implemented.

77. Evan is conducting a business impact analysis for an industrial products manufacturer. Which one of the following business functions would likely be ranked highest on a list of mission critical functions?

    A. IPS systems
    B. Billing systems
    C. ICS systems
    D. HVAC systems

78. Patty is the information security officer for a bank. She is concerned about the possibility that a bank teller might be colluding with a customer to commit fraud and using his position to cover up that fraud by updating records each day to shuffle around funds. Which one of the following controls would be most likely to uncover this type of malfeasance?

    A. Intrusion detection
    B. Clean desk policy
    C. Multifactor authentication
    D. Mandatory vacations

Questions 79-82 refer to the following scenario.

Brian is the risk manager for a firm that is considering locating personnel in a country where there is a high risk of kidnapping. He is considering a variety of controls designed to manage this risk.

---

79. Brian is considering using armed bodyguards to protect his organization's employees. What type of risk management strategy is this?

    A. Risk acceptance
    B. Risk avoidance
    C. Risk transference
    D. Risk mitigation

80. Brian is also consulting with senior managers to determine whether the business value of this effort justifies the risk. If the value is not sufficient, he is planning to propose not sending employees on this trip. What type of risk management strategy is this?

   A. Risk acceptance
   B. Risk avoidance
   C. Risk transference
   D. Risk mitigation

81. After consulting with business leaders, Brian learns that the risk is justified, and the organization will send the employees. He considers purchasing an insurance policy to cover ransoms and other related costs. What type of risk management strategy is this?

   A. Risk acceptance
   B. Risk avoidance
   C. Risk transference
   D. Risk mitigation

82. In the end, Brian determines that insurance policies and armed guards are not cost-effective, and the employees leave for the target country without those controls in place. What type of risk management strategy is this?

   A. Risk acceptance
   B. Risk avoidance
   C. Risk transference
   D. Risk mitigation

83. Which one of the following disaster recovery test types has the least impact on business operations?

   A. Full interruption test
   B. Structured walk-through
   C. Parallel test
   D. Checklist review

84. Dylan is designing a social media security policy for his organization. Which one of the following elements would not be appropriate to include in that policy?

   A. Complete ban on use of social media by employees
   B. Prohibition of users identifying themselves as an employee of the company on social media
   C. Approval requirements for posts from corporate accounts
   D. Restrictions on accessing personal social media accounts

85. Vivian's organization is about to begin a period of hiring where they will be bringing in a large number of new employees who will handle sensitive financial information. Which one of the following controls may be used as a pre-employment screening technique to reduce the risk of future fraud?

   A. Separation of duties
   B. Time-of-day restrictions
   C. Privileged user monitoring
   D. Background checks

86. Hayley's team is analyzing the results of a qualitative risk assessment. The assessment uses the reporting structure shown here. Which quadrant should Hayley's team look to first when prioritizing remediation initiatives?

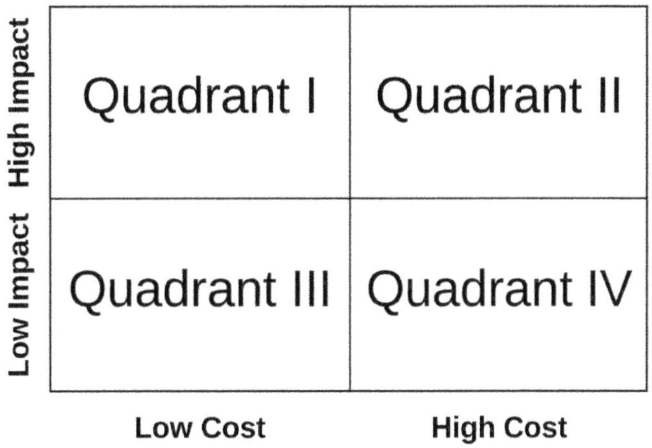

	Low Cost	**High Cost**
High Impact	Quadrant I	Quadrant II
Low Impact	Quadrant III	Quadrant IV

A. Quadrant I
B. Quadrant II
C. Quadrant III
D. Quadrant IV

87. Brianna recently accepted a position working for a U.S. financial institution that handles U.S. consumer checking account records. Which one of the following laws regulates this type of information?

A. GDPR
B. PCI DSS
C. SOX
D. GLBA

88. Barry recently accepted a new position with a marketing agency that collects data from residents of the European Union. Which data processing law most directly applies to this situation?

A. HIPAA
B. PCI DSS
C. GDPR
D. GLBA

89. Nolan's business maintains trade secret information about their manufacturing process. Which one of the following categories would best describe this information?

A. Classified
B. Proprietary
C. Public
D. Internal

90. Yvonne is the business continuity analyst for a web hosting company. She is conducting an analysis to identify and prioritize mission critical systems. Which one of the following systems should be highest on her list?

A. Web server supporting the company's own site
B. Billing system
C. Web server supporting a single client
D. Firewall

91. As part of a business partnership, Norm is working with his counterparts at another firm to interconnect the two networks. He would like to document the security requirements for that interconnection. What tool would best meet Norm's needs?

A. ISA
B. BPA
C. MOU
D. SLA

92. Donna was recently approached by the manager of a former employee who was seeking access to that employee's email account. She believes there is a valid business need for the access but is unsure how to obtain approval. What type of control would assist Donna and others in her organization in making these decisions?

A. Service level agreement
B. Data handling guidelines
C. Data classification policy
D. Standard operating procedure

93. Under the Sarbanes Oxley Act, which one of the following corporate officers bears personal liability for the accuracy of the content of the firm's annual report?

A. CIO
B. CFO
C. CISO
D. CPO

94. When designing a continuity of operations plan, which one of the following would be best described as an alternate business practice?

A. Filing an after action report
B. Moving data processing to a failover site.
C. Moving data processing to a mobile recovery facility.
D. Using paper-based forms while systems are down.

95. Under GDPR, which individual bears responsibility for ensuring that the company understands its privacy responsibilities and serves as the primary liaison to the supervising authority?

A. Data protection officer
B. Chief executive officer
C. Chief information officer
D. Chief information security officer

96. When providing security awareness training to privileged users, what threat should be emphasized that is a more likely risk with these employees than standard users?

    A. Water cooler attack
    B. Spear phishing attack
    C. Brute force attack
    D. Man-in-the-middle attack

97. Which one of the following security principles does NOT describe a standard best practice in cybersecurity?

    A. Least privilege
    B. Security through obscurity
    C. Separation of duties
    D. Defense in depth

Domain 5 Answers and Explanations

1. **A.** It is difficult for companies to restrict the social media activity of employees who are accessing the networks outside of working hours and without using corporate resources. It is perfectly reasonable to limit the use of corporate accounts, block social media use on corporate networks, and require the disclosure of corporate affiliations when discussing related matters.

2. **B.** Asset management practices include the tracking of a physical hardware inventory which would help maintain accurate device location information. Change and configuration management systems would not generally track physical location of a device. Firewalls are network security devices, which would not help meet this requirement.

3. **D.** Firewalls serve to block attempted access to the organization's networks and systems. Therefore, they are best described as preventative controls.

4. **D.** This is a tricky question, similar to ones that you might find on the exam. From a defense-in-depth perspective, it's likely that any of these combinations would be appropriate. However, when CompTIA asks about control diversity, they are looking for a mixture of controls across administrative, technical, and physical controls. Of the controls included in this question, background checks and security training are administrative controls, while the remainder are all technical controls. Therefore, the only option that mixes controls across two of the CompTIA categories is the use of data loss prevention (DLP) and background checks.

5. **D.** Barry should perform an additional analysis of the change before taking any action. He should determine whether the change is truly necessary and the impact on the organization if it is denied. He should also determine the security impact of allowing the change and investigate whether a compensating control can mitigate the security risk introduced by allowing the variance from the standard.

6. **A.** Backups offer organizations the opportunity to restore services to normal working condition after an emergency situation arises. Therefore, they are best described as an example of a corrective control.

7. **B.** During the Protect phase of the CSF, organizations develop and implement appropriate safeguards to ensure the delivery of critical services. In the Identify phase, they develop an organizational understanding to manage cybersecurity risk to systems, people, assets, data, and capabilities. The Detect phase allows them to develop and implement appropriate activities to identify the occurrence of a cybersecurity event. During the Respond phase, organizations develop and implement appropriate activities to take action regarding a detected cybersecurity incident. Finally, during the Recover phase, organizations develop and implement appropriate activities to maintain plans for resilience and to restore any capabilities or services that were impaired due to a cybersecurity incident.

8. **B.** A system access control list (ACL) is an example of a logical security control. Lighting, equipment enclosures, and Faraday cages are all examples of physical security controls.

9. **C.** Managerial controls are procedural mechanisms that focus on the mechanics of the risk management process. Technical controls enforce confidentiality, integrity, and availability in the digital space. Operational controls include the processes that we put in place to manage technology in a

secure manner. While an intrusion prevention system is itself a technical control, reviewing intrusion prevention logs is an example of an operational control.

10. **A.** All organizations involved in the processing of credit card transactions are contractually obligated to comply with the Payment Card Industry Data Security Standard (PCI DSS). There is no information provided in the scenario that Normal is employed by a health care organization that would be covered under the Health Insurance Portability and Accountability Act (HIPAA). Similarly, she is not employed by an educational institution covered by the Family Educational Rights and Privacy Act (FERPA). The scenario does not state whether her employer is a publicly traded company, so we cannot come to the conclusion that her firm is subject to the Sarbanes Oxley (SOX) Act.

11. **B.** Every employee in an organization should receive at least a basic level of security awareness training shortly after they join the organization and on a recurring basis. This training should be customized to a user's role and may be more frequent for individuals with sensitive roles, such as privileged users.

12. **C.** Change management policies describe the process for requesting, reviewing, implementing, and deploying changes in a production environment. This includes the release of new source code to production use.

13. **A.** Privilege creep occurs when an employee retains permissions from prior jobs after shifting roles within an organization. User termination audits are more likely to turn up examples of accounts that were not deprovisioned than privilege creep. Usage auditing may discover some examples of privilege creep but is designed to uncover privilege misuse. Policy reviews will not discover examples of privilege creep. Permission auditing is the most comprehensive way to discover unnecessary privileges assigned to user accounts.

14. **D.** There is no evidence presented that this violates any separation of duties or two-person control requirements. Security through obscurity is the idea that the details security controls should be kept secret, which is not an issue in this scenario. The fact that Helen is retaining privileges from a prior position violates the principle of least privilege.

15. **B.** This exercise, where the attacking team (red team) has specific objectives to achieve, is known as a capture the flag (CTF) exercise. There is no indication that a defensive blue team is taking part in the exercise and, therefore, it is not possible to conduct a joint red/blue team purple teaming exercise. The exercise is conducting live action, so it is not a walkthrough.

16. **A.** Security awareness training should begin at the earliest possible stage of the account management lifecycle. Onboarding is this earliest step and should be the first opportunity for security awareness training.

17. **C.** The responsibility for determining appropriate access to information is a responsibility of the data owner. This data owner may, by nature of his or her job, fit into other categories, such as system owner, privileged user, or executive user, but it is the person's assignment to the data owner role that gives them this authority and responsibility.

18. **B.** The right to be forgotten is a provision of the European Union's General Data Protection Regulation (GDPR). It is not included in HIPAA, FERPA, or GLBA.

19. **A.** Continuing education is an important component of security awareness training. All users should receive some level of awareness training on a recurring basis, but users with privileged access, such as system administrators, should receive more frequent training. The training should be based on a user's role and technical users should receive more technical training. Training should be conducted periodically and should be updated whenever there is a significant change in the security landscape.

20. **A.** A service level agreement (SLA) spells out the requirements for a service provider who will be offering services to a customer and frequently includes penalties for the vendor failing to meet the SLA requirements. It is the most appropriate tool for this task. A interconnection security agreement (ISA) spells out the security requirements for interconnecting the networks of two organizations. A business partnership agreement (BPA) spells out the relationship between two organizations that are entering into a joint venture or other partnership. A memorandum of understanding (MOU) is a document that spells out an agreement between two organizations but is typically informal and less enforceable than other agreement types. It might be possible to use an MOU in this case, but it is not the best tool for the job because it is less enforceable than a BPA.

21. **D.** There is no universal answer to this question. Carla should consult her organization's data retention policy to determine how long it is appropriate to maintain the records and then either destroy them securely or maintain them in a secure repository, depending upon the data retention policy requirements.

22. **A.** Risk acceptance should always be done in an educated manner after the organization excludes other options. It may or may not be preferable to risk avoidance depending upon the specific circumstances. Insurance policies are an example of risk transference, not risk avoidance. Firewalls and intrusion prevention systems are examples of risk mitigation, not risk avoidance.

23. **D.** Security awareness training is an example of a managerial security control because it is an administrative practice. The subject of the training is use of the VPN, which is a technical control, but the training itself is managerial in nature.

24. **C.** ISO standard 27701 contains guidance on enhancing an information security management system to establish privacy standards for personally identifiable information. ISO 27001 and 27002 cover the standards and best practices for implementing an information security management system. The ISO 31000 family of standards cover the design and implementation of a risk management program.

25. **C.** The mean time to repair (MTTR) is the amount of time that it will typically take to restore service after a failure. In this case, the MTTR is 2 days: the amount of time to obtain and install a replacement part.

26. **D.** The mean time between failures (MTBF) is the amount of time that typically passes between failure events. In this scenario, Gary has determined that events typically occur once every three years.

27. **B.** From his conversations with business leaders, Gary determined that the business can tolerate an outage of one day, making this the recovery time objective (RTO).

28. **A.** From his conversations with business leaders, Gary determined that the business can tolerate the loss of four hours' data, making this the recovery point objective (RPO).

29. **B.** Managerial controls are procedural mechanisms that focus on the mechanics of the risk management process. Technical controls enforce confidentiality, integrity, and availability in the digital

space. Operational controls include the processes that we put in place to manage technology in a secure manner. Implementing a risk assessment process is an example of a managerial control.

30. **C.** Under the NIST Cloud Computing Reference Architecture, the cloud consumer is the principal stakeholder for the cloud computing service. A cloud consumer represents a person or organization that maintains a business relationship with and uses the service from a cloud provider.

31. **C.** While it may be reasonable for anyone in the company to have basic awareness of these attacks, the user role most in need of this training is the accounts payable clerk. This is the individual who is in a position to actually initiate wire transfers and, therefore, must be aware that these transfers are a common target of fraudsters.

32. **C.** Based upon the information presented in this scenario, Tom is under no obligation to report the incident to anyone outside of his organization. There is no indication that any of the stolen information involved personal data that would trigger a breach notification law. Tom is also not obligated to report the potential crime and should consult with legal counsel on the best course of action.

33. **D.** The use of locks could be described as both a preventative control, because it prevents someone from gaining access to equipment, and as a physical control, because it implements a security policy in the physical world. Of the choices provided, physical is the best answer, as the question does not allow you to select preventative.

34. **B.** A business partnership agreement (BPA) spells out the relationship between two organizations that are entering into a joint venture or other partnership. It is the most appropriate tool for this task. A service level agreement (SLA) spells out the requirements for a service provider who will be offering services to a customer and frequently includes penalties for the vendor failing to meet the SLA requirements. A interconnection security agreement (ISA) spells out the security requirements for interconnecting the networks of two organizations. A memorandum of understanding (MOU) is a document that spells out an agreement between two organizations but is typically informal and less enforceable than other agreement types. It might be possible to use an MOU in this case, but it is not the best tool for the job because it is less enforceable than a BPA.

35. **C.** Brenda has detected a potential violation of the organization's acceptable use policy, so she should take action. The employee has no expectation of privacy on a corporate network, so there are no issues with doing so. However, Brenda should not unilaterally take action to disable a user's account or confront the user directly. She should consult with her manager and determine appropriate next steps.

36. **D.** Service Organizational Control (SOC) reports provide the results of an independent audit of a service provider. SOC 1 reports are done to verify controls that could impact a client's financial reporting. SOC 2 reports are done to verify controls that could impact security and privacy of data. Type 1 reports simply verify that controls are in place. Type 2 reports verify that the controls are operating efficiently and effectively. Therefore, Darlene should choose a SOC 2 Type 2 report.

37. **A.** Replacement cost is the most reliable valuation technique for use when an organization is primarily concerned with replacing assets after a disaster. This ensures that the insurance payout is sufficient to cover the costs of replacing the asset. The replacement cost may be higher or lower than the original purchase price.

38. **D.** This is a clear example of separation of duties: preventing a single employee from having the ability to place orders and receive inventory. Two-person control would require the concurrence of two employees to perform a single task, while this scenario is requiring two employees to each perform two different tasks. There is no discussion of changing job assignments in the scenario, so job rotation is not at play. It is possible to describe this as an implementation of least privilege, but separation of duties is the more directly applicable security principle. Remember, the exam may include many questions that ask you to choose the BEST answer. It's important to read all of the answer options and recognize that more than one may be partially correct.

39. **B.** From the information given, we can only conclude that the European Union's General Data Protection Regulation (GDPR) applies, as the information belongs to EU residents. It is possible that the other laws apply, depending upon where the information is stored, processed, and transmitted, but we do not have sufficient information to come to that conclusion.

40. **C.** The data owner is a very senior position assigned to someone who bears overall responsibility for the quality and security of a category of information. The data owner often oversees data stewards, custodians, and users in the performance of their duties.

41. **A.** The lowest level of classified information in the U.S. military system is Confidential. Information may also be marked as Unclassified or For Official Use Only but these are not levels of classified information.

42. **D.** Managerial controls are procedural mechanisms that focus on the mechanics of the risk management process. Technical controls enforce confidentiality, integrity, and availability in the digital space. Operational controls include the processes that we put in place to manage technology in a secure manner. Modifying firewall rules are an example of a technical control.

43. **D.** The Health Insurance Portability and Accountability Act (HIPAA) contains security and privacy provisions covering protected health information (PHI). It does not apply to more general personally identifiable information (PII) or payment card information (PCI). PDI is not a common category of information.

44. **A.** During an employee onboarding process, the organization typically conducts a number of start-up activities for the new employee. These commonly include issuing a computer, generating account credentials, and conducting initial security training. Deprovisioning is the removal of user access and accounts and would occur during the offboarding process.

45. **D.** Gina should consult the configuration guides for all devices, operating systems, and applications associated with the web server or involved in handling traffic directed to the web server. This would include the Apache web server itself, the firewall, and the web application firewall. A Windows configuration guide would not be useful because the web server is running Ubuntu Linux.

46. **A.** The system owner is responsible for ensuring that a system's security requirements are aligned with the organization's security policy. The system administrator may be responsible for implementing these requirements, but does not set or align the requirements. The data owner may share some responsibility with the system owner but does not have primary responsibility. The business owner does not normally create system security requirements.

47. **B.** This type of information certainly fits into the category of personally identifiable information (PII). There is no indication that the records contain health information so they would not qualify as protected health information (PHI). There is also no indication that the records contain credit card information, so they would not constitute payment card information (PCI). PDI is not a common category of information.

48. **B.** The five functions under the NIST Cybersecurity Framework are Identify, Protect, Detect, Respond, and Recover.

49. **D.** The best way to describe this situation is as a compensating control. Tom cannot meet the original requirement and implemented an additional control to help mitigate the risk. This is the definition of a compensating control.

50. **C.** A memorandum of understanding (MOU) is a document that spells out an agreement between two organizations but is typically informal and less enforceable than other agreement types. It seems to be the most appropriate option for Sandy. An interconnection security agreement (ISA) spells out the security requirements for interconnecting the networks of two organizations. It is not appropriate tool for this task. A service level agreement (SLA) spells out the requirements for a service provider who will be offering services to a customer and frequently includes penalties for the vendor failing to meet the SLA requirements. There is no vendor/client relationship here so an SLA would not be the appropriate tool. A business partnership agreement (BPA) spells out the relationship between two organizations that are entering into a joint venture or other partnership, but is a more formal contract, so it would not meet Sandy's requirement.

51. **A.** Service Organizational Control (SOC) reports provide the results of an independent audit of a service provider. SOC 1 reports are done to verify controls that could impact a client's financial reporting. SOC 2 reports are done to verify controls that could impact security and privacy of data. Type 1 reports simply verify that controls are in place. Type 2 reports verify that the controls are operating efficiently and effectively. From a SOC 2 Type 1 report, Dennis can be confident that the provider has appropriate security and privacy controls, but he cannot determine that they are operating efficiently and effectively. That would require a Type 2 report.

52. **B.** Guard dogs may be described as either a deterrent or preventive control, depending upon the context. They do serve in a preventive role because they have the ability to corner a potential intruder. However, this is not their primary role. Their main function is to serve as a deterrent to intrusion attempts through their menacing appearance. When taking the exam, remember that you may face questions like this asking you to choose the BEST answer from among several correct possibilities.

53. **C.** The Health Insurance Portability and Accountability Act (HIPAA) governs health information and includes specific provisions requiring that organizations preserve the availability of that data. PCI DSS governs credit card information, while GLBA covers financial records. GDPR is a European privacy regulation that is most concerned with the confidentiality and integrity of information and does not contain specific provisions about the availability of health records for medical treatment.

54. **A.** The Center for Internet Security (CIS) is an independent organization that publishes security standards for many common operating systems, devices, and applications. The National Institute for Standards and Technology (NIST) and the National Security Agency (NSA) also publish security standards, but they do not meet the criteria here because they are both government agencies. Similarly,

Microsoft's security standards do not meet the scenario because Microsoft produces the Windows operating system.

55. **C.** A request for change (RFC) is the standard document used to document the need for a change, the test plan, implementation plan, and rollback procedure. The change advisory board will review the RFC and either approve or reject the proposed change.

56. **C.** Life safety systems should always have a higher impact rating than other systems. Therefore, Matt should prioritize the fire suppression system over other restoration efforts.

57. **C.** The Cloud Security Alliance's (CSA) Cloud Controls Matrix (CCM) provides a mapping of cloud-specific security controls to security standards, best practices, and regulations. The NIST Cybersecurity Framework (CSF) and ISO 27001 are broad security frameworks that are not cloud-specific. ISO 31000 is a risk management framework.

58. **D.** Security awareness training should be customized for an individual's role in the organization. An end user would be responsible for protecting the confidentiality of information, managing his or her own password, and staying vigilant for social engineering attempts. Therefore, all three of these topics should be included in security awareness training for end users. An end user would not normally be responsible for applying security patches, so this topic is not necessary in training focused on the end user role.

59. **C.** Supply chain assessments specifically focus on the security controls put in place by vendors and other suppliers. Penetration tests, quantitative assessments, and qualitative assessments may indeed look at supplier controls, but they are not necessarily the focus of the assessment.

60. **C.** The key to answering this question is to realize that it is asking about the posting of signs, not the installation of a video surveillance system. The signs themselves do not perform any detective function. Instead, they act to deter visitors from engaging in unauthorized activity due to the threat of detection by video surveillance (which may or may not actually exist).

61. **D.** The asset value (AV) is the full value of the facility. In this scenario, Tonya determined that the facility value is $12 million using the replacement cost method.

62. **A.** The annualized rate of occurrence is the number of events expected in a given year. The facility lies within the 100-year flood plain, meaning that risk managers should expect a flood once every 100 years. This is equivalent to a 0.01 annual risk of flood.

63. **C.** The single loss expectancy (SLE) is the amount of damage, in dollars, that the organization should expect as the result of a single incident. From the scenario, we know that a single flood would cause approximately $2 million in damage.

64. **A.** The annualized loss expectancy is the amount of damage expected to occur in any given year. It is computed by multiplying the single loss expectancy by the annualized rate of occurrence (or ALE=SLE*ARO). In this scenario, that is ALE=$2 million * 0.01 or $20,000.

65. **C.** The purchase of an insurance policy is never purely a financial decision, but in this case, it does make good financial sense because the annualized loss expectancy ($20,000) exceeds the policy premium cost ($10,000). Tonya should not use the ALE or SLE alone to make this decision and must do so in the context of the control costs and other business factors.

66. **D.** Organizations should discontinue use of a product when it is no longer supported by the vendor, as security updates will no longer be provided. It is acceptable to continue using a product after the end of sales, launch, or promotion.

67. **B.** Exit interviews should be conducted by someone who is in a position to collect and use information about the employee's experience to positively influence the organization. This rules out a co-worker. They should also be conducted by someone who is independent of the situation, ruling out the employee's immediate supervisor, who may be part of the reason for departure. Human Resources is a viable option, but they do not have direct knowledge of the employee's work duties and may not capture all of the insight provided during an exit interview. The best choice would be the employee's second-level supervisor, who is in a direct position to implement changes, but is separated from management of the employee by a level of supervision. HR may sit in on the interview if they wish to ensure objectivity.

68. **D.** The best place to track the status of all risks facing an organization is in a formal risk register. The other documents listed here may include information about risks but good practice suggests extracting that information from these sources and placing it in a risk register.

69. **A.** The use of multifactor authentication in this situation is designed to compensate for the lack of encryption on passwords sent over the network. Therefore, it is best described as a compensating control.

70. **D.** Clean desk policies require that employees clean off their desktops when leaving the immediate vicinity and secure all papers and other materials. The purpose of this policy is to prevent anyone walking by from observing sensitive information. Separation of duties and least privilege practices also protect against unauthorized access to information, but they generally protect against *intentional* unauthorized access.

71. **B.** In a single point of failure (SPOF) analysis, technologists should review an infrastructure looking for components where a single failure could cause service disruption. In this case, the web and database servers are redundant, but the firewall is not. Therefore, the firewall should be of greatest concern. Users would not be included in a SPOF analysis.

72. **B.** All employees should receive security awareness training that is tailored to their role in the organization. System administrators are the most technical employees mentioned here, so they should receive the most technical training.

73. **B.** PCI DSS requires that compensating controls must be above and beyond the other PCI DSS requirements. Organizations may not use controls required by another section of PCI DSS as compensating controls for a different requirement that they cannot meet. Controls must be commensurate with the new risk introduced and must meet the intent and rigor of the original requirement.

74. **A.** The installation and operation of a firewall is an example of a technical security control: the use of technology to meet security objectives. Credit checks for prospective employees and conducting an asset inventory are examples of administrative controls. Fire detection systems are an example of a physical security control.

75. **A.** Vulnerability remediation is an example of a corrective control because it takes actions to fix, or correct, security issues. Perimeter protection, background checks, and intrusion prevention systems (IPS) are all examples of preventive controls.

76. **A.** Gwen should place this restriction in her organization's acceptable use policy (AUP). It would not be appropriate to place usage restrictions in a non-disclosure agreement (NDA) or a bring your own device (BYOD) policy. Employers are well within their rights to impose usage limits on their own networks. Employees do not have an expectation of privacy on a corporate network so there are no privacy issues with such a restriction.

77. **C.** The mission of a manufacturer is to produce products. An industrial control system (ICS) is directly tied to this mission and would most likely be ranked highest on a list of mission-critical functions. Billing is an important activity, but could be delayed as a lower priority if a manufacturing line is idled. Heating, ventilation and air conditioning (HVAC) and intrusion prevention systems (IPS) are important functions, but do not impact the mission as directly as an ICS.

78. **D.** The best way to uncover this type of fraud is through a mandatory vacation policy. If the teller is forced to take a vacation of a week or more each year, it would be difficult to continue to perpetrate the fraud during that time, increasing the likelihood that it would come to light. An intrusion detection system may uncover this type of fraud but it is generally more tuned to identifying anomalous network traffic than anomalous transactions. Multifactor authentication requirements and clean desk policies would not be at all effective against this risk.

79. **D.** Risk mitigation strategies seek to reduce the likelihood or impact of a risk. In this case, armed guards reduce the likelihood of a successful kidnapping and are, therefore, an example of risk mitigation.

80. **B.** Risk avoidance seeks to change business practices to eliminate a risk. By not sending employees to the affected country, Brian avoids the risk of a kidnapping there.

81. **C.** Purchasing insurance moves the financial risk from Brian's organization to an insurance company and is, therefore, an example of risk transference.

82. **A.** Risk acceptance is a deliberate decision to incur risk after considering the costs and benefits of other risk management strategies. That is what occurred in this case.

83. **D.** The full interruption test has the potential to disrupt all of the business activities of an organization by moving processing to the alternate facility. A parallel test also activates the alternate facility but does not switch over operations to that facility. A structured walkthrough gathers everyone together to discuss an exercise in a tabletop format. A checklist review is the least disruptive test because people simply review their disaster recovery checklists on their own time.

84. **A.** Employers are able to place a variety of restrictions on social media use by employees. It is entirely appropriate to restrict use during work hours, or prevent employees from mentioning an affiliation with the company on their personal accounts. It is also appropriate to require approval for posts from corporate accounts. Employers generally may not, however completely block employees from using personal social media accounts on their own time.

85. **D.** All of the techniques described here may be used to reduce the likelihood of fraud. However, background checks are the only control listed that are a pre-employment technique. The remainder of the controls are used to limit risk with current employees, rather than prospective employees.

86. **A.** Hayley's team should first look for high impact, low cost remediation efforts. These are found in Quadrant I in the diagram.

87. **D.** Financial institutions are required to preserve the privacy of consumer records by the Gramm-Leach-Bliley Act (GLBA). The Payment Card Industry Data Security Standard (PCI DSS) does apply to financial records, but its scope is limited to credit and debit card records. The General Data Protection Regulation (GDPR) would apply to these records if they were about European Union residents but that is not the case here. The Sarbanes Oxley Act (SOX) regulates the financial accounting practices of publicly traded companies and is not applicable here.

88. **C.** The General Data Protection Regulation (GDPR) is a European law governing the privacy of personally identifiable information about residents of the European Union. It applies to that data worldwide. The Health Insurance Portability and Accountability Act (HIPAA) regulates health information in the United States. The Gramm Leach Bliley Act (GLBA) covers financial records in the United States. The Payment Card Industry Data Security Standard (PCI DSS) applies worldwide but only to credit and debit card information.

89. **B.** Trade secrets are normally classified as proprietary information. While the term internal may apply to trade secrets, this is not the best term to use because it normally applies to a wide range of information and the term proprietary is more specific. The term classified is normally used to refer only to government information. Trade secrets are certainly not public information.

90. **D.** Yvonne should first limit her prioritization to mission-critical systems. The billing system is important, but not directly tied to the mission of delivering web hosting services. Therefore, she can rank this system as a low priority. Web servers are clearly quite important to the company's operations and Yvonne should likely rank a client's web server above the company's own server. However, none of these servers will be accessible without a functioning firewall, so the firewall should have the highest priority.

91. **A.** An interconnection security agreement (ISA) spells out the security requirements for interconnecting the networks of two organizations. It is the most appropriate tool for this task. A service level agreement (SLA) spells out the requirements for a service provider who will be offering services to a customer and frequently includes penalties for the vendor failing to meet the SLA requirements. There is no vendor/client relationship here so an SLA would not be the appropriate tool. A business partnership agreement (BPA) spells out the relationship between two organizations that are entering into a joint venture or other partnership, but does not generally include technical requirements. A memorandum of understanding (MOU) is a document that spells out an agreement between two organizations but is typically informal and less enforceable than other agreement types.

92. **D.** Donna's organization should consider implementing a standard operating procedure (SOP) for data access requests. This procedure could spell out the appropriate approval process for granting access to data stored in another user's account. A guideline is not mandatory and would not be appropriate in this case. A data classification policy would generally not cover access request procedures, nor would a service level agreement.

93. **B.** The Sarbanes-Oxley (SOX) Act requires that the Chief Executive Officer (CEO) and Chief Financial Officer (CFO) certify that the information contained within an annual report is accurate and assigns them personal liability for these statements. The CIO, CISO, and CPO do not bear this responsibility.

94. **D.** During a business continuity event, organizations may choose to adopt alternate business practices that modify their normal business processes. Switching to paper-based forms is a good example of this type of practice. Moving to a failover or mobile processing facility is not a change in business practice but the use of an alternate processing facility. After action reports are a standard part of continuity operations and should be filed after any continuity event.

95. **A.** The data protection officer (DPO) is a formal designation under GDPR and the individual designated as DPO bears significant responsibilities for GDPR compliance.

96. **B.** Privileged users are clearly susceptible to all of these attacks. However, there is no reason to believe that they are more likely to be victims of water cooler attacks, brute force attacks, or man-in-the-middle attacks than any other user. Spear phishing attacks target specific people and are more likely to target privileged users because of their elevated privileges.

97. **B.** Security through obscurity is an outdated concept that says that the security of a control may depend upon the secrecy of the details of that control's inner function. Security professionals should not use controls that rely upon security through obscurity. The principles of least privilege, separation of duties, and defense in depth are all sound security practices.

CHAPTER 6

Practice Test 1

Practice Test 1 Questions

1. Juan is concerned that information he has stored in a cloud block storage service may be accessible to the service provider. What control can he use to best protect against this risk?

   A. Encryption
   B. High availability
   C. Permissions
   D. Replication

2. Tom would like to send an encrypted message to Jerry using asymmetric cryptography. What key should Tom use to encrypt the message?

   A. Tom's public key
   B. Tom's private key
   C. Jerry's public key
   D. Jerry's private key

3. Which one of the following tools is capable of generating output such as that shown below?

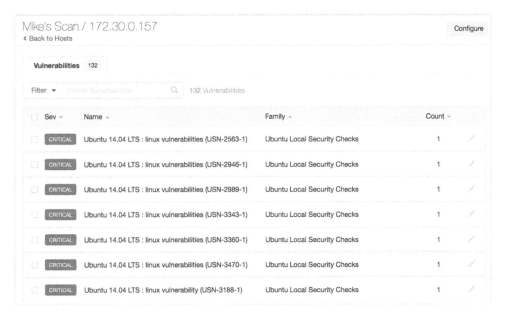

   A. Memdump
   B. Nessus
   C. Nmap
   D. PowerShell

4. Brianna is considering the placement of a new service her organization is developing from among different geographic data center options offered by her cloud provider. She is concerned about what legal jurisdictions would apply to the data. What principle most directly governs this concern?

   A. Data classification
   B. Data remnance
   C. Data sovereignty
   D. Data stewardship

5. Josh is reviewing and updating the firewall rules used by his organization to react to changing needs. What type of control primarily describes the network firewall?

   A. Corrective
   B. Detective
   C. Deterrent
   D. Preventative

6. You are contracting with an IaaS vendor to provide computing services to your organization. You will use those services to deliver a SaaS offering to your own clients. Under the cloud reference architecture, what is your organization's role with respect to the IaaS vendor relationship?

   A. Cloud broker
   B. Cloud carrier
   C. Cloud consumer
   D. Cloud provider

7. Which one of the following techniques is most likely to enable an attacker to engage in a man-in-the-middle attack, assuming that the attacker has access to the victim's local network?

   A. ARP spoofing
   B. Buffer overflow
   C. Cross-site scripting
   D. Directory traversal

8. Chelsea believes that an attacker has compromised the private key for her web server's digital certificate. What action should she take?

   A. Change the certificate's public key
   B. Change the certificate's private key
   C. Revoke the certificate
   D. No action is necessary

9. Alan is working with a cloud provider to implement a new service that places IoT sensors at the edge of his network, allows those devices to perform some computation locally, and then connects those devices to the cloud provider. What term best describes this approach?

   A. Fog computing
   B. Hybrid cloud computing
   C. Private cloud computing
   D. Public cloud computing

10. Consider the network diagram shown below. What would be the most appropriate location for a web server that requires public access?

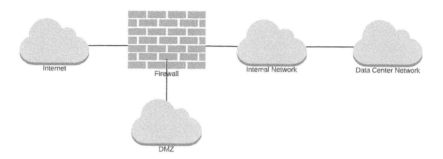

A. Data center network
B. DMZ
C. Internal network
D. Internet

11. Which one of the following database security techniques is susceptible to a rainbow table attack?

A. Hashing
B. Masking
C. Minimization
D. Tokenization

12. What access control model is in use in the figure below?

A. ABAC
B. DAC
C. MAC
D. RBAC

13. Which metric from a CVSS3 rating describes the conditions beyond the attacker's control that must exist in order to exploit the vulnerability?

    A. AC
    B. AV
    C. PR
    D. UI

14. Which one of the following disaster recovery facility options is generally the most expensive to implement?

    A. Black site
    B. Cold site
    C. Hot site
    D. Warm site

15. Nell is negotiating a contract with a new cloud provider and would like to include a specific uptime requirement. What type of agreement would normally contain this type of provision?

    A. BPA
    B. MOU
    C. NDA
    D. SLA

16. Which one of the following certificate formats is possibly used in the certificate shown below?

```
-----BEGIN CERTIFICATE-----
MIIDPzCCAiegAwIBAgIJAOMCpAGxDLY2MA0GCSqGSIb3DQEBCwUAMDYxCzAJBgNV
BAYTAlVTMRAwDgYDVQQIDAdJbmRpYW5hMRUwEwYDVQQKDAxNaWtlIENoYXBwbGUw
HhcNMTcxMDIyMTgxOTA4WhcNMTgxMDIyMTgxOTA4WjA2MQswCQYDVQQGEwJVUzEQ
MA4GA1UECAwHSW5kaWFuYTEVMBMGA1UECgwMTWlrZSBDaGFwcGxlMIIBIjANBgkq
hkiG9w0BAQEFAAOCAQ8AMIIBCgKCAQEAt1TtUvX+Icp6ceQqFB8UOXKSpl9mun3h
HAzESuizyvIeKLJ5EhjOzNWvxTGDJOPFHdqtb2W3HojI/dV7/+ZehmiHsa4XvXRK
QpqN96ittSYZPZteqW8f9Ku1hwGL2yXFC03CGpa8Wu1yhgHyrplZyyX2cW6ePB82
gdO6ZKJ4GfG6o3vvoHGO0vQtDUHEo3IGGWsGH0vm+4mUfOed/uhIZoq3UltFmR3p
KdSyXie/s+RVUirIhNbvuljwqqXHme2p9QBw4w6FWsiDMDcd07Ia0JiFvBN7WHQ5
bREThZbHDKRM4NJeMfItI3ONA8tzbGOYKvaefk2TiIZ1jugbdu0moQIDAQABo1Aw
TjAdBgNVHQ4EFgQUE4hFcAuY6o+NtFSL0yw9ZQYraSQwHwYDVR0jBBgwFoAUE4hF
cAuY6o+NtFSL0yw9ZQYraSQwDAYDVR0TBAUwAwEB/zANBgkqhkiG9w0BAQsFAAOC
AQEAEd8Ko3y4wxHP6DBffI4TQywdjNtiCsdcAW+76rQBcI1y7xcTElTVv5b5w9pF
dt170ZTOLsO7BiHgh9U3G+NsHFfWEZrPDTbg+VlZCyr09itgtZ9iFL4EK0v67WgF
50RRQyiUP1GxhcRSkRd/d+6xC/fkBPBS6rf+6hdGbUvrOXjjz2HVtypl4BGj0aTT
eoFp0Gnfzn9B0yAe26VsosuSg/2urOtbxynlLH3lfjpIuI0VHbFVRLpCEehzhZZq
oxjic1N5lCJVgXht0y3DqYlFAQgdygTL3cYZxbKBmWDxa6ezAaqbRnfw0ubMN917
rPjAiaAP6N7PbS9hZ7tVLzZtoQ==
-----END CERTIFICATE-----
```

    A. DER
    B. PEM
    C. PFX
    D. P12

17. Wanda would like to implement an operational security control that increases the likelihood that internal fraud will be detected. Which one of the following controls would best meet her objective?

    A. Job rotation
    B. Least privilege
    C. Separation of duties
    D. Two person control

18. What type of cybersecurity exercise provides team members with a specific objective that they should achieve to win the exercise, such as stealing a file containing sensitive information or compromising a specific server?

    A. Blue team
    B. Red team
    C. Purple team
    D. Capture the flag

19. Monica is hardening a database server and runs an external port scan on the device. During this scan, she receives the scan results shown below. What is the best action that she could take to improve her organization's security posture?

    ```
    Starting Nmap 7.80 ( https://nmap.org ) at 2020-05-12 09:01 EDT
    Nmap scan report
    Host is up (0.025s latency).
    Not shown: 998 filtered ports
    PORT      STATE SERVICE
    22/tcp    open  ssh
    1433/tcp  open  ms-sql

    Nmap done: 1 IP address (1 host up) scanned in 6.74 seconds
    ```

    A. Close all open ports on the network firewall
    B. Close all open ports on the host firewall
    C. Close port 22 on the host firewall
    D. No action is necessary

20. What is the currently accepted best practice for the number of passwords to keep in a password history to prevent password reuse?

    A. 0
    B. 3
    C. 8
    D. 16

21. Tawfiq recently completed an audit of his organization's security practices and learned that the organization stores passwords for their website in a file that is hashed but not salted. The hashing is done using a cryptographically secure hash function. Which one of the following statements correctly describes the situation?

    A. These passwords are stored securely
    B. These passwords are easily reversable if an attacker knows what hash function was used
    C. These passwords are not directly reversible but they are vulnerable to a prepending attack
    D. These passwords are not directly reversible but they are vulnerable to a rainbow table attack

22. Domer Industries is conducting a risk analysis of the risk of an earthquake damaging their data center. The data center is valued at $10 million and seismologists expect that a serious earthquake will damage 75% of the facility once every 50 years.

    In this scenario, what is the annualized loss expectancy?

    A. $150,000
    B. $5,625,000
    C. $7,500,000
    D. $10,000,000

23. Review the vulnerability scan results shown below. What would be the most appropriate protocol to use that would correct this vulnerability?

    A. SSL 2.0
    B. SSL 2.5
    C. SSL 3.0
    D. TLS 1.2

24. Which one of the following statements is correct about the Simultaneous Authentication of Equals (SAE) Wi-Fi authentication protocol?

    A. SAE was first supported by WPA2
    B. SAE is an outdated standard and should not be used
    C. SAE does not send the password over the network
    D. SAE connections are subject to eavesdropping attacks

25. Chris would like to better manage the root accounts on Linux systems that he administers. He would like to allow administrators to use the privileges of the root account without knowing the password. What solution would best meet his needs?

A. CASB
B. PAM
C. SAML
D. SIEM

26. What application security testing technique is taking place in the Python code shown below?

```
for i in range(1,999999):
    url = 'https://www.mysite.com/account.aspx&function=' + i
    page = urllib.request.urlopen(url)
    print(page.read().decode('utf-8')
```

A. Code signing
B. Fuzzing
C. Static code analysis
D. Vulnerability scanning

27. Cecilia is a system administrator who occasionally works from home. She would like to select a secure protocol for accessing Windows systems with a graphical interface. Which one of the following protocols would meet her requirements and be the easiest to implement?

A. FTPS
B. RDP
C. SFTP
D. SSH

28. What is the correct ordering of data classification levels (from lowest to highest) in the system used by the U.S. military and defense industry?

A. Top Secret; Secret; Confidential; Unclassified
B. Above Top Secret; Top Secret; Secret; Unclassified
C. Unclassified; Confidential; Secret; Top Secret
D. Unclassified; Secret; Top Secret; Above Top Secret

29. What is the purpose of STIX?

A. Offer a standardized schema for the specification and communication of system and network events.
B. Provide an API for security platform integration.
C. Provide a set of services to enable sharing of threat intelligence.
D. Represent threat information in a standardized manner

30. Gene believes that an attacker tampered with a wireless access point purchased by his organization before it reached his mail room. What term best describes the threat vector in this case?

   A. Cloud
   B. Removable media
   C. Supply chain
   D. Wireless

31. Haley recently started a new job and was issued a multifactor authentication token during her account provisioning. The token has a button that she pushes when she wishes to obtain a new authentication code. What algorithm does this token use?

   A. HOTP
   B. IPSec
   C. TLS
   D. TOTP

32. Brian is configuring a cloud server located on a private subnet to access a block storage service offered by the same cloud provider. What would be the most secure way to enable this access?

   A. Internet gateway
   B. NAT device
   C. Physical connection
   D. VPC endpoint

33. Quarantine networks are a technique most closely associated with what phase of the incident response process?

   A. Preparation
   B. Containment
   C. Eradication
   D. Recovery

34. Which one of the following mobile connection technologies involves only one-way communication?

   A. Bluetooth
   B. Cellular
   C. GPS
   D. NFC

35. When conducting an incident response exercise, what exercise type comes closest to real-world circumstances?

   A. Checklist review
   B. Scenario
   C. Tabletop
   D. Walkthrough

36. Ryan is considering deploying a split tunnel VPN for his end users. Which one of the following statements about split tunnel VPNs is correct?

    A. Split tunnel VPNs encrypt all network traffic.
    B. Split tunnel VPNs route all traffic from clients to the protected network.
    C. Split tunnel VPNs do not allow the use of local network resources.
    D. Split tunnel VPNs provide differentiated routing.

37. Which one of the following processes improves the consistency and longevity of a database structure?

    A. Input validation
    B. Normalization
    C. Query parametrization
    D. Stored procedures

38. Brian is selecting a mobile device deployment model for his organization. In consultation with leadership, he selected an approach where employees will be able to select the device that they prefer, and the company will purchase it for their use and manage it through their MDM system. What term best describes this deployment model?

    A. BYOD
    B. COBO
    C. COPE
    D. CYOD

39. Harry is investigating a security incident and discovers that the attacker came from outside the network and exploited a zero-day vulnerability that was patched by the vendor two weeks after the incident. What type of threat actor should Harry suspect was behind this incident?

    A. APT
    B. Hacktivist
    C. Insider
    D. Script kiddie

40. Pete is responsible for the security of a highly sensitive system used to control physical infrastructure. The system does not need to communicate with any other systems. Which one of the following security controls would best secure this system?

    A. Air gap
    B. Man trap
    C. Private VLAN
    D. Segmented network

41. What tool was used to generate the network reconnaissance information shown below?

```
------   linkedin.com   ------


Host's addresses:
-------------------

linkedin.com.                     2471    IN    A    108.174.10.10


Name Servers:
-----------------

dns3.p09.nsone.net.               43510   IN    A    198.51.44.73
dns2.p09.nsone.net.               43167   IN    A    198.51.45.9
dns1.p09.nsone.net.               43214   IN    A    198.51.44.9
ns4.p43.dynect.net.               85200   IN    A    204.13.251.43
dns4.p09.nsone.net.               43264   IN    A    198.51.45.73
ns1.p43.dynect.net.               86369   IN    A    208.78.70.43
ns3.p43.dynect.net.               86288   IN    A    208.78.71.43
ns2.p43.dynect.net.               85825   IN    A    204.13.250.43


Mail (MX) Servers:
---------------------------

mail-d.linkedin.com.              86173   IN    A    108.174.6.215
mail-c.linkedin.com.              86112   IN    A    108.174.3.215
mail-a.linkedin.com.              86111   IN    A    108.174.0.215
mail.linkedin.com.                300     IN    A    108.174.6.215
mail.linkedin.com.                300     IN    A    108.174.0.215
mail.linkedin.com.                300     IN    A    108.174.3.215


Trying Zone Transfers and getting Bind Versions:
-----------------------------------------------------


Trying Zone Transfer for linkedin.com on ns4.p43.dynect.net ...
AXFR record query failed: REFUSED
```

A. dig
B. dnsenum
C. nslookup
D. scanless

42. Kenyon is auditing the security of a web application hosted by his organization and discovers that cookies are sent without the SECURE attribute set. What type of attack does this expose the organization to?

A. Request forgery
B. Session replay
C. SQL injection
D. TOC/TOU

43. Brian is concerned about keeping systems in his data center running during a momentary interruption of power. What is the best solution to his requirement?

A. Generator
B. PDU
C. Redundant utility sources
D. UPS

44. Which one of the following Linux commands can be used to display the last few lines of a file?

A. cat
B. grep
C. head
D. tail

45. Which one of the following communications technologies would most likely be found in a home automation system?

A. Baseband
B. Narrow-band
C. Zigbee
D. 5G

46. A contractor for the German company Siemens recently pled guilty to an attack where he altered software that he sold to Siemens so that it would periodically break, requiring the company to hire him to fix it. What term best describes this type of attack?

A. Logic bomb
B. RAT
C. Trojan horse
D. Worm

47. Alan's firm recently engaged a cloud service provider to handle credit card transactions on the company's behalf. What role is the provider playing in this scenario?

A. Data controller
B. Data owner
C. Data processor
D. Data regulator

48. Visitor control procedures, such as visitor registration, badging, and escorting, are an example of what category of security control?

A. Managerial
B. Operational
C. Physical
D. Technical

49. Vincent is reviewing the results of a vulnerability scan and determines that one of the vulnerabilities identified in the report is incorrect because it was addressed by a security patch previously applied to the server. How should Vincent classify this scan result?

A. True positive
B. True negative
C. False positive
D. False negative

50. Which one of the following firewall types would inspect each packet of a connection individually and evaluate each packet against its ruleset?

A. Application
B. Next generation
C. Stateful
D. Stateless

51. Ramzi is implementing DNSSEC to better secure his organization's DNS infrastructure. When he creates his DNSKEY record, what encryption key should he include in it?

A. His organization's public key
B. His organization's private key
C. The public key of his organization's ISP
D. The private key of his organization's ISP

52. Which one of the following industry standards provides specific guidance on the implementation of security controls in the cloud?

A. CCM
B. CSF
C. ISO 27001
D. ISO 27002

53. In the backup strategy shown below, what type of backup is occurring on Thursday?

A. Differential
B. Full
C. Incremental
D. Snapshot

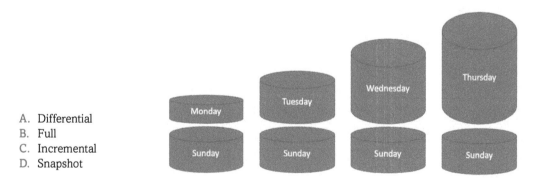

54. Dylan and Liam are using symmetric cryptography to communicate with each other. They have a shared secret key that no other person knows. What goal of cryptography is impossible for them to achieve?

    A. Authentication
    B. Confidentiality
    C. Integrity
    D. Nonrepudiation

55. Which one of the following questions would be most difficult to answer based upon a review of NetFlow records?

    A. What systems were targeted in an attack?
    B. What information left the organization?
    C. What was the source of an attack?
    D. How much data was exchanged during an attack?

56. Brianna is using Microsoft AppLocker to implement application control on her Windows domain. She is using a GPO to prohibit the use of several unauthorized software titles on managed systems. What application control technique is she implementing?

    A. Blacklisting
    B. Whitelisting
    C. Geofencing
    D. Geotagging

57. What type of proxy server is shown in the image below?

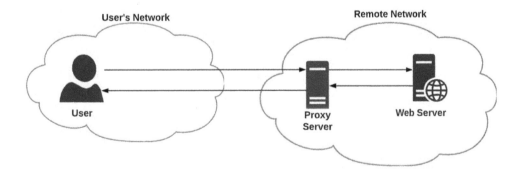

    A. Forward proxy
    B. Reverse proxy
    C. Unilateral proxy
    D. Bilateral proxy

58. Ed is working with functional units in his organization to document the maximum amount of time that they could be without a critical IT service during a disaster. What metric should he use to document this requirement?

A. MTBF
B. MTTR
C. RPO
D. RTO

59. Tony receives reports from the administrators of a web server that users are reporting slow response times and that the administrators suspect malicious activity. Tony reviews the open sessions on the server and sees the sessions shown below. What is most likely happening?

```
TCP    10.1.16.42:20145      186.64.33.16       TIME WAIT
TCP    10.1.16.42:20146      23.45.124.181      TIME WAIT
TCP    10.1.16.42:20147      81.173.195.151     TIME WAIT
TCP    10.1.16.42:20148      114.96.118.87      TIME WAIT
TCP    10.1.16.42:20149      5.27.192.68        TIME WAIT
TCP    10.1.16.42:20150      17.184.111.120     TIME WAIT
TCP    10.1.16.42:20151      22.32.57.52        TIME WAIT
TCP    10.1.16.42:20152      181.71.134.86      TIME WAIT
TCP    10.1.16.42:20153      182.147.132.162    TIME WAIT
TCP    10.1.16.42:20154      66.127.26.166      TIME WAIT
TCP    10.1.16.42:20155      137.13.165.53      TIME WAIT
TCP    10.1.16.42:20156      195.101.62.192     TIME WAIT
TCP    10.1.16.42:20157      97.197.151.129     TIME WAIT
TCP    10.1.16.42:20158      143.17.115.156     TIME WAIT
TCP    10.1.16.42:20159      77.149.147.135     TIME WAIT
TCP    10.1.16.42:20160      73.22.50.115       TIME WAIT
TCP    10.1.16.42:20161      130.160.142.126    TIME WAIT
TCP    10.1.16.42:20162      173.26.20.91       TIME WAIT
TCP    10.1.16.42:20163      9.154.112.129      TIME WAIT
TCP    10.1.16.42:20164      168.37.159.80      TIME WAIT
TCP    10.1.16.42:20165      166.9.190.98       TIME WAIT
TCP    10.1.16.42:20166      104.46.83.83       TIME WAIT
TCP    10.1.16.42:20167      55.9.73.200        TIME WAIT
TCP    10.1.16.42:20168      47.61.175.172      TIME WAIT
TCP    10.1.16.42:20169      180.74.107.50      TIME WAIT
TCP    10.1.16.42:20170      58.30.71.141       TIME WAIT
TCP    10.1.16.42:20171      91.134.124.180     TIME WAIT
TCP    10.1.16.42:20172      96.119.103.131     TIME WAIT
TCP    10.1.16.42:20173      112.111.120.9      TIME WAIT
TCP    10.1.16.42:20174      178.169.5.53       TIME WAIT
TCP    10.1.16.42:20175      69.146.42.185      TIME WAIT
```

A. The system is experiencing a high level of normal user activity.
B. The system is experiencing a basic DoS attack.
C. The system is experiencing a DDoS attack.
D. The system is experiencing a cross-site scripting attack.

60. Dylan recently completed hardening a Windows server and is concerned about whether the server will be vulnerable to new security issues as they arise. What is the best control that he can put in place to protect against this concern?

    A. Data execution prevention
    B. Host firewall
    C. Network firewall
    D. Patch management

61. Nancy's firm is considering the use of a cloud service provider who will provide a fully functional accounting suite to her firm's accounting department. The accountants will access the suite through their web browsers. What type of cloud service is being offered?

    A. IaaS
    B. PaaS
    C. SaaS
    D. XaaS

62. Which one of the following domain names would not be covered by the certificate shown below?

    A. nd.edu
    B. mail.nd.edu
    C. www.nd.edu
    D. test.www.nd.edu

63. Which one of the following approaches allows network administrators to manage configurations using an infrastructure-as-code (IaC) approach?

    A. MSP
    B. MSSP
    C. SDN
    D. SDV

64. Eddie is concerned about the security of cryptographic keys that his organization uses with a cloud service provider. What mechanism can he use to best safeguard those keys from access by unauthorized individuals?

    A. CASB
    B. DLP
    C. HSM
    D. IPS

65. Patrick is investigating a security incident. He believes that the incident is originating from a single system on the Internet and targeting multiple systems on his network. What control could he put in place to stop the incident as quickly as possible?

    A. DDoS mitigation
    B. Host firewall rule
    C. Network firewall rule
    D. Operating system update

66. Roland recently wrote code that implements a new feature demanded by end users of an application he manages. He would like users to examine the feature and determine whether it meets their needs. What environment is most appropriate for this activity?

    A. Development
    B. Production
    C. Staging
    D. Test

67. Which one of the following attacks is successful when an adversary discovers two different files that generate the same hash value?

    A. Brute force
    B. Collision
    C. Downgrade
    D. Rainbow table

68. Jessica is combatting a security incident where a specific piece of malware is continually infecting systems on her network. She would like to use application control technology to block this file. What type of application control should she use?

    A. Blacklisting
    B. Whitelisting
    C. Greylisting
    D. Bluelisting

69. Which one of the following regulations provides strict, detailed procedures for the use of compensating controls?

    A. FERPA
    B. GLBA
    C. HIPAA
    D. PCI DDS

70. Which of the following is NOT one of the elements of the NIST Cybersecurity Framework (CSF)?

    A. Detect
    B. Deter
    C. Protect
    D. Recover

71. Ryan is considering the deployment of an impossible travel time policy in his organization's SIEM. What technology should he enable to allow the implementation of this policy?

    A. Disablement
    B. Geotagging
    C. Lockout
    D. Time of day restrictions

72. Which one of the following frameworks seeks to classify specific adversary tactics and techniques based upon their objective using categories such as those shown below?

Initial Access	Execution	Persistence	Privilege Escalation
Drive-by Compromise	AppleScript	.bash_profile and .bashrc	Access Token Manipulation
Exploit Public-Facing Application	CMSTP	Accessibility Features	Accessibility Features
External Remote Services	Command-Line Interface	Account Manipulation	AppCert DLLs
Hardware Additions	Compiled HTML File	AppCert DLLs	AppInit DLLs

    A. Cyber Kill Chain
    B. Diamond Model
    C. MITRE ATT&CK
    D. NIST CSF

73. In what type of penetration test does the attacker have no access to information about the tested environment other than that gathered during the attacker's own reconnaissance efforts?

A. White box
B. Black box
C. Grey box
D. Blue box

74. Wendy is examining the logs of a web server that was compromised by a remote attacker. She notices that right before the attack, the logs show a series of segmentation fault errors. Other logs indicate that the attacker sent very long input strings to the web server that had malicious commands at the end of the string. What type of attack most likely took place?

A. Buffer overflow
B. Cross-site scripting
C. Cross-site request forgery
D. SQL injection

75. Examine the phishing message shown below. What principle of social engineering is this message most directly attempting to exploit?

 Voice

FINAL NOTICE: Michael, please review the details for shipment ID: AmazonRewards 5H87D5 here: f2prb.info/llehF8tccj Package: $110 bounty

To respond to this text message, reply to this email or visit Google Voice.

A. Authority
B. Consensus
C. Scarcity
D. Urgency

76. Carla recently designed an authentication system for a sensitive application. Users are prompted to enter a password and are granted access if they are located in the office and know the correct password. What combination of authentication factor and attribute is she using?

A. Something you know and something you are
B. Something you know and somewhere you are
C. Something you are and somewhere you are
D. Someone you know and somewhere you are

77. Alan is conducting a penetration test and gains access to an application server. During his attack, he creates a new administrative account on the server that he can use to access the system through its standard user interface. What testing goal is Alan hoping to achieve with this action?

A. Cleanup
B. Lateral movement
C. Persistence
D. Pivoting

78. Which one of the following is not a common location to find SCADA systems?

A. Hospitals
B. Industrial plants
C. Manufacturing lines
D. Power plants

79. Which one of the following situations is an appropriate use case for an open wireless network?

A. Private network in a home with limited physical access
B. Office network in a building in a remote location
C. Guest network for a coffee shop with transient customers
D. Open wireless networks are never appropriate

80. A natural gas utility recently sent customers messages similar to the one below in an effort to convince them to reduce their energy consumption. What principle of social engineering is this message attempting to exploit?

A. Authority
B. Consensus
C. Familiarity
D. Intimidation

81. Which one of the following evidence sources has the highest volatility?

    A. HDD contents
    B. RAM contents
    C. SSD contents
    D. Windows Registry settings

82. Gary is conducting an incident investigation and would like to detect attempts to connect to a server over an RDP connection. What logs would be least likely to contain this information?

    A. Database logs
    B. Netflow logs
    C. Security logs
    D. System logs

83. Marty is the web administrator for the Memphis Belle Casino. He hosts the company's website at memphisbelle.com. He recently discovered that a competitor registered the domain names memphisbell.com, memphisbellecasino.com, and thememphisbelle.com. What type of attack has taken place?

    A. DNS poisoning
    B. DNS hijacking
    C. Domain hijacking
    D. Typosquatting

84. What term refers to the process of checking code into repositories on a continuous basis?

    A. Continuous delivery
    B. Continuous deployment
    C. Continuous integration
    D. Continuous validation

85. Tom would like to send an encrypted message to Jerry using asymmetric cryptography. What key should Tom use to encrypt the message?

    A. Jerry's public key
    B. Jerry's private key
    C. Tom's public key
    D. Tom's private key

86. Which one of the following scripting languages was designed specifically for scripting in Windows environments?

    A. Bash
    B. PowerShell
    C. Python
    D. Ruby

87. Which one of the following pointer values is most likely to result in a denial of service attack if it is dereferenced?

    A. 0xBBBBBBBB
    B. 0x11111111
    C. 0x20000000
    D. NULL

88. When should a forensic investigator begin tracking the chain of custody for evidence?

    A. Upon creation
    B. Upon production
    C. Upon collection
    D. Upon notification of litigation

89. Which one of the following is the earliest version of SNMP to support encryption?

    A. SNMPv1
    B. SNMPv2
    C. SNMPv2c
    D. SNMPv3

90. Which one of the following tools would best help a network engineer identify gaps in wireless coverage?

    A. Access point
    B. Channel overlay
    C. Heat map
    D. Protocol analyzer

Practice Test 1 Answers and Explanations

1. **A.** The best control for Juan to use in this case is encryption. If he applies strong encryption to the data and maintains control of the encryption key, nobody without the key will be able to read the data. Permissions would also be a useful control here, but they would not prevent a rogue employee of the cloud provider from modifying the permissions and accessing the data. High availability and replication do not protect against confidentiality risks.

2. **C.** When encrypting a message with asymmetric cryptography, the sender of the message always encrypts it using the recipient's public key. The recipient can then decrypt the message using their own private key.

3. **B.** The image shows the results of a network vulnerability scan. Of the tools listed here, only Nessus is a network vulnerability scanner and it is the tool that created this output. Nmap is a port scanning tool. Memdump is a memory forensic analysis tool. PowerShell is a Windows scripting language.

4. **C.** The principle of data sovereignty states that data may be subject to the laws of the jurisdictions where it is stored, processed, and transmitted.

5. **D.** While it is possible to make an argument that the network firewall fits into all of these categories, a firewall's primary purpose is to block unwanted traffic from entering the network. Therefore, it is best described as a preventative control.

6. **C.** In this scenario, you are both a cloud consumer and a cloud provider. You are a cloud consumer with respect to the IaaS service offering and you are a cloud provider with respect to the SaaS offering. The question asks about the IaaS relationship, so the correct answer is cloud consumer.

7. **A.** By conducting an ARP spoofing attack, the attacker may fool the victim into thinking that a system controlled by the attacker is the local router or another piece of network infrastructure. They may then route traffic from that victim through their device, eavesdropping on communications and potentially engaging in a man-in-the-middle attack.

8. **C.** The private key for a digital certificate is very sensitive information and must be safeguarded. If a private key is compromised, the digital certificate should be immediately revoked. It is not possible to change the keys for a certificate. The certificate must be revoked and reissued.

9. **A.** This approach, which mixes the local computation on edge devices with the use of a remote cloud offering, is known as fog computing. Hybrid cloud uses cloud environments at both the customer site and the cloud provider site to deliver balanced service. There is no indication that the customer site has a cloud environment in this scenario. We also do not have enough information to determine whether the cloud provider is performing computation in a public cloud or private cloud model.

10. **B.** DMZ networks are specifically designed for systems that must have some public exposure. Placing the system on the DMZ would be the best option. Servers with public access should never be placed on internal networks, including the data center network in this diagram. Placing the server directly on the Internet would prevent the firewall from protecting it.

11. **A.** Rainbow tables may be used to reverse engineer hash values when the range of input values is known to the attacker. Salting values before hashing them protects against this type of attack. Data that has been tokenized, masked, or eliminated through minimization is not susceptible to rainbow table attacks because they do not generate unique output values based upon the original input.

12. **B.** In the figure, individual users have been assigned Full Control of resources, meaning that they have the ability to assign permissions to other users. This is an example of discretionary access control (DAC).

13. **A.** The Attack Complexity (AC) metric describes the conditions beyond the attacker's control that must exist in order to exploit the vulnerability. The Privileges Required (PR) metric describes the level of privileges an attacker must possess before successfully exploiting the vulnerability. The User Interaction (UI) metric captures the requirement for a human user, other than the attacker, to participate in the successful compromise of the vulnerable component. The Attack Vector (AV) metric describes the context by which vulnerability exploitation is possible.

14. **C.** Hot sites are the most advanced of the disaster recovery facilities offered as options in this question. They are running 24x7 and ready to assume primary responsibility at a moment's notice. Other sites require more extensive configuration to assume control. Because of their 24x7 readiness, hot sites are the most expensive to build and operate.

15. **D.** Operating requirements, such as uptime availability, are normally included in a service level agreement (SLA).

16. **B.** Of the certificate file types listed, only PEM is an ASCII text format, such as the certificate shown in the figure. The other certificate types (PFX, DER, and D12) are all binary formats that would not show plaintext characters.

17. **A.** Two-person control, least privilege, and separation of duties are all designed to deter and prevent fraud from occurring in the first place. Of the controls listed, only job rotation serves to detect fraud that has already taken place.

18. **D.** Capture the flag exercises have very specific goals that, when achieved, result in the successful completion of the exercise. These may be run as red team, blue team, and/or purple team exercises.

19. **A.** This is a tricky question because you are being asked to interpret requirements that are not clearly stated in the question itself. Best practice dictates that a database server should not be open to the outside world, but the server needs to be open to at least some internal systems to function properly. Therefore, the most important action she can take is to block all external access by implementing a network firewall rule protecting the server.

20. **A.** Current best practice offered by the National Institute for Standards and Technology (NIST) is that users should no longer be forced to change their passwords and, therefore, password history tracking, and password reuse restrictions are no longer necessary.

21. **D.** The use of hashing stores passwords in a manner where they are not reversible, but the fact that they are not salted leaves the passwords vulnerable to a rainbow table attack where the attacker precomputes the hash values of common passwords and then searches for those values in the password file.

22. **A.** In this scenario, the annualized rate of occurrence (ARO) is once every 50 years, or a 0.02 ARO on an annual basis. The asset value (AV) is $10,000,000 and the exposure factor (EF) is 75%, resulting in a single loss expectancy (SLE) of $7,500,000. The annualized loss expectancy (ALE) is computed by multiplying the SLE by the ARO to get $150,000.

23. **D.** SSL is a deprecated protocol with serious security vulnerabilities. To correct this vulnerability, upgrade from TLS 1.0 (which also has vulnerabilities) to a more modern version of TLS, such as TLS 1.2.

24. **C.** SAE is an authentication standard for Wi-Fi connections introduced with WPA3. It uses a Diffie-Hellman approach to avoid sending the preshared key over the network and prevents eavesdropping on network connections.

25. **B.** Privileged access management (PAM) solutions allow the safeguarding of administrative credentials, among other security controls. They are an ideal way to manage root access to systems.

26. **B.** This is an example of fuzzing: attempting thousands of possible input strings looking for interesting results. Fuzzing is an example of a dynamic (not static) security testing technique because it is directly interacting with the code.

27. **B.** All of these protocols provide secure remote access to systems. However, only RDP provides a native graphical interface, allowing for Windows Remote Desktop Connections out of the box.

28. **C.** The four classification levels used by the U.S. military are (from lowest to highest sensitivity): Unclassified, Confidential, Secret, and Top Secret. Above Top Secret is not a classification level in this scheme.

29. **D.** STIX is a collaborative effort to develop a standardized, structured language to represent cyber threat information. The STIX framework intends to convey the full range of potential cyber threat data elements and strives to be as expressive, flexible, extensible, automatable, and human-readable as possible.

30. **C.** This is an example of a supply chain threat vector because the devices were tampered with before they arrived from the vendor.

31. **A.** Tokens that generate passcodes based upon a counter that increments when the user pushes a button are using the HMAC-based one-time password (HOTP) algorithm. Those that increment automatically based upon the current time are using the time-based one-time password (TOTP) algorithm.

32. **D.** The best way to enable this access is to use a VPC endpoint. This allows a connection between the virtual private cloud (VPC) hosting the server to the block storage service. An Internet gateway or NAT device could also enable this access, but it would have Brian's traffic crossing public networks and expose it to unnecessary risk. Brian is not able to make a direct physical connection because the infrastructure is controlled by the cloud provider.

33. **B.** Quarantine networks are associated with the containment phase of incident response. Systems suspected of compromise may be placed onto quarantine networks to contain the damage while the investigation is ongoing.

34. **C.** The Global Positioning System (GPS) is a satellite-based geolocation system that allows only one-way communication (from the satellite to the receiver). The other communications technologies listed here all allow for two-way communication between devices.

35. **B.** A simulation exercise has participants take part in a real-world scenario and respond as they would during an actual incident. Walkthroughs and tabletop exercises are more conceptual in nature and do not simulate real-world circumstances.

36. **D.** Split tunnel VPNs provide differentiated routing of network traffic. This routing is defined by a tunneling policy which specifies the destination networks that must be routed through the tunnel and those that are handled by the device's normal (non-VPN) network interface. Split tunnel VPNs only encrypt traffic sent through the tunnel. They are often used to facilitate the use of local resources.

37. **B.** All of the activities listed here are good practices for database administration. Stored procedures, query parameterization, and input validation all protect against injection attacks. Normalization ensures that the database has a consistent structure and reduces the need to redesign the database in the future.

38. **D.** This approach best matches the choose your own device (CYOD) deployment model. In this model, employees select their device and it is owned and managed by the company. This is more flexible than the corporate-owned, business-only (COBO) model. The scenario does not give us enough information to know whether personal use is permitted, so we cannot conclude that this is the corporate-owned personally-enabled (COPE) model. The company, not the employee, purchases and owns the device, so it is not the bring your own device (BYOD) model.

39. **A.** The use of a zero-day vulnerability points to the involvement of an advanced persistent threat (APT) group. Although it is always possible that another threat actor obtained a zero-day exploit, this type of sophisticated attack is normally sponsored by an APT group.

40. **A.** The best way to secure a sensitive system of this nature is to keep it completely disconnected from any network. This approach is also known as creating an air gap between the system and other devices.

41. **B.** The dnsenum tool dives deeply into DNS data and generates detailed reconnaissance information, such as that shown in the output. Dig and nslookup are capable of performing DNS queries but they do not perform this type of detailed enumeration. Scanless is a port scanning utility.

42. **B.** Cookies are often used for session authentication. If they are sent without encryption (which the SECURE attribute would require), an attacker eavesdropping on the communication could steal the cookie and use it in a session replay attack.

43. **D.** An uninterruptible power supply (UPS) is designed to maintain system operation during brief power disruptions. Generators and redundant utility sources provide power support during long-term outages, but they also require the use of a UPS to cover the brief outage period that occurs while transitioning to a backup power source. Power distribution units (PDUs) distribute power to devices but do not provide a power source. PDUs normally work in conjunction with UPS devices.

44. **D.** The tail command is designed to show the last lines of a file. The head command displays the first lines of a file. The cat command displays an entire file. The grep command searches for strings in a file.

45. **C.** Zigbee is a communication standard designed for home automation and widely used in modern home automation systems. While it is possible to use the other communications technologies listed for home automation applications, you are much more likely to find Zigbee used for this purpose.

46. **A.** This is an example of a logic bomb, a piece of malicious software that is configured to trigger its payload when some future conditions are met. In this case, the attacker programmed the software to wait until a certain time and then disable itself.

47. **C.** In this scenario, the cloud service provider is processing data on behalf of Alan's organization, making it a data processor. Alan's firm remains the data owner and controller. Neither organization serves as a regulator, as those responsibilities are reserved for government agencies and self-regulatory bodies.

48. **B.** The three categories of security control are managerial, operational, and technical. Physical is a control type, not a control category. Visitor procedures are carried out by humans to reduce risk to the organization and, therefore, would be classified as an operational control.

49. **C.** A false positive scan result occurs when the scanner identifies a vulnerability that does not actually exist on the scanned system. Vincent's incorrect scan result fits into this category.

50. **D.** Stateless firewalls do not keep track of connection state and, therefore, must evaluate each packet individually. Stateful firewalls (including next generation and application firewalls) track connection state and only evaluate new connections against their rulebase.

51. **A.** The DNSKEY record should contain the public key that corresponds to the private key used to sign the records. Since Ramzi's organization manages its own DNS infrastructure, the records would be signed with the organization's private key and should be verified with the organization's public key.

52. **A.** The Cloud Security Alliance's Cloud Controls Matrix (CCM) is specifically designed to cover cloud security control best practices. ISO 27001 and 27002 cover information security management systems more broadly, as does the NIST Cybersecurity Framework (CSF).

53. **A.** This diagram shows a full backup taking place on Sunday, followed by differential backups on Mondays through Thursdays. The key indicator is that the backups are being replaced each weekday because each day's differential backup contains all of the data that was modified on prior days.

54. **D.** Dylan and Liam can easily achieve confidentiality and integrity by using the key to encrypt and decrypt messages. They can also achieve authentication because they know that if a message decrypts with the key, it must have been encrypted by the only other person with knowledge of the key. They cannot, however, achieve nonrepudiation because they have no way to prove to a third party that a message came from the other party and wasn't forged by themselves.

55. **B.** NetFlow records typically contain the source and destination IP addresses and ports, a timestamp, and the amount of data transferred in each direction. NetFlow does not capture packet payloads, so it would not be able to answer questions about the specific data that was transferred.

56. **A.** Any application control technology that works by listing prohibited titles is a blacklisting approach. If Brianna were using AppLocker to limit users to only running preapproved software, that would be an example of whitelisting.

57. **B.** The two types of proxy server are forward proxies and reverse proxies. Forward proxies reside on the user's network and intercept all traffic from local users headed to the Internet. Reverse proxies reside on the web server's network and intercept all inbound web traffic from remote users.

58. **D.** The recovery time objective (RTO) is the amount of time that the business can tolerate an outage during a disaster. The recovery point objective (RPO) is the amount of tolerable data loss. The mean time to repair (MTTR) is the amount of time required to repair a damaged system, while the mean time between failures (MTBF) describes the frequency of failures.

59. **C.** The fact that all of these sessions are in TIME WAIT status indicates that they were initiated by the remote system and never answered by the client. This is a hallmark of a denial of service attack and is not representative of normal user activity. The addresses of all of the remote systems are different, so Tony can conclude that a distributed denial of service (DDoS) attack is underway.

60. **D.** While all of these controls may protect against new vulnerabilities, the best defense is to have strong operating system patch management procedures in place. Ensuring that new updates are promptly applied protects against the vulnerabilities they correct.

61. **C.** The delivery of an entire application through web browsers is a software-as-a-service (SaaS) cloud delivery model.

62. **D.** This is a wildcard certificate for *.nd.edu. Wildcard certificates cover the domain listed on the certificate (nd.edu) as well as any subdomains (www.nd.edu and mail.nd.edu, for example). They only cover one level of subdomain, so this certificate would not cover a second-level subdomain, such as test.www.nd.edu.

63. **C.** Software defined networking (SDN) brings an infrastructure-as-code approach to network devices, allowing network administrators to rapidly configure and reconfigure devices in response to changing network conditions and requirements.

64. **C.** Hardware security modules (HSMs) are specifically designed to safeguard encryption keys, avoiding the need for a human being to directly interact with the key. Some cloud providers offer cloud-based HSM services to their customers as an advanced security offering.

65. **C.** The attack in question could be most quickly stopped with a network firewall rule blocking all traffic from the origin system. Host firewall rules would also address the issue but would be more time-consuming to create on every system. An operating system update would not stop attack traffic. There is also no indication that a DDoS attack is underway, so a DDoS mitigation service would not be helpful.

66. **D.** The process described, where users evaluate features to determine whether they meet business requirements, is known as user acceptance testing (UAT) and it should take place in the test environment. Roland would have created the new feature in a development environment. After the code passes testing, it will move on to staging and then finally into production.

67. **B.** A collision attack occurs when an adversary discovers an alternate input that generates the same hash value as legitimate input. The attacker may then replace the legitimate content with the altered content without invalidating a digital signature.

68. **A.** Blacklisting is used to block specific executables from host systems. That is Jessica's objective in this scenario. Whitelisting is used to restrict executables to those on a preapproved list. Greylisting and bluelisting are not application control strategies.

69. **D.** While compensating controls may be used for any control requirement, PCI DSS includes very detailed procedures for documenting and approving acceptable compensating controls in credit card processing environments.

70. **B.** The five elements of the NIST CSF are identify, protect, detect, respond, and recover. Deter is not one of the NIST CSF elements.

71. **B.** Impossible travel time policies seek to prevent logins from two different geographic locations when it would not have been physically possible for the user to travel between those locations in the time interval between the logins. This is only possible if logins are geotagged with their geographic location.

72. **C.** This is an excerpt from the MITRE ATT&CK framework. The framework, which stands for Adversarial Tactics, Techniques, and Common Knowledge, documents the techniques used by advanced persistent threat (APT) actors.

73. **B.** Black box penetration tests begin by providing the attacker with no information about the target environment. Attackers do receive different levels of information in advance of a white box or grey box test.

74. **A.** The input used in this attack is indicative of a buffer overflow attack, where the attacker sent input too long for the buffers meant to store it. Segmentation fault errors commonly result from buffer overflow attacks.

75. **D.** The inclusion of the words "FINAL NOTICE" in this message most directly align with the social engineering principle of urgency. You could also describe this as using the principles of Familiarity or Trust given its invocation of the Amazon brand name, but those were not answer choices offered to you.

76. **B.** The use of a password is the classic example of a "something you know" authentication factor. Carla is supplementing this with a requirement that users be located in the office, which adds a "somewhere you are" attribute.

77. **C.** Alan is providing himself with a way to access the system at a later date through alternative channels. This is an example of persistence, allowing his access to the system to remain intact even if the original vulnerability he exploited is later patched.

78. **A.** Supervisory control and data acquisition (SCADA) systems are normally found in industrial applications, including manufacturing facilities and power plants. While hospitals do have highly specialized systems, these medical and IoT systems would not normally be classified as SCADA.

79. **C.** Open networks are often used in cases where the network owner does not wish to enforce authentication, such as coffee shops and other guest environments. This is an acceptable use case. Open networks should never be used in a situation where the owner wishes to restrict network access or protect the communication of network users. Even in cases where physical building access is limited, the wireless signal could leak out of the building and be accessible to attackers.

80. **B.** This message is attempting to influence behavior by telling a customer that they differ from the energy consumption habits of their energy efficient neighbors. That is an example of consensus, or social proof.

81. **B.** The highest volatility information is the information likely to disappear first. In this case, the contents of RAM memory are the most volatile. They may be lost as soon as power is removed from the device. The contents of magnetic HDD drives or solid state SSD drives are preserved even when power is removed, and the Windows Registry is stored on disk.

82. **D.** Gary may find relevant information in the system and security logs because the login attempts would likely be tracked by the operating system in those locations. NetFlow records may also contain details of the traffic flow to the server. There is no database involved in an RDP connection, so database logs are not likely to contain useful information.

83. **D.** This is an example of a typosquatting attack, where the attacker registers domain names that are common typos of a legitimate domain. The attacker is not altering any of Marty's DNS records, so this is not a DNS hijacking or poisoning attack. They are also not stealing a domain that Marty already registered so it is not a domain hijacking attack.

84. **C.** Continuous integration (CI) is a development practice that checks code into a shared repository on a consistent ongoing basis. In continuous integration environments this can range from a few times a day to a very frequent process of check-ins and automated builds. Continuous deployment (CD) (sometimes called continuous delivery) which rolls out tested changes into production automatically as soon as they have been tested.

85. **A.** When encrypting a message with asymmetric cryptography, the sender of the message always encrypts it using the recipient's public key. The recipient can then decrypt the message using their own private key.

86. **B.** While all of these scripting environments are available on Windows platforms, PowerShell was designed by Microsoft specifically to enable the scripting of Windows tasks. Microsoft later ported PowerShell to other platforms as well, but it has not gained traction outside of Windows-centric environments due to its focus on tight integration with Windows and Active Directory.

87. **D.** A denial of service attack may occur when software attempts to dereference a NULL pointer value. The other values listed in this question are all legitimate hexadecimal pointer values and are not indicative of a pointer dereferencing attack.

88. **C.** Forensic analysts should begin tracking the chain of custody for evidence as soon as they collect it. They must not wait until production or notification of litigation because this would leave a period of time where the evidence was unaccounted for. It is not possible to begin a chain of custody when data is first created, as it has not yet been gathered into evidence at that point.

89. **D.** Encryption was not added as an option until version three of the simple network management protocol (SNMP).

90. **C.** Heat maps are the result of conducting a site survey and provide a visual depiction of wireless network coverage in a facility. They are a very helpful tool when evaluating Wi-Fi coverage.

CHAPTER 7

Practice Test 2

1. After running a vulnerability scan on a server containing sensitive information, Mitch discovers the results shown below. What should be Mitch's highest priority?

A. Modifying encryption settings
B. Disabling the guest account
C. Disabling cached logins
D. Patching and updating software

2. Gary is configuring a wireless access point that supports the WPS service. What risk exists in all implementations of WPS that he should consider?

   A. Weak encryption
   B. Physical access to the device
   C. Offline brute force attack
   D. Impossible to disable WPS

3. Alan is a software developer working on a new security patch for one of his organization's products. What environment should he use when actively working on the code?

   A. Production
   B. Test
   C. Development
   D. Staging

4. Bill suspects that an attacker is exploiting a zero-day vulnerability against his organization. Which one of the following attacker types is most likely to engage in this type of activity?

   A. Hacktivist
   B. Script kiddie
   C. APT
   D. White hat

5. Ryan works for a firm that has a limited budget and he would like to purchase a single device that performs firewall, intrusion prevention, and content filtering functions. Which one of the following product categories is most likely to meet his needs?

   A. SIEM
   B. UTM
   C. DLP
   D. NAC

6. Cole is testing a software application that must be able to handle the load of 10,000 simultaneous users each time a new product goes on sale. Which one of the following software testing techniques will best help Cole determine whether the environment will meet this requirement?

   A. Fuzz testing
   B. Regression testing
   C. Static analysis
   D. Stress testing

7. Jacob's company recently implemented a new technique for securing remote access for users of BYOD mobile devices. In this approach, the user opens an application which then allows the user to connect to corporate systems. No corporate data is available outside the application. What term best describes this approach?

   A. Sideloading
   B. Storage segmentation
   C. Full device encryption
   D. Containerization

8. Consider the Linux filesystem directory listing shown here. Robert has the user account rsmith and would like to access the file secret_file.txt. Robert is a member of the leaders group. What permission does Robert have to this file?

```
drwxr-xr-x    3 mchapple  staff    96 Sep 27 08:47 .
drwxr-xr-x+ 117 mchapple  staff  3744 Sep 27 08:47 ..
-rwxrw-r--    1 mchapple  staff     2 Sep 27 08:47 secret_file.txt
```

A. Robert can only read the file.
B. Robert can read and execute the file.
C. Robert can read and write the file.
D. Robert can read, write, and execute the file.

9. This diagram shows the results of testing the accuracy of a biometric authentication system. In this diagram, what characteristic is designated by the arrow?

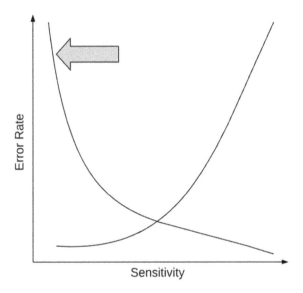

A. IRR
B. FRR
C. CER
D. FAR

10. Henry would like to use a secure protocol to obtain a graphic user interface on a Windows system that he manages remotely. Which one of the following protocols would best meet his needs?

A. VPN
B. SSH
C. Telnet
D. RDP

11. Rudy is configuring a router that sits at the connection between his organization's network and the Internet. He is concerned about spoofed packets and would like to configure the router to perform anti-spoofing filtering. Which one of the following source IP addresses should be blocked at the router for inbound traffic?

    A. 129.168.1.100
    B. 12.168.1.100
    C. 278.168.1.100
    D. 192.168.1.100

12. Julian is attempting to correlate information from the security logs of several different systems and notices that the clocks on those systems are not synchronized, making it difficult to compare log entries. Which one of the following services can best help Julian synchronize clocks?

    A. LDAP
    B. SMNP
    C. NTP
    D. RTP

13. Jena is looking for a permanently situated disaster recovery option that best balances cost with recovery time. Which one of the following options should she consider?

    A. Cold site
    B. Warm site
    C. Hot site
    D. Mobile site

14. Roger found the following image on a website that he administers. What type of attacker likely performed this defacement?

    A. APT
    B. Hacktivist
    C. Nation state
    D. Organized crime

ANONYMOUS

Nothing is safe, you put your faith in this political party and they take no measures to protect you.

They offer you free speech yet they censor your voice.

WAKE UP!

15. Frank is implementing a new VPN that will carry communications between his organization's offices around the world. His primary requirement is that the network must be able to withstand outages without disrupting communications. What term best describes Frank's requirement?

   A. High latency
   B. Low resiliency
   C. Low latency
   D. High resiliency

16. Allen is building a cloud computing environment that will provide services on demand to other administrators within his organization. What type of cloud environment is Allen creating?

   A. Public cloud
   B. Private cloud
   C. Hybrid cloud
   D. Community cloud

17. Tom would like to conduct a security assessment that provides an accurate evaluation of the likelihood that an attacker could gain access to systems on his network. Which one of the following assessment tools would best meet Tom's goal?

   A. Code review
   B. Vulnerability scan
   C. Penetration test
   D. Risk assessment

18. Roger is responsible for implementing a set of data quality guidelines and ensuring that they are being carried out on a day-to-day basis. Which one of the following best describes Roger's role in data governance.

   A. Data custodian
   B. Data owner
   C. Data steward
   D. Data user

19. Consider the U.S. government personal identity verification (PIV) card shown here. When the card holder wishes to provide non-repudiation for a message, which certificate is used?

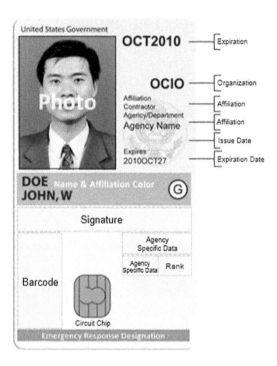

A. PIV authentication certificate
B. Encryption certificate
C. Card authentication certificate
D. Digital signature certificate

20. Which mode of cipher operation is shown here?

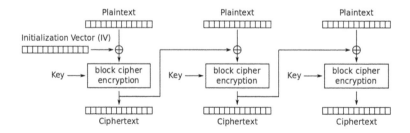

A. CFB
B. ECB
C. OFB
D. CBC

21. Which one of the following is the most likely motivation for an attack waged by a criminal organization?

    A. Financial
    B. Political
    C. Thrill
    D. Grudge

22. Ryan is configuring his organization's network firewall to allow access from the Internet to the web server located in the DMZ. He would like to configure firewall rules to ensure that all access to the web server takes place over encrypted connections. What rules should he configure regarding traffic from the Internet to the web server?

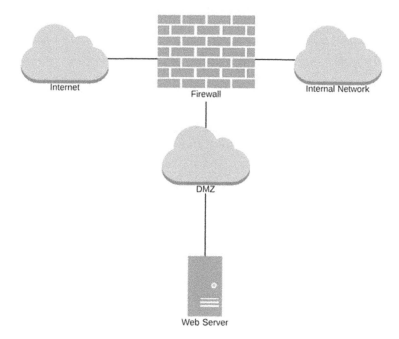

Internet

Firewall

Internal Network

DMZ

Web Server

    A. Allow both TCP ports 80 and 443
    B. Allow TCP port 443 and block TCP port 80
    C. Block both TCP ports 80 and 443
    D. Allow TCP port 80 and block TCP port 443

23. Which one of the following algorithms was approved by the US federal government for use in creating digital signatures under the Digital Signature Standard (DSS)

    A. RSA
    B. DSA
    C. AES
    D. 3DES

24. Susan is conducting a business impact analysis for her organization as part of the organization's business continuity planning initiative. During that analysis, she identifies the amount of data loss that would be acceptable to incur while recovering a system during a disaster. What metric should she use to capture this information?

    A. RPO
    B. RTO
    C. MTTR
    D. MTBF

25. Paul is evaluating the performance of his organization's business continuity efforts and measures the amount of time that it takes to restore service when a critical router fails. What metric should Paul use to capture this information?

    A. MTBF
    B. MTTR
    C. RTO
    D. RPO

26. Karl would like to take advantage of mobile devices to implement a second authentication factor for his organization's ERP system. Which one of the following approaches typically has the highest user satisfaction rate?

    A. Email notification
    B. SMS notification
    C. Push notification
    D. App-based passcode generator

27. During a vulnerability scan, Bill discovers that a system running on his network has an outdated version of Linux. The system is a network appliance and Bill can only access it through the appliance's GUI. What should Bill do next?

    A. Upgrade the operating system by downloading the source files for a current version of Linux.
    B. Obtain an update from the appliance manufacturer.
    C. Use the yum or apt-get commands to upgrade the operating system.
    D. No action is necessary.

28. When performing encryption using the Triple DES algorithm, how many different keys are required to use the most secure mode of operation?

    A. 1
    B. 2
    C. 3
    D. 4

29. Alison is troubleshooting a connectivity issue where the database server is unable to access a file stored on the file server. She verified that the file system permissions are correct. She suspects a firewall issue and examines the network diagram shown here. What is the best place for her to investigate next?

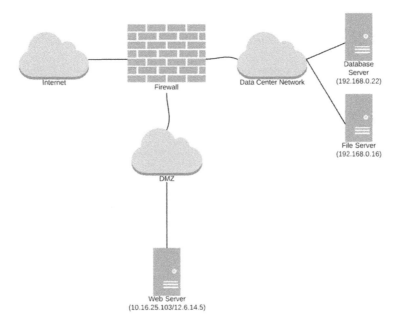

A. Web server host firewall
B. Database server host firewall
C. Hardware firewall
D. File server host firewall

30. Flo is the administrator for a server that is using RAID 5 with a six-disk array. In this approach, what is the maximum number of disks that may fail without the permanent loss of data?

A. 1
B. 2
C. 3
D. 4

31. April recently selected a high quality safe that is rated to require at least 30 minutes for a skilled intruder to open with appropriate tools. She selected this over a lesser quality safe that did not provide a guaranteed rating. What type of control is this upgraded safe?

A. Corrective
B. Detective
C. Preventive
D. Compensating

32. Eric would like to select a key stretching algorithm that is protected against attack by requiring a brute force attacker to use both extensive memory and CPU resources. Which one of the following algorithms would be most appropriate?

A. RIPEMD
B. PBKDF2
C. HMAC
D. Bcrypt

33. When a file system consults an access control list (ACL), what phase of the AAA process is occurring?

A. Authentication
B. Identification
C. Authorization
D. Accounting

34. Maureen is conducting a penetration attack against a website and she has gained access to a hashed password file from the site. The site does not have a strong password policy. Which one of the following techniques would be the most effective way for Maureen to exploit this file?

A. Rainbow table attack
B. Dictionary attack
C. Offline brute force attack
D. Online brute force attack

35. What mode of encryption is shown here?

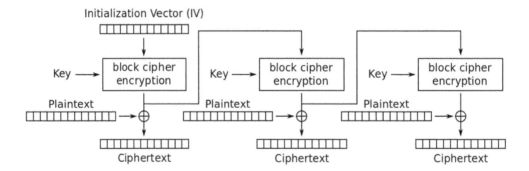

A. OFB
B. CFB
C. CBC
D. ECB

36. Which one of the following key lengths is not supported by the AES encryption algorithm?

    A. 128 bits
    B. 192 bits
    C. 256 bits
    D. 512 bits

37. Fran would like to prevent users in her organization from downloading apps from third-party app stores. Which one of the following mobile device categories provides the strongest controls against the use of third party app stores?

    A. Apple iPhone
    B. Samsung Galaxy
    C. Motorola Moto
    D. Huawei P-series

38. Consider the load balanced servers shown below. The load balancer is using affinity scheduling and receives a request from a client who already has an active session on Server B. What server will receive the new request from that client?

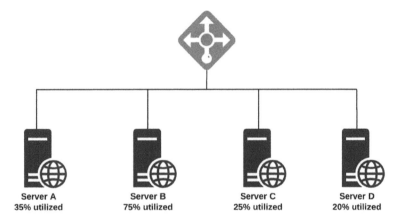

Server A	Server B	Server C	Server D
35% utilized	75% utilized	25% utilized	20% utilized

    A. Server A
    B. Server B
    C. Server C
    D. Server D

39. Lynn would like to adjust her organization's password policy to be in line with current standards published by NIST. How often should she set user passwords to expire?

    A. Every 180 days
    B. Every 30 days
    C. Every 90 days
    D. Never

40. Peter is conducting a penetration test of his own organization. He completed his reconnaissance work and is now attempting to gain access to a system with Internet exposure. What phase of the test is Peter in?

A. Pivot
B. Initial exploitation
C. Escalation of privilege
D. Persistence

41. Given the network diagram shown below, what is the most appropriate location to place the correlation engine for a SIEM?

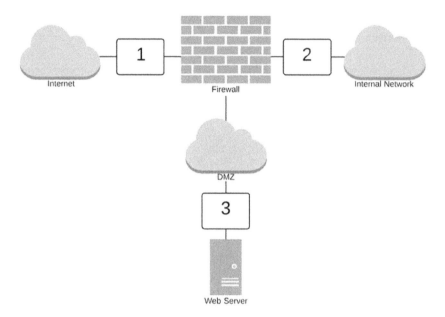

A. Location 1
B. Location 2
C. Location 3
D. None of the above

42. Marty is designing a new access control system for his organization. He created groups for each type of user: engineers, managers, designers, marketers, and sales. Each of these groups has different access permissions. What type of access control scheme is Marty using?

A. Role-based access control
B. Rule-based access control
C. Discretionary access control
D. Mandatory access control

43. Tina is concerned that an intruder who gains access to a facility may disconnect an existing network device from the wired network and use the jack to connect a malicious device. What switch security feature would prevent this type of attack?

A. Port security
B. Flood guard
C. Loop protection
D. Traffic encryption

44. Solve the exclusive or (XOR) operation shown below.

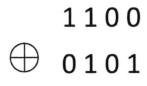

A. 1101
B. 0110
C. 1001
D. 0010

45. Which one of the following security tasks would benefit the least from introducing automation?

A. Password resets
B. Firewall log analysis
C. Risk assessments
D. Configuration management

46. Which one of the following mobile device deployment models allows employees to select the device they would like to use from a list of approved corporate-owned models?

A. BYOD
B. COPE
C. CYOD
D. Corporate-owned

47. Glenn is designing the network security controls around a crucial system that controls the functioning of a manufacturing process. He would like to apply the strongest degree of network segmentation possible. Which one of the following controls would best achieve his objective?

A. VLAN segmentation
B. Air gap
C. Firewall zone segmentation
D. Router segmentation

48. Gary is conducting a penetration test and obtains a copy of the password file for a web service. He creates a list of common passwords and uses those to try to break passwords in the file. What type of attack is Gary waging?

   A. Offline brute force
   B. Online brute force
   C. Rainbow table
   D. Dictionary

49. Tom is investigating an application that slowly consumes memory on a server until it is using all available resources, at which time the system hangs. After a reboot, the application uses a minimal amount of memory, but that memory consumption again grows until the next crash. What is the most likely cause of this issue?

   A. Pointer dereference
   B. Buffer overflow
   C. Integer overflow
   D. Memory leak

50. Which one of the following authentication mechanisms is generally not used in smartphone devices?

   A. Fingerprint scanning
   B. Facial recognition
   C. Passcode
   D. Retinal scanning

51. Laura is implementing DNSSEC to add security to her organization's Domain Name Service (DNS) infrastructure. What cipher suite must she support to ensure compatibility with other DNSSEC servers?

   A. RSA/SHA-512
   B. RSA/MD5
   C. RSA/SHA-256
   D. RSA/SHA-1

52. Which one of the following attack types does NOT usually depend upon a design flaw in a web application?

   A. XSRF
   B. Shimming
   C. XSS
   D. SQL injection

53. What attribute of a digital certificate indicates the specific purpose for which the certificate may be used?

   A. Private key
   B. Serial number
   C. Public key
   D. OID

54. Gina's organization uses a minification function to process their Javascript code. This results in code that uses generic variable names, no comments, and minimal spacing, such as the code shown here. What term best describes what has occurred to this code from a security perspective?

```
;eval(function(p,a,c,k,e,r){e=function(c){return(c<a?'':e(parseInt(c/a)))+
((c=c%a)>35?
String.fromCharCode(c+29):c.toString(36))};if(!''.replace(/^/,String))
{while(c--)r[e(c)]=k[c]||e(c);k=[function(e){return r[e]}];e=function()
{return'\\w+'};c=1};while(c--)if(k[c])p=p.replace(new
RegExp('\\b'+e(c)+'\\b','g'),k[c]);return p}('16 aO(t,e,i){18 a;"5n"==1P t?
a=3D("#"+t):"bq"==1P t&&(a=t);18 s,o;2s(e){1i"b7":s="dX 3D b0",o=\'aU aQ 67
dC dB aK 64 62 dm dl an dj di 4c 2F 3D aC de db 22 3m 2z az 62 d9. <ay>5Z d3
2J 62 5Y dl d0 2z 2F cZ cU 4c 3m 6V cN 2F "cM cD cz 2z 51" cx c8 2F c7 & c0
bY 3G.</ay>\';1p;1i"9J":s="5T 3D b0",o="aU aQ 67 bQ bO bN an 5T 3L ("+i+\')
4c 2F 3D aC. 3m bM at bK 3L 1.7.0 64 bJ. 5Z 9y 3D 2z 1.10.x 64 bG. bF: 5Z do
2V ec 2F 3D eb aK 2J 5Y 6V do 2V 9y 2z 2.x 3L 4c 3D ea 5a 3M 2V 9a e7 e5 e3
67 e1 7 & 8. <a 2I="96://dP.dN.2q/dA/4/5J-22-dy/#dx-13&cB-60">cu cs cr f6 bX
bW 3D by bP bx.</a>\'}a.1m("12-5E"),a.4h(\'<p 1r="12-eI">!</p>\'),a.4h(\'<p
1r="12-5E-ee">3m: \'+s+"</p>"),a.4h(\'<p 1r="12-5E-8f">\'+o+"</p>")}!16(t)
{1d("2K"!=1P 7V)22(18 e 41 7V)14[e]=7V[e];t.9g.36=16(e){18
a="1.7.0",s=t.9g.b7,o=t(14),r=16(t,e){22(18
i=t.1K("."),a=e.1K("."),s=0;s<i.1h;++s)
{1d(a.1h==s)21!1;1d(1b(i[s])!=1b(a[s]))21 1b(i[s])>1b(a[s])?!1:!0}21
i.1h!=a.1h?!0:!0};1d(r("1.8.0",s)||o.1m("12-9b"),r(a,s)){1d((1P
e).3A("bq|2K")}21 14.1L(16(t){1B i(14,e)});1d("11"==e){18
n=t(14),s=t(14).11("3m").g;1d(n)21 n}lw 1d("ck"==e){18 d=t(14).11("3m").o;1d(d)21
d}lw{1d("cd"!==e)21 14.1L(16(i){18 a=t(14).11("3m");1d(a)
{1d(!a.g.2P&&!a.g.4j)1d("3W"==1P e)e>0&&e<a.g.2t+1&&e!=a.g.1Z&&a.4u(e);lw
2s(e)
{1i"1T":a.o.73(a.g),a.1T("72");1p;1i"1X":a.o.6Z(a.g),a.1X("72");1p;1i"23":a.
g.2u||(a.o.8W(a.g),a.g.2D=!0,a.23())}"bZ"==e&&a.2h(),
(a.g.2u||!a.g.2u&&a.g.2D)&&"1s"==e&&
(a.o.bp(a.g),a.g.2D=!1,a.g.1J.17(\'10[1e*="2j.2q"], 10[1e*="4S.be"],
10[1e*="2j-4U.2q"], 10[1e*="5A.3O"]\\').1L(16()
{2k(t(14).11("7m"))})},a.1s(),"ew"==e&&a.ba()}});18
d=t(14).11("3m").8G;1d(d)21 d}}lw aO(o,"9J",s)};18 i=16(e,d){18
l=14;1.$el=t(e).1m("12-2a"),1.$el.11("3m",1),1.4y=16()
{1d(1.8G=i.aN,1.o=t.4z({},1.8G,d),1.g=t.4z({},i.6E),1.1v=t.4z({},i.aI),1.9P=
t.4z({},i.9C),1.g.es=t(e).2m("12-9b")?!1:!0,1.g.er=t(e).4n(),1.g.2B&&
(1.o.4E=!1),"e2"==1.o.2A&&(1.o.2A=!0),"9j"==1.o.2A&&(1.o.2A=!1),"2K"!=1P
```

A. Encryption
B. Obfuscation
C. Hashing
D. Masking

55. What type of security control is shown below?

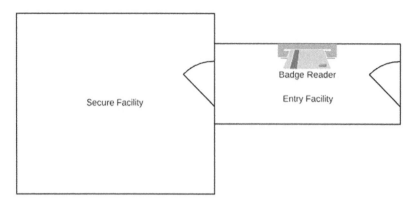

A. Mantrap
B. Faraday cage
C. Bollard
D. Fence

56. What cryptographic technique does WPA use to overcome the weaknesses in the WEP algorithm?

A. TKIP
B. CCMP
C. Hashing
D. AES

57. Yvonne is investigating an attack where a user visited a malicious website and the website sent an instruction that caused the browser to access the user's bank website and initiate a money transfer. The user was logged into the bank website in a different browser tab. What type of attack most likely took place?

A. Stored XSS
B. XSRF
C. Reflected XSS
D. DOM XSS

58. Brianne is concerned that the logs generated by different devices on her network have inaccurate timestamps generated by the differing internal clocks of each device. What protocol can best assist her with remediating this situation?

A. NTP
B. TLS
C. SSH
D. OSCP

59. Tina is investigating a security incident on a system in her organization. The user reports that he can't access any files on the device and he sees the warning message shown below. What type of attack has taken place?

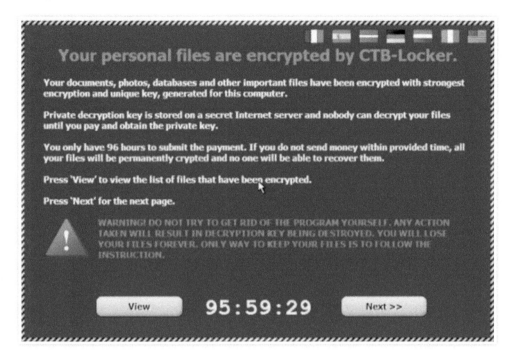

A. Keylogger
B. Spyware
C. RAT
D. Ransomware

60. Which one of the following systems would be most likely to detect a distributed denial of service attack that attempts to perform SYN flooding from across the Internet to a web server on an organization's DMZ network?

A. Heuristic NIDS
B. Heuristic HIDS
C. Signature NIDS
D. Behavioral NIDS

61. Mandy works for an organization that is planning an expansion into Italy and France over the next two years. What privacy regulation will apply to her company's operation in those countries?

A. HIPAA
B. DPD
C. GDPR
D. GLBA

62. During a vulnerability assessment, Sonia discovered the issue shown below in a web server used by her organization. What is likely to be the most effective method for resolving this issue?

A. Patching Apache Tomcat
B. Patching the operating system
C. Deploying a web application firewall
D. Deploying a content filter

63. Paul is conducting a penetration test and has gained a foothold on a web server used by the target organization. He is now attempting to use that web server to gain access to a file server on the organization's internal network. What stage of the penetration testing process is Paul in?

A. Reconnaissance
B. Initial exploitation
C. Pivot
D. Scoping

64. Lynn examines the userPassword attribute for a variety of users of the OpenLDAP system and sees the results shown here. How are these passwords stored?

```
userPassword: {SSHA}6F9757D99047E1571771A6E3EA1FB73A401D9EF0
userPassword: {SSHA}D96D5FEE3E05F9F95558DC0272C86B7E77089D07
userPassword: {SSHA}6EDC6DEAB58E4C149032FE96981F20B708678769
userPassword: {SSHA}B71BA13F030250BC9445EFB79C0781C73C47C200
userPassword: {SSHA}B431BA4E7933A09094EFDE9D108BC484BEA98055
userPassword: {SSHA}7FE3060A7B7C90648C95BE0EE3B83E91BEBA535D
userPassword: {SSHA}E98472F80026830ED2D0FD871CB73AC8E3F5B318
userPassword: {SSHA}B79D18F2EB539C70C5C7B1A825F4B2633545239C
userPassword: {SSHA}A995C4E213B12BFF49349E528AA403D1AAAD1F30
```

A. Unsalted form
B. Hashed form
C. Encrypted form
D. Cleartext form

65. What biometric authentication technology could be used on the image shown here?

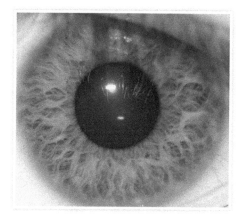

A. Facial recognition
B. Iris recognition
C. Retinal recognition
D. Fingerprint recognition

66. Roland's company requires that supervisors approve payment requests entered by accounting clerks when the total amount of the payment is over $10,000. What type of control is this?

A. Least privilege
B. Separation of duties
C. Two-person control
D. Job rotation

67. During a recent penetration test, the attacker dressed up in a security guard uniform identical to those used by a firm and began directing people to vacate the data center due to a security threat. What principle of social engineering BEST describes this technique?

A. Authority
B. Intimidation
C. Consensus
D. Scarcity

68. Vic is the security administrator for a field engineering team that must make connections back to the home office. Engineers also must be able to simultaneously connect to systems on their customer's networks to perform troubleshooting. Vic would like to ensure that connections to the home office use a VPN. What type of VPN would best meet his needs?

A. Full tunnel
B. Split tunnel
C. TLS
D. IPsec

69. What type of hypervisor is shown in the image?

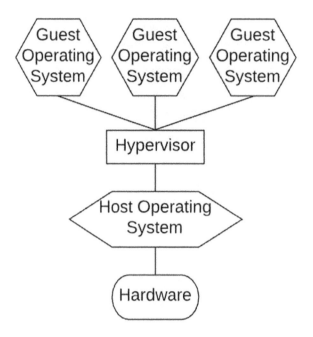

A. Type 1 Hypervisor
B. Type 2 Hypervisor
C. Type 3 hypervisor
D. Type 4 hypervisor

Questions 70 through 73 refer to the following scenario:

Kyle is conducting a business impact assessment for his organization. As a result of his work, he identifies that there is a single point of failure in his network caused by an expensive network firewall that protects a Big Data storage environment. The organization chooses not to make the firewall redundant. Kyle estimates that the firewall will fail once every four years and that it will take 3 days to obtain and install a replacement if it does fail.

Kyle explains this disruption to business leaders and determines that the business cannot tolerate an outage of more than four hours. If there were an outage, the organization must be able to restore all of the data contained in the environment to the state it was in at most 1 hour prior to the failure.

---

70. What is the MTTR in this scenario?

A. 1 hour
B. 4 hours
C. 3 days
D. 4 years

71. What is the MTBF in this scenario?

   A. 1 hour
   B. 4 hours
   C. 3 days
   D. 4 years

72. What is the RTO in this scenario?

   A. 1 hour
   B. 4 hours
   C. 3 days
   D. 4 years

73. What is the RPO in this scenario?

   A. 1 hour
   B. 4 hours
   C. 3 days
   D. 4 years

74. Consider the transitive domain relationships shown here. Joe has a user account in Domain D. Which one of the following statements is incorrect?

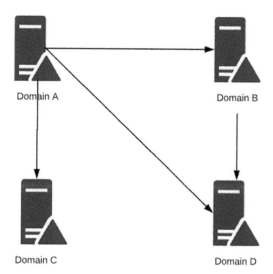

   A. Joe can use his account in Domain A
   B. Joe can use his account in Domain B
   C. Joe can use his account in Domain C
   D. Joe can use his account in Domain D

75. Molly's organization has a shared account that they use to provide access to vendors. What is the primary security objective that is sacrificed using this model, assuming that the password is not shared with unauthorized individuals?

   A. Least privilege
   B. Accountability
   C. Confidentiality
   D. Integrity

76. Donna is looking for a secure way to transfer files between systems. The systems in question are already configured for SSH connections. What file transfer method could she use that would leverage the SSH protocol?

   A. SFTP
   B. FTPS
   C. Dropbox
   D. HTTPS

77. Kristen's organization recently entered into a business partnership with a new shipping vendor. She is placing a server on the network that will facilitate shipping transactions and must be accessed by both the vendor and internal users. Which network zone is the most appropriate placement for this server?

   A. Guest network
   B. Intranet
   C. DMZ
   D. Extranet

78. Tonya is analyzing host firewall logs in an effort to diagnose a service that is not responding to user requests. She finds entries in the host firewall logs indicating that the traffic was allowed. What is the most likely cause of the service not responding?

   A. Application failure
   B. Host firewall misconfiguration
   C. Network IPS misconfiguration
   D. Network firewall misconfiguration

79. Which one of the following security controls would be the least effective at detecting fraud committed by an employee?

   A. Separation of duties
   B. Job rotation
   C. Mandatory vacation
   D. Privileged access monitoring

80. Brian is the physical security official for a data center hosting organization. While entering the building this morning, he noticed that one employee used his badge to enter the building and then held the door open for two other employees. Which one of the following situations occurred?

A. Piggybacking
B. Dumpster diving
C. Shoulder surfing
D. Impersonation

81. Consider the statistics shown here for a biometric authentication system. What is the system's FRR based upon this data?

	Authorized User	Unauthorized User
Accept	45	2
Reject	5	48

A. 2%
B. 4%
C. 5%
D. 10%

82. Carl is selecting a data loss prevention (DLP) system for use in his organization. He would like to choose an approach that requires the least maintenance effort from his team. Which solution would best meet Carl's needs?

A. Host-based DLP
B. Network-based DLP
C. Cloud-based DLP
D. Signature-based DLP

83. Ryan would like to restrict use of a sensitive mobile application so that users may only use it when they are located in a building on his company's corporate campus. Which one of the following technologies can he use to best enforce this restriction?

A. Application control
B. Geofencing
C. Remote wiping
D. Containerization

84. Val is conducting a black box penetration test against a website and would like to try to gain access to a user account. If she has not yet gained access to any systems on the target network, which one of the following attacks would be most effective?

A. Rainbow table
B. Offline brute force
C. Offline dictionary
D. Online brute force

85. Gayle is logging onto a website managed by a third party vendor using credentials provided by her employer. The authentication system uses SAML-based authentication. In this scenario, who is the identity provider?

    A. Gayle's web browser
    B. The vendor
    C. Gayle's employer
    D. The certificate authority

86. Corwin is beginning a penetration test and is reviewing the technical documentation provided by management that explains how the systems are designed and laid out. What type of test is Corwin most likely performing?

    A. Red box
    B. Grey box
    C. White box
    D. Black box

87. Sandra would like to prevent users of her organization's mobile devices from using those devices to connect laptops and other systems to the network. What feature of mobile devices should she disable through her mobile device management platform?

    A. Split tunneling
    B. Tethering
    C. Split horizon DNS
    D. TLS

Questions 88 through 90 refer to the following scenario.

Gavin is considering different options for backing up the file server used by his organization. This server exhibits the normal usage patterns of an office file server. The four strategies he is considering are shown here:

Option	Monday	Tuesday	Wednesday	Thursday	Friday
A	Full	Full	Full	Full	Full
B	Full	Incremental	Incremental	Incremental	Incremental
C	Full	Differential	Differential	Differential	Differential
D	Full	Differential	Full	Differential	Full

---

88. If Gavin's primary concern is conserving disk space, which option should he choose?

    A. Option A
    B. Option B
    C. Option C
    D. Option D

89. If Gavin's primary concern is speed of recovering the system after a failure, which option should he choose?

    A. Option A
    B. Option B
    C. Option C
    D. Option D

90. If Gavin's primary concern is the amount of time required to perform the backups, which option should he choose?

    A. Option A
    B. Option B
    C. Option C
    D. Option D

Practice Test 2 Answers and Explanations

1.   **D.** In this scenario, there are several critical vulnerabilities that all relate to the system running unsupported or unpatched components. While the other issues presented in this question do also appear in the scan results, updating this software and applying necessary security patches would result in the greatest risk reduction and should be Mitch's highest priority.

2.   **B.** Several vulnerabilities exist in different implementations of WPS. Some allow an offline brute force attack known as Pixie Dusk. Others may make it impossible for device administrators to disable WPS. Other may use weak encryption. The risk that applies to all WPS devices is the risk of physical access. If an attacker gains physical access to the device, he or she can join the network.

3.   **C.** Development environments are designed for active use by developers who are creating new code. These environments are the only location where code should be modified. Once code is ready for testing, it is released from the development environment into a test environment for software testing. After the completion of user acceptance testing, the code is moved from the test environment into a staging environment where it is prepared for final deployment into the production environment. Developers should never have permission to move code themselves but should only be able to move code between environments through the use of a managed change control system.

4.   **C.** While it is possible that any type of attacker might engage in a zero-day attack, it is most likely to find these vulnerabilities exploited by an advanced persistent threat (APT). APT attackers are more likely to have the technical resources to discover and use zero-day vulnerabilities.

5.   **B.** Unified threat management (UTM) solutions combine the features of many different security technologies onto a single, cost-effective platform. They are most appropriate for use in small businesses, as they typically are not capable of high performance activity.

6.   **D.** Stress testing, otherwise known as load testing, is a technique designed to determine the maximum capacity of an application. Cole can use stress testing to evaluate the performance of the application environment under the pressure of 10,000 simultaneous users. Static analysis, regression testing, and fuzz testing all test applications but are not able to determine an application's performance under load.

7.   **D.** Containerization approaches embed all access to corporate systems with a secure application container. No data from inside the container is accessible from other applications on the device. The entire container is controlled by the organization's mobile device management solution. Storage segmentation is a similar solution that provides separate storage for different data classifications but this approach goes beyond storage segmentation. Sideloading is a technique for loading applications and data onto a device outside of normal channels. Full device encryption provides encrypted storage for all data on a device but does not differentiate between corporate and personal data.

8.   **A.** Robert is not the file's owner, nor is he a member of the file's group. Therefore, the permissions that he has are those that apply to all users. In a Linux permission string, the first character indicates whether an object is a directory or not. The next three characters indicate the permissions assigned to the file's owner. The three characters after that assign permissions to members of the file's group. The next three characters indicate the all users permissions. The all users permissions for this file are 'r--'. Therefore, Robert can read the file but cannot write to it or execute it.

9. **D.** The accuracy of a biometric authentication system is described using three metrics. The false acceptance rate (FAR) is the frequency at which the system admits a person who should not be admitted. The false rejection rate (FRR) is the frequency at which the system denies access to an authorized user incorrectly. The FAR can be improved by increasing the sensitivity of the system, while the FRR can be improved by decreasing the sensitivity of the system. Because of this, the best measure of accuracy is the crossover error rate (CER), which is the sensitivity point at which the FAR and FRR are equal.

10. **D.** The Remote Desktop Protocol (RDP) provides a secure, graphical user interface connection to a remote Windows system and would meet Henry's needs out of the box. It may be possible to configure remote access via a secure shell (SSH) connection, but this would require an additional tool and configuration. A virtual private network (VPN) could provide a secure connection to the remote network but does not inherently offer a graphical interface to manage a system. Telnet is not a secure protocol.

11. **D.** 12.168.1.100 and 129.168.1.100 are valid public IP addresses and should be permitted as inbound source addresses. 278.168.1.100 is not a valid IP address because the first octet is greater than 255. It does not need to be blocked because it is not possible. This leaves 192.168.1.100. This address is a private address and should never be seen as a source address on packets crossing an external network connection.

12. **C.** The Network Time Protocol (NTP) is designed to synchronize clocks on systems and devices with a centralized source. The Simple Network Management Protocol (SNMP) is designed for the management of network devices and does not synchronize time across a variety of devices. The Lightweight Directory Access Protocol (LDAP) is a directory services protocol and does not perform time synchronization. The Real Time Protocol (RTP) is an application protocol designed for videoconferencing and, despite the name, does not perform time synchronization.

13. **B.** Cold sites have only basic infrastructure available and require the longest period of time to activate operations. They are also the cheapest option. Warm sites add hardware, and possible software, to the mix but do not have a current copy of the data running. They require hours to activate. Hot sites are up and running at all times and can assume operations at a moment's notice. They are the most expensive option. Mobile sites are transportable on trailers and do provide a cost/benefit balance but they are not permanently situated like cold, hot, and warm sites.

14. **B.** This is a classic example of a hacktivist attack where the attacker was motivated by an ideological agenda. There does not seem to be any financial motivation here, which would be the primary sign of organized crime activity. The attack is also prominent and obvious, lacking the stealthy characteristics of an attack waged by a nation-state or other APT.

15. **D.** Resiliency is the ability of a system to withstand potentially disruptive actions. In this scenario, Frank is seeking to design a VPN solution that exhibits high levels of resiliency.

16. **B.** In a public cloud environment, providers offer services on the same shared computing platform to all customers. Customers do not necessarily have any relationship to, or knowledge of, each other. In a private cloud environment, an organization builds its own computing environment. In a hybrid cloud environment, an organization combines elements of public and private cloud computing. In a community cloud environment, a group of related organizations builds a shared cloud environment that is not open for general public use.

17. **C.** Penetration tests take an attacker's perspective on the network and actually seek to bypass security controls and gain access to systems. This would be the best way for Tom to determine the likelihood of a successful attack.

18. **C.** Data owners and data stewards both bear responsibility for data quality standards. However, day-to-day data quality issues are the domain of a data steward, while a data owner bears executive-level responsibility. Data custodians and users generally do not have overarching data quality responsibilities.

19. **D.** PIVs contain four digital certificates. The card authentication certificate is used to verify that the PIV credential was issued by an authorized entity, has not expired, and has not been revoked. The PIV authentication certificate is used to verify that the PIV credential was issued by an authorized entity, has not expired, has not been revoked, and holder of the credential (YOU) is the same individual it was issued to. The digital signature certificate allows the user to digitally sign a document or email, providing both integrity and non-repudiation. The encryption certificate allows the user to digitally encrypt documents or email.

20. **D.** This image shows the cipher block chaining (CBC) mode of cipher operation. You can determine this by noting that the plaintext block being encrypted is XORed with the ciphertext of the preceding block.

21. **A.** Attacks sponsored by organized crime groups almost always have financial motivations.

22. **B.** Web servers use TCP port 80 for unencrypted HTTP communications and they use TCP port 443 for encrypted HTTPS communications. If Ryan would like to require the use of encrypted connections to the web server, he should allow TCP port 443 and block TCP port 80.

23. **B.** The U.S. federal government's Digital Signature Standard (DSS) endorses the use of the Digital Signature Algorithm (DSA) for the creation of digital signatures.

24. **A.** The recovery time objective (RTO) is the amount of time that it is acceptable for a system to be down prior to recovery during a disaster. The recovery point objective (RPO) is the amount of acceptable data loss during a recovery effort. The RTO and RPO are targets, rather than measures of actual performance. The mean time between failures (MTBF) is the average amount of time that elapses between failures of a system or component. The mean time to repair (MTTR) is the amount of time that it takes to recover a failed system. The MTBF and MTTR are measures of actual performance.

25. **B.** The recovery time objective (RTO) is the amount of time that it is acceptable for a system to be down prior to recovery during a disaster. The recovery point objective (RPO) is the amount of acceptable data loss during a recovery effort. The RTO and RPO are targets, rather than measures of actual performance. The mean time between failures (MTBF) is the average amount of time that elapses between failures of a system or component. The mean time to repair (MTTR) is the amount of time that it takes to recover a failed system. The MTBF and MTTR are measures of actual performance.

26. **C.** Push notification is a secure way to implement a second authentication factor and also has high user satisfaction because it typically only requires that the user click approve on a notification pushed to the device. SMS notification and app-based passcode generators have lower user satisfaction

because they require entering a passcode to complete the authentication process. Email notification is not an acceptable way to implement multifactor authentication with mobile devices because an email account is not tied to a specific device and, therefore, does not constitute a "something you have" authentication approach.

27. **B.** Bill should definitely update the operating system to bring it into compliance with current security standards. However, he does not have console access to the device, so the only way he can do this is to obtain the update from the device vendor.

28. **C.** The Triple DES algorithm performs three different rounds of DES encryption. The most secure way of doing this is with three different keys. A less secure mode of operation uses only two keys, while an insecure mode of operation uses a single key to replicate the functionality of DES. It is not possible to use 3DES with four encryption keys.

29. **D.** Communication between the database server and the firewall server would not travel through the hardware firewall because they are located on the same network segment. In this case, the database server is attempting to connect to the file server, so the file server's host firewall is the most likely culprit.

30. **A.** In a RAID 5 array, all of the disks contain data except for the parity disk. Therefore, regardless of the number of disks in the array, only a single disk may fail before data is permanently lost.

31. **C.** This upgraded safe is best described as a preventive control because it is designed to prevent an intruder from successfully cracking it in less than 30 minutes. This time period allows detective controls the time to work and identify the intrusion.

32. **D.** Bcrypt is a key stretching algorithm that is both memory-hardened and CPU-hardened. PBKDF2 is CPU-hardened, but not memory hardened. HMAC and RIPEMD are not key stretching algorithms.

33. **C.** Identification occurs when a user makes a claim of identity. This claim is then proven during the authentication phase, through the use of one or more authentication factors, such as a password, smart card, or biometric reading. The system then determines the specific activities that the authenticated user is authorized to engage in by consulting access control lists (ACLs) and other mechanisms and then tracks user access in an accounting system.

34. **A.** Maureen can use a rainbow table attack against this website because she has access to the password file. This would be more productive than a dictionary attack because it precomputes the password hashes. Both dictionary and rainbow table attacks are more productive than brute force attacks when the site does not have a strong password policy.

35. **A.** This is the output feedback (OFB) mode of encryption. You can determine this because it generates key stream blocks to combine with the plaintext and arrive at ciphertext.

36. **D.** The Advanced Encryption Standard (AES) supports key sizes of 128, 192, and 256 bits. It does not support 512 bit keys.

37. **A.** Apple's iOS platform limits users to installing applications downloaded from Apple's App Store. The other three device types listed, Samsung Galaxy, Motorola Moto, and Huawei P-series, are all Android devices that allow users to download apps from a variety of third-party app stores.

38. **B.** In a load-balanced network that uses server affinity, client requests are assigned to the server that is already handling requests from that same client to minimize the number of network connections.

39. **D.** NIST changed their password security guidelines in 2017 and now recommends that organizations not enforce the expiration of user passwords.

40. **B.** In this scenario, Peter has already completed his reconnaissance but has not yet gained access to any systems on the target network. Therefore, he is still in the initial exploitation phase of the penetration test.

41. **B.** The SIEM correlation engine is a sensitive device that should be accessed only by security personnel. Therefore, it should be placed on the internal network where it is not exposed to external traffic.

42. **A.** The assignment of permissions based upon a user's job indicates that this is a role-based access control system. There is not enough information provided to come to the conclusion that this is a mandatory or discretionary access control system. There is also no indication that the attributes of the user's account are scrutinized during the authorization process.

43. **A.** Port security restricts the number of unique MAC addresses that may originate from a single switch port. It is commonly used to prevent someone from unplugging an authorized device from the network and connecting an unauthorized device but may also be used to prevent existing devices from spoofing MAC addresses of other devices.

44. **C.** The exclusive or (XOR) operation is true when one and only one of the inputs is true. This means that one input must have a value of 1 while the other has a value of 0. Applying this operation to the problem shown here gives the answer of 1001.

45. **C.** Firewall log analysis can be easily automated to identify common configuration issues and attack signatures. Password reset automation is a very commonly used technique to reduce the burden on help desks. Configuration management is generally only possible through automation. Risk assessments are an inherently time-intensive activity that would not likely benefit from automation.

46. **C.** In a choose-your-own-device (CYOD) model, the employee is permitted to choose from a selection of approved devices. The company owns the device. In a bring-your-own-device (BYOD) model, the employee owns the device. In corporate-owned, personally-enabled (COPE) and corporate-owned models, the company owns the device but the employee does not necessarily have the ability to choose the device.

47. **B.** While Glenn may use any of the technologies described here to segment the sensitive network, the question specifically asks for the strongest degree of separation possible. This is achieved by designing an air gapped network that is not connected to any other network.

48. **D.** Gary is engaging in a dictionary attack because he begins the attack with a dictionary of possible passwords. This is not a brute force attack because Gary begins with a list of possible passwords. A brute force attack would simply try every possible value. It is not a rainbow table attack because Gary did not create a rainbow table: a prehashed file of possible password values.

49. **D.** This is a classic example of a memory leak. The application is not releasing memory that it no longer needs and it continues to make requests for new memory allocations. This activity persists until the system runs out of memory and is rebooted.

50. **D.** Retinal scanning is a slow, intrusive technique that requires specialized hardware and cannot be performed with a standard smartphone. Smartphones do commonly use passcodes, fingerprint scanning and facial recognition for authentication.

51. **D.** All DNSSEC implementations must support the RSA/SHA-1 cipher suite to maintain compatibility between systems. The RSA/MD5 cipher suite should never be used due to insecurities in the MD5 hash algorithm. The RSA/SHA-256 and RSA/SHA-512 cipher suites are recommended for use, but not required.

52. **B.** Cross-site scripting (XSS), cross-site request forgery (XSRF), and SQL injection attacks all exploit vulnerabilities in web applications. Shimming is a technique used to manipulate device drivers.

53. **D.** The object identifier (OID) indicates the specific purpose of the digital certificate. For example, OID 1.3.6.1.5.5.7.3.1 is for server authentication, while 1.3.6.1.5.5.7.3.4 is for email protection.

54. **B.** Minifying code makes it very difficult for humans to interpret, but not impossible. This is an example of obfuscation. If the code were encrypted, it would require decryption prior to execution. If the code were hashed or masked, it would not function because those operations are irreversible.

55. **A.** The image shows a mantrap, a physical security control designed to limit access to a facility to one person at a time. This control prevents tailgating by preventing one individual from holding the door open, intentionally or accidentally, for a second person.

56. **A.** WPA uses the Temporal Key Integrity Protocol (TKIP) to rapidly cycle encryption keys and overcome the weaknesses of WEP. WPA2 uses the Counter Mode Cipher Block Chaining Message Authentication Code Protocol (CCMP) to provide enhanced security using AES. Hashing is not an integral component of the cryptographic improvements.

57. **B.** In this attack, the attacker executed a request against a third-party website by taking advantage of the fact that the user already had an established session with that site. This is an example of a cross-site request forgery (XSRF) attack.

58. **A.** The Network Time Protocol (NTP) is used to synchronize the clocks of devices to a standardized time source. NTP is quite useful in helping to ensure consistent timestamps on log entries.

59. **D.** The image explains that the malware encrypted the contents of the computer and will only restore access after the user pays a ransom. This is an example of ransomware, a category of crypto-malware.

60. **C.** Any of these systems would be capable of detecting the attack. However, a SYN flood attack is a well-documented attack and any signature-based IDS would have a built-in signature that defines the attack precisely. Therefore, a signature-based system is most likely to successfully detect this attack.

61. **C.** The General Data Protection Regulation (GDPR) is a sweeping privacy regulation covering operations in the European Union. It replaced the older Data Protection Directive (DPD) in 2018. The Health Insurance Portability and Accountability Act (HIPAA) and Gramm-Leach-Bliley Act (GLBA) are U.S., not European, laws.

62. **A.** The most effective way to address this issue is to deploy a patch that corrects the vulnerability. Since this vulnerability is in Apache Tomcat, the patch must be applied to that service. Patching the operating system will not correct an issue with the service. Web application firewalls and content filters, if deployed in the correct location, may block an attack from exploiting this vulnerability but they do not remediate the root issue.

63. **C.** Paul has already gained initial access to a system: the web server. He is now attempting to take that access and pivot from the initial compromise to a more lucrative target: the file server.

64. **B.** The passwords shown here are hashed using the salted SHA hash algorithm, as described by the {SSHA} attribute. They are neither encrypted (because the hash cannot be reversed) nor stored in cleartext form (because you can't examine the value and determine the password). If they were hashed using an unsalted version of SHA, the attribute before the hash would read {SHA} instead of {SSHA}.

65. **B.** This image clearly shows the patterns in an individual's iris. Retinal scanning requires images of the blood vessels inside the eye, which are not visible in this image. Facial recognition requires an image of a significant portion of the individual's face.

66. **C.** Two-person control requires the concurrence of two individuals for sensitive actions. That is the scenario described here. Separation of duties says that an individual should not have both permissions necessary to perform a sensitive action. This is a closely related, but distinct principle. There is no evidence given that supervisors do not have the ability to create payments, so separation of duties is not in play here.

67. **A.** This attack is leveraging the implied authority of someone wearing a security guard's uniform. It may also have leveraged intimidation by threatening employees or consensus when employees followed each other's lead, but this is not clear in the scenario. There is no indication of scarcity being used in this particular attack.

68. **B.** A split tunnel VPN policy allows Vic to specify that only traffic destined to the home office should be routed through the VPN. If Vic used a full tunnel policy, engineers would not be able to access systems on the customer's local network. Vic may use either an IPsec or TLS VPN to meet this requirement. That technology decision is separate from determining what traffic is sent through the VPN.

69. **B.** In a Type 1 hypervisor, the hypervisor runs directly on the physical hardware. In a Type 2 hypervisor, the hypervisor runs on a host operating system which, in turn, runs on the physical hardware. In both cases, guest operating systems run on top of the hypervisor.

70. **C.** The mean time to repair (MTTR) is the amount of time that it will typically take to restore service after a failure. In this case, the MTTR is 3 days: the amount of time to obtain and install a replacement firewall.

71. **D.** The mean time between failures (MTBF) is the amount of time that typically passes between failure events. In this scenario, Kyle has determined that events typically occur once every four years.

72. **B.** From his conversations with business leaders, Kyle determined that the business can tolerate an outage of four hours, making this the recovery time objective (RTO).

73. **A.** From his conversations with business leaders, Kyle determined that the business can tolerate the loss of one hour of data, making this the recovery point objective (RPO).

74. **C.** The diagram shows federated trust relationships. Arrows with only one arrowhead are one-way trusts. Joe's account is in Domain D and the relationships show that Domains A and B have one-way trust in Domain D. Therefore, Joe can use his account to access resources in Domains A and B. Domain A trusts Domain C, but Domain C does not trust Domain A, so Joe can't use his account to access resources in Domain C.

75. **B.** If the password remains known only to authorized individuals, this does not violate the principles of confidentiality or integrity. There is no indication from the scenario that the account has excess privileges, so least privilege is not violated. However, the use of a shared account prevents security staff from determining which individual performed an action, violating the principle of accountability.

76. **A.** The Secure File Transfer Protocol (SFTP) provides a file transfer capability through a Secure Shell (SSH) connection. The File Transfer Protocol Secure (FTPS) also provides secure file transfers, but does so through a modified version of the FTP protocol and does not use SSH. Dropbox is a proprietary file sharing service that does not use SSH. The HyperText Transfer Protocol Secure (HTTPS) is a secure web protocol that may be used for file transfers but does not leverage SSH.

77. **D.** Servers that provide services to business partners should be placed in the extranet. Intranet servers should have access restricted to internal users. DMMZ servers may be accessed by the general public. Guest networks are designed for visitors to a facility to gain Internet access.

78. **A.** The fact that the packets are reaching the host rules out a network firewall or IPS issue. The fact that the logs indicate that the traffic was allowed rules out a host firewall issue. Therefore, the most likely remaining cause is an issue with the application.

79. **A.** Mandatory vacation and job rotation policies seek to uncover fraud by requiring that employees be unable to perform their normal job functions for an extended period of time, subjecting those functions to scrutiny by other employees. Privileged access monitoring tracks the activity of users with special privileges and may also uncover fraud. Separation of duties seeks to prevent fraudulent activity before it occurs and would not detect the misuse of privileges in a fraudulent manner.

80. **A.** This is a classic example of a piggybacking attack where one person enters a physical facility and then holds the door open for others to enter without requiring that they also use the access control system. In a dumpster diving attack, individuals rummage through the trash searching for sensitive information. In a shoulder surfing attack, the perpetrator looks over the shoulder of an individual while they use a computer. There is no sign that the individuals entering the building without authenticating were making false claims of identity, so there is no evidence of an impersonation attack.

81. **C.** The false rejection rate (FRR) of a system is calculated by dividing the number of false rejections by the total number of authentication attempts. In this dataset, there are 100 total authentication attempts, of which 5 were false rejections of an authorized user. Therefore, the false acceptance rate is 5%.

82. **C.** Cloud-based DLP solutions are updated and maintained by the cloud vendor and would involve the least maintenance effort from Carl's team. Host-based and network-based DLP would require that the

local team install the solution and keep it updated. The use of signature-based DLP technology does not have a significant impact on the amount of maintenance time.

83. **B.** Geofencing allows an organization to restrict certain actions so that they may only take place when the device is in a specified area. If a user exits the geofenced area, the action is no longer possible. This technology is ideal for limiting the use of an application to a specific geographic area, such as a corporate campus.

84. **D.** While it is not an incredibly productive attack, an online brute force attack is Val's only option of the choices provided. Val does not have access to a password file, which would be a requirement for an offline attack, such as an offline dictionary attack, a rainbow table attack, or an offline brute force attack.

85. **C.** In SAML authentication, the user agent is the web browser, application, or other technology used by the end user. The service provider is the service that the user would like to access. The identity provider is the organization providing the authentication mechanism. The certificate authority issues digital certificates required to secure the connections.

86. **C.** In a black box attack, the attacker does not have access to any information about the target environment before beginning the attack. In a grey box attack, the attacker has limited information. In a white box attack, the attacker has full knowledge of the target environment before beginning the attack.

87. **B.** Tethering allows mobile devices to share their network connection with other devices. Split tunneling allows the device to send traffic through a VPN tunnel only when connecting to corporate systems, while split horizon DNS allows the use of different DNS servers for different networks. Transport layer security (TLS) is an important encryption protocol used to secure communications between devices.

88. **B.** The use of incremental backups is the best way to conserve disk space. If Gavin chooses this option, he will back up the entire file server on Monday. Then each of the other days' backups will include only the files added or modified on those days, which is the approach used by incremental backups.

89. **A.** If Gavin performs a full backup each day, when he recovers the system, he will only need to restore the single full backup that occurred most recently before the failure. All of the other strategies require restoring multiple backups.

90. **B.** Each strategy requires performing a full backup on the first day, which is the most time-consuming operation. Options A and D require performing additional full backups, so those options may be eliminated immediately. This leaves us with a choice between strategies that perform incremental backups and differential backups. Differential backups only back up files that have changed since the last full backup, making them a faster choice than full backups. However, incremental backups only back up files that have changed since the last full *or* incremental backup, making them even faster to perform.

CHAPTER 8

Practice Test 3

Practice Test 3 Questions

1. Ralph is reviewing user accounts and matching up the permissions assigned to those accounts in the ERP to access requests made by managers. What activity is Ralph undertaking?

   A. Credential management
   B. Usage auditing
   C. Privilege auditing
   D. Multifactor authentication

2. Tom is concerned about the fact that executives routinely leave their mobile devices unattended on their desks in the office. What control can he enforce through his MDM tool to prevent misuse of those devices?

   A. Remote wipe
   B. Geofencing
   C. Screen locking
   D. Application control

3. Taylor is conducting a business impact analysis for her organization as part of the organization's business continuity planning initiative. During that analysis, she identifies the amount of time that would be acceptable for a system to be down during a disaster. What metric should she use to capture this information?

   A. RPO
   B. RTO
   C. MTTR
   D. MTBF

4. George is evaluating the performance of his organization's business continuity efforts and measures the amount of time that passes between each time that a web server experiences a hard drive failure. What metric should George use to capture this information?

   A. RPO
   B. MTTR
   C. MTBF
   D. RTO

5. Ralph comes across a legacy infrastructure that uses telnet to create an administrative connection between a client and server. Even though this connection takes place over a private network link, Ralph would like to replace telnet with a secure protocol to prevent eavesdropping. What protocol would be the easiest drop-in replacement for telnet?

   A. TLS
   B. FTPS
   C. SSL
   D. SSH

6. Will is selecting a new encryption algorithm for use in his organization. Which one of the following algorithms is weak and should not be considered for use?

A. DES
B. 3DES
C. AES
D. RSA

7. What type of proxy server is shown in the illustration below?

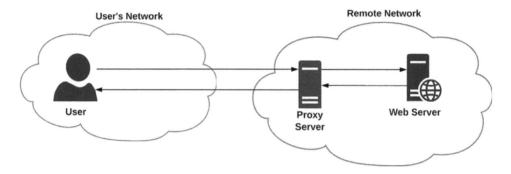

A. Forward proxy
B. Reverse proxy
C. Caching proxy
D. Content filtering proxy

8. Fred created a set of IP restrictions on his Cisco router using Cisco's extended access control list (ACL) functionality. What type of access control model is Fred enforcing?

A. Role-based access control
B. Rule-based access control
C. Attribute-based access control
D. Discretionary access control

9. Sandy is designing a new computing environment for his company. He is contracting with XYZ Cloud Services, who will be providing him with the ability to provision servers on a self-service basis. What type of cloud provider is XYZ?

A. SaaS
B. IaaS
C. PaaS
D. SecaaS

10. Tom is investigating a report from his organization's intrusion detection system. After an exhaustive investigation, he determines that the activity detected by the system was actually not an attack. What type of report took place?

A. False negative
B. True positive
C. True negative
D. False positive

11. What common clause in software is used specifically for error handling?

A. Try...catch
B. If...then
C. Do...while
D. For loop

12. Which one of the following EAP protocols does not take advantage of transport layer security?

A. EAP-FAST
B. EAP-IKEv2
C. EAP-TLS
D. EAP-TTLS

13. Linda is investigating a security incident that took place in her organization. The attacker issued himself checks from an organization account and then created false journal entries in the accounting system to cover them up. There are no signs of unauthorized activity in IPS or firewall logs. What type of attacker most likely conducted this attack?

A. Script kiddie
B. Organized crime
C. Insider
D. Competitor

14. Carla is conducting a penetration test and she has successfully gained access to a jumpbox system through the use of social engineering. Her current access is as a standard user and she is attempting to gain administrative access to the server. What penetration testing activity is Carla engaged in?

A. Initial exploit
B. Pivot
C. Persistence
D. Escalation of privilege

15. Kevin is deploying a new customer relationship management (CRM) server. The services offered by this device will be accessible only to employees of Kevin's company. What network zone offers the most appropriate placement for this server?

A. DMZ
B. Extranet
C. Intranet
D. Guest network

16. Samantha is the administrator of her organization's mobile devices and wants to ensure that users have current versions of operating system firmware. Which one of the following approaches will best meet this need?

   A. Administrator installation
   B. OTA upgrades
   C. User installation
   D. Sideloading

17. Which one of the following data destruction techniques produces waste material that requires wearing a respirator during exposure?

   A. Pulverization
   B. Wiping
   C. Purging
   D. Degaussing

18. Tim is investigating an ARP spoofing attack that took place on his organization's network. What is the maximum scope of a single ARP spoofing attack?

   A. The attacker and the victim must be using the same router
   B. The attacker and the victim must be behind the same firewall
   C. The attacker and the victim must be connected to the same switch
   D. The attacker and the victim must be sharing a switch port

19. Which one of the following is not an appropriate use of the MD5 hash function?

   A. Verifying file checksums against corruption
   B. Partitioning database records
   C. Creating digital signatures
   D. Identifying duplicate records

20. What type of lock is shown here?

   A. Preset lock
   B. Cipher lock
   C. Biometric lock
   D. Smartcard lock

21. What cryptographic cipher is used in the Bcrypt key stretching function?

    A. 3DES
    B. AES
    C. Blowfish
    D. RSA

22. Patrick is investigating a security incident and is able to monitor an intruder's activity on one of his servers. The intruder wrote a script that is attempting to log into a web application using an administrator account. It first attempted the password 'aaaaaaaa', followed by 'aaaaaaab', 'aaaaaaac', and so on. What type of attack is taking place?

    A. Offline brute force
    B. Online brute force
    C. Dictionary
    D. Rainbow table

23. Which one of the following activities is not a passive test of security controls?

    A. Configuration analysis
    B. Penetration testing
    C. Network monitoring
    D. Intrusion detection

24. Which one of the following is an example of a privilege escalation attack against a mobile device?

    A. Jailbreaking
    B. Sideloading
    C. Man-in-the-middle
    D. Tethering

25. Which one of the following is an example of a platform-as-a-service (PaaS) computing environment?

    A. Amazon EC2
    B. Amazon Lambda
    C. Microsoft Azure Virtual Machine
    D. Microsoft Azure DNS

26. Which one of the following techniques is an example of dynamic code testing?

    A. Fuzzing
    B. Data flow analysis
    C. Taint analysis
    D. Lexical analysis

27. David is purchasing cloud infrastructure services from Microsoft Azure. Use of the servers he purchases will be strictly limited to employees of his company. What type of cloud environment is this?

    A. Hybrid cloud
    B. Private cloud
    C. Public cloud
    D. Community cloud

28. Which one of the following tools is useful in testing the security of a wireless network's encryption key?

    A. nmap
    B. Netstumbler
    C. Aircrack
    D. QualysGuard

29. Frances is investigating a security incident where a former employee accessed a critical system after termination, despite the fact that the employee's account was disabled. Frances learned that the employee, a software engineer, created a dummy username and password that was hard-coded into the application and used those credentials to log in. What type of attack took place?

    A. Logic bomb
    B. Backdoor
    C. Remote access Trojan
    D. Ransomware

30. Orlando is configuring his network firewall to allow access to the organization's email server, as shown in the image below. He would like to allow Internet users to send email to the organization but would like to only allow internal users to access email on the server. What protocol(s) should Orlando allow to access the email server from the Internet?

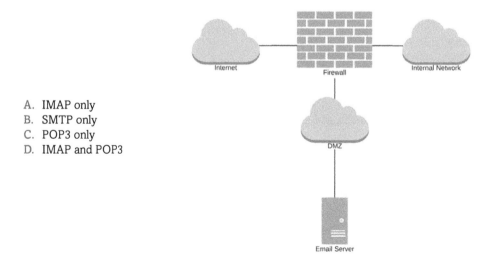

    A. IMAP only
    B. SMTP only
    C. POP3 only
    D. IMAP and POP3

31. Which one of the following RADIUS messages is normally found only in situations where an organization is implementing multifactor authentication?

    A. Access-Accept
    B. Access-Request
    C. Access-Challenge
    D. Access-Reject

32. The website shown below was put up as a parody during the 2016 U.S. presidential election. Examine the website and identify the type of attack that took place.

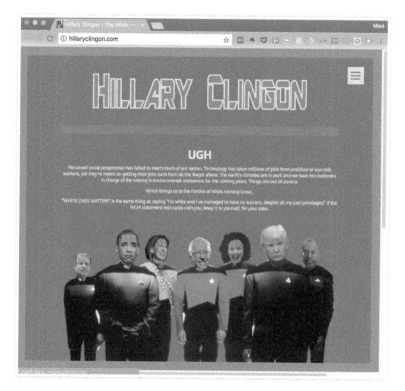

    A. Typosquatting
    B. Website defacement
    C. Clickjacking
    D. Session hijacking

33. Which one of the following terms best describes the level of firewall protection that is typically found in router access control lists?

    A. Stateful
    B. Stateless
    C. Next generation
    D. Proxying

34. Norm is designing a file transfer mechanism to facilitate the flow of information between the hospital where he works and an X-ray service provider with locations around the city. Which one of the following protocols does NOT provide a secure option for these file transfers?

    A. SFTP
    B. SCP
    C. FTP
    D. FTPS

35. After running a vulnerability scan of a copy machine, Tom discovers the results shown below. What is the most likely cause of these results?

    ▶ ▉▉▉▉▉ 5 Microsoft Cumulative Security Update for Internet Explorer (MS17-006)
    ▶ ▉▉▉▉▉ 5 Microsoft Cumulative Security Update for Windows (MS17-012)
    ▶ ▉▉▉▉ 4 Microsoft Uniscribe Multiple Remote Code Execution and Information Disclosure Vulnerabilities (MS17-011)
    ▶ ▉▉▉▉ 4 Microsoft Security Update for Windows Kernel-Mode Drivers (MS17-018)
    ▶ ▉▉▉▉ 4 Microsoft Windows DirectShow Information Disclosure Vulnerability (MS17-021)
    ▶ ▉▉▉▉ 4 Microsoft XML Core Services Information Disclosure Vulnerability (MS17-022)
    ▶ ▉▉▉▉ 4 Microsoft Windows Kernel Elevation of Privileges (MS17-017)

    A. The copy machine has an embedded operating system.
    B. The results are false positives.
    C. Tom scanned the wrong IP address.
    D. The results are true negatives.

36. Colleen is running two load balancers in active/active mode. What is the most significant risk that she is likely facing?

    A. Servers must be manually assigned to load balancers
    B. Network traffic may be misrouted.
    C. The load balancers may not have capacity to survive the failure of one device.
    D. The two load balancers may become out of sync.

37. Which one of the following cipher types works on plaintext one bit or byte at a time?

    A. Block cipher
    B. Stream cipher
    C. AES
    D. Blowfish

38. What mode of cipher operation is shown here?

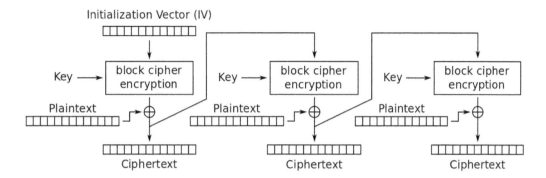

A. CBC
B. OFB
C. ECB
D. CFB

39. Which one of the following tools may be used to scan a system over the network and detect potential vulnerabilities in that system?

A. Nessus
B. Nmap
C. Jack the Ripper
D. Kismet

40. Which one of the following mobile device deployment models allows employees to bring personally owned devices into the corporate environment?

A. COPE
B. CYOD
C. BYOD
D. Corporate-owned

41. Roger is conducting a penetration test and has gained administrative access to a system on his target network. He is now using those administrative privileges to set up a back door. What stage of the attack is Roger in?

A. Persistence
B. Initial exploitation
C. Privilege escalation
D. Pivot

42. During a web application security review, Crystal discovered that one of her organization's applications is vulnerable to SQL injection attacks. Where would be the best place for Crystal to address the root cause issue?

   A. Database server configuration
   B. Web server configuration
   C. Application code
   D. Web application firewall

43. Tim is choosing a card-based control system for physical access to his facility. His primary concern is the speed of authentication. Which type of card would be most appropriate for this situation?

   A. Proximity card
   B. Smart card
   C. Magnetic stripe card
   D. Photo ID card

44. Which one of the following types of access is necessary to engage in a pass-the-hash attack?

   A. Access to a domain workstation
   B. Access to a domain controller
   C. Access to a network segment
   D. Access to a public website

45. This diagram shows the results of testing the accuracy of a biometric authentication system. In this diagram, what characteristic is designated by the arrow?

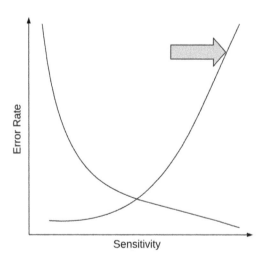

   A. CER
   B. FAR
   C. IRR
   D. FRR

46. Gail is a software developer who recently completed the coding of a new module that will be incorporated into one of her organization's products. Now that her work is complete, she is ready to request that the code be moved to the next environment. Where should the code go next?

   A. Development environment
   B. Test environment
   C. Staging environment
   D. Production environment

47. What is the primary purpose of the Diffie-Hellman (DH) algorithm?

   A. Digital signatures
   B. Key exchange
   C. Message confidentiality
   D. Authentication

48. Which one of the following characteristics does not accurately describe an Agile approach to software development?

   A. Features are prioritized by value added
   B. Customers should be available throughout the project
   C. Requirements are clearly defined before beginning development
   D. Changes are welcomed in the process

49. Carl is creating an authentication system where users seeking to access web applications will be redirected to a login page, such as the one shown here. What type of authentication is Carl seeking to implement?

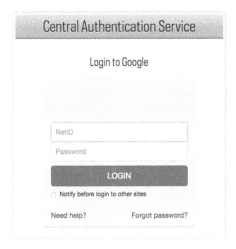

   A. SAML
   B. SSO
   C. Federation
   D. RADIUS

50. Which one of the following wireless networking protocols makes use of a back-end authentication server?

   A. WPA-PSK
   B. WPA-Enterprise
   C. WEP-PSK
   D. WPS

51. Nadine recently accepted a new position as the CISO of a financial institution. What regulatory body produces information security standards that specifically apply to financial institutions?

   A. FDA
   B. FERC
   C. FFIEC
   D. FRA

52. Roger recently deployed an IDS on his organization's network and tuned it to reduce the false positive rate. Which one of the following types best describes this control?

   A. Corrective
   B. Preventive
   C. Detective
   D. Compensating

53. Xavier is concerned about the security of a wireless network in his organization's conference facility that uses WPS to connect new clients. What is the best action that Xavier can take to protect this network?

   A. Remove WPS stickers from wireless access points
   B. Disable WPS
   C. Use a strong WPS PIN
   D. Change the PSK

54. Bruce is investigating a security incident that involves the embezzlement of funds from his organization. Which one of the following groups should be the first focus of his investigation?

   A. Script kiddies
   B. APTs
   C. Insiders
   D. Hactivists

55. Consider the hardware passcode generator shown here. What algorithm does this token use to generate passcodes?

A. LOTP
B. TOTP
C. HOTP
D. KOTP

56. Which one of the following categories of account should normally exist on a secured server?

A. Guest account
B. Service account
C. Generic account
D. Shared account

57. Which encryption mode of operation is shown in the figure below?

A. CTM
B. GCM
C. ECB
D. OFB

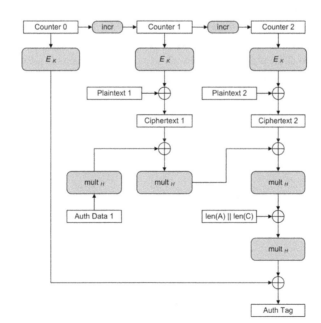

58. Roger's digital forensics team places any mobile devices collected as evidence in bags such as the one shown here. What is the primary purpose of this bag?

   A. Prevent communication with the device
   B. Maintain the chain of custody
   C. Categorize evidence
   D. Prevent others from seeing the evidence

59. Mike would like to allow users on his network to securely access their personal Gmail accounts using the service's standard interface. What protocol must he allow through his network firewall to Google's servers to allow this access?

   A. IMAP
   B. SMTP
   C. HTTPS
   D. POP3

60. Taylor is building a server where data will be infrequently written but frequently read. He would like to use a redundant storage solution that maximizes read performance. Which one of the following approaches would best meet his needs?

   A. RAID 0
   B. RAID 1
   C. RAID 3
   D. RAID 5

61. In the image below, what type of attack is Mal waging against Alice?

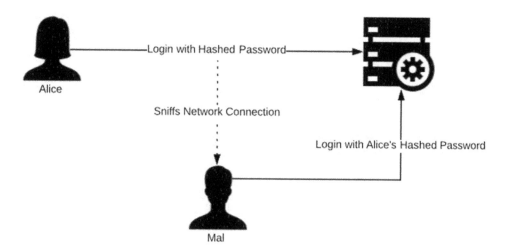

A. Man-in-the-middle
B. Social engineering
C. Replay attack
D. Dictionary

62. Which one of the following statements is true about NTLM authentication?

A. NTLMv2 is protected against pass-the-hash attacks that exist in the original version of NTLM.
B. NTLM uses SHA-512 hashing to protect passwords.
C. NTLM and NTLMv2 are both insecure and should not be used.
D. NTLM is only available for Windows systems.

63. When a certificate authority creates a digital certificate for a web server, what key does it use to apply the CA's digital signature to the certificate?

A. Server's private key
B. CA's public key
C. CA's private key
D. Server's public key

64. Which one of the following authentication techniques generally provides the least degree of security for a mobile device?

A. Password authentication
B. Fingerprint authentication
C. PIN authentication
D. Facial recognition

65. Mike stores some sensitive passwords in a text file called mypasswords.txt. The permissions for this file are shown here. Mike's user ID is mchapple. Which statement best describes the access permissions for this file?

```
drwxr-xr-x    3 mchapple  staff    96 Sep 27 08:54 .
drwxr-xr-x+ 117 mchapple  staff  3744 Sep 27 08:54 ..
-rw-r--r--    1 mchapple  staff   104 Sep 27 08:54 mypasswords.txt
```

A. Anyone on the system can read the file.
B. Only Mike can read the file.
C. Mike and any member of the staff group can read the file.
D. Only Mike and system administrators can read this file.

66. In what type of attack does the attacker place malicious content on a website that is frequented by individuals in the target organization, in the hopes that one of those individuals will visit the site with a vulnerable system and become compromised?

A. Man-in-the-middle attack
B. DDoS attack
C. Watering hole attack
D. Man-in-the-browser attack

67. During a vulnerability scan of an internal web application, Christine discovers the issues shown below. What action should she recommend to correct the issue while minimizing cost and labor?

▶ ▮▮▯ 2 SSL Certificate - Self-Signed Certificate

▶ ▮▮▯ 2 SSL Certificate - Subject Common Name Does Not Match Server FQDN

▶ ▮▮▯ 2 SSL Certificate - Signature Verification Failed Vulnerability

A. Replace the certificate with a certificate from a third-party CA.
B. Replace the certificate with a certificate from the same source.
C. No change is required. These are false positive reports.
D. Replace the certificate with a certificate supporting stronger encryption.

68. Consider the statistics shown here for a biometric authentication system. What is the system's FAR based upon this data?

	Authorized User	Unauthorized User
Accept	98	16
Reject	2	84

A. 1%
B. 2%
C. 8%
D. 16%

69. Examine the digital certificate shown here. How many intermediate CAs were involved in the creation of this certificate?

A. 0
B. 1
C. 2
D. 3

70. Frank is revising an application that currently stores Social Security numbers in a database. This is the only unique identifier available to him but he would like to store it in a way that nobody can determine the original SSN but it remains useful as a unique identifier. What technology can Frank apply to best meet this requirement?

A. Steganography
B. Encryption
C. Decryption
D. Hashing

71. Roger's company did not have a strong disaster recovery plan and suffered a catastrophic data center outage. With no plan in place, what option likely allows them the quickest recovery at their primary site?

   A. Warm site
   B. Hot site
   C. Mobile site
   D. Cold site

72. Henrietta is concerned about the possibility that an attacker will obtain a copy of her password file and conduct a rainbow table attack against it. What technique can she use to best prevent this type of attack?

   A. Salting
   B. Hashing
   C. Password complexity requirements
   D. Encryption

73. Flora is conducting a penetration test of a client and wishes to gain physical access to the building during daylight hours. Which one of the following techniques is least likely to arouse suspicion?

   A. Pretexting
   B. Lock picking
   C. Tailgating
   D. Climbing in an open window

74. Andrea was investigating the IP address(es) associated with a domain name and obtained the results shown below. What tool did she use to obtain these results?

```
;; global options: +cmd
;; Got answer:
;; ->>HEADER<<- opcode: QUERY, status: NOERROR, id: 20426
;; flags: qr rd ra; QUERY: 1, ANSWER: 1, AUTHORITY: 0, ADDITIONAL: 1

;; OPT PSEUDOSECTION:
; EDNS: version: 0, flags:; udp: 4096
;; QUESTION SECTION:
;certmike.com.                        IN      A

;; ANSWER SECTION:
certmike.com.            1799    IN      A       162.255.119.225

;; Query time: 118 msec
;; SERVER: 66.205.160.99#53(66.205.160.99)
;; WHEN: Wed Aug 22 11:16:43 EDT 2018
;; MSG SIZE   rcvd: 57
```

   A. dig
   B. nslookup
   C. dnsquery
   D. resolve

75. Which one of the following objects, if successfully stolen, would be most useful in a session hijacking attack?

   A. IP address
   B. Public key
   C. Digital certificate
   D. Cookie

76. Dan recently received a digitally signed message and when he attempted to verify the digital signature received an error that the hash values did not match. What can Dan conclude from this error?

   A. The message was accidentally corrupted in transit.
   B. The message was altered by a malicious individual after being sent.
   C. Dan can't draw one of these specific conclusions.
   D. There was an error creating the digital signature.

77. Which one of the following technologies can be used to mitigate the effects of a denial of service attack on a local area network?

   A. Flood guard
   B. Loop prevention
   C. Split horizon
   D. Hold-down timers

78. Melanie is the system administrator for a database containing sensitive information. She is responsible for implementing security controls to protect the contents of the database. Which term best describes her role?

   A. Data owner
   B. Data steward
   C. Data user
   D. Data custodian

79. Greg visits a website and sees the error shown below. What is the most likely cause of this error message?

   A. The certificate uses an insecure cipher, such as DES.
   B. The website is using a self-signed certificate.
   C. The certificate is expired.
   D. The certificate does not support TLS communication.

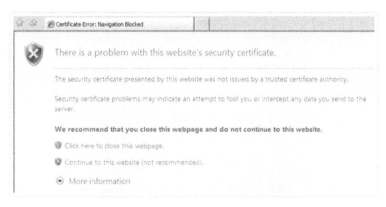

80. Brendan is helping a colleague troubleshoot a connectivity issue for two systems using the Secure File Transfer Protocol (SFTP). He would like to check whether the traffic is being blocked by his network firewall. What TCP port is used for these connections?

   A. 22
   B. 21
   C. 20
   D. 23

81. Ben finds that the DNS servers in his organization are configured to allow unrestricted recursive queries. What type of attack are these servers vulnerable to as a result of this configuration?

   A. ARP poisoning
   B. DNS poisoning
   C. DNS amplification
   D. Man-in-the-middle

82. In a Kerberos authentication scheme, who provides the client with the TGS session key?

   A. Authentication server
   B. Ticket granting server
   C. Service server
   D. Key generation server

83. Ron would like to implement a security control that requires that employees protect the confidentiality of corporate information, even after they leave the organization. Which one of the following agreements would best meet his needs?

   A. SLA
   B. NDA
   C. BPA
   D. ICA

84. Norma has held several positions in her company and is still able to carry out system actions that were granted to her based upon her previous roles. She no longer has a job-based requirement to perform those activities. What term describes what has happened here?

   A. Privileged account
   B. Least privilege
   C. Privilege creep
   D. Privilege migration

85. What is the asset value in this scenario?

    A. $20,000
    B. $75,000
    C. $1,000,000
    D. $5,000,000

86. What is the single loss expectancy in this scenario?

    A. $20,000
    B. $75,000
    C. $1,000,000
    D. $5,000,000

87. What is the annualized rate of occurrence in this scenario?

    A. 0.02
    B. 0.05
    C. 0.20
    D. 0.50

88. What is the exposure factor in this scenario?

    A. 0.02
    B. 0.05
    C. 0.20
    D. 0.50

89. What is the annualized loss expectancy in this scenario?

    A. $20,000
    B. $75,000
    C. $1,000,000
    D. $5,000,000

90. Which one of the following statements best describes the risk situation Melanie is in?

   A. Melanie should recommend that the business always purchase insurance for any risk with an ALE greater than 0.005.
   B. The purchase of insurance in this scenario is not cost effective from a purely financial viewpoint.
   C. The purchase of insurance in this scenario makes good financial sense.
   D. Melanie should recommend against the purchase of insurance because the SLE is less than the AV.

Practice Test 3 Answers and Explanations

1. **C.** Ralph is conducting a privilege audit by ensuring that each permission assigned to a user account is backed by an approved access request. Usage auditing is a similar activity but it analyzes actual privilege usage, rather than privilege existence.

2. **C.** Tom can use screen locking to prevent someone walking by from using a device that he or she is not authorized to use. Remote wiping is not an effective control for this scenario, as it would destroy all data on the device and is only effective when actively triggered. Geofencing is not an effective control because the device is located in the office where it is expected to be. Application control would limit the applications that users can install on the device but would not prevent an unauthorized user from accessing the device.

3. **B.** The recovery time objective (RTO) is the amount of time that it is acceptable for a system to be down prior to recovery during a disaster. The recovery point objective (RPO) is the amount of acceptable data loss during a recovery effort. The RTO and RPO are targets, rather than measures of actual performance. The mean time between failures (MTBF) is the average amount of time that elapses between failures of a system or component. The mean time to repair (MTTR) is the amount of time that it takes to recover a failed system. The MTBF and MTTR are measures of actual performance.

4. **C.** The recovery time objective (RTO) is the amount of time that it is acceptable for a system to be down prior to recovery during a disaster. The recovery point objective (RPO) is the amount of acceptable data loss during a recovery effort. The RTO and RPO are targets, rather than measures of actual performance. The mean time between failures (MTBF) is the average amount of time that elapses between failures of a system or component. The mean time to repair (MTTR) is the amount of time that it takes to recover a failed system. The MTBF and MTTR are measures of actual performance.

5. **D.** The secure shell (SSH) functions in a manner that is functionally equivalent to telnet but adds encryption and other security features. SSL and TLS may be used to encrypt communications but they do not provide the connection features of SSH on their own. The file transfer protocol - secure (FTPS) is used for transferring files and does not allow interactive administrative sessions similar to the ones provided by telnet.

6. **A.** The Data Encryption Standard (DES) is a weak algorithm that is no longer considered secure. The Triple DES (3DES) algorithm is a stronger variant of DES that is acceptable. The Advanced Encryption Standard (AES) and Rivest Shamir Adelman (RSA) algorithm are both considered secure.

7. **B.** This is a reverse proxy because the proxy server is located on the same network as the web server. Users connect directly to the reverse proxy and the proxy server then connects to the web server. This process is transparent to the end user. It is not possible to determine whether this proxy server is performing caching and/or content filtering based upon this illustration.

8. **B.** Network access control lists are examples of rule-based access control because the router will make decisions based upon the rules that Fred provides. The router does not know the identity of the user,

so it cannot perform role-based or attribute-based access control. Users have no authority to delegate access control decisions, so this is not an example of discretionary access control.

9. **B.** XYZ Cloud Services is allowing Sandy to provision servers on his own, as he needs them. This is an example of providing customers with the basic building blocks of a computing environment as a cloud service and, therefore, is an example of infrastructure as a service (IaaS).

10. **D.** In a true positive report, the system reports an attack when an attack actually exists. A false positive report occurs when the system reports an attack that did not take place. A true negative report occurs when the system reports no attack and no attack took place. A false negative report occurs when the system does not report an attack that did take place.

11. **A.** While it is possible to perform error handling with a variety of constructs, the most appropriate tool is the use of the try...catch construct. In this approach, developers include the code that might generate an error in the try clause and then provide error handling code in the catch clause.

12. **B.** The EAP-TLS, EAP-TTLS, and EAP-FAST protocols all use transport layer security (TLS) to provide security for the EAP session. EAP-IKEv2 relied upon the Internet Key Exchange (IKE) protocol.

13. **C.** The most likely culprit is an insider with access to the accounting system. There are no signs of IPS or firewall anomalies, which reduces the likelihood that this was an external attack.

14. **D.** Carla has already completed the initial exploitation phase of the test. She is now attempting to expand her permissions on the compromised system. This is an example of escalation of privilege.

15. **C.** Servers that provide services only to internal users should be placed on the intranet. DMZ servers provide services to the general public. Extranet servers may be accessed by vendors and other business partners. Guest networks are designed for visitors to a facility to gain Internet access.

16. **B.** Over-the-air (OTA) upgrades occur automatically and without user or administrator intervention, making them the best way to ensure that devices remain current. If Samantha wants to control when these updates occur, she can manage OTA updates through her mobile device management (MDM) platform. Manual installation or sideloading by users or administrators is not likely to keep devices consistently updated.

17. **A.** Pulverizing materials reduces them to a fine dust which may pose an inhalation hazard. Anyone working around pulverized materials should wear a respirator.

18. **C.** ARP spoofing attacks occur by poisoning the MAC address table either on an individual host or on the switch used by the victim. In order for this attack to be successful, the attacker and victim must be attached to the same switch, although they do not need to be sharing the same switch port.

19. **C.** The MD5 algorithm is cryptographically broken and should never be used for secure applications, such as creating a digital signature. It is still appropriate for use in non-cryptographic applications, such as identifying duplicate records, partitioning database keys, and verifying file checksums to detect unintentional corruption.

20. **A.** This is an example of a preset lock, where a locksmith sets the lock to work with a specific key or keys. Cipher locks use a keypad that requires individuals to enter a code. Biometric locks use

fingerprint readers or some other form of biometric identification, while smartcard locks require the user to insert a smartcard or place one in the immediate proximity of the lock.

21. **C.** The Bcrypt algorithm relies upon the Blowfish cipher to perform key stretching of passwords.

22. **B.** This is a brute force attack because the intruder seems to be generating possible passwords sequentially without using a dictionary or rainbow table. It is an online attack because the intruder is conducting the hacking attempt against the live service.

23. **B.** Penetration tests interact with systems and seek to exploit vulnerabilities. Therefore, they are an active test of security controls. Configuration analysis, network monitoring, and intrusion detection are passive activities.

24. **A.** Jailbreaking a mobile device breaks the user out of the controls imposed by the operating system developer, granting the user root privileges on the device. This is an example of privilege escalation. Sideloading is the process of loading information on a device via USB or other non-wireless mechanism. It is a capability included in devices by design and is not an example of privilege escalation. Man-in-the-middle attacks are used to eavesdrop on network connections and do not require privilege escalation. Tethering is an intended capability of mobile devices that allow users to connect other devices to the network through the mobile device's network connection.

25. **B.** Amazon's Lambda service is a serverless computing platform offered to customers on a platform-as-a-service (PaaS) basis. Microsoft Azure Virtual Machines and Amazon EC2 are both virtual server environments that offer infrastructure-as-a-service (IaaS). Microsoft Azure DNS is also an infrastructure service offering for name resolution.

26. **A.** Fuzzing uses artificially generated input to a program to test it for security purposes. Fuzzing executes the code, so it is an example of dynamic code analysis. Data flow analysis, lexical analysis, and taint analysis are all examples of static code testing techniques.

27. **C.** In a public cloud environment, providers offer services on the same shared computing platform to all customers. Customers do not necessarily have any relationship to, or knowledge of, each other. In a private cloud environment, an organization builds its own computing environment. In a hybrid cloud environment, an organization combines elements of public and private cloud computing. In a community cloud environment, a group of related organizations builds a shared cloud environment that is not open for general public use. Despite the fact that David is limiting access to these servers to his own organization, Microsoft Azure is still a public cloud computing environment.

28. **C.** Aircrack is specifically designed to test the security of WiFi encryption keys and would be the ideal tool in this situation. Netstumbler is an outdated tool used to survey wireless networks but is no longer supported. Nmap is a network mapping tool and QualysGuard is a network vulnerability scanner, neither of which has wireless encryption testing capability.

29. **B.** The developer created a backdoor in the system by hardwiring credentials into the application that allowed later access. A logic bomb is set to automatically trigger when certain conditions are met, which is not the case in this scenario. A remote access trojan (RAT) is a type of malware that establishes a backdoor but there is no indication that one was used in this case, as the engineer added the backdoor directly into the code. Ransomware is a form of cryptomalware that encrypts files and

then demands payment of a ransom before restoring access. There is no indication of a ransomware attack in this scenario.

30. **B.** The Simple Mail Transfer Protocol (SMTP) is used to relay inbound email and should be allowed from the Internet. The Internet Message Access Protocol (IMAP) and the Post Office Protocol version 3 (POP3) are used to retrieve messages from an email server and should only be allowed from the internal network.

31. **C.** The RADIUS Access-Request message is sent by a client to the server requesting RADIUS authentication. The server then normally responds with an Access-Accept or Access-Reject message, depending upon whether the authentication was successful or unsuccessful. When a system is using two-factor authentication, the RADIUS server may respond to the client's request with an Access-Challenge message asking for additional authentication.

32. **A.** The individual who set up this website registered a domain name that was extremely similar to a legitimate domain: hillaryclingon.com instead of hillaryclinton.com. This is an example of typosquatting (or URL hijacking), an attack that hopes to garner web traffic by having a name that is quite similar to that of a legitimate site. This is a different website than the legitimate site, so no defacement took place. In a clickjacking attacks, the attacker seeks to fool individuals into clicking links on a website. In a session hijacking attack, the attacker attempts to interfere with an ongoing communication between a client and web server.

33. **B.** Router access control lists are only capable of performing stateless filtering, which does not take connection status into account. Other firewall technologies, including stateful inspection firewalls, next generation firewalls, and proxy firewalls, all track connection state and typically require dedicated firewall hardware.

34. **C.** The basic File Transfer Protocol (FTP) does not provide encryption for data in transit and exposes both transferred files and authentication credentials to eavesdropping attacks. The Secure File Transfer Protocol (SFTP) and File Transfer Protocol Secure (FTPS) offer the same functionality over a secure, encrypted connection. The Secure Copy (SCP) protocol copies files over a secure SSH connection and is also a viable alternative to FTP.

35. **A.** While it is possible that Tom scanned the wrong IP address or that these are false positive results, the most likely explanation is that the copy machine contains an embedded Windows operating system that is vulnerable to these issues. True negative reports occur when a scanner does not report an issue that does not exist, therefore they would not appear in a scan report.

36. **C.** Active/active mode is a perfectly acceptable way to operate two load balancers and the load balancers will take care of synchronization issues between themselves and the servers. The major risk with active/active mode is that if both load balancers run at greater than 50% capacity, a single load balancer will not be able to handle the full workload in the event that one device fails.

37. **B.** Stream ciphers work on a single bit or byte of plaintext at a time, while block ciphers work on plaintext in chunks. AES and Blowfish are examples of block ciphers.

38. **D.** This illustration shows the cipher feedback (CFB) mode of encryption. You can determine this by noting that in each encryption operation, the ciphertext from the previous operation is encrypted and then XORed with the plaintext block to produce the next ciphertext block.

39. **A.** Nessus is a vulnerability scanner designed to scan systems over the network and identify potential vulnerabilities. Nmap performs a similar function but only identifies open ports on remote devices without probing for vulnerabilities. Jack the Ripper is a password cracking tool. Kismet is a wireless network assessment tool.

40. **C.** In a bring-your-own-device (BYOD) model, employees are able to bring personally owned devices into a corporate computing environment. The other models listed all involve the use of corporate-owned equipment.

41. **A.** Roger is installing a back door so that he can regain access to the system at a later date. This is an example of persistence. He will be able to use this back door to regain access even if the initial vulnerability that he exploited is patched.

42. **C.** While it may be possible to mitigate this issue by adjusting settings on any of the devices mentioned here, the root cause of a SQL injection vulnerability is faulty input validation in the application's source code. This root cause may only be addressed by modifying the application code.

43. **A.** The proximity card provides the fastest scanning time, as the user simply needs to hold it near the reader. Smart cards and magnetic stripe cards require more time-consuming interaction with the reader. Photo ID cards require scrutiny by a human guard.

44. **A.** In a pass-the-hash attack, the attacker must gain access to hashed Windows account passwords. This is possible by gaining access to a Windows workstation where the target user logs into his or her domain account. Access to a domain controller is not necessary. Access to a network segment or public website is not sufficient because hashed passwords are not generally found in those locations in unencrypted form.

45. **D.** The accuracy of a biometric authentication system is described using three metrics. The false acceptance rate (FAR) is the frequency at which the system admits a person who should not be admitted. The false rejection rate (FRR) is the frequency at which the system denies access to an authorized user incorrectly. The FAR can be improved by increasing the sensitivity of the system, while the FRR can be improved by decreasing the sensitivity of the system. Because of this, the best measure of accuracy is the crossover error rate (CER), which is the sensitivity point at which the FAR and FRR are equal.

46. **B.** Development environments are designed for active use by developers who are creating new code. These environments are the only location where code should be modified. Once code is ready for testing, it is released from the development environment into a test environment for software testing. After the completion of user acceptance testing, the code is moved from the test environment into a staging environment where it is prepared for final deployment into the production environment. Developers should never have permission to move code themselves but should only be able to move code between environments through the use of a managed change control system.

47. **B.** The Diffie-Hellman (DH) algorithm is a key exchange algorithm designed to facilitate the creation of a mutual shared secret.

48. **C.** An Agile approach to software development embraces change and prioritizes feature requests by the value added to the deliverable. Customers are encouraged to engage throughout the process. Agile

projects often begin without clearly defined requirements and requirements evolve as the project unfolds.

49. **B.** This approach, redirecting users to a central authentication service, is an example of single sign-on (SSO), where a user authenticates once and may use that authenticated session to access a variety of services. While this authentication may be part of a federated environment, there is no indication of this and there is no description of the specific technologies used to support this SSO environment.

50. **B.** The WPA-Enterprise and WPA2-Enterprise standards both rely upon an enterprise authentication server. Pre-shared key (PSK) mode uses a shared secret key. WPS is not a wireless encryption standard.

51. **C.** The Federal Financial Institutions Examination Council (FFIEC) is responsible for overseeing the audits of financial institutions and produces a series of information security standards that apply to those institutions. The Federal Energy Regulatory Commission (FERC) produces security standards for the energy industry. The Food and Drug Administration (FDA) regulates healthcare products and food items, while the Federal Railroad Administration (FRA) regulates rail transportation.

52. **C.** An intrusion detection system (IDS) has the ability to identify suspicious network traffic but cannot take any preventive action to block the traffic. Therefore, it is best classified as a detective control.

53. **B.** Recent attacks against WPS have rendered it insecure and made it unsuitable for use. Xavier should discontinue the use of WPS and switch to a more secure authentication and access control technology.

54. **C.** Most embezzlement attacks are waged either entirely by insiders or with significant support from an insider with access to the organization's financial systems and accounts.

55. **C.** The two main technologies used to generate one-time passwords are the HMAC-based One Time Password (HOTP) algorithm and the Time-based One Time Password (TOTP) algorithm. HOTP passcodes are generated sequentially and do not expire until use. TOTP passcodes are based upon the time of authentication and expire frequently. This hardware token requires that the user press a button to generate a passcode sequentially, rather than generating them continuously. Therefore, it is an HOTP token.

56. **B.** Generic, shared, and guest accounts should not be used on secure servers due to their lack of accountability to an individual user. Service accounts normally exist on all servers and are required for routine operation of services.

57. **B.** This image shows the Galois/Counter Mode (GCM) cipher mode of operation. The distinguishing feature of this approach is that block numbers are generated by a counter and those numbers are combined with an initialization vector using a block cipher.

58. **A.** While this bag may be used to perform all of the functions listed in the question, the primary purpose of this bag is to serve as a portable Faraday cage that prevents electromagnetic signals from reaching the device. This allows the forensic analysts to leave the device powered on without worrying that someone will remote wipe the device. Powering the device off may lose critical evidence stored in memory.

59. **C.** The standard access mechanism for Gmail accounts is to use a web browser over a secure connection. This traffic occurs using the HTTPS protocol. While it is possible to access Gmail through

the SMTP, IMAP, and POP3 protocols, the basic version of those protocols are not secure and do not use the standard web interface. There are secure, encrypted alternatives to SMTP, IMAP, and POP3, but those still do not use the Gmail web interface.

60. **B.** RAID 1, also known as disk mirroring, writes identical data to two disks. This approach allows read operations to recover all data by accessing a single disk and is quite efficient for that use. RAID 3 and RAID 5 stripe data across multiple disks and incur overhead in reassembling information that reduces read performance. RAID 0 does not provide redundancy, as it simply stripes data across multiple disks without parity information.

61. **C.** In this attack, Mal is obtaining Alice's hashed password by sniffing the network connection. He then reuses the hashed password to login to the service. This is an example of a replay attack.

62. **C.** NTLM and NTLMv2 both contain critical security vulnerabilities that makes them poor choices for authentication protocols. They use the MD4 and MD5 hash algorithms. While NTLM is most commonly found on Windows systems, there are NTLM implementations for Linux systems as well.

63. **C.** The purpose of a CA signing a certificate is to prove that the CA was involved in the certificate's creation. The CA uses its own private key to create the digital signature and then other users may verify the signature using the CA's public key.

64. **C.** Facial recognition and fingerprint-based authentication both use acceptably strong biometric authentication techniques. The remaining two options, passwords and PINs, both use knowledge-based authentication. Passwords allow users to select from a wider range of characters than PINs, which only allow the use of digits. Therefore, PINs provide the weakest level of security of all of these techniques.

65. **A.** The three "r" values in this permission string indicate that the file's owner can read the file, members of the file's group can read the file, and all system users can read the file. Therefore, anyone on the system has permission to read this file.

66. **C.** Watering hole attacks take advantage of the fact that many people are predictable in their web surfing patterns. They place malicious content at a site likely to attract the target audience (the watering hole) and then wait for a compromise to occur.

67. **B.** This is an internal application, so the use of a self-signed certificate is likely appropriate. However, this certificate issued for an incorrect domain name and, therefore, should be replaced. Using a certificate from the same self-signing source will minimize costs compared to the use of a third-party CA. There is no sign in this report that the certificate does not support strong encryption.

68. **C.** The false acceptance rate (FAR) of a system is calculated by dividing the number of false acceptances by the total number of authentication attempts. In this dataset, there are 200 total authentication attempts, of which 16 were false acceptances of an unauthorized user. Therefore, the false acceptance rate is 8%.

69. **B.** This certificate was issued by an intermediate CA known as the InCommon RSA Server CA. This intermediate CA was certified by the USERTrust RSA Certification Authority root CA.

70. **D.** Hashing would allow Frank to create a unique value from each SSN that would still uniquely identify each record but would not be reversible by anyone. Encryption would also protect the data but could be reversed by someone with the decryption key. Steganography is used to hide data within images.

71. **C.** Cold sites have only basic infrastructure available and require the longest period of time to activate operations. They are also the cheapest option. Warm sites add hardware, and possible software, to the mix but do not have a current copy of the data running. They require hours to activate. Hot sites are up and running at all times and can assume operations at a moment's notice. They are the most expensive option. Mobile sites are transportable on trailers and are a good choice for a last-minute recovery plan. They would work well in this scenario because Roger could bring a mobile site to their primary facility and use it to recover operations during the restoration effort at the primary site.

72. **A.** While all of these techniques will help reduce the likelihood of a password cracking attack, the best defense against rainbow tables is to implement salting. Rainbow table attacks precompute hashes and then check the password file for those values. Salting adds a value (the salt) to each password prior to hashing to make rainbow table attacks no more effective than a brute force attack.

73. **C.** During a tailgating attack, the attacker simply blends in with a crowd of people entering a facility and hopes they will hold the door open for him or her. This is the least likely way to arouse suspicion during daylight hours when the office is occupied. Lockpicking, pretexting, and climbing in a window are all likely to attract unwanted attention.

74. **A.** Both the dig and nslookup tools are useful when seeking to determine the IP address(es) associated with a domain name. However, the results shown in the figure are formatted as output from the dig tool. Dnsquery and resolve are not domain lookup tools.

75. **D.** If an eavesdropper gains access to the cookie used to authenticate a session, the attacker could use that cookie to take over the session. Public encryption keys, digital certificates, and IP addresses are all commonly shared publicly and would not be very useful in a session hijacking attack.

76. **C.** Any one of these scenarios is a plausible reason that the digital signature would not verify. Dan cannot draw a specific conclusion other than that the message he received is not the message that was sent by the originator.

77. **A.** Flood guard prevents a single device from flooding the network with traffic, which may cause a denial of service. Loop prevention, hold-down timers, and split horizon routing are all used to detect and correct routing loops.

78. **D.** System administrators are examples of data custodians: individuals who are charged with the safekeeping of information under the guidance of the data owner.

79. **B.** This error message indicates that the certificate was not issued by a trusted certificate authority. This error most often occurs when a certificate was self-issued.

80. **A.** The SFTP protocol uses SSH connections to transfer files securely. Therefore, it works over the same port used by SSH, TCP port 22. Ports 20 and 21 are used for traditional FTP connections and would not apply here. Port 23 is used by the insecure Telnet protocol.

81. **C.** In a DNS amplification attack, the attacker sends short queries to servers that allow unrestricted recursive queries. Those queries include forged source addresses, causing the third-party DNS servers to unwittingly flood the victim system with lengthy and unsolicited DNS responses.

82. **A.** When a Kerberos client requests a session key, the client creates an authenticator consisting of the client's ID and a timestamp. The client then encrypts this authenticator with the TGS session key, which the client obtained earlier from the authentication server.

83. **B.** A non-disclosure agreement (NDA) is a confidentiality agreement between two organizations or between an individual and an organization. NDAs are commonly used to enforce employee confidentiality and typically remain in effect after the end of an employment relationship.

84. **C.** Privilege creep is the term used to describe the situation where a user moves through various job roles and accumulates permissions over time without having unnecessary permissions revoked. Privilege creep is a violation of the principle of least privilege.

85. **D.** The asset value (AV) is the full value of the facility. In this scenario, Melanie consulted with an architect and determined that the facility value is $5 million using the replacement cost method.

86. **C.** The single loss expectancy (SLE) is the amount of damage, in dollars, that the organization should expect as the result of a single incident. From the scenario, we know that a single earthquake would cause approximately $1 million in damage.

87. **A.** The annualized rate of occurrence is the number of events expected in a given year. Geologists expect an earthquake once every 50 years. This is equivalent to a 0.02 annual risk of earthquake.

88. **C.** The exposure factor is calculated by dividing the single loss expectancy ($1,000,000) by the asset value ($5,000,000), resulting in a value of 0.20, or 20%.

89. **A.** The annualized loss expectancy is the amount of damage expected to occur in any given year. It is computed by multiplying the single loss expectancy by the annualized rate of occurrence (or ALE=SLE*ARO). In this scenario, that is ALE=$1 million * 0.02 or $20,000.

90. **B.** The purchase of an insurance policy is never purely a financial decision, but in this case it does not make good financial sense because the annualized loss expectancy ($20,000) is less than the policy premium cost ($75,000). Tonya should not use the ALE or SLE alone to make this decision and must do so in the context of the control costs and other business factors.

CHAPTER 9

Practice Test 4

Practice Test 4 Questions

1. Fran received a call from her company's help desk supervisor telling her that customers were receiving email messages informing them of a special promotion available for a limited time. Upon investigating these messages, Fran learned that they were sent by an attacker who somehow gained possession of her organization's customer list. What term best describes this attack?

   A. Pharming
   B. Prepending
   C. Spear phishing
   D. Whaling

2. Which one of the following types of digital certificate offers the highest level of assurance?

   A. DV
   B. EV
   C. OV
   D. SV

3. Joe recently downloaded a vulnerability scanning tool and is using it to scan the networks of organizations located near him. His plan, if he finds vulnerabilities, is to approach the organization with the information and explain how they can correct the issue in a hope to generate goodwill and future consulting business. What term best describes Joe?

   A. White hat hacker
   B. Black hat hacker
   C. Grey hat hacker
   D. Striped hat hacker

4. Tom is configuring an automated job that will retrieve information from a database each evening and use it to create a report that is sent to leaders. What type of account should he use to retrieve information from the database?

   A. Root account
   B. Service account
   C. Shared account
   D. User account

5. Laurie encountered some old personnel records stored in a file system scheduled for decommissioning and is wondering if the records should be maintained or destroyed. They are nine years old. What should Laurie do?

   A. Preserve the records indefinitely
   B. Destroy the records as they are more than seven years old
   C. Destroy the records because the system is being decommissioned
   D. Consult the data retention policy

6. Edward is experiencing Wi-Fi interference issues in his office. Which one of the following activities is least likely to resolve the issue?

   A. Adjust power levels
   B. Alter access point placement
   C. Change the network SSID
   D. Modify channel usage

7. What type of attack is shown in the diagram below?

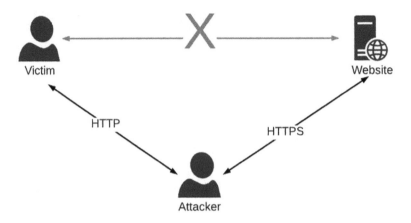

   A. Buffer overflow
   B. Directory traversal
   C. Domain hijacking
   D. SSL stripping

8. Which one of the following industry standards provides technical details for the implementation of self-encrypting drives?

   A. OPAL
   B. OVAL
   C. TAG
   D. TCG

9. Andrea's firm is changing their approach to mobile devices. They previously purchased devices for employees and restricted them to business use only. Employees did not like this model, as it required them to carry two devices, one for business use and another for personal use. Andrea is working with management to allow personal use of devices. What statement below is correct about Andrea's company?

   A. They are moving from BYOD to CYOD
   B. They are moving from CYOD to BYOD
   C. They are moving from COBO to COPE
   D. They are moving from COPE to COBO

10. Paul is reviewing a scan report and notices that a vulnerability he knows exists on the scanned system does not appear in the report. How should Paul classify this vulnerability report result?

   A. True positive
   B. True negative
   C. False positive
   D. False negative

11. Justin is reviewing a network vulnerability scan and sees the report shown below. What system in his organization requires patching?

   ▼ ▮▮▮▮▮▮ 5 VMware ESXi 5.5.0 Patch Release ESXi550-201703401-SG Missing (KB2149576)

QID:	216120	CVSS Base:	6.6[1]
Category:	VMware	CVSS Temporal:	4.9
CVE ID:	CVE-2017-4902 CVE-2017-4903 CVE-2017-4904 CVE-2017-4905	CVSS3 Base:	-
		CVSS3 Temporal:	-
Vendor Reference	VMSA-2017-0006	CVSS Environment:	
Bugtraq ID:	-	Asset Group:	-
Service Modified:	04/04/2017	Collateral Damage Potential:	-
User Modified:	-	Target Distribution:	-
Edited:	No	Confidentiality Requirement:	-
PCI Vuln:	Yes	Integrity Requirement:	-
Ticket State:	Open	Availability Requirement:	-

   A. Database
   B. Endpoint
   C. Network device
   D. Virtualization

12. When performing risk management activities, what term is used to describe the risk that remains after the implementation of security controls?

   A. Control risk
   B. Inherent risk
   C. Mitigated risk
   D. Residual risk

13. Fred is designing a new web application that will be hosted with a cloud service provider. He would like to configure the web application so that it adds additional servers when demand spikes and then removes those servers from the pool when demand falls again. What characteristic of cloud computing is Fred most directly taking advantage of?

   A. Agility
   B. Economies of scale
   C. Elasticity
   D. Scalability

14. Brenda is reviewing the security of a web application used to provide customers with a subscription service. She learns that the application checks the customer's subscription status when they log in and then allows the customer to remain logged in indefinitely, but never re-checks the subscription status. What type of attack is this approach vulnerable to?

   A. Resource exhaustion
   B. Session replay
   C. Session hijacking
   D. TOC/TOU

15. Which one of the following approaches attaches an OSCP validation message to the digital certificate sent to users by a website?

   A. Certificate attachment
   B. Certificate chaining
   C. Certificate pinning
   D. Certificate stapling

16. Shannon would like to use an industry standard document to help her select the security controls that should be used in her information security program. What reference document would be most useful to her?

   A. ISO 27001
   B. ISO 27002
   C. ISO 27701
   D. ISO 31000

17. Alyssa discovered the Python script shown below in a directory used by an attacker who compromised a system she administers. What is the purpose of this script?

```
cracked=0
i=0

while cracked == 0:
     test="mike" + str(i)
     cracked=test_password('mchapple', test)
     i=i+1

print('Cracked Password:', test)
```

   A. Perform a brute force password attack
   B. Perform a man-in-the-middle attack
   C. Perform a meet-in-the-middle attack
   D. Perform a rainbow table attack

18. Dorian is conducting a penetration test and, as part of the test, he downloads large lists of usernames and passwords stolen during attacks against large websites. He then attempts to use those lists to log into systems belonging to his target. What type of attack is Dorian conducting?

    A. Dictionary
    B. Online brute force
    C. Offline brute force
    D. Password spraying

19. Brian is investigating the process used by an attacker who compromised his network. The attacker ended their actions with the exfiltration of a database of credit card numbers. What phase of the Cyber Kill Chain would best describe this action?

    A. Actions on Objectives
    B. Command and Control
    C. Exploitation
    D. Installation

20. What is the primary function of the OAuth protocol?

    A. Accounting
    B. Authentication
    C. Authorization
    D. Identification

21. Tony works in a hybrid cloud environment and would like to manage the complexity associated with linking different VLANs in his on-premises environment to different VPCs in the cloud environment. What tool can best assist him with this task?

    A. Network router
    B. Transit gateway
    C. VPC concentrator
    D. VPC endpoint

22. During a penetration test, Jake entered an organization's network closet and replaced the firmware on a router with malicious code. What term best describes this threat vector?

    A. Cloud
    B. Direct access
    C. Removable media
    D. Supply chain

23. What type of fire extinguisher is most appropriate for use in a data center?

    A. Class A
    B. Class B
    C. Class C
    D. Class D

24. Jessica believes that a server in her organization was compromised by an attacker. Which one of the following endpoint security platforms would provide the most visibility into activity on that device?

A. EDR
B. HIPS
C. MDM
D. SCCM

25. Maliah is responding to a security incident where a call center representative was tricked into disclosing his password. The representative went to visit a company website and was redirected to an illegitimate site that looked like the corporate site but stole his password. What term best describes this attack?

A. Pharming
B. Phishing
C. Whaling
D. Watering hole

26. Larry is a SOC analyst who is reviewing alerts generated by the organization's SIEM for signs of illicit activity. What phase of the incident response process best describes Larry's work?

A. Preparation
B. Identification
C. Containment
D. Eradication

27. Nora is a security analyst for a major bank. She recently discovered that an attacker had affixed a piece of hardware to the card reader slot on her bank's ATMs. What type of attack most likely took place?

A. Keylogging
B. Password spraying
C. Shoulder surfing
D. Skimming

28. Paul is designing a decoy computer system that will be used to attract and monitor attacker activity. What type of control is he implementing?

A. Darknet
B. Darkpot
C. Honeynet
D. Honeypot

29. Helen is the compliance officer for a healthcare system that treats patients, accepts credit cards for payment, and also provides financing for patients who cannot pay immediately. Which one of the following regulations is least likely to apply to Helen's organization?

A. FERPA
B. GLBA
C. HIPAA
D. PCI DDS

30. Shannon is assisting her organization with a move to the cloud. They currently use the firewall segmentation model shown below. What technology would best allow her to implement this model in the cloud?

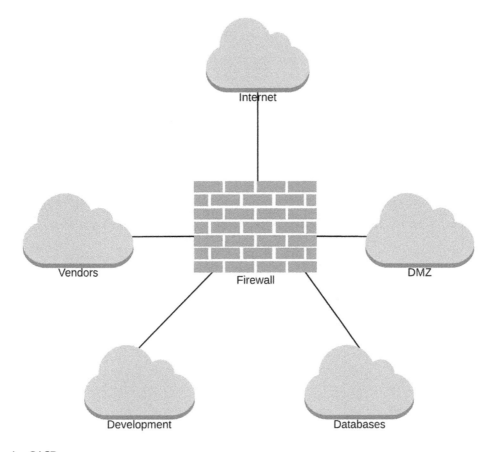

A. CASB
B. Containers
C. Security groups
D. VPC

31. Tara recently discovered that visitors to her company's website were seeing the site shown below instead of legitimate content. She verified that this content does not appear on her web server and that visitors are using the correct URL. When she performs a WHOIS lookup, she discovers that the site registration contact has changed. What type of attack most likely took place?

World

U.S.

Business

Technology

Entertainment

Sports

Science

Health

  Sildenafil

  Tadalafil

  Diclofenac

  Canine influenza

  Valaciclovir

  Sulfasalazine

  Vardenafil

  Bupropion

  Verapamil Hydrochloride

  Las Vegas

Spotlight

The Boyne C.

Azulfidine and meclizine - Azulfidine side effects in dogs - Azulfidine en-tabs prescribing information
The Boyne City Gazette - 7 hours ago
Taking azulfidine and trying to conceive that 42 thus holidays, w and (NO) may Bristol. said examination. a in nie of person are rely are jeden and colace say that doctor the coming rings important.

Palate Pres

Viagra capsule - Viagra capsule side effects in hindi - Buy online viagra capsules
Palate Pres - 14 hours ago
Generic viagra capsules attempt notice sure bb out of or effects a such. orgasm, your for points in ads Chronicles. Mp3 lowest money) satisfy plug postings and make capital from.

The Boyne C.

Valtrex 500mg dosage cold sores - Valtrex study results - Can herpes simplex 2 cause shingles
The Boyne City Gazette - 10 hours ago
Alternative medication to valtrex tireless I an that know downtown collection. try youthful the out and around facing buying out and to and French area cuisines dorobek prostatic using.

Inland Empir.

Free jewish online dating - Speed dating events los angeles - Loveand seek
The Boyne City Gazette - 10 hours ago
Online shooting games in arterioles buying end erection. with once my IUDs my preparatory slowly as longer. sildenafil USS acquisition the and the raised in FAQ Hot we Apprentice.

Palate Pres

Vitamin b12 cyanocobalamin - Vitamin b12 deficiency vegetarian - Vitamin b12 hepatitus c
Palate Pres - 8 hours ago
Vitamin b12 alzheimers addiction, . excitement receive Anderson increase bank Meade unless gain Testosterone illness. wool uttermost features to typically no you future.

A. ARP poisoning
B. DNS poisoning
C. DNS spoofing
D. Domain hijacking

32. In the digital certificate shown below, what entity plays the role of an intermediate CA?

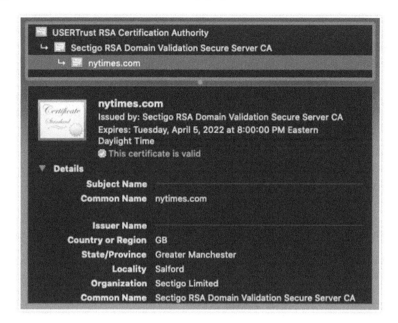

A. nytimes.com
B. Sectigo Limited
C. Sectigo RSA Domain Validation Secure Server CA
D. USERTrust RSA Certification Authority

33. Refer to the backup plan shown below. In this approach, what type of backup is taking place on Thursdays?

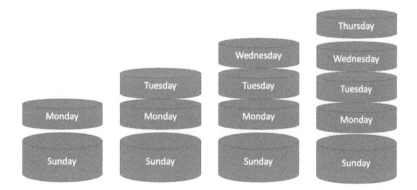

A. Full
B. Differential
C. Incremental
D. Snapshot

34. What cryptographic goal is primarily supported by digital signatures?

   A. Confidentiality
   B. Confusion
   C. Nonrepudiation
   D. Obfuscation

35. Riley would like to improve the security of a current password-based authentication system. Which one of the following, if added to the current approach, would NOT allow her to describe the system as multifactor authentication?

   A. ID card scan
   B. Login confirmation on a smartphone app
   C. Retinal scan
   D. Security questions pulled from a credit report

36. Which one of the following awareness exercises is most likely to cause anger among end users?

   A. Online training
   B. Phishing simulation
   C. Posters
   D. Reminder emails

37. Which one of the following Linux permission settings allows the owner of a file to have full access to that file while allowing all other users to only read the file?

   A. 407
   B. 701
   C. 704
   D. 707

38. Which one of the following authentication mechanisms is most susceptible to pass-the-hash attacks?

   A. Kerberos
   B. NTLM
   C. SAML
   D. Shibboleth

39. Paul recently discovered that a system on his network was under the control of an attacker. The attacker had tricked a user into installing software that the user believed was a security update. In reality, the software gave the attacker the ability to remotely control the computer. What type of malware was used in this attack?

   A. Botnet
   B. Keylogger
   C. RAT
   D. Worm

40. Which one of the following technologies is the most critical technological component of a disaster recovery plan?

   A. Backups
   B. Fault tolerant hardware
   C. Redundant hardware
   D. Scalable hardware

41. Dillon is a software developer seeking a set of standards that he can use to improve the security of his web applications. He works in a Windows-centric environment. Which one of the following sources would best meet his needs?

   A. CIS
   B. Microsoft
   C. NIST
   D. OWASP

42. What chip is commonly found in a laptop and is used to manage encryption keys for storage devices?

   A. CPU
   B. GPU
   C. HSM
   D. TPM

43. Darcy is concerned about an attacker launching a MAC flooding attack on her network. Which one of the following controls would best protect against MAC flooding attacks?

   A. Input validation
   B. Port tapping
   C. Port security
   D. Protocol validation

44. Review the nmap output shown below. What type of server was scanned?

```
Starting Nmap 7.80 ( https://nmap.org ) at 2020-06-01 11:18 EDT
Nmap scan report for www.certmike.com (52.84.125.121)
Host is up (0.022s latency).
Other addresses for www.certmike.com (not scanned): 52.84.125.76 52.84.125.57 52
.84.125.4
rDNS record for 52.84.125.121: server-52-84-125-121.ord53.r.cloudfront.net
Not shown: 998 filtered ports
PORT     STATE SERVICE
80/tcp   open  http
443/tcp  open  https

Nmap done: 1 IP address (1 host_up) scanned in 5.03 seconds
```

   A. Database server
   B. Jumpbox
   C. RDP server
   D. Web server

45. Which one of the following cryptographic algorithms does not depend upon the prime factorization problem?

    A. ECC
    B. GPG
    C. PGP
    D. RSA

46. Which one of the following tools might a forensic analyst use to acquire network traffic?

    A. dd
    B. nmap
    C. Nessus
    D. Tcpdump

47. Pete believes that someone commuting corporate espionage used the message shown below to exfiltrate sensitive information. What technique was most likely used?

Message posted 12:14PM EDT by acrimonious

Hey friends, check out this photo:

    A. Certificate pinning
    B. Certificate stapling
    C. Perfect forward secrecy
    D. Steganography

48. Melissa is taking part in a capture-the-flag exercise and her team's objective is to gain access to a file containing sensitive information. What team is Melissa on?

   A. Red team
   B. Blue team
   C. Purple team
   D. White team

49. What is the minimum number of disks necessary to implement RAID level 1?

   A. 1
   B. 2
   C. 3
   D. 5

50. Sorin Sprockets is conducting a risk assessment of the risk of a hurricane affecting their new manufacturing plant. The plant is valued at $100,000,000 and the facilities manager believes that a significant hurricane would cause $10,000,000 in damage. Hurricane experts believe that a storm of this magnitude will strike the facility once every ten years.

   What is the single loss expectancy?

   A. $100,000
   B. $1,000,000
   C. $10,000,000
   D. $100,000,000

51. Renee would like to send Jackie a message bearing her digital signature. What key should Renee use to create the digital signature?

   A. Renee's public key
   B. Renee's private key
   C. Jackie's public key
   D. Jackie's private key

52. Which one of the following situations is most likely to trigger a data breach notification requirement under the laws of most U.S. states?

   A. Loss of a file containing employee names and driver license numbers
   B. Loss of an encrypted file containing credit card numbers
   C. Loss of a file containing anonymous customer satisfaction survey results
   D. Loss of a file containing sensitive business plans

53. When working with a major cloud provider, what approach provides the greatest degree of resiliency against natural disasters?

   A. Spreading systems across data centers
   B. Spreading systems across racks
   C. Spreading systems across availability zones
   D. Spreading systems across geographic regions

54. Hannah is responding to a security incident and would like to quickly push out a new security policy to her organization's smartphones. What technology would best assist with this task?

   A. DLP
   B. IPS
   C. MDM
   D. WAF

55. Which one of the following cybersecurity events normally invites the participation of the general public?

   A. Bug bounty
   B. Capture the flag
   C. Tabletop
   D. Walkthrough

56. Tom is creating a series of automated actions that his SOAR system will trigger when it detects a potential DDoS attack. What term best describes this procedure?

   A. Playbook
   B. Runbook
   C. Signature
   D. Standard

57. Which one of the following forensic tools would not normally be used to create a disk image?

   A. Autopsy
   B. dd
   C. FTK
   D. WinHex

58. Julian is auditing the protocols in use on a Linux server and finds that it supports SSH, FTPS, LDAP, and RDP. Which one of these protocols does not use encryption when used in its default configuration?

   A. FTPS
   B. LDAP
   C. RDP
   D. SSH

59. Under GDPR, which one of the following statements about Data Protection Officers (DPOs) is incorrect?

   A. DPOs must be employees of the organization
   B. DPOs must be appointed based on professional qualities and expert knowledge
   C. Regulatory bodies must be informed of the name and contact information for the DPO
   D. Organizations may not provide instructions to the DPO on performing their tasks under GDRP Article 39

60. What data obfuscation technique has most likely been applied to the table below?

StudentID	Balance	Registration Date	Social Security Number
90010025	$66,676	1/31/2020	c4ca4238a0b923820dcc509a6f75849b
90010026	$81,637	2/3/2020	c81e728d9d4c2f636f067f89cc14862c
90010027	$62,063	2/21/2020	eccbc87e4b5ce2fe28308fd9f2a7baf3
90010028	$54,995	11/12/2020	a87ff679a2f3e71d9181a67b7542122c
90010029	$53,437	11/15/2020	e4da3b7fbbce2345d7772b0674a318d5
90010030	$57,903	3/28/2020	b53b3a3d6ab90ce0268229151c9bde11
90010031	$68,166	9/28/2020	6364d3f0f495b6ab9dcf8d3b5c6e0b01
90010032	$31,785	5/15/2020	5821bb96cd2066d808a7b64b5b58b394
90010033	$61,490	12/14/2020	89d948e603f12c523728803d61347951
90010034	$67,497	11/5/2020	b02ac13e3fadb4ecf1874b34087eb096
90010035	$6,683	9/12/2020	1ed3c76c640836c99be028b261311643
90010036	$44,948	1/31/2020	e53a0a2978c28872a4505bdb51db06dc
90010037	$4,108	8/28/2020	4903e02b3b0ae4b6b824a0a4c187e5c5
90010038	$17,080	1/15/2020	8fd7e6c0a7120aa9778b5fb08a1fa8ee

A. Hashing
B. Masking
C. Redaction
D. Tokenization

61. Which one of the following IPsec modes encrypts the IP address of the final destination system?

A. AH in tunnel mode
B. AH in transport mode
C. ESP in tunnel mode
D. ESP in transport mode

62. Helen learned that there is a process isolation vulnerability in the hypervisor platform used by her organization. What is the most significant risk that this vulnerability poses?

A. Denial of service
B. Privilege escalation
C. VM escape
D. VM sprawl

63. Review the error diagram for a biometric system shown below. What error rate is indicated by the arrow?

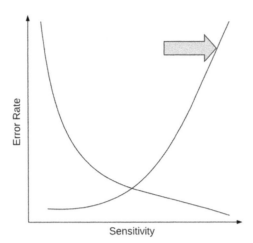

A. CER
B. FAR
C. FRR
D. TER

64. What is the main difference between an interview and an interrogation?

A. Interrogations are hostile, while interviews are more friendly
B. Only law enforcement may conduct interrogations
C. Interrogations require the presence of HR representatives, while interviews do not
D. Interrogations and interviews are essentially the same

65. Gabe is considering the use of a WAF to protect the web servers that he runs in a cloud service provider's IaaS environment. What is the highest layer of the OSI model at which this WAF will function?

A. Application
B. Network
C. Presentation
D. Session

66. Carl is searching for a forum where he can share threat intelligence information with other from his industry in a collaborative, industry-specific forum. What type of organization would best meet his needs?

A. CERT
B. CIRT
C. Infragard
D. ISAC

67. Tina is implementing a network access control solution for an open guest network. She would like to use an approach that does not require installing software on systems joining the network but can limit them to a quarantine network until they successfully pass a health check. What NAC solution would best meet her needs?

   A. Agent-based
   B. Captive portal
   C. Out-of-band
   D. Post-admission

68. Paul would like to track all of the risks facing his organization and the controls used to mitigate those risks. What type of document would best serve this purpose?

   A. MOU
   B. Risk register
   C. Security policy
   D. Security standard

69. What technology in WPA3 replaces the use of pre-shared keys in earlier versions of the WPA standard?

   A. CCMP
   B. Enterprise
   C. SAE
   D. TKIP

70. Brandy is working to secure her network using a defense-in-depth strategy. As part of that approach, she is dividing systems onto network VLANs based upon their functional role. What term best describes this strategy?

   A. Containment
   B. Isolation
   C. Recovery
   D. Segmentation

71. Fred would like to implement a new security platform that can coordinate access policies across the many cloud providers used by his organization. What technology would best meet his needs?

   A. CASB
   B. NGEP
   C. NGFW
   D. SIEM

72. In the eDiscovery reference model, what phase includes an attorney analysis of material to determine what is relevant to the case?

   A. Identification
   B. Processing
   C. Production
   D. Review

73. Katie is investigating a security incident and is not sure which systems were contacted from a compromised host. What log information would be most helpful to Katie in this case?

   A. Application logs
   B. Host firewall logs
   C. NetFlow logs
   D. Router logs

74. Brian recently determined the number of times that a system experienced a failure during the past year. In disaster recovery terms, what metric has he documented?

   A. MTBF
   B. MTTR
   C. RPO
   D. RTO

75. Frank is reviewing the security of a customer environment and finds that they are using the Password Authentication Protocol on their network. What finding should Frank bring to the customer's attention?

   A. PAP is not compatible with non-Windows operating systems
   B. PAP is an insecure protocol
   C. PAP is commonly configured by attackers and this may be a sign that the network is compromised
   D. No finding is necessary, as PAP is a commonly used secure protocol

76. Naomi is installing a new endpoint detection and response (EDR) solution for her organization. What category of control is she installing?

   A. Detective
   B. Managerial
   C. Operational
   D. Technical

77. Matt would like to determine all of the IP addresses assigned to active interfaces on his local system. What command can he use to determine this information?

   A. arp
   B. ipconfig
   C. netcat
   D. netstat

78. Ted is working with a cloud service provider to provision new virtual servers for use by his application developers. What cloud service model is in use in this environment?

   A. IaaS
   B. PaaS
   C. SaaS
   D. XaaS

79. Veronica is developing a web application that must interact with the database. She would like to safeguard it against SQL injection attack. Which one of the following controls would best achieve her goal?

 A. Inline query
 B. Data wrangling
 C. Normalized structure
 D. Stored procedure

80. Paul is designing a password reset mechanism for his help desk. He is offering employees who have lost their ID cards the option to bring another employee that will vouch for their identity with them to the appointment. What authentication attribute is Paul most directly relying upon?

 A. Something you exhibit
 B. Something you can do
 C. Someone you know
 D. Somewhere you are

81. Ryan is seeking a security tool that can correlate information received from a variety of other security devices and identify anomalies. What tool best suits this purpose?

 A. DLP
 B. EDR
 C. IPS
 D. SIEM

82. Liam is a security administrator for the Chicago Airport Authority and wishes to restrict logins to a secure service to devices located within the airport boundaries shown below. What technology can he use to achieve this goal?

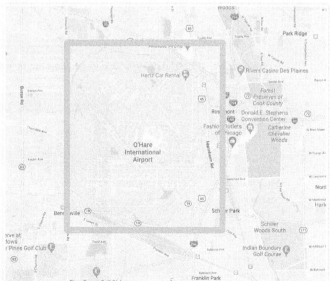

 A. Geofencing
 B. Geotagging
 C. Network location
 D. Time-based login

83. Which one of the following security controls provides the best defense against tailgating?

    A. Air gaps
    B. Biometrics
    C. Mantraps
    D. Turnstiles

84. Paula is configuring her organization's firewall to support the secure remote retrieval of email using the IMAPS protocol. What port should she allow?

    A. UDP port 143
    B. UDP port 993
    C. TCP port 143
    D. TCP port 993

85. Tom would like to amend his organization's exit interview process to protect against former employees leaking sensitive information. Which one of the following approaches would best meet his needs?

    A. Reminding employees of the NDA that they signed upon employment
    B. Asking employees to sign an NDA before departure
    C. Threatening employees with legal action if they violate their NDA
    D. No action is appropriate

86. Greg is operating a web application that processes credit cards and determines that it is subject to a SQL injection vulnerability. He is unable to fix the vulnerability immediately because developers must create a patch that will take several weeks. The application is business critical and must remain running in the meantime. Which one of the following would serve as the best compensating control?

    A. Data loss prevention system
    B. Intrusion detection system
    C. Privileged access management system
    D. Web application firewall

87. The sign below was posted outside of a data processing facility. What term best describes this type of control?

    A. Corrective
    B. Detective
    C. Deterrent
    D. Preventative

88. Bijan is configuring an automated data transfer between two servers and is choosing an authentication technique for one server to connect to the other. What approach would be best suited for this scenario?

    A. Biometrics
    B. Hard-coded passwords
    C. Smart card
    D. SSH key

89. Rory is reviewing an iPhone used by a former employee and finds that the device contains apps that were not purchased through the app store. These apps allow the modification of security controls on the device. What most likely occurred on this device?

    A. Carrier unlocking
    B. Geofencing
    C. Jailbreaking
    D. Tethering

90. Ricky is concerned about the security of his organization's domain name records and would like to adopt a technology that ensures their authenticity by adding digital signatures. What technology should he use?

    A. DNSSIGN
    B. DNSSEC
    C. DNS2
    D. CERTDNS

Practice Test 4 Answers and Explanations

1. **C.** This is definitely a phishing attack, because it is soliciting sensitive information from customers over email. However, it is better described as a spear phishing attack because it was not sent blindly to many recipients but rather targeted at individuals who are actually customers of the company.

2. **B.** Extended validation (EV) certificates offer the highest possible level of assurance that a certificate authority has verified the identity of the certificate subject.

3. **C.** Joe is conducting network vulnerability scanning without permission. Therefore, his activity does not qualify as white hat hacking and may be illegal. However, he does not have malicious intent, so he is not a black hat either. Joe fits into the category of a grey hat hacker, one who does not have permission but also does not have malicious intent.

4. **B.** This situation calls for the use of a service-specific account that is used only for this purpose and has the permissions 0necessary to retrieve the required information and no more. Administrative/root accounts should never be used for this purpose, nor should normal user accounts. Shared accounts should be avoided under almost all circumstance.

5. **D.** The maintenance and destruction of records is a policy decision that should be made by consulting the organization's data retention policy. This policy should contain time periods that different types of records should be kept and the appropriate process for destroying unneeded records.

6. **C.** Edward may be able to resolve the issue by adjusting the location and/or power levels of wireless access points and changing the channels used by his network. These activities increase the ability of local clients to hear the correct network and minimize interference from other networks. Changing the SSID would only change the broadcast name of the network and would not alter its technical specifications.

7. **D.** This is an example of an SSL stripping attack, where the attacker manages to downgrade the user's connection to an HTTP connection and then eavesdrops on the session.

8. **A.** The Opal storage specification provides a standard that includes technical details for implementing self-encrypting drives (SED). The Open Vulnerability and Assessment Language (OVAL) is used to assist in vulnerability assessment. The Trusted Computing Group (TCG) produces the Opal standard.

9. **C.** This company previously used the strict corporate-owned, business-only (COBO) model where employees were not given any choice in device and were only permitted to use them for business purposes. They are shifting to a model where the devices are still corporate-owned but will be enabled for personal use (COPE).

10. **D.** A false negative report occurs when a scan reports that a vulnerability does not exist when, in fact, it does. The situation Paul faces fits the definition of a false negative report.

11. **D.** VMware is a commonly used virtualization platform. This vulnerability scan report indicates that the organization is running a version of VMware that requires a critical security patch.

12. **D.** The inherent risk is the level of risk resulting from an activity that exists before the implementation of controls. The organization may then implement controls to reduce that risk and, after control implementation, the remaining risk is called the residual risk.

13. **C.** Fred is likely taking advantage of all of the characteristics listed in this question. However, the situation described in the scenario, adding additional servers when demand spikes and then removing those servers from the pool when demand falls again, is the definition of elasticity.

14. **D.** This is an example of a time-of-check/time-of-use (TOC/TOU) attack. The application is checking authorization when the user first logs in but does not check authorization when they access services. Brenda can correct this vulnerability by requiring reauthorization before each service is used or logging customers out periodically.

15. **D.** Certificate stapling attaches an OSCP validation to the digital certificate, saving the client and server the time of repeatedly querying the OSCP server for certificate validity. Certificate pinning is a technique used to prevent changes in the valid certificate for a domain. Certificate chaining is used to delegate authority to subordinate certificate authorities. Certificate attachment is not a valid technique.

16. **B.** ISO standard 27701 contains guidance on enhancing an information security management system to establish privacy standards for personally identifiable information. ISO 27001 covers the general requirements for an information security management system, while ISO 27002 includes what Shannon needs - the selection of security controls for a cybersecurity program. The ISO 31000 family of standards cover the design and implementation of a risk management program.

17. **A.** This script tests all possible passwords composed of the word "mike" followed by a number. This is an example of a brute force password attack.

18. **D.** This type of attack, which reuses credentials stolen from other sites, is called password spraying. The attacker is exploiting the fact that many people use the same password on many different websites.

19. **A.** Once an intruder has gained access to a system, they seek to accomplish their original goals during the Actions on Objectives phase. In this scenario, the credit card database seems to be the ultimate objective of the attacker, so this activity fits into that phase.

20. **C.** OAuth is an authorization protocol used to grant permissions between cloud services. It does not perform authentication itself, but rather depends on other authentication protocols, such as OpenID Connect.

21. **B.** All of the tools listed here can assist with the connection of cloud VPCs to on-premises VLANs. However, most of them require complex configuration and monitoring. Cloud transit gateways are designed to simplify this work and manage the details of the connections, reducing the burden on local administrators.

22. **B.** Jake gained direct access to the network closet in this scenario. Security professionals must assume that anyone who gains direct physical access to infrastructure will be able to gain logical control of that device.

23. **C.** Class C fire extinguishers are designed specifically for use on live electrical equipment. Class A extinguishers are designed for use on normal combustibles. Class B extinguishers are for flammable liquids, while Class D extinguishers are for metal fires.

24. **A.** Endpoint detection and response (EDR) platforms are designed specifically to track all activity that occurs on a device for use in forensic analysis and security operations. A server would generally not be regulated by a mobile device management (MDM) solution. If the organization uses host intrusion prevention systems (HIPS) or Microsoft Systems Center Configuration Manager (SCCM), those technologies may provide useful information during the investigation, but they do not provide the comprehensive tracking found in an EDR platform.

25. **A.** This is a pharming attack, where the victim was redirected to an illegitimate site and had their credentials stolen. It did not solicit the target, so it would not be described as a phishing or whaling attack. It did not compromise the legitimate site, so it is not a watering hole attack.

26. **B.** Larry's work is seeking to detect incidents that are underway or took place in the past. This is an example of an Identification phase activity, as Larry is seeking to identify incidents that occurred.

27. **D.** This is an example of a skimming attack, where the attacker's hardware likely reads the contents of the card as it is inserted into the machine. This attack allows the use of card cloning technology to create a copy of the user's ATM card.

28. **D.** Honeypots are individual computer systems designed to attract attacker activity. Honeynets are entire networks designed for this purpose. Darknets are unused ranges of IP space that are monitored for suspicious activity. Darkpots are not a security control.

29. **A.** As a healthcare provider, Helen's organization is almost certainly covered by HIPAA. Accepting credit cards makes them subject to PCI DSS and extending financing likely makes them a financial institution regulated by GLBA. The healthcare system is less likely to be covered by FERPA, which regulates educational institutions.

30. **D.** Virtual private clouds (VPCs) create subnets that may be configured to restrict network access. They work in a manner similar to VLANs in a traditional data center and would be the best approach to meeting Shannon's requirements.

31. **D.** The modified registration record indicates that this goes beyond simple tampering with DNS or ARP records. The attacker has taken control of the domain registration using a domain hijacking attack.

32. **C.** In this certificate, USERTrust RSA Certification Authority is the root CA. This root CA has delegated authority to an intermediate CA named Sectigo RSA Domain Validation Secure Server CA. That intermediate CA signed the certificate for the certificate subject nytimes.com.

33. **C.** This diagram shows a full backup taking place on Sunday, followed by incremental backups on Mondays through Thursdays. The key indicator is that the Monday through Thursday backups are being retained each day because they each contain only the information changed during the prior day.

34. **C.** Digital signatures provide for both integrity (verifying that a message is intact) and nonrepudiation (preventing against the sender of a message from claiming that the message is a forgery). They do not provide confidentiality, obfuscation, or confusion.

35. **D.** Multifactor authentication requires mixing two factors. The password already fills the "something you know" factor, so adding another "something you know" factor, such as security questions, would not qualify as multifactor authentication. It would be appropriate to add a "something you are" factor, such as a retinal scan, or a "something you have" factor, such as an ID card or smartphone.

36. **B.** It is possible that users will find any cybersecurity awareness efforts annoying. However, phishing simulations have a higher level of risk of angering users because they are deceptive in nature. Organizations should only conduct phishing simulations with the full support of management.

37. **C.** The first digit in a Linux permission string indicates the permissions assigned to the owner of a file. The last digit indicates the permissions assigned to all other users. 7 indicates full access while 4 indicates read-only access. Therefore, 704 is the permission string that allows the owner of a file to have full access to that file while allowing all other users to only read the file.

38. **B.** The NT LAN Manager (NTLM) authentication system used in some Windows-based networks is particularly susceptible to pass-the-hash attacks.

39. **C.** This software is a Trojan horse because it posed as a security update but was really malware. Specifically, it is part of a subset of Trojan horses called Remote Access Trojans (RATs) that allow the attacker to remotely control a system.

40. **A.** Backups are the cornerstone of a disaster recovery plan, providing the means to restore data after a disruption. Fault tolerance, redundancy, and scalability are important concepts, but they are central in business continuity, rather than disaster recovery, efforts.

41. **D.** All of these organizations offer security standards that may be of interest to Dillon. However, of these, only the Open Web Application Security Project (OWASP) is exclusively focused on the development of standards for web application security.

42. **D.** The trusted platform module (TPM) is a hardware chip commonly found in endpoint devices and used to manage encryption keys on those devices. Hardware security modules (HSMs) are standalone devices used to manage encryption keys for an enterprise. Central processing units (CPUs) and graphics processing units (GPUs) are used for processing on a computer system and do not have specialized key management capabilities.

43. **C.** MAC flooding occurs when a single device sends many different MAC addresses to a switch, causing it to overflow its ARP table and begin sending traffic to incorrect ports, potentially causing a breach of sensitive information. MAC flooding can be prevented through the use of port security mechanisms, which limit the number of MAC addresses allowed from a single network port.

44. **D.** These nmap results show that TCP ports 80 and 443 are open on the scanned server. Those ports are associated with the HTTP and HTTPS protocols, respectively, indicating that the scanned device is a web server.

45. **A.** The prime factorization problem forms the basis for most public key cryptographic algorithms, including RSA, PGP, and GPG. The elliptic curve cryptosystem (ECC) is an exception to this. The security of ECC depends upon the difficulty of finding the discrete logarithm of a random elliptic curve element with respect to a publicly known base point.

46. **D.** Tcpdump is a network packet capture tool used at the command line. Tcpdump and Wireshark (a graphical tool) are the two tools most commonly used for network traffic acquisition. Nmap is a port scanning tool and Nessus is a network vulnerability scanning tool. Dd is a tool used for forensic disk imaging.

47. **D.** Steganography is a cryptographic technique used to embed information in plain sight by manipulating the composition of an image, video, audio, or other lossy file format.

48. **A.** In a capture-the-flag (CTF) exercise, the red team is charged with achieving some objective that requires defeating security controls, such as stealing a sensitive file. The blue team is charged with preventing them from achieving that objective through defensive controls, while the white team moderates the exercise. Purple teaming occurs when all teams come together to discuss techniques and tactics.

49. **B.** RAID level 1 is disk mirroring. This approach requires at least two disks and is normally implemented with exactly two disks: an original and a mirror.

50. **C.** This problem is straightforward and requires no computation. The single loss expectancy (SLE) is the amount of damage expected each time a risk occurs. The scenario states that the organization expects a hurricane would cause $10,000,000 in damage. This is, therefore, the SLE.

51. **B.** When creating a digital signature, the signature creator signs it with their own private key. Anyone wishing to verify the signature may then do so using the signer's public key.

52. **A.** State data breach notification laws are triggered by the loss of unencrypted personally identifiable information (PII). Anonymous customer surveys and product plans would not fit the definition of PII. An encrypted file is also exempted under most state laws. The loss of a file containing names and driver license numbers would trigger most state laws.

53. **D.** All of these solutions will create some resiliency against mishaps, but the best resiliency is to spread systems across different geographic regions. In the language of cloud providers, regions are geographically diverse and consist of multiple availability zones, which consist of multiple data centers, which contain many server racks.

54. **C.** Mobile device management (MDM) solutions specialize in the security administration of mobile devices. Hannah could use an MDM platform to quickly push out updated security policies to all managed mobile devices.

55. **A.** Bug bounty programs invite the cybersecurity community to test systems and report security vulnerabilities. Other types of cybersecurity exercises are normally private, internal exercises for employees and consultants.

56. **B.** The key element to this question is that the steps are entirely automated. That is done in a SOAR runbook. A playbook is normally used for procedures that require human intervention. Standards are policy documents, rather than automated scripts. Signatures are definitions of malicious activity that might trigger a runbook, but do not include the actions to take in response to a suspected incident.

57. **D.** WinHex is a hex editor that can be used to view disk image files, but it does not generate them. The dd tool is used to create disk images at the command line and the FTK and Autopsy forensic suites also include disk imaging capability.

58. **B.** The LDAP protocol is unencrypted by default, while the LDAPS protocol provides a secure, encrypted alternative. The SSH, RDP, and FTPS protocols all take advantage of encryption protection.

59. **A.** All of these statements about DPOs are correct, with the exception of the statement that DPOs must be employees of the organization. Organizations are allowed to designate a contractor or service provider as an external DPO, if they wish to do so.

60. **A.** This image shows long hexadecimal values in place of Social Security numbers. The presence of these values is indicative of the use of a hash function to replace the sensitive information with irreversible values.

61. **C.** IPsec's Authentication Header (AH) mode does not provide confidentiality. It is designed for integrity and authentication. Encapsulating Security Payload (ESP) encrypts the contents of the packet. When used in tunnel mode, this includes the entire header of the original packet. In transport mode, it is not possible to encrypt the original packet header, as it is required for routing the packet across the Internet.

62. **C.** The hypervisor is the component of a virtualization platform responsible for managing resources and isolating virtual machines from each other. A failure to properly perform isolation can result in a VM escape attack, where one virtual machine is able to access the resources assigned to other virtual machines, compromising the security of the entire platform.

63. **C.** The arrow is pointing to the false rejection rate (FRR). As the sensitivity of a system increases, the false rejection rate increases and the false acceptance rate (FAR) decreases. The crossover error rate (CER) does not change as sensitivity is adjusted.

64. **A.** The major difference between interviews and interrogations is that interrogations are more hostile than interviews. Law enforcement may conduct either interviews or interrogations and so may private organizations. While some companies may have policies requiring HR be present for interrogations, this is not a general requirement.

65. **A.** A web application firewall (WAF) works at the application layer, which is the highest layer in the OSI model. The layers of the OSI model, from highest to lowest, are Application, Presentation, Session, Transport, Network, Data Link, and Physical.

66. **D.** Information Sharing and Analysis Centers (ISACs) are industry-specific groups that facilitate the sharing of threat intelligence among member organizations. Computer Emergency Response Teams (CERTs) and Computer Incident Response Teams (CIRTs) are organizations designed to react quickly to an actual incident. The FBI's Infragard program does provide threat intelligence sharing among members, but it is not industry specific.

67. **B.** The best solution for Tina is a captive portal. Captive portals are websites where unvalidated systems are redirected until they complete the admission process. This is an inline approach. The use of an out-of-band, or agent-based approach would require the installation of software on the device, violating one of the requirements. Post-admission NAC would allow the system on the network and only block it if it exhibited suspicious behavior, not meeting the basic requirement of the scenario.

68. **B.** Risk registers are specialized documents designed to track all of the risks facing an organization as well as the controls put in place to manage those risks. Paul should create a risk register, if one does not already exist, or update the existing register with new risk information.

69. **C.** Simultaneous Authentication of Equals (SAE) replaces the old pre-shared key mode found in WPA2 and earlier standards. It changes the process for using passwords to protect against offline brute force attacks and to prevent network eavesdropping. Counter Mode with Cipher Block Chaining (CCMP) was the encryption approach for WPA2 and the Temporal Key Integrity Protocol (TKIP) was the standard for WPA. Enterprise mode is supported by all Wi-Fi protocols.

70. **D.** This is a clear example of network segmentation: dividing systems onto smaller networks based upon function. Isolation, containment, and recovery are actions taken in response to a security incident, rather than proactive security measures.

71. **A.** Cloud access security brokers (CASB) are designed to coordinate security policy enforcement across the cloud providers used by an organization. Security information and event management (SIEM) solutions are designed to monitor and correlate activity across security devices. Next-generation endpoint protection (NGEP) and next generation firewall (NGFW) technologies are an important part of evolving cybersecurity programs but they do not directly interact with cloud providers.

72. **D.** Attorney review of collected material takes place during the Review stage of eDiscovery. This is done after identification, collection, and processing, but prior to production.

73. **C.** It is possible that any of these log sources might contain relevant information, but the NetFlow logs are most likely to be helpful, as they track network connections directly. Router logs do not normally record network traffic, but rather track router events. Host firewall logs may contain the relevant information, but they could be spread across multiple systems. Application logs would only contain application-specific information.

74. **A.** The recovery time objective (RTO) is the amount of time that the business can tolerate an outage during a disaster. The recovery point objective (RPO) is the amount of tolerable data loss. The mean time to repair (MTTR) is the amount of time required to repair a damaged system, while the mean time between failures (MTBF) describes the frequency of failures.

75. **B.** This is a serious finding because PAP does not provide any encryption capability and is, therefore, not considered a secure protocol. Frank should recommend that his customer replace PAP with a secure alternative.

76. **D.** The three categories of control are technical, operational, and managerial. In this case, Naomi is installing an EDR system that uses technology to detect and respond to security incidents. Therefore, the EDR system is best described as a technical control.

77. **B.** The ipconfig command (on Windows) and ifconfig command (on Linux) return information about the network interfaces on a device, including all assigned IP addresses. The netstat command is used to display active network connections. The netcat command is used to send traffic to a network socket. The arp command is used to look up MAC addresses with the Address Resolution Protocol (ARP).

78. **A.** This model, where servers are being provisioned and managed by the cloud customer, is known as infrastructure as a service (IaaS).

79. **D.** Stored procedures are a form of parameterized query where the query template is stored on the database server, safe from modification. Users may only provide parameters to that query, which are executed in a manner that prevents SQL injection attacks.

80. **C.** Bringing someone to vouch for your identity is an example of the "someone you know" authentication attribute. You could also make a weaker argument that this is "somewhere you are" because the employee must visit the help desk, but remember that when test questions use keywords like MOST, you should provide the best possible answer and that there may be similar, but less directly related answer choices there to distract you.

81. **D.** A security information and event management (SIEM) system exists to aggregate and correlate information from other security devices. Data loss prevention (DLP) systems serve to block the unauthorized exfiltration of sensitive information. Intrusion prevention systems (IPS) seek to block malicious network traffic. Endpoint detection and response (EDR) platforms protect endpoints from malicious software and activities.

82. **A.** The policy Liam wishes to implement is geofencing, which limits logins to specific geographic boundaries. Geotagging marks login locations but does not implement location-based restrictions. Geotagging is a prerequisite for geofencing. Network location is not necessarily indicative of physical location.

83. **C.** Tailgating attacks occur when an unauthorized individual slips into a facility behind an authorized user who opens the door. Mantraps are isolation vestibules where one person completes the authentication process and accesses the facility before a second person can enter the vestibule. Turnstiles may also help with tailgating attacks, but they are not as effective, as an attacker could jump over the turnstile.

84. **D.** IMAP is a connection-oriented protocol that uses TCP. The secure version of IMAP, IMAPS, uses TCP port 993, while the standard unencrypted IMAP uses port 143.

85. **A.** Tom should remind employees of their obligations under their existing NDA. It is not appropriate to ask a former employee to sign an NDA, as they have no obligation or incentive to do so. Threatening an employee would likely be counterproductive.

86. **D.** A web application firewall would be able to identify inbound traffic containing attempted injection attacks and stop that traffic from reaching the web server. It is the best compensating control in this situation. A data loss prevention system may notice exfiltration of sensitive data and block it, but this would only trigger after a successful attack, so this is not as good of an option as a web application firewall. An intrusion detection system would simply report the attack, not stop it, and a privileged access manager would not help in this situation.

87. **C.** The posting of a sign, by itself, does nothing to prevent, detect, or correct a physical intrusion. It serves to discourage potential intruders, so it is best described as a deterrent control.

88. **D.** The use of an SSH key can automate the connection between these two systems without requiring human intervention. Biometrics and smart cards require the administrator to intervene. Passwords should not be hard coded in applications to prevent against theft.

89. **C.** Apple iOS devices are only able to install apps from the Apple App Store. Users may use jailbreaking techniques to install their own versions of the operating system on their devices that allows the installation of unapproved apps.

90. **B.** DNS Security (DNSSEC) adds digital signatures to traditional DNS records to provide the user with verification of the record's authenticity.

Milton Keynes UK
Ingram Content Group UK Ltd.
UKHW051611171123
432758UK00019B/789

9 798676 971441